"Gerhard Lohfink is a superb scholar and a beautiful writer who helped many readers see the Son of God in an entirely new light with his brilliant book *Jesus of Nazareth*. Now, in a series of wise, provocative, and inspiring essays, backed by vast learning and deep prayer, Lohfink reveals Jesus as he was and is, and the church as it was and is meant to become."

James Martin, SJ
Author of *Jesus: A Pilgrimage*

"*No Irrelevant Jesus* is a profound meditation on what Jesus means for the church and our world today. In probing metaphors of the church as a sacrament, as the eschatological Israel, Lohfink explores the church's newness, its proper name as an assembly, how a sacrament works, and how faith works. He carefully parses for us how to pray as a way to get access to reality. Readers will not only be deeply enlightened but also feel a call for a genuine and deep conversion (as individuals and the church) against any taming of Jesus."

John A. Coleman, SJ
Associate Pastor
St. Ignatius Church
San Francisco, California

"Following his highly successful *Jesus of Nazareth*, Gerhard Lohfink delivers another stunning achievement with this passionate set of essays about why Jesus remains relevant. Originally a series of public lectures, the chapters retain their oral flair, reflected in the excellent translation. They also impart a wealth of sophisticated information on a variety of themes tied to Jesus and his ministry: miracles, the love commandment, salvation, sin and reconciliation, the nature of the church, the episcopacy, and more. This book demonstrates once more Lohfink's eminent status as a seasoned scholar who nonetheless has the ability to communicate a meaningful pastoral message. In short, a superb book on Jesus' significance for the church today!"

Ronald D. Witherup, SS
Superior General of the Society of the Priests of
Saint Sulpice and author of *Saint Paul and the
New Evangelization*

"Gerhard Lohfink is to theology what Flannery O'Connor is to literature: a voice calling us to be aware of what really matters. O'Connor shouts to a culture deaf to grace; Lohfink confronts anyone trying to tame and domesticate Jesus. Modern-day prophets they are."

Auxiliary Bishop Emeritus Robert F. Morneau
Diocese of Green Bay, Wisconsin

"*No Irrelevant Jesus* by Gerhard Lohfink is an excellent complement to the author's *Jesus of Nazareth*. It highlights the mystery of Jesus Christ and his message in relation to the church's nature and mission. Speaking to general readers as well as to scholars, it illumines the living Lord's 'good news' in its biblical setting and also in the context of our contemporary world. Its short, clear, down-to-earth essays challenge us to orient our lives and the church to the coming of God's reign."

Robert A. Krieg
Professor of Theology
University of Notre Dame

"Gerhard Lohfink not only demonstrates that Jesus and his church are unquestionably relevant for life today, his essays also offer readers clear and theologically wise responses to critical issues of our day. While his writing is solid and sophisticated, it is accessible to scholar and seeker alike. Brilliantly written and translated, this work should be on the reading list of everyone interested in updating their understanding of Jesus and his church with fresh and stimulating insights."

Stephen J. Binz, independent scholar, speaker,
and author of biblical theology and spirituality

Gerhard Lohfink

No Irrelevant Jesus

On Jesus and the Church Today

Translated by

Linda M. Maloney

A Michael Glazier Book

LITURGICAL PRESS
Collegeville, Minnesota

www.litpress.org

A Michael Glazier Book published by Liturgical Press

Cover design by Ann Blattner. Illustration by Br. Martin Erspamer, OSB, a monk of Saint Meinrad Archabbey, Indiana. Used with permission.

This volume was originally published in German as *Gegen Die Verharmlosung Jesu* (Freiburg im Breisgau: Verlag Herder GmbH, 2013). This English-language edition has been slightly abridged, by permission of the author.

1   2   3   4   5   6   7   8   9

Library of Congress Control Number: 2013955285

ISBN 978-0-8146-8264-7
ISBN 978-0-8146-8289-0 (ebook)

To the memory of
Rudolf Pesch

Contents

Preface

Jesus is being rendered irrelevant nowadays in many ways. It happens, for example, when Jesus is appraised as a somewhat unusual rabbi or a prophet, certainly one mighty in word and deed, but ultimately just one of the many prophets throughout history. It happens when posters in Augsburg invite people to journey through the ages and the religions: "We will meet Rama, Krishna, Buddha, and Jesus, and sing their names. Circle dances from the Sufi tradition will help us to incorporate our bodies, too, into our meditation and to experience deep peace in the harmony of body and soul." That kind of peace was something Jesus definitely did *not* promise.

But resistance is called for above all when Christians act as if the church were a kind of club to serve religious needs. That too is part of the long series of ways of making Jesus irrelevant, because the eschatological people of God for which, in the end, he died, was something he conceived quite differently.

Therefore at many points this book is not only about Jesus himself but also about the church. Where else could we see who Jesus really was, if not in the life of the church and of Christians who dare to name themselves after him? The book is derived from talks I have given over the last several years. Originally they had no common theme, but in retrospect it appears that there is a fairly stout "scarlet thread" running through them: they all fall quite easily and without much alteration under the title of this book.

Public talks force the speaker not to be boring. Otherwise the audience will fall asleep, and next time they will stay home. Still more important is that they force one to get to the point quickly, because an hour is all one has, at the most. So it is not a problem to read a book made up of talks. For that reason I have deliberately retained the oral style and have not attempted to turn transparent talks into abstract disquisitions.

I dedicate this book in profound gratitude to my deceased colleague, Professor Dr. Dr. Rudolf Pesch, with whom I was able to work for many years in the Catholic Integrierte Gemeinde.

Bad Tölz, 6 January 2013   Gerhard Lohfink

Acknowledgments

First and primarily I want to thank my bishop, Dr. Franz-Peter Tebartz-van Elst, who invited me to give a lecture to the priests and deacons of the diocese of Limburg on the feast of the Holy Cross in 2012. On that day, the tenth of September, I chose the theme "On Not Making Jesus Irrelevant." That lecture became the introductory chapter to this book and also gave it its title. The chapter "Prayer as Access to Reality" was also shaped in response to a gracious invitation from my bishop.

Thanks are due also to my brother, Professor Dr. Norbert Lohfink, SJ. He read the whole manuscript and encouraged me, as he always does. I am grateful also to my friend, Professor Dr. Marius Reiser, and to Professor Dr. Georg Braulik, OSB, in Vienna and Professor Dr. Christian Troll, SJ, in Frankfurt for a great deal of helpful information.

As in the case of my book *Jesus of Nazareth*, I want to again thank my student, the Reverend Dr. Linda M. Maloney. She has translated this book also, applying all her professional exegetical knowledge as well as a great deal of care and attention. Without her, and the kind support of Hans Christoffersen, academic publisher of Liturgical Press, this American edition would not have been possible.

The next-to-last chapter of this book speaks of "a place for faith." For the last twenty-five years I have made my home in such a place. For this I thank my many brothers and sisters in the Katholische Integrierte Gemeinde with all my heart.

Chapter 1

On Not Taming Jesus

In March 1969 I copied three sentences from Karl Rahner into my diary. At that time I was reading with lip-smacking glee everything of his I could get my hands on. Those three sentences read:

> Christianity has not been given any guarantee by God that it will be unable to sleep through the Present. Christianity can be old-fashioned, it can forget that the old truths and the values of yesterday can be defended only if and when one conquers a new future. And it has actually to a great extent fallen into this error, so that today's Christianity often gives rise to the painful impression that it is running mopishly and in a disgusted, critical mood behind the carriage in which the human race drives into a new future.[1]

At that time I must have agreed entirely with those statements (which certainly do not represent the whole of Rahner's theology). Otherwise I would not have copied them down. They expressed what I myself felt in that restless time, at the end of the 1960s, and what many others felt as well: that the church must finally clear out its dusty old traditions and learn from modern society. Five pages earlier, in the same diary, I had copied from somewhere: "Traditions are like lampposts. They light the way we are supposed to follow, but only drunkards hold on to them."

That is the way we thought back then. There was a tingling mood of upheaval in the air. Not only in society, but in the church as well there were many who were pushing for renewal, change, revolution—and that impulse was justified. It still is. For every living organism must renew itself; otherwise it will turn into a rapidly decaying corpse.

Ten years later I find in the diary, still ongoing, a new entry on the theme of "tradition," this time in a quotation from the Polish philosopher Leszek Kolakowski. In an essay that has since become famous, he wrote:

> There are two circumstances we should always keep simultaneously in mind: First, if the new generations had not continually revolted against inherited tradition we would still be living in caves; second, if revolt against inherited tradition should become universal, we would soon be back in the caves. . . . A society in which tradition becomes a cult is condemned to stagnation; a society that tries to live entirely through revolt against tradition condemns itself to destruction.[2]

As radically as this text also points in the direction of revolt, it is at the same time filled with a deep skepticism toward a one-sided demolition of tradition. A society that destroys its traditions—its collected, concentrated, and inherited experiences—destroys itself. The same is true, obviously, of the church. It must not do away with its traditions, but at the same time it must continually clarify, renew, and deepen them.

The Standard of Renewal

The question is only what the church should take as a standard for its continual renewal. Should that standard really be found in society, which according to Rahner is driving toward the future in a fast and apparently elegant vehicle?

Rahner cannot have meant that, but apparently I understood him to be saying that at the time. Today I think differently on this point. I certainly do not want to deny that society can also have a prophetic function for the church. There are secular prophets like Friedrich Nietzsche or Karl Marx, and many others, from whom the church is still learning much and has much more to learn. But the church's true standard cannot be the swift vehicle of society: it swerves fearfully, doesn't always manage the curves, and in the twentieth century only too often became a hearse.

The church's true measure lies somewhere else. Taking the secular prophets and the critics of Christianity seriously is by no means the same thing as running behind society with our tongues hanging out. Our true measure, the only one by which the church can renew itself, is Jesus Christ as the gospels present him to us. He is the center of the church, and church renewal can only mean coming closer to what was given to the church with Christ as its heart and center.

If Jesus is the *logos* of God, the final and ultimate word spoken by God, the Word in which God has spoken God's self totally and without exception, then, certainly, Jesus is always far ahead of us all and ahead of all times. In that case we must not model his figure according to our time-conditioned standards—as long as they correspond to our ideas. We can only try to follow him. And it is only in this constant discipleship within the church, in the midst of many sisters and brothers, that we will really understand him—and then we will also understand the church's precious tradition.

The New Message of Self-Acceptance

This process of understanding Jesus is not an easy one, for we are all children of our own time. We are much more powerfully influenced by the guiding images, ideas, and shifting values of the society in which we live than we even begin to suspect. And that very naturally shapes how we perceive Jesus. Let me illustrate this with an example.

Nowadays we regularly hear that "you can only love others if you first learn to love yourself." Not only psychologists and psychotherapists tell us that; it is constantly repeated by the religious "inspirational literature" of the twenty-first century. I can go into any bookstore and pull one of these new books on religious "lifestyle" off the religion shelf, open it up, leaf through it, and invariably come across statements like this:

> You have to get in touch with yourself.
>
> Self-accusation is pointless.
>
> You have to accept yourself as you are.
>
> Accept yourself unconditionally.
>
> Accept yourself, with everything that is in you.
>
> You can feel confident that you are good.
>
> Choose yourself.
>
> Everything in you is good, just as it is.
>
> You have to be reconciled with yourself.
>
> You should live in peace with yourself.
>
> You can forgive yourself.

You can live in harmony with yourself.

You must experience Jesus as the door into yourself.

It is important that you be one with yourself.

Show yourself compassion.

You have to love yourself.

Be good to yourself.

All those are literal quotations from a single book that I looked through, more or less by accident, in a bookstore in my town. There are heaps of such books nowadays in every bookstore—and especially on the shelves devoted to religion and the esoteric.

I don't want to condemn the quoted statements out of hand. They do contain some truth; self-acceptance can be profoundly Christian. For example, I must accept myself as God's creature, as someone whose guilt God has forgiven, again and again. I can accept myself as loved and led. That kind of self-acceptance is healthy and healing. But the sentences I have quoted are written in a different tone. In the vehemence with which they are spoken by many people today, and in their isolation from what the New Testament understands by reconciliation, they are seductively false.

Interestingly enough, these statements are almost entirely identical with the advertising texts of today's "wellness" industry, and it is striking that they correspond exactly to the search of people today for pleasurable self-discovery. It is just that they don't correspond in any way to the Bible, which speaks not of self-acceptance but of repentance, of reconciliation not with oneself but with God and one's neighbor.

The Bible says, "Change! Turn your life around!" In contrast, the quoted lines all tend toward the adage, "Stay the way you are!" I don't think it is any accident that a few days ago I found these very words in my mailbox on an advertisement for a major bank. "Stay the way you are!" it said, in huge, bright-colored letters. Slick advertising slogans and pseudo-Christian self-acceptance spirituality flow into one another without a hitch.

In the fog of such a contemporary spirit, the Bible's words vanish as though covered with an opaque veil. The twofold love commandment is suddenly no longer perceived in the way the church understood it for two thousand years. "You shall love your neighbor *as yourself*" is now distilled primarily and urgently into the command to love yourself. Thus, the twofold biblical commandment becomes a "threefold commandment":

You shall love God,
you shall love your neighbor
and you shall love yourself—
in fact, you shall first of all love yourself,
because otherwise you can love neither God
nor your neighbor.

This commandment to love yourself is comforting and promotes good middle-class sleep. Consequently, in the last few decades this interpretation has enjoyed enormous success.

But that kind of exegesis has not the least thing to do with the biblical twofold commandment, because there "as yourself" does not refer to the individual "you" in the modern sense. The "you" of the twofold commandment is, rather, one's own family. This is very clearly illustrated in the call of Abraham, when God says to him: "I will make of you a great nation, and I will bless you, and make your name great, so that you will be a blessing" (Gen 12:2). Who is this "you"? Abraham, of course, but not Abraham alone, because he is leaving his homeland together with his wife Sarai, his nephew Lot, and the menservants and maidservants they had acquired in Haran (Gen 12:4-5). Abraham travels with his whole extended family, his cattle and tents, toward Canaan.

Against this background, which the Old Testament simply takes for granted, the commandment to love the neighbor in Leviticus 19:18, 34 says: the help and solidarity that every individual in Israel owes to her or his own relatives, and especially one's own family, is to be extended to all Israel. The boundaries of the family are to be broken and extended to all brothers and sisters in the people of God, even to strangers, even to those who are regarded as enemies to your family and relations. That is the intent of Leviticus 19, and it is light-years from the individual self-love that is preached to us today from all sides.

Meanwhile, this whole phenomenon has crept into our prayers. Not long ago I read a theologian's address to God: "You, the power who enables me to appreciate myself."

But enough of this! I have already spoken of the difficulty in understanding Jesus because we are so powerfully shaped by our own times. The remarkable transformation of the commandment to love one's neighbor into an urgent appeal for self-love is only one small example of the metamorphosis of biblical texts that goes on nowadays, silently and almost as a matter of course. A great many other examples could be given. But it is not my purpose to enter into a critique of contemporary mentalities in church and society. That is not the idea behind this chapter. What I want to talk about is the Jesus of the gospels.

Positively, I want to develop two crucial points in Jesus' message and practice that nowadays are often watered down or even suppressed: first, Jesus' call to follow him and to discipleship and, second, his expectation of the imminent end.

Jesus' Call to Follow Him and to Discipleship

Let us take another quick look at Leviticus 19:18: "You shall love your neighbor as yourself." This statement marks a revolution in religious history. We can scarcely imagine the significance, in the ancient Near East, of the family and the larger kinship group. Every person was bound into a clan to which she or he owed obedience and solidarity, receiving from it in return community, aid, and a home. This strong incorporation within the clan was as obvious to the minds of that society as the primacy of self-expression and "the good life" have become in our Western society today.

In Leviticus 19, as we have already seen, the internal solidarity owed to "us," that is, the family and the clan, is exploded and expanded to include all of Israel. Even the stranger within the people of God now has a claim to the same solidarity as the blood relative. Even the foreigners in the land are to become brothers and sisters to the longtime inhabitants, Leviticus 19 says. That was anything but obvious. It went contrary to all the values and rules of the time.

Jesus takes up precisely this revolutionary step in Israel's exilic theology; in fact, he radicalizes it still further. In the Pentateuch the commandments to love God and the neighbor remain unconnected. The former is in Deuteronomy 6, the latter in Leviticus 19. Jesus joins the two commandments; more than that, he gives the command to love the neighbor the same weight and importance as the command to love God (Matt 22:39). For him, the two commandments are inseparable; together they constitute for him the center of the Torah.

But that is not simply a lovely theory in Jesus' mind; it becomes the center of his actions. When Jesus appeared, the people of God was profoundly divided and split into Samaritans, Sadducees, Pharisees, Zealots, and Essenes. Each of these groups and religious parties declared enmity to the others and claimed to be the "true Israel," the only one corresponding to God's will. If we look closely, we see that Jesus was confronted with exactly the same scandal we endure today: the division of the people of God.

What did he do in that situation? His whole activity, his whole practice of the reign of God was aimed at gathering, uniting, and renewing this divided Israel in light of the nearness of the reign of God. But how can such a thing be done? We all know how hugely difficult it is to unite a parish, a diocese, the Catholic Church, the many Christian churches according to the will of God. It was just as hard back then.

What did Jesus do? What did he undertake in view of the mortal divisions in Israel? To put it anachronistically: he did not assemble a committee of experts. He did not introduce a process of dialogue. He did not seek a formula of compromise. He certainly did not have a consensus paper drawn up. He did not undertake any of those things or any of the comparable measures of his own time.

What did he do? He proclaimed the reign of God throughout the land, and he placed twelve men demonstratively before the crowds and said: this is the beginning of the eschatological Israel. Beyond that, he gathered disciples who would follow him. This gathering of disciples is what interests me now. What did Jesus intend by it? Why was this circle of disciples of such crucial importance to him?

First of all, obviously Jesus was concerned with the whole of Israel, with all the people of God—the hated Samaritans as much as the orthodox in Galilee and Judea, the Sadducees as much as the Pharisees, the anti-Roman Zealots as much as the profit-hungry collaborators, the scribes as much as the ordinary people. Consequently, the movement Jesus began in Israel did not include just Jesus' disciples. The Jesus movement was much more colorful and multifaceted. It incorporated not just the disciples who followed Jesus, that is, who were on the road with him throughout the land from village to village, from town to town. The Jesus movement also included a great many local followers of Jesus who remained at home but placed their houses at his disposal: think, for example, of the family of Lazarus, Martha, and Mary in Bethany.

Still more, the Jesus movement also included sympathizers and occasional helpers who may have met Jesus only once in their lives but who were on the spot when they were needed. I think of Joseph of Arimathea, who after Jesus' execution made an expensive cave tomb available, and I think of Jesus' saying that anyone who would give one of his thirsty disciples so much as a cup of water would receive a full reward (Matt 10:42).

But the Jesus movement included not only sympathizers and occasional helpers; there were also those who sought healing and those who were healed, people who were interested or curious, hangers-on and even beneficiaries. Then as now, the church included not only those who are actively engaged and regularly attend worship but many others who only occasionally participate or are somewhere on the margins or themselves do not really know where they belong. If there is to be freedom, it cannot be otherwise. As the Jerusalem temple had many outer courts, so does the church.

I want to be clear that the gathering of Israel that Jesus set in motion offered a vivid and multifaceted picture. Many people belonged to it "in some way." But what is crucial is this: all that would not have been enough. It would all have remained "up in the air" if it had not been for the circle of disciples, which was the center of Jesus' enormous project of gathering all of Israel and uniting it in the reign of God.

Those who literally followed Jesus and who also had left everything were thus not a special, separate community, an esoteric club, a closed ghetto, and most certainly not a cozy group of the like-minded or of exalted worshipers of Jesus. Rather, they were the beginning of the eschatological Israel, the growth center of the people of God that Jesus had in mind. They were the yeast that was to leaven the whole lump.

If we read the gospels closely we will see that Jesus expended an extraordinary amount of time on instructing this "center" of Israel. In Mark, our oldest gospel, a relatively long section, encompassing chapters 8–11, is reserved for the instruction of the disciples. The other gospels also contain major discourses that are addressed primarily to the disciples: think, for example, of Matthew's Sermon on the Mount (Matt 5–7) and Luke's Sermon on the Plain (Luke 6:20-49).

Besides that, we should note that a great many texts in the gospels that we assume as a matter of course were addressed to all the people in Israel, or even "globally" to the world in general, were originally intended for the disciples. Their *Sitz im Leben*, their place in the real world, as biblical scholars like to say, was instruction of the group of disciples.

For example: In lectionary Year A, on the eighth Sunday of the year, we hear the gospel of freedom from anxiety. "Do not worry, saying 'What will we eat?' or 'What will we drink?' or 'What will we wear?' For it is the Gentiles who strive for all these things; and indeed your heavenly Father knows that you need all these things" (Matt 6:31-32). Every preacher must shudder when confronted with these words. Can he really tell the audience that they should not worry? Obviously, they have to worry and take care. Everyone who is head of a household, and in fact everyone who has any kind of responsibility, has to be careful to keep control of the bank balance, fill the refrigerator, order heating oil before the prices go up, plan ahead and follow up, budget rationally—and all that takes wisdom, prudence, and careful planning. We are right to be angry nowadays at politicians who are unconcerned about the simplest principles of responsible budgeting and burden the state with unimaginably huge debts.

Some preachers find a way out of this situation by saying that, of course, we have to take care and plan in many areas of life, but we should not do it *anxiously*. A Christian must indeed be prudent and look to the future but should do it *with confidence*. That may be true, but it does not get at the heart of this saying of Jesus. Its addressees were not simply the crowds of people around Jesus; they were the disciples who traveled with him throughout Israel.

They were constantly and repeatedly on the road, with Jesus and sometimes without him. They were on the road so that the beginning of the reign of God could be proclaimed throughout the land. Most often they did not know in the morning where they would be at night. Would they find people who would receive them into their homes in the evening and give them something to eat? I mentioned the localized followers of Jesus, his sympathizers, friends, and those he healed, his helpers and supporters. It is precisely *this* large group within the Jesus movement who played their specific role here. For Jesus and his disciples were by no means solitary. They could count on a whole network of friends and sympathizers throughout the land. And this is precisely where we should locate the freedom from worry that Jesus asks of his disciples. Jesus' disciples who traveled with him throughout Israel and those of his followers who remained tied to their homes mutually augmented one another, supported and helped one another, and thus constituted an inseparable unit.

Jesus and his disciples needed people who would prepare a meal for them in the evening and offer them shelter for the night. In turn, the localized followers needed vital contact with Jesus and his disciples so that the new thing, the silent revolution of the reign of God, could enter into their families. So there was a profound relationship between the two groups, a mutuality and community. The disciples lived not for their own sake but for the sake of the people of God, and the localized followers no longer lived only for themselves and their children. So something new came into existence throughout the villages and small towns of Israel: a new community of many people, a new family that extended beyond the old physical relationships and clan mentality.

Thus what Jesus says about freedom from anxiety does not betray some kind of alienation from the world and most certainly not eccentricity.

The disciples' non-anxious trust, of which Jesus speaks, has a genuine basis: namely, the houses of Jesus' followers throughout the land in which Jesus and his disciples were received at night. The disciples can be worry free and trust in God because they are not alone. They are surrounded by a network of adherents and sympathizers, a multitude of people who, like them, believe in the coming of the reign of God.

In this way there was created in Israel a new community, a new form of society in which all help one another. The goal of this community, this being-together, this mutual support and help, was to make apostolic work possible. The goal of this community is that Jesus' messengers may be able to proclaim the Gospel.

I am convinced that precisely here we are all challenged by the Gospel of non-anxiety: do we want community in this sense—as a being-together of many who support one another, a communion of many brothers and sisters who are present for one another so that engagement on behalf of the Gospel will be possible? This would be a change from solitary parishes staffed by single persons and self-sacrificing individuals to communities in which there are mutual aid, mutual claims and commitments, mutual advice, mutual consolation, mutual correction, continually renewed and common repentance—and precisely, therefore, no anxiety.

I think it has become obvious that Jesus did not preach his Gospel of the reign of God blindly and optimistically. He had a clear strategy. The proclamation of the reign of God is not simply and solely proclamation, not simply and solely preaching, not simply "word." It calls for a people, a renewed people of God, a new society—and this eschatological renewal of the people of God has as its indispensable precondition disciples, or more precisely, a community of disciples.

The Gospel is full of sayings about this new way of life for Jesus' disciples, because that is precisely where we find portrayed what the reign of God truly is. Jesus' disciples have to forgive one another seventy-seven times a day, that is, constantly and again and again (Matt 18:21-22). They are not to look for the splinter in the eye of their sister or brother in the faith, but deal with the plank in their own eye (Luke 6:41-42). No one is to try to rule over another. Whoever wants to be first must serve the others like a menial (Luke 22:24-27). No one is to seek special recognition and praise. If they are deathly tired in the evening, they must say: "We have only done what we ought to have done" (Luke 17:10).

In all this, the disciples are to learn constantly from Jesus (Matt 23:10). They will never learn everything there is to know. That is why the gospels call them *mathetai*, students. Our word "disciple" used to say that plainly, because it comes from medieval *discipulus,* which then meant an apprentice. So when the gospels speak of Jesus' *mathetai* they mean to say that they remain lifelong students, learners, apprentices, trainees.

Jesus' pupils are supposed to proclaim the Gospel everywhere and attest to it by their way of being together, but they do not reside in fixed locations. If some place will not accept the Gospel, they are to move on (Luke 10:10-12). The New Testament nowhere speaks of "comprehensive pastoral care."

Jesus' students were not permitted to exercise any kind of force; they were to proclaim the Gospel in a spirit of absolute nonviolence. As a sign of their nonviolence they—in contrast to the Zealots, the warriors for God of that time—should not so much as carry a staff for self-defense (Matt 10:10). They were not even to wear sandals, with which they could run away rapidly (Luke 10:4).

But there was something even more severe: Jesus asked them to leave their families and follow him (Matt 10:37). In that way he radically brought into being what Leviticus 19 had already contemplated: the mentality of mere family ties, of the clan, was ruptured. The result was a "new family" ordered toward all Israel.

Jesus himself followed the path he had demanded of his pupils: when his relatives tried to carry him home by force because they were convinced that "he has gone out of his mind" (Mark 3:21), he separated himself from his family and in positively juridical language called all those who were now hearing the word of God through him his sisters and brothers (Mark 3:31-35). That is, he created a "new family" and thus definitively made a reality of Leviticus 19.

The new community thus created is more than a mere matter of common life. It is a community with a common fate, to the extent that Jesus' students had to be ready to suffer as Jesus did: just as people called Jesus a "glutton" and a "drunkard" (Matt 11:19), even a eunuch (cf. Matt 19:12), so also Jesus' disciples would be ridiculed. They would be slandered, despised, excluded. They would have to "take up their cross" (Matt 10:38).

It should be clear by now that the life of discipleship Jesus demanded as the indispensable basis for the renewal of the people of God was no game, and it was altogether contrary to the well-known list of demands that are loudly proclaimed by many today as *essentials* for the renewal of the church: from renunciation of celibacy to active support of euthanasia. The list is familiar enough. If we look at it carefully we can see that from beginning to end it is an accommodation to the ways of life of contemporary society. It has very little to do with the Gospel.

But the people of God has never yet been renewed through accommodation. Israel's prophets had to constantly defend against a saying that was one of Israel's greatest temptations: "we want to be like the other nations" (Deut 17:14; 1 Sam 8:5, 20; Ezek 20:32). This demand has sounded repeatedly through the whole history of the people of God: "we want to be like the other nations," that is, like the rest of society. Jesus, contemplating Gentile society, had to tell his disciples: "but not so with you" (Luke 22:26).

At present we run the deadly risk of separating the renewal of the church from Jesus, or else of accommodating Jesus to the thinking of our own time and watering down his demand. This applies especially to the *way* in which Jesus wanted to renew the people of God, a way that led to the gathering of disciples, the community of people who desired to serve the reign of God with their whole existence. Do we still have the courage to regard such a discipleship of women and men, married and celibate, young and old as the most urgent thing the church today needs?

If we read the gospels attentively and without presuppositions, however, we not only stumble unceasingly over Jesus' call to follow him, to discipleship, but also over something else that appears again and again, just as urgently, and that we even more urgently suppress: Jesus' expectation of the nearness of the end. So I come to my second point.

Jesus' Urgent Expectation of the End

For me there can be no question: we cannot understand Jesus' preaching and his gathering of Israel unless we pay attention to the uncanny expectation of the end that shaped everything he did. These two things—Jesus' educational work with his circle of disciples and his expectation of the imminent end—are intimately connected. Jesus does not speak of a reign of God that will come someday. His preaching of the reign of God is announcement, proclamation: God's new world is coming *now*, is at the door, is intent on happening now, in this very hour. And his preaching of the reign of God was not spoken into empty space. It had to find, corresponding to it, a newly forming people of God in which the reign of God could already be a reality.

How else can we understand Jesus' calling the poor, the sorrowing, and the hungry "blessed"? "Blessed are you who are hungry now, for you will be filled" (Luke 6:21). That is, of course, not a reference to eternal life in heaven. No, it means that the transformation is about to happen, right away. The reign of God is coming *now*, and then there will be the kind of abundance that exists when God acts and when all in Israel help one another in solidarity. Therefore, Jesus calls the poor who follow him "blessed." They will at last have enough to eat, they will at last be able to laugh again, and they will have a share in the reign of God.

For Jesus, all that is already beginning. God's new world no longer lies in an absolutely to-be-awaited future. On the other hand, the whole fullness of the reign of God is not yet present. Hence the parable of the fig tree, the only tree in Israel that drops its leaves in winter. Jesus points it out in order to show how things stand with the reign of God: within a few days its twigs soften and take on a reddish glow; that means that summer is coming, when the fig tree's leaves unfold. So it is with the reign of God, Jesus says. It is already breaking through; its signs can already be seen; its abundance is about to come (cf. Luke 21:29-31).

How can we deal with Jesus' urgent expectation? Certainly not like all the sects who equate the coming of the reign of God with the end of the world and Jesus' return, and then set particular dates for it to happen. Sooner or later the predicted day arrives, and neither Jesus nor the reign of God has come. Oddly enough, for the most part there is no great frustration within these sects. Could it be because, hidden in all these crass projections and calculations, there remains a bit of genuine expectation that can still be taken seriously, even when the superficial projections have proved false?

As we have said, the church cannot follow this fundamentalist path of chronological calculation; it is totally irrational. But how tempting it is, then, to simply suppress all the texts in the New Testament that speak of imminent expectation! When they appear, most preachers do not touch them, let alone interpret them. Usually they are simply passed over in silence. As a whole, the theme of "imminent expectation" is rather embarrassing, and it has long since vanished from the faith consciousness of Catholic congregations.

Nevertheless, this method of suppression is, in view of contemporary exegesis, not as easy as it once was. In the year 1892 there appeared a now-famous book by the Protestant exegete Johannes Weiss, *Jesus' Preaching of the Reign of God*. That book showed anew how deeply Jesus' preaching of the reign of God was shaped by imminent eschatological expectation. Since then theologians have tried to deal with the phenomenon of "imminent expectation." Some say that in this Jesus was simply deceived. He was, after all, a child of his times like all of us. He too was deeply embedded in the ideas and ways of thinking appropriate to the Jewish worldview of the time. And at that time many Jews thought in apocalyptic terms, that is, they expected the complete re-creation of the world in the very near future. Jesus thought that way too—and in doing so he was fundamentally mistaken. We should honestly admit that and simply ignore the relevant texts. I am convinced that this is one of the many diminishing "clarifications" used today to make Jesus irrelevant.

Other theologians, however, are quite clear about the fact that this simple ignoring of the New Testament texts of imminent expectation is no solution. So they take another tack: they reduce Jesus' imminent expectation to a matter of ethics. They quote from the well-known book on Jesus by Herbert Braun, formerly professor of New Testament in Mainz:

> The essential intention of Jesus' preaching about the end is not entertaining advice about events in the near future but an unprecedented sharpening of accountability. . . . Jesus did not intend to give *information* about the imminent end but to *summon* people because of it. . . . The preaching about the nearness of God's reign seeks to warn people lest they themselves miss out on it.[3]

That doesn't sound so bad. But Braun's crucial deficiency is his reduction of the basic eschatological structure of Jesus' discourse to ethics. If Jesus' preaching of the end time is rightly translated in Braun's terms—we could also say: if it is proper to transform it into our current way of speaking—then time and history play no role in it. Jesus' proclamation thus becomes ahistorical. The living hope in his preaching becomes "accountability." There is no longer any salvation that approaches people out of the future, indeed, out of the future-already-in-fulfillment.

More subtle is the argument of all those who, following Rudolf Bultmann, give an existential interpretation to Jesus' eschatological preaching, that is, they read it in terms of human eschatological existence. An especially impressive example of this type of exegesis is found in Hans Conzelmann's *An Outline of the Theology of the New Testament*, where he writes:

> Jesus is not interested in the question of the interval of time in itself. If the expectation of the kingdom is understood radically, then *ēggiken* [having come near] does not represent a primarily neutral statement about the length or brevity of an interval of time, but a fact which determines human existence: man has no more time left for himself. He must respond to the kingdom in the present moment. It is still not there; otherwise the opportunity for this response, for repentance, would be past. The kingdom would no longer be preached. But it is so near that a man can no longer ask, "For how

long can I postpone repentance?" There is no more time. Now is the
last moment for those who are addressed. For this reason, the question of time cannot be put in neutral terms.[4]

I find this development of the existential aspect of Jesus' eschatological
preaching very good. It reveals some important elements in Jesus'
preaching of the reign of God. Above all, Conzelmann's interpretation
makes it understandable why the delay of the approaching end presented
no problem to the early church: within it the constant repentance of all
the many people who believed with their whole existence was taking
place, and thus they were repeatedly living this "last hour."

Nevertheless, the existential interpretation also reveals a profound
deficiency: Jesus' eschatology is now formulated in terms of individuals.
Church and community are almost entirely absent. Therefore, history is
also absent, a history conceived in terms of God's action and taking seriously the "already" and "not yet" of the reign of God. I need to explain
this more precisely.

God always acts eschatologically, because—paradoxically—there has
been no instant since the creation of the world in which God has not
encompassed and sustained this world with divine action, care, mercy,
and love that anticipates all. In Jesus of Nazareth this grace, always given
to the world, reached its ultimate goal. That is the end time. But if the
reign of God is still not present in its full abundance, it is not because
God is holding it back but because we have not yet fully grasped it. There
is still unbelief everywhere. The reign of God cannot yet be fully real.
What is already present in Christ has not yet been completely established.
But that is not God's fault. It is ours, with our lack of repentance. From
God's point of view, everything is present, everything is offered. We
would only have to take hold of it.

At this point Hans Conzelmann's existential interpretation also makes
sense. Its deficiency is only that it does not really take into account the
historical dimension of this salvation (and judgment) that is always approaching us in every moment of our lives.

After all, the world does not consist only of individuals who repent
or not. Individual decisions are, instead, sustained by the decisions of
many others with whom she or he is connected and in whose steps she
or he follows—and every individual, with every decision, in turn creates
history, opens doors to others or closes them. To put it another way: we
find ourselves in a history of salvation and no salvation that is decisively
shaped by whether we live as church, as a believing community, or not.

In our communities, the eschatological salvation of God is constantly approaching us, seeking to change the world. Here, then, we are constantly living in a state of imminent expectation, in a space in which God's promises earnestly seek fulfillment. But we can constantly fall out of that space, and in that case God's promises are not fulfilled in us and the arrival of Christ is delayed.

We have to interpret the New Testament texts of imminent expectation against this horizon of salvation history, always being fulfilled and at the same time repeatedly held at bay. In that light, all these texts are absolutely true. They belong to Jesus' core proclamation: that the whole salvation of God is on its way to us today.

This can only be met by imminent expectation. This kind of expectation is an awareness of the need to act, because it is all about the "now," and there is no time thereafter. Then every hour is precious; time has to be fully exhausted precisely because it has eschatological quality. Then imminent expectation, accurately interpreted, means at every moment taking into account that the Spirit of Christ desires to show the church new ways. It means at every moment reckoning with the fact that the Spirit is opening new doors. It means expecting at every moment that the Spirit can change evil into good. It means hoping at every moment that the impossible will become possible. And it means never saying, later! but always saying, now!

Then the texts of imminent expectation in the New Testament are not something embarrassing that we ought to be ashamed of; nor are they time conditioned, something we can leave behind us. Rather, they belong at the center of what it is to be Christian.

From this point of view, I would never say that Jesus and the early church were mistaken in their imminent expectation. Jesus was certain to his very core that God is acting now—acting definitively and unsurpassably. He was sure that God, in this action, was speaking God's self into the world—entirely and without reservation. This "entirely" and "definitively" are, however, confronted by the fact that human beings normally have no use for such an "entirely" insofar as it touches them and their response. They do not want to commit themselves definitively but prefer to delay their own decisions and, for the time being, leave everything open.

So there arises a deep discrepancy between God's "already" and the human "not yet." But because God has spoken God's self entirely and absolutely in Jesus, there is no more time for this "putting off the decision." Jesus' hearers have to decide: now, this minute. And they must not only decide because of God but also because of Israel's crisis and the immeasurable suffering of the world.

I ask myself whether, in the context of the eschatological thought of his environment, in which he himself was deeply rooted, Jesus could have shaped other language for this urgent "now" of decision or expressed it any differently than in terms of imminent expectation. And we ourselves, with our imagined horizon of endlessly unfolding time in which there is no real *kairos* any more but only *events*—are we really, with our concept of time, any closer to the truth of our existence and of human history than Jesus was with his eschatological emphasis?

I doubt it very strongly indeed. Obviously we have to translate the eschatological language of Jesus and the early church. When we do, it is apparent that it was not Jesus who was mistaken. We, in fact, deceive ourselves uninterruptedly, not only about the fragility and exposure of our lives, but also about the nearness of God.

Taming Jesus

Jesus is tamed and made irrelevant in a terrible way when we cease to speak about his imminent expectation. The same is true of a great many other aspects of his proclamation and his actions that for the sake of brevity I cannot speak of here. Jesus is rendered irrelevant when his preaching of judgment, which makes up a significant portion of the gospel tradition, is ignored and there is talk only of the loving and tender Jesus.

Jesus is tamed when there is no more preaching about his sharp words against the rich. "It is easier for a camel to go through the eye of a needle than for someone who is rich to enter the kingdom of God," Jesus said (Mark 10:25). We generally treat his critique of riches and the wealthy[5] as erratic blocks that poke up strangely and irregularly in the landscape. We prefer to take the long way around them.

Jesus is tamed when it becomes taboo to speak of his celibacy. It was not accidental and not a matter of fate; it is connected with his absolute devotion to the people of God. According to Matthew 9:15, he is the bridegroom, and the wedding feast with Israel has already begun.

Jesus is also tamed when we sharply criticize the treatment of divorced and remarried persons by Rome and yet keep silent about the altogether clear and thoroughly well-attested words of Jesus against divorce. Can we no longer see that here the Catholic Church is trying to remain true to Jesus, despite all the difficulties it causes for the church? The solution of this difficult and complex question, on which many points of view must be considered, can at any rate not be achieved by putting aside or whitewashing Jesus' demand.

Above all, Jesus is tamed and rendered irrelevant when he is presented only as a sympathetic rabbi, a prophet mighty in word and deed, or a gifted charismatic—or as the first feminist, a radical social revolutionary, or a gregarious social worker. All that conceals his true claim. In all these categories Jesus is shrunken, distorted, twisted into shape, planed smooth, disempowered, and accommodated to our secret desires.

I could have talked about many other things, but I had to concentrate on two points: Jesus' call to discipleship and his imminent expectation. Those were the two that seemed to me most important.

Please permit me, in concluding, to say something about the current crisis of faith. In 1948 and 1949 Ludwig Erhard still had to fight for the "free market" in Germany against market regulations and state control of the economy. In the interim the free market has long since become our reality, characterized above all by the freedom to produce and consume, free competition, an open balancing of supply and demand, and above all the principle of performance: whoever performs best conquers the market. Today all that—with a number of restrictions such as the suppression of monopolies—is a matter of course.

But at the same time we now have a free market in beliefs, including the corresponding competition and an unimaginable supply of scintillating projections of meaning. The media, especially the Internet, give evidence. Anyone can propound the religion she is persuaded to embrace—and that is a good thing. Each can choose the religion that appears right to him—and that is also a good thing. Still more: anyone can put together, out of various pieces of existing religions, an individual religion focused on herself or himself—and there is nothing to prevent it.

All that has led to a profound crisis of faith in Europe. It is no longer a matter of course that one is a Christian. Nowadays Christianity has to claim its own identity in the supermarket of religions and worldviews. Or should I say, it has to rediscover that identity? In any case, it needs to show what makes it distinctively Christian. Still more, it has to show that it is not *a* religion but the redemption of all religion.

But the situation within which we have to preach Jesus Christ is still more difficult. There is not just the religious supermarket with its proposals and bargains. Beyond that, there is the philosophy, nowadays almost a matter of course, that occupies countless heads today and can be reduced to this formula: "There is no such thing as truth, but only constructions of personal truths."

If, in this highly complex situation, we do not preach what is distinctively Christian and witness to it with our lives, we have no chance in the marketplace of chummy offerings of meaning. And if we want to be like society, our chances will be even slimmer. Then we as Christians are simply superfluous. Then we are salt that has lost its savor, to be thrown away and trodden on (Matt 5:13).

Wouldn't it be better, instead of accommodating ourselves, to hope, with Psalm 126, that God will take notice of Christianity's crisis of faith? Wouldn't it be better to count on it that what the psalm says will then happen for us?

> Restore our fortunes, O LORD,
>   like the watercourses in the Negeb.
> May those who sow in tears
>   reap with shouts of joy.
> Those who go out weeping,
>   bearing the seed for sowing,
> shall come home with shouts of joy,
>   carrying their sheaves. (Ps 126:4-6)

That certainly does not mean sitting with our hands in our laps: after all, the sowing comes first. But at the same time it means being able to expect everything from God: a superabundant harvest—if only we remain true to Jesus and the church.

Chapter 2

Jesus Revolutionizes Linear Time

When, on September 11, 2001, the two World Trade Center towers in New York City were brought down by a fundamentalist Islamist attack, taking with them nearly three thousand human lives, a breathless, hectic activity broke out in the media. The world was flooded with images, film clips, eyewitness accounts, commentary, and background analyses. Immediately after the event, a great many commentaries included the statement: "After September 11 nothing will ever be the same."

We could, of course, argue about that. Not very long afterward one of the major German dailies began a commentary with, "Much is already the same as it was before September 11." That, in fact, was also true, and yet at the same time there was a powerful feeling, on September 11, that for an instant history had held its breath—and then changed course. There was a similar feeling when the Berlin Wall fell on the evening of November 9, 1989. At that time a great many people were overcome by the feeling that history was happening: *now*! That's how it is when history happens.

It may also be that quite a few people reflected on what history really is. Perhaps they concluded that there are events that are simply unpredictable, that break upon us suddenly and unexpectedly. But they may have come to a quite different conclusion and said that there are moments when something deeply hidden but in preparation for a long time suddenly and viciously appears. Moods, trends, hidden developments can condense, coalesce, combine, and bring something new into the world.

And if there are people at hand who are courageous and valiant or fanatical and criminal, things can happen that have never occurred in this world in such a form.

We might ask ourselves whether it is really so obvious that we are all aware of something called "history," historical events, historical upheavals. Have the peoples of the world always experienced it as "history" in the way we do today? Or were there cultures that experienced the flow of time very differently?

We can be sure that for a long time people did not and could not perceive history in the modern sense. They certainly had no such concept as "history." They experienced the world, the universe, the rhythms of life, and the flow of time differently from the way we do.

Cyclical Time

Animals have no notion of history, although we can suppose that, within their limitations, they have a sense of time that is difficult for us to understand. Chimpanzees, for example, can organize tools they will need the next day. But that is not a concept of history. Besides, we can never know precisely how, in such a case, the experimental situation itself influences their behavior.

In any case, our ancient ancestors lived like animals for many, many years, as far as a concept of history is concerned, even long after they had descended from the trees. Nietzsche, in his *Untimely Meditations*, wrote:

> Consider the cattle, grazing as they pass you by: they do not know what is meant by yesterday or today; they leap about, eat, rest, digest, leap about again, and so on from morn to night and from day to day, fettered to the moment and its pleasure or displeasure, and thus neither melancholy nor bored.[1]

Human beings, developing out of the animal world over an unimaginably long period of time, probably had for many ages little or no awareness of history. For far longer than we can grasp, they were "fettered to the moment." Of course, they had an awareness of time, but at first it was cyclical. Some primitive peoples and nature religions even today have a cyclical view of time.

If we try to make a schematic picture of this notion of time, we would have to draw a circle on which an arrow turns, returning again and again to its starting point. Why? This kind of idea of time was inspired by the phenomena of nature: the cycle of day and night, the phases of the moon, the seasons, the regular rhythms of the hunt and of birth and death. All events were contained in nature and conditioned by it. Therefore the festivals of early cultures were also nature feasts celebrating birth and death, sowing and harvest, success in the hunt, and above all the cycles of the sun and moon.

But we should not make things too easy for ourselves in imagining the cyclical notions of some societies. It could also be the case that there were cultures in which profound changes, social revolutions, and historical catastrophes were experienced as pervasive evil that people sought to resist through cyclical time constructs. Concretely, in festivals and periodically repeated rituals people therefore celebrated above all the eternal return of the known in order to counter the horrors of real history and secure the continuity of social institutions. In that case cyclical time would not have been simply the dominant basic experience of a society but a cultural construct.

But however that may have been, cyclical thinking is still burned deeply into us, much more deeply than we suppose. We can see it in the fact that in neosecular society Christian feasts are being slowly transformed back into nature festivals: for many people Easter has long since become nothing but a spring holiday, Ascension Day is Fathers' Day, and at Christmas we celebrate the natural mystery of "mother and child." The spread of the notion of reincarnation in formerly Christian lands is also connected to cyclical notions of time or, rather, to the longing for ever-new cycles of life.

The Ages of the World

We can ponder how it was that humanity first arrived at a genuine notion of history. Was it through terrifying natural catastrophes that buried themselves deep in people's consciousness, stories which were handed on and so broke apart the cyclical idea of time—such things as huge floods like that described in the story of Noah? Was it brought about by the migrations of tribes to new regions? Or victorious battles that then survived in the form of sagas? We need not go into that in this context. More important is the rise of the historical model of the ages of the world, because that indicates the first notions of history. It was still cyclical, but it began to reflect an experience of history and reflection on it.

Nearly all high cultures have some periodization of continuing time into "ages of the world" or "world eons." The Greek poet Hesiod, in his instructional poem "Works and Days," describes five ages succeeding one another: first the gold, then the silver, then the bronze age, followed by the age of the heroes, that then devolved into the iron age. The Roman poet Ovid counted four ages: golden, silver, bronze, and iron. There were, as we have said, similar models of world time in almost all cultures, for example, in India or ancient Mexico. At the end of these models there is usually not a complete collapse or end of the world; rather, the course begins again from the beginning. Everything is repeated in endless succession. When the worst, the iron age, has reached its nadir, everything turns back and the golden age shines forth once more.

The silent model for such thinking was, obviously, the maturing and then the long downward course of living things, including human beings, who grow to the fullness of their strength and then slowly decline. Characteristic of most models of the ages of the world is their pessimism: the present condition is always part of the worst age. We could describe it as follows: "Things have never been worse than they are now, but some day they will get better."

Linear Time

Genuine historical thinking presupposes a linear experience of time. What is crucial is an awareness of the irreversibility of the processes of time and history. A graphic illustration of this kind of notion of time requires a linear arrow showing the direction-orientation of all events. The arrow can be subdivided into sections: A, B, C, D, etc., but what is crucial is that B will never again be A, and D will never again be C. If time were reversible, all events would return to their beginning. The Greek philosopher Heraclitus is supposed to have said, "You cannot step twice into the same stream."[2]

It is true that Heraclitus was talking about the unity of the world and thus the unity of being. But within that unity everything is in flux, in constant motion, and forms change uninterruptedly. The world is a process, and that must also mean that the course of time is irreversible. So Heraclitus is not simply uttering a banality when he says that no one steps into the same river twice. He is expressing an experience that was "relatively" new as an observation on human development.

There was linear historical thinking in Egypt, with the Hittites, in Babylon, and then of course also in Greek and Roman culture. Characteristic of such thinking was the recording of important events in annals written and continued by local officials. Israel took up this linear notion of history and made it central to its faith. It was not just a matter of course for Israel, because its great feasts were originally harvest festivals or those connected with the annual transhumance, the shift from one pastureland to another; thus they derived from cyclical thinking. Only bit by bit were they transformed into historical feasts.

In this the exodus of Moses' group from the oppressive structures of Egypt must have played a key role. This exodus experience was a historical one through and through, and it permanently shaped Israel's thought. Nowhere, in no other nation and in no other culture, was history taken as seriously as in Israel—and by way of Israel, in Christianity.

Obviously, Greek historical thought was of fundamental consequence for Western concepts of history. I need only mention the great names Herodotus and Thucydides. The world's first work of truly scientific historical writing is Thucydides' *Peloponnesian War*. Nonetheless, Israel's experience of history played an immense role in shaping Western thought. That was connected with Israel's secularization of the world.

I don't know whether you have ever asked yourself why the industrial revolution developed in Europe and not in India, where supposedly the best mathematicians and programmers live today. Or why not in China, where paper and gunpowder were invented? It cannot have been a lack of intelligence. Why not in Mali, once the most powerful empire in West Africa? Why not among the Aztecs in Mexico? Why Europe?

Scholars have any number of explanations for it: Europe had fertile soils, moderate rainfall, a temperate climate, the right kind of domestic animals. But the explanations that rest on Europe's different worldview are much more illuminating: In Christian Europe the world was no longer a numinous reality in which everything is divine; rather, it was the "creation" of a God who also works at creation, where there is, therefore, a history of creation.

When faith in the Creator of the world drained the world itself of its divinity, it was placed at the disposal of scientific thought and creative work. Ultimately this worldview stems from the biblical tradition. Israel, at the nodal point between Asia, Africa, and Europe, was the flashpoint for an unimaginable development to which we are all witnesses and in which we are all involved. Now human beings could get to the bottom not only of nature but also of society, and not only society but the course of history itself.

Accordingly, in Europe the idea of linear time developed its full power: it made possible, for example, the idea of progress within history. This notion reached its apogee in the nineteenth century's faith in progress. At that time Europeans were convinced that the world was steadily becoming more humane. This notion was only shattered by the experience of World War I.

History as Chaos

But then it broke with a crash. For many, from that time on history was only confusion and obscurity, an utter chaos. The arrow of linear development by no means vanished from people's minds; they continued to experience the unbelievable advances of technology and the way nearly all nations adopted the industrial civilization of the West and "developed" themselves faster and faster. Add to this the gigantic advances in physics and biology: the ideas of an exploding universe and a universal evolution of living things.

But that is only part of the consciousness characteristic of modern people. In another part of their thinking, the picture of an orderly and meaningful history has been shattered. There is no universal meaning any longer, and therefore there is essentially no clear history aiming toward a goal. What remains is only the disconnected chaos of infinitely many contending and crisscrossing "narratives." At the center stands one's own experience of the moment, one's own momentary world, one's own momentary feeling, which only says: "I like it," "I don't like it," "I love it," "I hate it."

Many of our contemporaries are convinced that no unified history is possible any longer because the world and its development consist of an infinite number of partial points of view. If we were to schematize this view, we could use not a single arrow but only countless mini-arrows swirling around, crossing over one another, eliminating one another, and thus resembling the chaos of molecules in a gas cloud. In this worldview there is no such thing as meaningful development. The world has no purpose or goal.

Existential Experience of Time

Philosophy after World War I both glorified this worldview and—anticipating the consequences—elevated it to a higher level: the past is past and cannot be repeated; the future is inaccessible to me and cannot be planned. All that remains is the "now" of my existence, which has precedence over all definitions of human nature. This "now" is characterized by disgust and fear, boredom and worry, absurdity and freedom. It is being toward death—and yet, this "now" must be lived.

Of course, this worldview is nothing entirely new. It existed even in antiquity, in a more trivial and less philosophically developed form. *Carpe diem*, the ancients said: "Seize [enjoy] the day." A good many ancient tomb inscriptions speak an almost existential language, for example, the following, found on a Roman tombstone:

> We are nothing; we were only mortals. You who read this, consider:
> in the briefest of times we descend from nothing to nothingness.[3]

In somewhat more banal form, another Roman tomb's writing reads:

> Make an enjoyable life for yourself, comrade! Why? After death
> there is no more laughter and no lovers' game or any other kind
> of pleasure.[4]

Or, on another Roman gravestone we read this still more mundane
thought:

> As long as you are alive, see to it that you will be handsomely buried.
> And live the way you want to, for down here [in the underworld]
> you can no longer light a fire or eat well. I tell you all this from my
> own experience: no dead person will be awakened from here.[5]

How much we moderns have recurred to this ancient worldview and
philosophy is evident from a book by Fernando Savater, professor of
philosophy in Madrid, titled *Do What You Want*.[6] Its basic statement is
this: "Trust yourself. Make a good life for yourself. Find something en-
joyable in everything there is. Do what you want to do!" That is, of
course, far from the ethos of existential philosophy, but the worldview
is much the same: there is only "now." Human beings stagger along from
moment to moment, and in the unending shuttling between boredom
and fulfillment of desire they are almost living in cyclical time again.

Christian Experience of Time

It is against this whole background that we must attempt to grasp the
Christian understanding of time and history. It may well contain residual
cyclical elements, but its fundamental structure is no longer such.

Everything, the whole universe, is God's creation, and that creation
is processual. It has a goal: fulfillment by God. Within this overall process
there is a real history, an irreversible march of events. Like the whole
universe, the history of nations has perfection by God as its goal. This
history cannot be conceived as a cycle, an eternal return of the same
things, for the fundamental Jewish and Christian experiences—the call
of Abraham and Israel's being led out of Egypt—aim toward a clear end:

a great nation in which all the nations of the earth will be blessed, and a new order of society for which Sinai is the symbol.

Matching this irreversible goal-directedness of history as a whole, the history of individuals also aims toward a definite end: each human person is not only a product of evolution that comes and then departs but at the same time God's creation, and each one's goal is perfection in God. Therefore the individual does not have many lives but only one, with a clear beginning and end. From this point of view there can be no such thing as reincarnation or transmigration of souls. Each person has a unique and unrepeatable history. That is each one's dignity, but also each one's obligation. With death, one's life has given its full witness; it is what it has become.

If the fundamental direction of this life was to the praise of God, with death it will be finally and forever a joyous glorification of God. If its basic aim was the search for truth, it has now finally arrived at ultimate Truth. If it was based on a longing for the good, it has at last discovered the absolute Good that is God. If its fundamental orientation was a search for human community, it has arrived in the communion of saints in the presence of God.

And as we have said, the same is true of history as a whole. It is goal-directed. It moves toward its gracious fulfillment. It does not run off into nothingness. It has a hidden meaning, a goal that, however, can only be fully perceived in faith.

For Christians, the ultimate and most profound basis for the goal-directedness of history is that it culminates in Jesus Christ. In him all the beginnings, all the longings, all the hopes of the time before him are fulfilled. "All things have been created through him and for him" (Col 1:16). The medieval world expressed this faith by dubbing the time before Christ *ante Christum natum*, the years "before the birth of Christ."

This, of course, does not mean that subsequent time is no longer directed to a goal. In the language of the New Testament, the Body of Christ, the church, is to grow more and more "to the measure of the full stature of Christ," its head (Eph 4:13-16) and, through the church, the whole world, until everything is subjected to Christ and finally God will be "all in all" (1 Cor 15:23-28).

"Brave New World"

The Christian concept of time, therefore, gives linear history, its goal-directedness, its unrepeatable character, its anticyclical sense of direction, and above all its positive character an immeasurable power. It is no accident that in the society painted in Aldous Huxley's famous dystopia, *Brave New World*, a threatened scenario of horror, neither God nor history plays any part. Both have been eliminated from the minds of this society. Why?

Horrible wars have thrust humanity into profound misery. Because of the fearful experience of constant wars, a world empire has arisen to organize a new society. All the people in it are biologically altered so that they live only in the "now." The highest goal of this "brave new world" is unity, peace, endurance, and absolute stability. Henceforth changes are regarded as threatening, and therefore any passion that does not serve the purposes of consumption and the fulfillment of private desires is absolutely despised. Science and the search for truth are condemned as a danger to the public good. "Truth" is only the feeling of pleasure that is achieved primarily by the use of highly developed drugs.

The leading figures in this "brave new world" know that religion, especially the Christian religion, would create passion for changes in society. Therefore every memory of God has been erased, and a refined religion of consumption has replaced the old religions. The museums have been closed; all historical monuments blown up; all books published before the advent of the new unity regime destroyed. When the narrator swallows *soma*, "[r]oots and fruits were abolished; the flower of the present rosily blossomed," reads one passage in the novel.[7] And one of the most important sayings, spoken by the highest levels of the government, is "History is bunk."[8]

Huxley's 1932 novel has lost none of its contemporary power. The insight that the history of humanity cannot continue on its present course is evoked in the novel not only through steadily worsening wars but also by disastrous economic collapses. For that reason the highest aim of the new society is absolute social stability. It can only be achieved by freezing research and industrial development at a high level, demonizing every memory of the past, and ruthlessly eliminating any thought of the religions of the peoples and most certainly the God of the Bible. Evidently Christian faith is inextricably bound up with the experience of history and its dynamic.

But to return to our topic, let me again summarize: for Christians, the history of the world and that of the individual are both goal-directed. There are no cycles of the world, no eternal return to the same point. There is no arrested, frozen history. For the individual after death as well, there is no new beginning, no circling from rebirth to rebirth. In that light, time's arrow seems the only possible representation of Christian history—and up to a point that is also true.

Altered Past

Still, there are serious reasons why a schematic depiction of the Christian view of history cannot be represented by a simple, unmodified arrow. The first is that the past does not remain purely past. A Christian *cannot* say, "What is past is past; I have no control over it any longer." Such a statement is true only insofar as, from a chronological point of view, we in fact cannot relive the past. I myself, for example, am by no means young anymore, and I know that I cannot begin again from the beginning, nor do I want to. I don't want to go back to the school bench and start to learn all over again. I don't want to relive my education and all the other phases of my life. The mere idea that I would have to undergo all that past experience again fills me with horror. But I cannot do what I don't want to, anyway. I cannot turn back the clock on my life.

And yet, from the right point of view, I do have my past at my disposal: I can turn back, and in the process of this turning back, this "repentance," I can remember. I can put everything before my own eyes—the previous course of my life, my crises, my guilt, all my confusion and sin. And what is decisive: I can confess my guilt before God and in the sacrament of reconciliation can have it all forgiven by God. In this way years long past can be placed in a new context and thereby transformed.

But it is not only that I can confess previous guilt so that it can thus be transformed and made a "happy fault." I can do still more: I can thank God for everything that has happened in my life—for my parents, my siblings, good friends, happy days, many little blessings. I can recognize God's deeds of kindness to me as *God*'s deeds and glorify God for them. I can trace lines in my life that were previously hidden from me, and with thanksgiving and praise I can place them in God's light. And in just that way I can recover and take possession of what is past.

In a certain sense, I can in this way even change the past I have lived, namely, by placing it confidently in God's hands once again. From the right perspective, as a Christian I have power over my past.

Making the Past Present

We must even go a step further. Retrieval of the past affects not only one's personal, individual history. Every Jewish and Christian feast brings the past of the whole people of God into the present. At every Seder, Jews recall the night of the exodus from Egypt, and each is to remember it as if she or he had been personally present. This making present is more than mere superficial recollection.

On January 16, 1996, Israeli president Ezer Weizman addressed the German parliament (Bundestag). His speech has not been forgotten to this day—not only because it was the first time an Israeli president had visited the Federal Republic of Germany, but above all because Ezer Weizman spoke in biblical language, as one who remembers. Early in his speech he said:

> Only one hundred fifty generations have passed from the Pillar of Fire of the Exodus from Egypt to the pillars of smoke from the Holocaust. And I, a descendant of Abraham, born in Abraham's country, have witnessed them all.
> I was a slave in Egypt.
> I received the Torah at Mount Sinai.
> Together with Joshua and Elijah, I crossed the Jordan River.
> I entered Jerusalem with David, was exiled from it with Zedekiah, and did not forget it by the rivers of Babylon.
> When the Lord returned the captives of Zion, I dreamed among the builders of its ramparts.
> I fought the Romans and was banished from Spain.
> I was bound to the stake in Mainz.
> I studied Torah in Yemen and lost my family in Kishinev.

He concluded with these words:

> Ladies and gentlemen, we are a people of memory and prayer. We are a people of words and hope. We have neither established empires nor built castles and palaces. We have only placed words on top of each other. We have fashioned ideas; we have built memorials. We have dreamed towers of yearnings—of Jerusalem rebuilt, of Jerusalem united, of a peace that will be swiftly and speedily established in our days. Amen.[9]

This way of remembering moved many at the time. Others found it inaccessible and simply stared blankly. But those who still knew what happens in the Easter Vigil celebration understood Ezer Weizman, for here too there is memory that makes present, causes what once happened to exist in the "now," and gives us a share in it. The same thing happens whenever the Eucharist is celebrated. It is a real participation in the death and resurrection of Christ.

All that should make it clear that while for Christians history is fundamentally irreversible and the arrow of time remains an arrow, still the past is not purely past; it can be brought forward into the present.

Anticipated Future

But that is still not enough. We have to make a further distinction, because Christian understanding of time is still more complex: it is not only the past that can be retrieved. The future can also be anticipated. I have already said that every celebration of the Eucharist is a real participation in the death and resurrection of Christ.

It is true that the resurrection of the dead, for those who dare to speak of it, normally remains something purely future. In the Nicene Creed we say: "I look for the resurrection of the dead and the life of the world to come." The "resurrection of the dead" is thus associated with the "life of the world to come" and so with what a believing Christian expects in the future. But this apparently obvious time structure is disrupted in the New Testament. The "world to come" does not arrive in the distant future, at the end of time, but instead begins already, in the midst of this world. Our resurrection is already beginning. With Jesus Christ, the "firstborn from the dead" (1 Cor 15:20), it has already begun; at any rate, that is what the baptismal theology of the New Testament says.

That baptismal theology, unfortunately, remains *terra incognita* on the map of Christian faith. While the applicable texts are read in worship, for the most part they no longer enter our Christian awareness—to say nothing of altering it. We simply blot them out. Hence I have to expand a little on my remarks at this point.

According to common Christian thinking, the new creation that is the resurrection happens only at the end of the world, and since none of us expects the world to end very soon, the resurrection, the new creation of the world, is something that for Christians is quite distant, not to say unreal. But for Paul it has already happened—in baptism. For him, baptism is the true turning of the eons. Baptism is the place where the new creation begins. Therefore he can say in 2 Corinthians 5:17: "if anyone is in Christ, there is a new creation; everything old has passed away; see, everything has become new!" Paul is clearly speaking of baptism here. In it, Christians are torn out of the old world, the old society. They receive a share in the life of the Risen One and thus in God's new creation. The reference to baptism is still clearer in Romans 6:3-4:

> Do you not know that all of us who have been baptized into Christ Jesus were baptized into his death? Therefore we have been buried with him by baptism into death, so that, just as Christ was raised from the dead by the glory of the Father, so we too might walk in newness of life.

The author of the letter to the Ephesians formulates still more keenly and urgently:

> But God, who is rich in mercy, out of the great love with which he loved us even when we were dead through our trespasses, made us alive together with Christ—by grace you have been saved—and raised us up with him and seated us with him in the heavenly places in Christ Jesus. (Eph 2:4-6)

These texts make clear the radical way in which baptism was understood in the New Testament. It is more than the blessing of a child. It is participation in a new life. It must, indeed, be accepted in faith as one grows, and thus ratified. But this believing acceptance of baptism is itself more than a moral elevation. It is a being incorporated into something new that lies altogether outside one's own existence and that those affected by it could never produce of themselves.

The adult seeking baptism, or the Christian taking hold of her or his baptism, encounters Jesus Christ—his Gospel, his practice of the reign of God, his death, and his resurrection. The New Testament baptismal theology speaks not only of turning away from sin, not only of the old person's dying and being buried, but also of resurrection to a new life. It does so circumspectly, without false enthusiasm. It says, for example, that the baptized are "as those who have been brought from death to life" (Rom 6:13). And all this is formulated not only in the indicative but always at the same time in the imperative as well, to avoid the impression that the baptized no longer live in this world.

The Schema of Two Eons

A glance at certain forms of Jewish apocalyptic from the first century CE shows how revolutionary all that was. We need to say something at this point about this late form of Jewish apocalyptic writing, because that in itself will reveal what is revolutionary about the Christian view of history. Just as later in Christianity, so also in Judaism there was a wealth of written books parallel to those accepted into the canon of Sacred Scripture and extending far beyond them. In this connection two books are especially important, namely, 2 Esdras [4 Ezra] and the Syrian Apocalypse of Baruch; they deal with the destruction of Jerusalem in the year 70 CE. In these two books, though not only there, we find the schema of the Two Eons, which can be characterized as follows.

The present age, the current eon, is an evil time, an era in which the good is destroyed, a time of social corruption and crying injustice. At the same time, it is a time of temptation and persecution for the people of God. The powers of evil are becoming more and more aggressive; they seem to be conquering. But this very accelerating crisis is a sign that the present old eon is hastening to its end. God is coming to the aid of God's people and will create a "new eon," the "future eon" in which the devout will experience no more tears or pain. This coming eon is a "new creation." It is the renewal of all creation, the new, definitive world of God.

All that sounds familiar, and rightly so. The New Testament Revelation of John talks the same way. A great many concepts and images from Jewish apocalyptic made their way into Christian eschatology. When we say that at the end of the world the dead will be raised and then the new, transformed world of God will appear, and from then on there will be no more death or sorrow for those who believe in Christ, we are speaking to a certain degree within the time scheme and imagery of apocalyptic.

And yet, despite all these common features, there is a profound difference between Jewish first-century apocalyptic, with its Two-Eons schema, and Christian eschatology. To make that difference clear, let me quote a text from the seventh chapter of 2 Esdras. It marks the exact point in time when the old eon disappears and the new eon appears. It reads:

> Then the world shall be turned back to primeval silence for seven days, as it was at the first beginnings, so that no one [among the living] shall be left. After seven days the [future] world [= eon] that is not yet awake shall be roused, and that which is corruptible shall perish. The earth shall give up those who are asleep in it, and the dust those who rest there in silence; and the chambers shall give up the souls that have been committed to them. The Most High shall be revealed on the seat of judgment, and [then comes the end]. (2 Esdr 7:30-33)

What is decisive is that the seven days of Genesis 1:1–2:4a repeat themselves at this borderline between the old and the new eon. The future eon thus appears as God's new creation. The old eon is destroyed by fire. Why is it destroyed? Why does it lose all significance? The answer is found in 2 Esdras 4:26-27: "the [old] age is hurrying swiftly to its end. It will not be able to bring the things that have been promised to the righteous in their appointed times, because this age is full of sadness and infirmities." So a deep chasm opens between the present age and the future. The present eon was once God's good creation, but it has sunk down in wickedness. Therefore God cannot perfect it; nor is there a fulfillment for the complex history of humanity. God has to create a new age for the righteous of the present eon, and God's true plan for creation will only be fulfilled in the new eon.

It is of fundamental significance that the New Testament does not and cannot see the present world, "this age," in that way. Paul can also speak of the "present evil age" (Gal 1:4) to which Christians must not conform (Rom 12:2). But he would never say that God's promises cannot be fulfilled in "this world." The New Testament does not join late Jewish apocalyptic in positing a profound difference between the old and new eons. It does not disavow the creation and history in which we live.

A New Concept of Time

On the basis of the experience of Jesus' death and resurrection, the New Testament achieves a completely new idea of time. If we state it sharply and pointedly, it is as follows: The end of the world does not come "at the end," for we are already in the midst of the "end of the world." We already live in the end time. Every moment is "the last hour." But I have to speak more precisely, because even the author of 2 Esdras or the Syrian Apocalypse of Baruch were convinced that they lived in a time shortly before the end. The real difference is that in this new concept God's new creation does not arrive only when the old creation has passed away; it begins already within the old world. In the death and resurrection of Jesus, God's new world has already begun, and in baptism every Christian receives a share in it.

So the New Testament brings into the "now," into today what Jewish apocalyptic and, with it, a very common Christian conception of time locates at the end of the world. It thus creates a new notion of time and history. The events that for us are decisive, namely, death, judgment, and resurrection, do not happen only in the absolute future; no, they are happening now. In this way the future is already being constantly anticipated in our existence. It is drawn into our present.

But for that very reason today, and everything we do in this moment, acquires an extraordinary weight and endless significance. It is not that the perfection of the whole world is already present, but the material of that fulfillment is being experienced now. In every moment of our existence God is creating, and we ourselves are creating, the "material" of eternity. Nothing of what we do is lost. In contrast to apocalyptic, present history is taken with absolute seriousness and acquires an enormous power.

Resurrection, then, is collected history, preparing itself already in our daily dying and rising. What does not happen in this life, in this history, cannot be raised at the end. If there is no *communio*, no communion among us now, there can be none in eternal life. If reconciliation does not happen here, it will not happen after death. If the reign of God does not begin here and transform our lives, then it will not do so in the "great beyond." If rejoicing in the Holy Spirit does not take fire here, it will not be so in heaven. If the common table of the Eucharist does not exist here, there can be no heavenly wedding banquet.

And the same is true in reverse: every yes to God and neighbor, every repentance, every reconciliation, every creation of community is already a morsel of resurrection. Resurrection from the dead is gathered and transformed history, and therefore everything depends on what happens here, in this history.

Certainly theologians would never have dared to formulate anything so revolutionary if they had not found it in the theology of the New Testament. And the theologians of the New Testament would not have dared to write as they did if they had not experienced all this as reality in their communities. And they could not have experienced all that if Jesus Christ had not preceded them with his proclamation of the reign of God, because this "now already," this "today" comes from the preaching and practice of Jesus. "If it is by the finger of God that I cast out the demons, the kingdom of God has come to you," Jesus says (Luke 11:20). Thus he was the one who, with his proclamation of the reign of God, his deeds of power and miracles, his death, and then above all his resurrection, broke open the old, dragged-out time. With Christ, every concept of time has been once again radically transformed.

Israel had already broken through purely cyclical thought long before Jesus. In considering Abraham and in reflecting on its Exodus experience, Israel had begun to think in an excessively historical manner, that is, to regard time as linear and progressive. Israel began to transform its nature festivals into historical feasts. At the same time, these very historical feasts brought the past into the present and so recovered it.

But Jesus then made the last, the most radical step: he revolutionized "linear time" at the root. He drew the whole future into the "today" of the reign of God and thus gave the present ultimate weight. This weight of "now" was already being sensed in Israel. "O that today you would listen to his voice! Do not harden your hearts, as at Meribah, as on the day at Massah in the wilderness!" said Psalm 95:7-8 (cf. Heb 3:7-8). But Jesus made this "today" of the reign of God, and thus the presence of God, the center of his preaching. This shifting of the way to look at the flow of time—still more, the transformation of time itself—is part and parcel of the revolution that came with Jesus, and that too we constantly play down and make irrelevant.

So we as Christians no longer live in iron circles, no longer in the eternal return to the beginning. But neither do we live in the chaos of intricate and empty "stories." We are caught up in a history with a clear goal: its fulfillment in God. Still more, we are incorporated in a history that can retrieve the past and even now draw the whole future into today.

All that complicates a schematic depiction of the Christian idea of history. It is no longer sufficient simply to draw out an arrow showing time and history, with fulfillment at the end. Linear time has been transformed. The arrow of history points toward Christ and ends with him. The timeline running on beyond him must repeatedly turn back toward the "Christ" point, because in him the end is already present, in him everything has been achieved, and all that remains is for all ongoing history to be transformed in light of him and gathered together in him.

Chapter 3

How Will the Hungry Be Filled in the Reign of God?

In Mark 6:30-44 we find a challenging story. In the older Bibles it was titled "First Miracle of the Multiplication of Loaves." That was not so very wrong, because the text belongs to the genre of so-called multiplication miracles, which we find elsewhere in the Bible also. Speaking of a "miraculous multiplication of loaves" does not make it at all clear, however, that Mark is describing a banquet.

A Banquet

In many newer translations the miracle is now called "Feeding the Five Thousand." That still skips over what is crucial here. "Feeding" makes us think of "feeding the poor," "soup kitchens," "feeding the pets," and so on. It does not evoke the idea of a feast, a festival dinner, a banquet. And Mark really does want to speak of a "feast." When a translation reads, "[Jesus] ordered them to get all the people to sit down in groups on the green grass," it is much too closely accommodated to today's table customs. What Mark 6:39 really says is that Jesus ordered the disciples to see to it that everyone should "recline," that is, make themselves comfortable for a banquet.

We must not overlook the fact that in antiquity people had two very different meal customs. Ordinary, everyday meals were taken, as they are now, seated at table. But when they celebrated a feast or invited guests to a special meal they reclined at table, lying on bolsters and pillows, supporting themselves on the left arm and eating with the right. So when Mark writes that Jesus ordered his disciples to "have them all lie down" (6:39), it means that a feast is about to begin, a banquet at which people may eat their fill, a great dinner to be taken at leisure, an evening supper accompanied by long and happy discussions.

It is true that the bolsters and pillows are lacking, but they are replaced by fresh grass, which Mark names explicitly (v. 39), even though he otherwise gives such details only rarely. The author of the Fourth Gospel then expands on it, writing, "there was a great deal of grass in the place" (John 6:10). Jesus' solemn introduction to the meal also shows that the narrative really means to describe a banquet. Mark writes, "Taking the five loaves and the two fish, he looked up to heaven, and blessed and broke the loaves, and gave them to his disciples to set before the people, and he divided the two fish among them all" (Mark 6:41).

This part of the narrative speaks of a fixed and ordered ritual introducing the main course at a Jewish festival meal: the host sat up, took the bread, and spoke the table prayer: "Blessed be the LORD our God, ruler of the universe, who brings forth bread from the earth." The host then broke the bread and gave it to each guest. In our story Jesus keeps exactly to this meal ritual. He acts as a host introducing a festival meal.

Finally, the end of the story also shows that this is really a banquet; it says explicitly that the disciples gathered up the pieces that were left over. That too was a fixed ritual after an ancient Jewish banquet: after the main course the dining hall was "cleansed" by gathering up all the crumbs larger than an olive. In our story the disciples collect twelve baskets of remnants of the bread and fish (6:43).

Why was so much left? It was not because the food had not appealed to the participants in the meal or because they had not eaten their fill but for the very reason that it was a banquet. After a festival meal there are always leftovers, as every householder knows. For a banquet there is always more food cooked, baked, and broiled than is really necessary. Excess is part of feasting: there can be no stinginess; preferably, one offers too much food rather than too little. The fact that at the end of the meal in our story there are twelve baskets of food left over is meant to say that Jesus was a good host who gave a marvelous dinner, a banquet overflowing with food. This is very similar to the story of the marriage at Cana, where the wine Jesus provides is not only of superb quality but amounts to somewhere between five hundred and seven hundred liters (John 2:6).

Of course, we have to ask by this point: why did the early Christian communities tell such stories? What did Jesus have to do with feasting, and what do banquets have to do with God or the reign of God? According to biblical theology, a great deal! In Isaiah 25:6-8 we read:

> On this mountain the LORD of hosts will make for all peoples
> a feast of rich food, a feast of well-aged wines,
> of rich food filled with marrow, of well-aged wines strained clear.
> And he will destroy on this mountain
> the shroud that is cast over all peoples,
> the sheet that is spread over all nations;
> he will swallow up death forever.
> Then the LORD God will wipe away the tears from all faces,
> and the disgrace of his people he will take away from all the earth,
> for the LORD has spoken.

This text from Isaiah presumes that God's eschatological royal reign (cf. Isa 24:21-23) has begun. God's enthronement is followed by a great banquet on Mount Zion, at which Israel shines with a new dignity. All the nations are invited to this enthronement banquet, and at the feast the shrouds of sorrow and suffering that lie over the nations are torn away. Eschatological joy shines throughout the whole world, joy that will never end.

For the prophets that is all in the future. Jesus, however, announces that the future is already present; it is *now*. The joy of the end time has begun. God's banquet with God's people Israel, which is to expand into a festival meal for all nations, is now beginning. Therefore in one of his parables he compares the reign of God to a great banquet that is about to begin, even if those invited excuse themselves, one after the other (Luke 14:15-24), and so he says, in a threat to those in Israel who refuse to understand, that this has already begun and that they will most certainly not be partakers in the meal to which the Gentile nations will very soon be flocking (Matt 8:11-12). Jesus is so firmly convinced that the reign of God is now reality in the form of a sumptuous dinner that he calls his poor and hungry hearers blessed: "Blessed are you who are hungry now, for you will be filled" (Luke 6:21).

As a soothing comment on a reign of God that will come *sometime or other*, such a statement represents a horrible cynicism and even a mockery of the audience. To promise the starving that they will be filled—that is something only someone can do who awaits the reign of God, not just in the world to come and not in some uncertain future, but in a future that is already beginning. In fact, Jesus quite simply defends himself against the accusation that he and his disciples do not fast like the devout in Israel by saying: what do you mean? A wedding feast has begun, and no one can fast at a wedding (cf. Mark 2:19)! Jesus lived like someone who knows that the great wedding banquet of the reign of God has already begun, and for that very reason he can say to the hungry, "You will be filled."

We must, of course, affirm that the hunger to be satisfied in the reign of God is not merely that of the body. It is also the hunger for righteousness, for peace, for festival. It is hunger for everything necessary for human life. But it is likewise and first of all physical hunger. It makes no sense to resolve the problems that arise from Jesus' positively alarming present eschatology by reinterpreting the hunger of the poor that Jesus promises will be satisfied as a longing for an inner realm, thus spiritualizing the beatitude. The reign of God that Jesus proclaims comes not only now; it comes also with an utterly offensive materiality: lepers are cleansed, the lame can walk again, those with neurotic obsessions are made normal once more, and the starving finally get enough to eat.

The Dialogue at the Heart of the Narrative

But how is that supposed to happen? How will the hungry be filled in the reign of God? Mark 6:30-44 gives the answer to precisely this question, but we will not find it if we only ask the text: did all that really happen? Obviously that question must arise at some point, but we should not rush to it too quickly. Modern textual criticism ought to have taught us at least *one* thing: before addressing questions to a truly great and beautiful text from outside, we must first have a precise understanding of the text itself. So, what does the text itself have to say? Where are its interests? Where does it move deliberately? Where does it pause? What does it tell, and what does it not tell?

If we pose our questions at that level, it appears immediately that the text says nothing about how the multiplication of the loaves and fishes took place. We would love to know. We are dying to ask whether people could dig into the baskets over and over and take out new rolls and fish again and again. Then we would be getting close to the Grimms' "The Wishing-Table, the Gold-Ass, and the Cudgel in the Sack." Or was it as enlightened exegetes love to say: Jesus shared the little that he and his disciples had with those right next to them, and that softened the hearts of all the people, especially the wealthy, so that they took their lunches out of their cloaks and shared them in the same familial fashion, so that on this unforgettable day everyone was filled?

We should not immediately pillory such exegesis as primitive rationalism. Its mistake is not that it rests on group psychology but that it blows up the text at one point and elsewhere makes it shout when the text itself is completely silent. Incidentally, by remaining silent the narrative remains true to its genre, because tales of miraculous multiplications never report how the miracle was performed. Neither is Mark interested in such details. In the miracle of the multiplication of the loaves his focus is on a very different point.

Mark's true interest is revealed when he introduces the miracle itself by means of a dialogue between the disciples and Jesus (6:35-39). In the context of the Synoptic Gospels this dialogue is unusually long. While in other miracle stories in the first three gospels there is for the most part only statement and counterstatement, here the dialogue moves back and forth three times. First the disciples say that it is late and the people should be sent away so they can buy something to eat. Jesus responds: You give them something to eat. The disciples answer: Should we buy bread for them? Jesus asks: How many loaves do you have with you? The disciples say: Five loaves and two fish. Then Jesus says, definitively: See to it that they all recline for a banquet.

To repeat: that is, for the Synoptic Gospels, a remarkably long and carefully constructed dialogue. Its first task is to present the situation and prepare for the miracle. Instead of a long explanation by the narrator, the story is set in motion in the course of a vivid dialogue. But the skillfully constructed dialogue does much more. It not only organizes an important part of the story; at the same time, it clarifies the meaning of the miracle to follow and does so on the theological level. It gives a precise answer to the question that presented itself to us: how will the hungry be filled in the reign of God?

The text, in the course of the three exchanges in the dialogue, offers three possible solutions. The first two, from the disciples, are rejected. They do not correspond to the nature of the reign of God. Only the third suggestion—Jesus' solution—is carried out. Let us take a closer look at these three possibilities.

Jesus has been speaking at length to the crowds about the reign of God. The text says literally, "he began to teach them many things" (Mark 6:34). But now the disciples come and ask him to stop teaching the crowds: "send them away so that they may go into the surrounding country and villages and buy something for themselves to eat" (6:36).

That is sober and realistic. The disciples know that nobody can listen forever, not even to Jesus. They know it is time for the people to eat something; otherwise they will collapse. Therefore Jesus should dismiss the crowd. The reign of God must be preached, but people have to eat too. These are things that can be cleanly separated. Jesus is responsible for preaching, and the people themselves ought to see to their meals, if you please.

As succinctly and simply as Mark presents it, we cannot avoid noticing that the disciples here separate reality into two clear areas: that of the reign of God and that of the rest of life. Both spheres—we could also say both "realms"—are as cleanly separated in the disciples' suggestion as they would be again and again in the course of the church's history. Basically, the modern isolation of faith from life, the separation of reality into autonomous subsections, is already anticipated here.

What is fascinating is how Jesus destroys that clean separation, which seems so sober and realistic, with a single statement: "*You* give them something to eat" (6:37). So much for the comfortable path, simply preaching to society and otherwise leaving it to its own devices. Jesus refuses to cooperate with dividing reality into separate zones. He emphatically shows his followers that everything belongs within the reign of God, the whole of human existence, including food. Therefore, "*You* give them something to eat." That ends the first dialogue.

The disciples think they have understood: it seems they are responsible to see that the masses do not go hungry. As practical people, they quickly envision a new solution: if the crowds are not to be sent away to obtain their own provisions but are to be provided for in this place through the disciples' initiative, that must be immediately organized. They will have to make a rough calculation of the total number, estimate how much bread they will need and what that amount will cost, and then some of the disciples will have to get underway quickly to buy bread. A clear organizational plan!—and hence the very precise question to Jesus: "Are we to go and buy two hundred denarii worth of bread, and give it to them to eat?" We can see how exact the calculation is here from the fact that in the Mishnah (*Pesaḥ* 8.7) a loaf costing one-twelfth of a denarius is said to be the daily requirement for a poor person. Thus two hundred denarii would buy 2,400 daily rations or 4,800 rations for half a day. That would be just about enough for five thousand people.[1]

We can only admire the initiative and organizational ability behind the disciples' second suggestion. The text assumes that it would have been possible for them, after making their quick calculation, to collect the two hundred denarii from the crowd and then get on the road right away.

Later, with the same zeal and pleasure in organizing things, the church would take to itself the world's suffering—once it had grasped that it had to give the poor not only the Gospel but bread as well. At present we are aware how the great church missionary societies organize help for the hungry and do so in impressive fashion. In the meantime, the disciples' second suggestion for solving the problem has become the accepted model in the church for providing bread for the world—either directly or as "helping them to help themselves." It is anything but accidental that the titles of Bread for the World and Misereor (= "I have compassion") are derived from the texts describing the multiplication of the loaves (cf. John 6:51; Mark 8:2).

What is strange is that Jesus does not accept the second suggestion either. He seems to be convinced that the poor can by no means be adequately fed in this way. It may be that with 4,800 half-day's rations for five thousand mouths the worst hunger can be allayed; at most, people can be temporarily satisfied. But the reign of God is much more than that! It will not only alleviate critical need; superfluity is of its very essence. In the reign of God, divine abundance will shine brightly. But above all, the action of well-organized aid such as the disciples suggest would not really change the world at all. What would be distributed would be mere bread, and society would remain just as it is, continually reproducing its structures of misery. The disciples would have to run back and forth, panting and never stopping, to organize aid to alleviate hunger, and even so they would never put an end to the suffering.

Therefore in our story Jesus does not accede to the disciples' second suggestion either, no matter how well meant it is. For him, the satisfaction of the hungry in the reign of God is something quite different. He had greater things in mind when he spoke his beatitude. Jesus, consequently, pursues a third solution, that of the reign of God. And because he knows that his disciples are utterly incapable, by themselves, of understanding this particular solution coming from God's generous abundance, he himself takes the initiative. He asks them: "How many loaves have you? Go and see" (6:38). It is not necessary to send the people away, nor is it necessary to obtain food for them from somewhere else. The festive banquet in the reign of God will spring forth as a miracle—and it will emerge from what already exists.

Something crucial has to take place, however, before the miracle can happen. Jesus orders the disciples to divide the crowds into "meal groups"

(6:39). The next verse explains this: "So they sat down in groups of hundreds and of fifties" (6:40). This is a clear allusion to Exodus 18:13-26, where the people of God journeying through the wilderness are divided into smaller units. As we know from the manuscripts found at Qumran, the Essenes deliberately imitated the divisions in Exodus when they held their community meals. But above all, this structuring of the people was expected to be necessary for the eschatological messianic meal (cf. 1QSa 2.11-22).

Against this background, Mark's text can only intend to say that Jesus is forming the crowds of people, who are without goal or orientation, who go about like sheep without a shepherd (6:34), into the eschatological people of God. It is apparently necessary that this end-time people of God should be visibly structured and divided into table groups. Only when the scattered people of God is assembled, and only when it is gathered in clear order around Jesus, its eschatological shepherd, can the miracle occur. Only then can the festival meal in the reign of God begin. Only then can the glory of that meal emerge. But then all will truly be satisfied. Then they will not be given only a morsel; they will experience a feast. Then twelve baskets of bread will be left over, a symbol of the people of the twelve tribes in its eschatological fullness.

The Truth of the Narrative

Only after the structural lines of the text have been clarified in this way can we legitimately ask whether all that really happened. And then the answer can only be: yes, it all happened, and it continues to happen, over and over again.

It has really happened that the church has only preached and then sent the people home hungry. It has really happened, and it continues to happen, that the church has cared for the hungry through admirable charitable actions and organizations and in the process has not changed the world's sick society, nor can it ever change it by such means—if all it shares is food.

But it has also happened, and continues to happen, that the church becomes what, according to the Gospel, it should be: the eschatological people of God that allows Jesus to gather it into a new society in which something of the abundance of the reign of God is already visible. This eschatological form of the people of God began to take shape with Jesus himself and was also experienced in the first church communities through the Spirit of the crucified and risen Jesus. After Easter the church in Jerusalem gathered "by houses," that is, in a clearly visible form, to "break bread" (Acts 2:46) with eschatological joy. It assembled for common meals in which everyone shared with one another not only their food but their whole existence. Luke dares to say of this church: "There was not a needy person among them" (Acts 4:34). At these festive meals of the first communities they would also have told the story of the miraculous feast at the beginning, which interpreted the foundational experience of these communities.

But it seems that even decades later, when Mark wrote his gospel, this story of the feast in the reign of God corresponded to a remarkable degree with the experiences of the Christian communities. There are a number of indications that Mark wrote his gospel in Rome, and there were already quite a few Christian house churches there. Mark could not have overlooked the correspondence between the organized "table" communities in the miracle story handed down to him and the gatherings of the Roman house churches.

The whole history is even more interesting when we go beyond this similarity and compare Mark 6:30-44 with banquets in pagan Rome, because then we can observe a revealing contrast: the wealthy Romans had a special dining room, the *triclinium*, where they ate with their guests.

> The dinner party was the main event of Roman social life, and it adhered closely to a traditional form. In the *triclinium* were usually three couches, each capacious enough to hold three reclining persons. When the Roman planned a small party, he composed his guest list so as to have between three and nine people dining, including members of the family. "Not less than the Graces, nor more than the Muses," was the formula he went by.[2]

These fancy meals, which featured many courses, began in the afternoon and lasted late into the night, and the number of participants was strictly limited. But above all, it should be noted that only the wealthy could afford such banquets. So when, according to Mark, Jesus the messianic shepherd invites to a banquet table groups that are much larger than was customary in antiquity (namely, fifty to one hundred each), but above all a feast in which the poor also participate, the contrast with the pagan world is quite obvious.

Thus our story must have reflected the experience of Mark's church as well: great crowds of people could enjoy solidarity and a festive atmosphere in the church at Rome; indeed—in contrast to pagan society, in which the elite class of the wealthy isolated itself from the rest—great crowds of needy and poor. A genuine "new family" arose in contrast to the old, and the many communities made up one people.

So the story of the festive banquet in the reign of God is true. It happened, and it happens again and again in the history of the church. It happens even today, wherever Christians allow themselves to be gathered together as the people of God, where they live with one another in visible ways—one group sharing the meal here, another alongside it there—where they share their lives and care for one another in a true *convivere*.

Where that happens, then today, just as in the early church, the miracle happens: all have what they need; they have it in the quiet glow of the abundance that characterizes the gifts of God. The solution, the reign of God, which alone can feed and satisfy the poor of the world, has long since been given us. We only have to live it.

Chapter 4

How Did Jesus Heal?

There can be no question about the fact that during his public life in Israel Jesus healed a great many sick people. The gospels attest to that so clearly that no serious historian doubts it. In the time when an extreme rationalistic theology was dominant there was such doubt, but today the numerous healing phenomena described by ethnologists everywhere among ancient peoples and cultures serve to put doubt to rest.

But the question remains: how, in what manner did Jesus himself heal? Differently from the countless shamans and medicine men and women in early cultures? Differently from the healers who follow in the footsteps of the shamans nowadays, though with markedly less personal commitment? Differently from twenty-first-century physicians who, although they are able to apply an unbelievable wealth of modern research to the healing process, still find that the power of personality continues to play a role that should not be underestimated? So, how did Jesus heal?

In what follows I want to make it clear that this is by no means a marginal question; rather, it has to do with the center of Jesus' proclamation and the nature of faith. I will begin with a concrete story of a healing related in the gospels. It can show us a great deal.

The Captain of a Company Asks for Help

"Only speak the word, and my servant will be healed!" This statement of belief is found in the story of the centurion at Capernaum. In its Matthean version, the whole story reads:

> When [Jesus] entered Capernaum, a centurion came to him, appeal-
> ing to him and saying, "Lord, my servant is lying at home paralyzed,
> in terrible distress." And he said to him, ["Shall I come and cure
> him?"] The centurion answered, "Lord, I am not worthy to have you
> come under my roof; but only speak the word, and my servant will
> be healed. For I also am a man under authority, with soldiers under
> me; and I say to one, 'Go,' and he goes, and to another, 'Come,' and
> he comes, and to my slave, 'Do this,' and the slave does it." When
> Jesus heard him, he was amazed and said to those who followed
> him, "Truly I tell you, in no one in Israel have I found such faith. I tell
> you, many will come from east and west and will eat with Abraham
> and Isaac and Jacob in the kingdom of heaven, while the heirs of the
> kingdom will be thrown into the outer darkness, where there will
> be weeping and gnashing of teeth." And to the centurion Jesus said,
> "Go; let it be done for you according to your faith." And the servant
> was healed in that hour. (Matt 8:5-13)[1]

A centurion, that is, the head of a company of soldiers, approaches
Jesus. Nothing is said about his nationality, but in any case he is not a
Jew. His servant—some translations say his "boy"—is seriously ill. There
is no precise information about his illness, although physicians are always curious about such details in the stories. The narrative says only
that the servant is lying at home, paralyzed and suffering. "He is in
terrible distress" is an ancient phrase; we should add: "he is being tor-
tured by the demons of sickness."

The peoples of antiquity, and that includes Israel, were convinced that
illnesses, especially those we primarily define nowadays in psychological
terms, were caused by demons. It would be well not to dismiss this
worldview immediately as naïve, unenlightened, and outdated, because
behind such ideas lies the knowledge that there are compulsions, forces,
often hideous ones, that come from without, and indeed sometimes from
evil sources. They are released by environments and circumstances that
can make people unfree and even ill. (Naturally we cannot exclude the
possibility that such illness can also arise through one's own fault.) In
the ancient Near East and in antiquity generally these forces were called
"demons." The sick person is like someone who is in chains. Such a one
is no longer himself or herself and has been made ill.

The centurion has someone in his house who is ill in this sense, who
lies bound and incapable of moving. But he needs him. What use to an
officer is someone who is bedridden? So he has made his way to Jesus.
He must have heard that there is a Jew who can heal and to whom sick

people are being brought from all the surrounding area. When he finds Jesus, he asks him to make his servant well.

Jesus' answer is not, "I will come and cure him."[2] This common translation is possible but unlikely. Jesus' response can also be translated as a question, which fits better with the centurion's subsequent argument. Thus we read not, "I will come and cure him," but, "Should I [perhaps] come and cure him?" With this hesitant response, tending to the negative, Jesus is saying, "Are you really asking me to go to your house with you—that I, a Jew, should enter a Gentile house and heal your servant?"

Once when a woman from Syro-Phoenicia begged Jesus to heal her daughter, Jesus at first reacted with similar negativity (Mark 7:27), since in general he did not preach and heal in Gentile territory; his concern was with Israel. In addition, because of the purity laws he, as a Jew, was not permitted to enter the houses of Gentiles. Only if one interprets Jesus' reaction in this narrative in the same sense—namely, as a negative response—does the centurion's subsequent speech acquire its appropriate contour and meaning. He says, in the sense of the situation, "You have no need to enter my house and so make yourself unclean. You can give the required command from here, and my servant will be healed." Then, also in the sense of the situation, he adds the marvelous explanation: "*I* am one who gives orders, and *you* are one who gives orders—*I* to my soldiers, and *you* to the demons of sickness. You only have to command the demons, and my servant will be healed. So just say the word!"

This is followed by a so-called healing at a distance, as the exegetes call it. But what interests me here, more than the distance healing, is the expression "just say the word!" The sick person is apparently cured by Jesus' word alone.

The Myth of the "Word Alone"

Theologians have always been impressed by the fact that Jesus heals the centurion's boy with a simple word of command. In this story of the centurion at Capernaum there is no touch, no laying on of hands, not even a gesture of blessing in the direction of the centurion's house. And theologians like that, because, for heaven's sake, they want nothing to do with magic, with any kind of hocus pocus, gestures, machinations that could indicate some sort of magical ritual. Since the Enlightenment anything too physical, intimate, ritual, or sacramental is suspect.

I am not talking here about ordinary people. They have always liked such things. They want contact with the healer, with healing relics; they like the St. Blaise blessing and want to feel the doctor's hands on their bodies. When they go to St. Peter's, they don't reverence the bronze statue of Peter from a distance but stroke and kiss the feet of the enthroned figure, so that over time his feet have been not only polished but even shrunk.

But then came the Reformation, followed by the European Enlightenment and rationalism. And with rationalism came dismissal of popular belief as a remnant of magic or even hideous superstition. Hence, from the modern period onward, the fear on the part of many theologians of anything that might look like magic. And hence the joy of these theologians when they finally discovered the bridge by which they thought they could escape from all things magical: the pure, effective word. Now they said, "Jesus always, or primarily, healed by a mere word. Can't we see that from the story of the centurion at Capernaum? Here we find the basic pattern for all Jesus' healings." And the theologians of the word alone did not notice that a whiff of contempt for the body, a pinch of Manichaeism, had wormed its way into their theology.

From a purely historical point of view this theology's approach cannot function over time, because when Jesus healed sick people he much more frequently used physical gestures and actions and not mere words. Jesus took sick people by the hand (Mark 1:31). He laid hands on them (Mark 6:5). He put his fingers into deaf people's ears (Mark 7:33). He touched the tongues of sick people with saliva (Mark 7:33). He spat on the ground, made a mud paste, and spread it on the eyes of the blind (John 9:6).

So Jesus' healing words were very often accompanied by sign-actions, which reach deep into human physicality and take it seriously. The human being is dust and earth, and so Jesus could make a paste of mud and put it on a blind man's eyes. Such a procedure is more than "natural healing." It makes clear that healing and liberation are not something purely spiritual or internal. The earth comes to the rescue of human beings, and the body is just as much in need of redemption as the soul. Jesus took the body and its needs seriously.

It is precisely in Jesus' deeds of healing that the incarnational nature of his activity is visible: God's salvation must come into the world and penetrate every aspect of reality. It is not simply a matter of consciousness; it is just as much about the material. Nothing can be neglected. Redemption is for the whole of creation. God has come to us skin-on-skin for our sake.

So the word alone is not only the opposite of magic, especially since magic can also make powerful and extensive use of words. There are piles of magical papyri surviving from late antiquity, filled with incomprehensible secret formulae, magical codes, the abracadabra of Gnosticism.

The Phenomenon of Magic

Then if reduction to words alone is not the criterion, what distinguishes Jesus' healing, and that of Christians, from magic? To answer this, we must first examine what magic in fact is.

Recent research extends the concept of "magic" quite broadly. It can include all the rituals in which earlier peoples celebrated their myths, that is, their interpretation of the world and being. In these rituals the elemental events were repeated anew and brought into the present, giving a comprehensive horizon of meaning to life. Only secondarily, many ethnologists today would say, were these early magical rituals diverted to the purposes of magic in the strict sense and applied to particular purposes.

In contrasting magic and faith, which is the principal issue in what follows, I am speaking of magic in this narrower, utilitarian sense, the magic that seeks to achieve something: heal an illness, catch bears, ensnare a man with a love spell, damage one's neighbors, cripple an approaching enemy. Instead of a dry definition of magic in the utilitarian sense, let me offer an example. In 2 Kings 13:14-19 we find the following story:

> Now when Elisha had fallen sick with the illness of which he was to die, King Joash of Israel went down to him, and wept before him, crying, "My father, my father! The chariots of Israel and its horsemen!" Elisha said to him, "Take a bow and arrows"; so he took a bow and arrows. Then he said to the king of Israel, "Draw the bow"; and he drew it. Elisha laid his hands on the king's hands. Then he said, "Open the window eastward"; and he opened it. Elisha said, "Shoot"; and he shot. Then he said, "The LORD's arrow of victory, the arrow of victory over Aram! For you shall fight the Arameans in Aphek until you have made an end of them." He continued, "Take the arrows"; and he took them. He said to the king of Israel, "Strike the ground with them"; he struck three times, and stopped. Then the man of God was angry with him, and said, "You should have struck five or six times; then you would have struck down Aram

until you had made an end of it, but now you will strike down Aram
only three times."

This story is a classic example of magic. Ethnologists would speak
here of "sympathetic magic" or "analogous magic." As in the magic
ritual an arrow is shot, so will in reality the Aramean enemies be shot to
nothing. And as the ground is ritually struck, so will the Arameans soon
be stricken.

In Egypt it was the custom, before a decisive battle, to make a clay
figure of the opponents, inscribed with a curse, and then to break the
figure and bury it. The Egyptians were convinced that the curse connected with this action would influence the impending battle. That too
was analogous magic in its purest form, exactly as in the case of Elisha.
It is worth noting the emphasis the prophet puts on the necessity of
carrying out the prescribed *rite*: "Elisha said to [the king of Israel], 'Take
a bow and arrows'; so he took a bow and arrows. . . . Elisha laid his
hands on the king's hands." In this way the *mana*, the magic power in
Elisha, was transferred to the king of Israel. But the king made a serious
mistake by striking the earth only three times. If he had struck six times
the effect would have been immeasurably more destructive. But why
were the three missing blows not simply added? That simply could not
be done. The ritual has its own laws; it cannot simply be repeated, and
the effect comes from the power of the ritual, that is, with the automatic
working of magic—unless there is a counterspell.

This method of magical interference in the world is very ancient. Earlier anthropologists and students of the history of religions supposed
that the oldest phase of human history was altogether dominated by
magic. People of old sought to take charge of every difficult situation,
everything they could not themselves master, by means of magic or
conjuring. For example, in that era hunting spells played a crucial role.
It was only much later, scholars said, that magic was replaced by religion.
Now people no longer relied on magical powers but instead called on
higher beings, namely, gods, and implored them to grant success.

More recent scholarship tends to reject this two-phase division. They
say that magic and religion have existed since the dawn of human history and are almost inseparably intertwined. In fact, magic plays a remarkable role in all the religions we know. We have just seen that it can
be observed in the Old Testament itself.

Although biblical faith is something other than religion, religious and
magical remnants endured in Israel with great tenacity. Despite the
claims of the prophets, there were sorceresses and sorcerers among the

people for quite a long time (Exod 22:17; Mal 3:5), as well as conjurors (Ps 58:6), people who cast evil spells (1 Kgs 18:17), fortune tellers, and mediums who consulted the spirits of the dead (Deut 18:11). Israel's theologians condemned these practitioners of magic in increasingly dire terms. Deuteronomy 18:9-13 is especially clear:

> When you come into the land that the LORD your God is giving you, you must not learn to imitate the abhorrent practices of those nations. No one shall be found among you who makes a son or daughter pass through fire, or who practices divination, or is a soothsayer, or an augur, or a sorcerer, or one who casts spells, or who consults ghosts or spirits, or who seeks oracles from the dead. For whoever does these things is abhorrent to the LORD; it is because of such abhorrent practices that the LORD your God is driving them out before you. You must remain completely loyal to the LORD your God.

The context makes it clear that this is a list of the magical and superstitious practices Israel encountered in the land of Canaan and among neighboring religions: the "abhorrent practices of the nations." Israel must not adopt these widespread practices that inquire into the future and interpret the present—otherwise it will no longer be a countersociety. After all, it has the prophets whom God again and again sends to the people. That is enough. Israel's faith is something different from magical interpretation and exploitation of the world: it rests solely on the one God. Therefore Israel may not call on any other powers, subject itself to them, or make use of them. "You must remain completely loyal to the LORD your God."

It is precisely in this turning away from magic and sorcery that we see in Israel the distinction between religion and faith. For me, it is highly revealing that it is always in those times when the difference Israel had discovered between religion and faith faded and retreated from people's consciousness that the ancient magical patterns for interpreting the world returned.

In these decades when, in Europe and North America, Christian faith is being replaced for many by superstition and private religion, magic is also making its return. It is amazing to find, in the enlightened and highly rational "Kursbuch" series, a positively programmatic plea for superstition and magic, and this only a few years ago:

> Modern superstition is domesticated, tolerant, and this-worldly; in times that are still and always will be unfathomable, it takes away some of people's anxiety over the unpredictability of everyday life.

> It is time, finally, to stop disparaging it. A little private magic is highly recommended.[3]

Magic, according to this author, is needed as a help against the uncertainty of life. We may well add: it is needed in a time when our world is increasingly rationalized throughout, functionalized, robbed of its mystery. In such an era good old magic is called upon to restore a bit of a religious atmosphere, a home—which in reality faith and the church ought to be. But my point here is not to critique the variations and abstruse features of post-Christian culture. I think we have reached a point at which I can summarize some of the characteristics of the typical "magical" worldview.

The whole world is a unit, a unified whole, and all of it is invisibly connected. Interwoven through this world are mysterious forces and energies. Shamans, medicine women and men, magicians, or whatever they are called know these forces and can influence them through particular techniques and rituals that may consist of the right words, actions, long meditations, and even ecstasies and heavenly journeys. But what is important in every case is that the proper ritual be performed *correctly*; otherwise it will not produce its power.

We all know Goethe's wonderful poem, "The Sorcerer's Apprentice" (probably most familiar in America in the Disney version with Mickey Mouse as the apprentice). This apprentice magician has sent a broom to bring water—and then he forgets the right formula for stopping the process!

> Stop! Stand still!
> Heed my will!
> I've enough
> of the stuff!
> I've forgotten—woe is me~
> what the magic word may be.
>
> Oh, the word to change him back
> into what he was before!
> Oh, he runs, and keeps on going!
> Wish you'd be a broom once more!
> He keeps bringing water
> quickly as can be,
> and a hundred rivers
> he pours down on me!

The apprentice is unable to stop the broom or to contain the floods of water. It is only when the master arrives that the correct formula is uttered:

> Back now, broom,
> into the closet!
> Be thou as thou
> wert before!
> Until I, the real master
> call thee forth to serve once more.[4]

Obviously, the apprentice lacks the magical competence of the master, though of course that competence does not consist merely in knowing the right formula. It is, rather, the ability to engage the "spirits" for one's own purposes, that is, to govern them and have power over them.

Goethe's tale echoes only indirectly the idea that a magician can not only rescue but also do damage with his or her techniques. There are spells for saving and healing, and there are spells to do harm. These harmful spells played at least as great a role in the magical rites of ancient cultures as those for healing. The ancient Near East has provided us with countless cursing texts. We know the story of the prophet Balaam, who was sent by the king of Moab to curse Israel; it was supposed to be a curse that would cause Israel to be defeated in war. But Balaam was unable to effect the curse because of the glory that lay upon Israel. He could only stammer out blessings (Num 22–24).

So much for the magical worldview: the world is a unity of powers and energies, and the magicians or medicine men and women can influence those powers, unless there are mightier forces contending against them. If they are in possession of the correct rituals, the effective words, they can bring about blessing or misfortune.

Magic and Natural Science

If we compare the worldview of magic with that of the natural sciences, we reach the unavoidable conclusion that there are some amazing resemblances between them. From the point of view of the natural sciences, the whole world is a unity, a single complex reality governed by inalterable laws. Like the shamans, natural scientists know these laws and apply them. They can influence nature. They can, for example, split atoms or alter genes. This influence is exercised through particular techniques that must be "correctly" employed; otherwise nothing will happen, or a false result will emerge that may even be deadly.

We can see from this comparison that magic and natural science are not as far removed from one another as we might suppose at first glance. The medicine woman, the shaman, did something that natural scientists do even today: they knew what holds the world together at its core, and they tried to influence it. In that sense modern ethnological research is correct is regarding the magic of early human beings as not merely something negative but as an attempt to control the world, something that for humans at the beginning was certainly a bitterly necessary business.

And it may be that our earliest ancestors, so close to nature, had opportunities to control the world through their magic that are no longer available to us to such a degree of concentration and clarity. Perhaps our highly cultivated rationality conceals many of the possibilities within us.

Obviously this magical control of the world could always turn into superstition, especially from the point in time when enlightened ways of controlling the world began to appear. Let us consider a much later period, when the first high cultures established themselves on the Nile and between the Tigris and the Euphrates. The ancient magical worldview still ruled, but rational structures that correspond in a great many points with our modern natural science were already developing.

For example, we know from cuneiform texts that among the Sumerians and Hittites, the Assyrians and Babylonians, lists were composed with true scientific thoroughness in order to get control of the imponderables in history. In the case of every battle, every flood, and everything that was important to these people, a careful record was made of the synchronous constellations in the heavens and the shapes in the entrails of the animals slaughtered as sacrifices to the gods.

For example, they would record that before this or that battle the liver of the ox that was sacrificed appeared in such and such a way. The battle was then successful. So when the liver had the same appearance, they thought, a future battle would also turn out well. That is a gross simplification. In reality, thousands of patterns of this kind were observed and compared in an attempt to arrive at a sense of regularity, of law.

Assyriologists call that "the science of lists." These "lists" were compiled according to a pattern: "If this and that is visible in the omens, such and such can be expected." Then, before important events, the constellations and the entrails of sacrificial animals were consulted, compared with the existing lists, and a conclusion was drawn about the course of the impending battle or other event.

The Bible would call that magic and superstition, and it was. But at the same time it was an attempt to achieve a rational control over reality. It was the infancy of natural science. The Babylonians, for example, made a great many observations of the stars in the course of their investigations; those observations were thoroughly scientific in nature and remain valid today. That was possible because their "magi" proceeded on the assumption that everything in the world is internally connected and we, as learned specialists, can interpret those connections and use our knowledge to intervene in the course of events.

That is all we can say here about the magical worldview. In current research it is judged more positively, and perhaps also more justly, than by earlier generations. But Israel's highly critical judgment on all magic remains correct, because at the moment when the image of the true God could be grasped in history the criteria are sharpened and magic becomes an unenlightened superstition. Then to continue to cling to the "powers" of the world is reprehensible.

So, now that we have laid the groundwork, we can return to our real question: what about Jesus' miracles? What about the action he did for the centurion at Capernaum? What was it? Was it magic? Or was magic at least a part of it? Time for a closer look!

Jesus and Magic

To begin with: nowhere do the gospels say that Jesus had supernatural powers or employed them to his own advantage through higher knowledge and practices of which he was master. Certainly his opponents accused him of it: he was said to drive out the demons of sickness with the help of demons (Mark 3:22). In saying this, the opponents characterized him primarily as a conjurer who made use of demonic powers to exercise mastery over harmful demons—and that would only work if one were oneself possessed, that is, at home in the demon world.

Jesus rejected this calumny, which within the horizon of Jewish faith was not only dangerous for the accused but ultimately lethal. He not only rejected it; he refuted it with a highly rational argument: driving out demons with the aid of demons would presuppose that the demonic world was deeply divided against itself. If the demons were warring among themselves, they could not prevail; their power would be at an end (Mark 3:23-25). It was not with the aid of demons but "by the finger of God" (Luke 11:20) that he cast out demons, Jesus said, and by that means he healed the sick and those with mental illnesses.

Thus Jesus wanted nothing to do with the shady realm of magical worlds between worlds. That does not exclude the presence of natural powers in harmony with God's creative power in the hands of Jesus. The gospels say nothing, however, about such natural powers. They speak of the *exousia* of Jesus' authority (Mark 1:27; 3:15), meaning that everything Jesus had came from his heavenly Father. This corresponds with the fact that Jesus himself relied absolutely on God and not on any numinous powers.

It is within this context that we should also speak of Jesus' powerlessness. His enemies mocked him: "He saved others; he cannot save himself. Let the Messiah, the King of Israel, come down from the cross now, so that we may see and believe" (Mark 15:31-32). Jesus did not come down. He performed no miracle to aid himself. He could not. He was not a magician.

Jesus' powerlessness was also manifest in the fact that where he found no faith he could not work any miracles of healing. He was elementally dependent on faith in extending help to others. He said again and again, "Your faith has saved you" (Luke 7:50; 8:48; 17:19). He could work no signs in Nazareth because he came face-to-face there with the unbelief of his native village (Mark 6:5).

The obvious difference between Jesus' work and magic, however, is that his works of healing took place in the context of his preaching of the reign of God. They were not primarily help for individuals; they served God's plan to bring peace and salvation to the world through Israel. God's will is that peace should prevail in the people chosen for God's self, a peace that rests on constant reconciliation with God. So also salvation that grows out of inner and outer peace will spread, and to salvation belongs health.

I have attempted to describe as accurately as possible the difference between faith and magic. It lies in the difference of context, that of the reign of God. There may certainly be commonalities between Jesus' miracles of healing and what was achieved by other healers and wonder-workers. The most striking example may be the healing of the woman with a hemorrhage (Mark 5:24-34). Jesus does not even notice that she touches his garment, but he does feel power go out from him. That, at least on the level of the narrative, certainly reminds us of the notion of *mana* described above. Nevertheless, it does not put Jesus within the sphere of magical healing. The crucial difference is that Jesus' healings occur within a different realm of meaning, namely, the context of the reign of God.

The gospels define that different sphere of meaning most clearly in the story of Jesus' temptations. During his time in the wilderness Jesus is tempted to go precisely in the direction that makes magic so dangerous: instrumentalizing the powers of the world for oneself and exploiting the authority that is given to one for one's own purposes: "If you are the Son of God, command these stones to become loaves of bread!" (Matt 4:3). Demonstrations are also essential to magic, because the practitioner lives on miracles and needs them in order to advertise her or his own power. So Jesus is tempted to leap from the pinnacle of the temple: "If you are the Son of God, throw yourself down!" (Matt 4:6).

All magic tends also to the desire for independent power, which has nothing to do with the honor of God: "Again, the devil took him to a very high mountain and showed him all the kingdoms of the world and their splendor; and he said to him, 'All these I will give you, if you will fall down and worship me'" (Matt 4:8-9). Jesus withstands this third temptation also, by confessing the central article of Israel's faith: "Worship the Lord your God, and serve only him" (Matt 4:10). In this absolute worship of God alone a new context emerges, and it is only this context, which changes everything, that ultimately decides whether we are looking at faith or magic. The criterion for us can only be a theological one.

But will that criterion suffice? Can we really make such a clean distinction between faith and magic? Don't shamans and medicine men and women also demand faith? Do they achieve their effects through ritual alone? Do the rites work automatically? Is it not also requisite that their "customers" believe in the ritual and the corresponding "means"?

Babylonian medicine had some defined therapies for depression. Thus, for example, we read in the Diagnostic Handbook of Esagil-kin-apli or Borsippa (eleventh c. BCE) of the following therapy:[5]

> A businessman is in crisis. His sales are declining, his subordinates are grumbling, he suffers from impotence, loss of sleep and appetite, and signs of paralysis. The doctor is called and prescribes a cleansing ritual. After the sick man has confessed his sins and faults in night-long conferences a clay figure is shaped to embody the divine curse under which he is suffering. Then the sick man "marries" the figure by having it sewn to his garment by torchlight while music is played. Afterward the healer cuts the thread, the figure is buried, and the grave is sealed with a magic formula. Sunrise, the return of the god Shamash, announces that healing has begun.

No one would say that in all these rituals the faith of the priestly healer and certainly the belief of the sick person played no part! We know that African magicians could kill people by symbolically destroying a doll representing the person on whom the spell was cast. Quite often, the person died; the spell worked. But it only worked because the victim believed in the spell and fear consumed that person's soul. If one does not believe in such practices and lives in the enlightenment of the Jewish-Christian tradition, the spell is ineffective.

On the other hand, ethnologists tell us that African healers often can only help if the sick people who come to them open themselves in trust and are prepared to change things in themselves and their environment so as to restore harmony. Often the corresponding consultations and invocatory rituals intended to effect such changes take days or even weeks. Apparently the intent is to begin a process of change. Enlightened Americans or Europeans would call such a thing "psychotherapy."

And now let me leap directly from Africa to ourselves. How does it go with our doctors and their patients? I am no expert here, but I read, for example, of series of experiments that have shown that if patients have a positive attitude and are hopeful, their bones take up to one-third less time to heal than do those of patients who are uneasy, depressed, and worried about the outcome. And I read constantly about the placebo effect, the observation that an intense expectation of being healed can activate the self-curing powers of the body, even if no effective pharmacological substances are applied. But it seems that even when completely normal prescriptions are used, the expectation of the patient that she or he will be cured supplies one-third of the success of the treatment.

The strength of such self-curative powers constantly arouses amazement, even among sober medical practitioners. They are therefore inclined to posit such a placebo effect also in the cases of so-called miraculous cures. Apparently this self-healing power exists in every animal and human, but it requires the *kairos*, the right time, the right constellation of circumstances. In the case of human beings there is a need, above all, for the right person to release these powers and bring them into action—namely, the healer.

Jesus and Faith

Can we exclude such things in the case of Jesus? Did the power of suggestion play any role in his healing? If not, then why did he require faith and the trust of those who sought to be healed by him? Can we exclude all these hard-to-name components, partly physical, partly mental, partly social, which today are part of a holistic medicine, from the story of the centurion at Capernaum? Is it wrong to ask why the centurion's servant had become ill?

After all, this person is a subordinate, one who lives in elementary dependence. He is, as it were, chained by forces that deny him any ability to move on his own. Is it an accident that his superior describes this tension between command and obedience with such striking clarity in saying, "I say to one, 'Go,' and he goes, and to another, 'Come,' and he comes, and to my slave, 'Do this, and the slave does it' "? Is not the servant's paralysis a crying symbolic action giving somatic expression to these binding forces?

In any case, the superior takes notice of his boy's cry for assistance. He sees that he himself cannot help, and therefore he goes in search of a helper he has heard about. In doing just that he takes a decisive step. By asking for something he makes himself dependent on someone else, for the benefit of his subordinate, and in doing so he is already breaking apart the pattern in which he only gives orders. Now he himself is the one making a request, the one in need of help.

When Jesus refuses to enter his house the centurion has to redouble his plea. He must also change his heart and adopt an attitude of pure faith in the man who stands before him. He has to arrive at a belief that Jesus' *word* can of itself heal. Can we not say that it is not only Jesus' word but also the centurion's faith that has made the servant well? The servant is made well through the fact that his superior comes to believe. The true miracle in the narrative is the faith of the centurion. His faith changes a part of the world.

But now the question arises again, still more urgently: if that is the case, what is the difference between shamanism and faith, between Aesculapius and Christ, between the placebo effect and a miracle? Are faith and trust not always necessary?

Let me repeat the answer I have already given: the difference is not primarily that "faith" plays a role in Jesus' healings and not in others, or that there are no world-immanent powers of self-healing at work in Jesus' healings, while in other cases they are brought to bear. If Jesus, as Christian faith affirms, is not only true God but also truly human, his humanity incorporates all the abilities, all the natural powers that are or can be at the disposal of a human being—including whatever we can observe in great "healers" that, at least so far, is not explained on the basis of pure natural science. I must here add that in this area medicine is progressing, though slowly: we now know that neurotransmitters play a role in placebo and nocebo effects and that there are measurable molecular processes at work in the brain and spinal cord.

All these things must also have played their part in Jesus' healings; otherwise he would not have been a real human being. But there was something more in him, and this "more," this difference, is what I have called the "context." The new context, the wholly other thing is the coming of the reign of God. Jesus lived for God alone. He was absolutely one with the will of God, with God's plan for the world. And that plan, as I have said, is that there should be a people in the world that serves God with its whole love and its whole passion and glorifies God alone. That is the salvation of the world, for the fact that human beings and society are so torn apart, so poisonous, is directly connected with the truth that each seeks to be her or his own master and god, with all the destructive claims to authority and power that implies. But where God is master, there is salvation and healing.

Jesus surrendered himself entirely and with an unfathomable insight to this divine mastery of the world. This is the source of the differences between him and other healers in the history of religions, despite all the commonalities of which I have spoken. The differences are very obvious:

1. Jesus performed an unusually large number of healing miracles. The time when a liberal exegesis generally explained them away as fictional narratives without a historical foundation is past. The historical evidence that Jesus must have healed sick and possessed people in extraordinary numbers is simply too weighty. Besides, it is more clearly evident today than in the past that the objections to Jesus' miracles were derived not from historical arguments but from ideological presuppositions. There is no figure in antiquity of whom so many miracles of this type are attested.

2. A striking feature of Jesus' miracles is the speed with which they occur. There is never an account of a long procedure like those characteristic of many medicine women and men, shamans, and healers. We must assume that the miracle stories in the gospels depict many things in summary and are condensations of more complex events. Nevertheless, the "immediacy" of most of these narratives is apparent. The eyewitnesses were moved and shaken by Jesus' power and authority.

3. Jesus' miracles are clearly directed to the context of the *reign of God* now coming to pass; we should not overlook the fact that this is at the same time a revelation of God's *sovereignty over creation*. With the coming of the reign of God, creation regains the brilliance with which God endowed it from the first. In all this, Jesus' healing miracles are unique when viewed against the horizon of the history of pagan religions. Jesus' healing acts surpass all magic; in fact, they redeem and liberate it.

4. From this point of view, obviously the *faith* Jesus demands is more than a sick person's trust in the therapist. In the Bible, faith is reliance on the fulfillment of God's promises, trust that God is acting *now* and that we can entrust ourselves to that action in and on God's people. Here again we find a profound difference between faith and magic.

If we apply what we have observed about Jesus' healing miracles to the healing that ought to be happening in the church as well—for Jesus' injunction, "heal the sick" (Matt 10:8), must be valid today as well—we can say that everything natural, all serious regard for human wholeness, all the depth dimensions of the human person that are part of creation, all the enlightened rationality of modern medicine must play their appointed parts. But at the same time and above all, the Wholly Other must be present as well, what I have called the "context of the reign of God," that full surrender to God's project that is only possible in a trusting communion of believers. This is the truly healing element in miracles within the church.

Here at the end, however, we must face the question: do we really still believe in the healing powers that emanate from Jesus and his message? Do we still believe that Christian faith heals, and that in the church there must be not only "salvation" (or "hale-ing") but also "healing"[6]—for the very reason that the saving and healing Christ is the church's center? Are we not guilty in this regard as well of making Jesus and the power that goes out from him irrelevant?

Chapter 5

What Does the Love Commandment Mean?

Rendering Jesus' message irrelevant also impairs the love commandment and its expansion in the commandment of love of enemies. Most Christians, and even many non-Christians, are aware that Jesus and the love commandment belong together somehow, but this central commandment is often understood to require a kind of "universal love," and in that very way it loses its power and becomes a kind of sentimental emotion. To exaggerate somewhat: anyone who tries to love all people everywhere falls all too easily into the peril of loving those at a distance but not those close at hand. As Linus once remarked to Charlie Brown: "I love mankind. It's people I can't stand." But let us take a closer look.

The Crucial Text

First let us look at the text that is of primary interest here: Jesus' commandment to love one's enemies, in Luke's version. This is a careful composition by the evangelist; we can see this immediately when we compare Luke's text with the parallel in Matthew 5:38-48—though behind all the compositions of Luke, Matthew, and the so-called Sayings Source (Q) from which Luke and Matthew drew at this point are the words of Jesus himself.

> I say to you that listen, Love your enemies, do good to those who hate you, bless those who curse you, pray for those who abuse you.

> If anyone strikes you on the cheek, offer the other also; and from anyone who takes away your coat do not withhold even your shirt. Give to everyone who begs from you; and if anyone takes away your goods, do not ask for them again. Do to others as you would have them do to you.
>
> If you love those who love you, what credit is that to you? For even sinners love those who love them. If you do good to those who do good to you, what credit is that to you? For even sinners do the same. If you lend to those from whom you hope to receive, what credit is that to you? Even sinners lend to sinners, to receive as much again. But love your enemies, do good, and lend, expecting nothing in return. Your reward will be great, and you will be children of the Most High; for he is kind to the ungrateful and the wicked. Be merciful, just as your Father is merciful. (Luke 6:27-36)

These sayings leave us speechless, for we live them either not at all or only partially, in fragments sometimes. If in some blessed hour we succeed in really living them, we know immediately that they are right. They are only questioned by those who consider them merely in their heads. Those who have never surrendered themselves to the commandment to love enemies will regard Jesus as an extravagant dreamer who had no idea of the realities of life.

Of course, even a little reflection shows that the sayings quoted are not those of a naïve young man, because we experience every day what mutual hatred does and where it has brought humanity thus far. The Austrian poet and essayist Erich Fried wrote:

> Naïve?
> Anyone who thinks
> that love of enemies
> is impractical
> has not considered
> the practical
> consequences
> of the consequences
> of hatred of enemies.[1]

Not a Set of Operating Instructions

It should also be said that Jesus' statements on love of enemies are not a formula to be applied like a recipe. They cannot be easily reduced to an ethical system, and they are unwieldy for moral philosophers. They are more like an axe designed to cut through our indifference and hardness of heart.

May I, should I, give to everyone who asks of me? Jesus would have said this with an eye to the situation in Israel, where small farmers and day laborers repeatedly needed help from their neighbors to overcome a bad harvest or times of unemployment. "Give to everyone who asks of you!" has not lost any of its significance for us either, but we cannot apply the principle mechanically. Should I fulfill every wish voiced by my child as we make our way through the supermarket—desires created by the cleverest of advertising means? The child suddenly stops, fascinated by a shelf of alcoholic beverages, and wants a particular bottle because of its beautiful label. She begs her mother to buy it. The mother remains adamant. Should she hold to Jesus' injunction to "give to everyone who asks of you" in this case? That would be the most unloving thing she could do for her child. She would be acting with hatred for her child if she bought her everything she would like to have.

The same is true of all the other parts of the sayings on love of neighbor and of enemies. We cannot use them like operating instructions to be applied mechanically. Rather, we must ask where they are at home, what their proper place is. That is precisely what I want to develop in this essay.

Greeks and Love of Enemies

In 1989 Mary W. Blundell, a professor of classical philology, published a book entitled *Helping Friends and Harming Enemies*, in which she wrote:

> Greek popular thought is pervaded by the assumption that one should help one's friends and harm one's enemies. These fundamental principles surface continually from Homer onwards and survive well into the Roman period, and indeed to the present day, especially in international relations.[2]

This states the essentials. Blundell arrived at her conclusions as a result of her outstanding knowledge of the ancient Greek world. She assembles a multitude of texts that all attest to the same principle: one should love one's friends and help them, but it is perfectly all right to hate one's enemies, and in fact, whenever possible, one should do them harm. The Greek poet Archilochos wrote, in the seventh century BCE, "I know how to love those who love me, how to hate. My enemies I overwhelm with abuse." What he confesses is nothing special; that is, in fact, what pretty much the whole of antiquity thought. Only rarely do we glimpse the idea that one really should not surrender to hate. The Stoics, for example, considered whether it was good for people to succumb to hate or anger. Perhaps this was contrary to the dignity of one's person, and it might also be harmful to the peace of one's soul if one were to hate one's fellow human beings. That was not stupid. Bertolt Brecht uttered a similar reflection in "The Mask of Evil":

> On my wall hangs a Japanese carving,
> The mask of an evil demon, decorated with gold lacquer.
> Sympathetically I observe—
> The swollen veins of the forehead, indicating
> What a strain it is to be evil.[3]

That is quite in line with what the Stoics said, but it is a long way from Jesus. His command to love enemies is more than a suggestion for the good of the soul. Certainly we cannot say that the love commandment has nothing at all to do with the soul's good. Imagine the following situation: a person has been deeply wounded by another and cannot sleep. Wrath, anger, bitterness—waves of emotion heave ceaselessly through heart, stomach, and brain and permit the person no rest. Shouting, imagining what he or she should have said to the other person, tossing and turning, this person is a bundle of aggression and self-pity. That can go on all night.

But what if such a person were to forgive the other one? What if she or he tried to look away from his or her personal situation and view the whole with new eyes?—maybe even with God's eyes? Probably sleep would come. So Jesus' command to love even one's enemies does have a little to do with peace of soul. And yet this commandment is infinitely greater. It is the consequence of the reign of God, now coming to pass; it is the consequence of the love with which God loves the world—even those in it who are the enemies of God.

Because the coming of the reign of God is something so incomprehensibly new, the love that corresponds to its coming stands athwart the usual course of things in the world. What the Greeks formulated is the normal, the usual, the obvious, what one finds in every society: love your friends, hate your enemies; help your friends, refuse all help to your enemies. We hear it again in the words of the Greek poet Hesiod:

> Be friends with the friendly,
> and visit him who visits you.
> Give to one who gives,
> but do not give to one who does not give.[4]

Poorly Informed Christians

One step further! Many Christians have rightly learned that one of the specifics of being a Christian is to love even one's enemies, but they proceed to make this correct statement into a formula that is easily misunderstood. That is, they say, "The Christian must love everyone." This formula is fascinating both in its universality and its apparent radicality. Such love claims to extend to the ends of the earth, to the Pashtun in Pakistan and the Inuit in the Arctic: everyone is included in this all-encompassing love.

But if we ask how such a universal love should look in the concrete, we very quickly see that as a *universal* love it does not work—or better, it can only work if it remains a mere feeling, pure emotion, a diffuse love for humanity in the sense of Friedrich Schiller's verses: "Be embraced, Millions! Take this kiss for all the world!" These verses from the "Ode to Joy" are impossible to fulfill, at least without the aid of alcohol, and they are utterly implausible in daily life—as implausible as the statement "all men will become brothers" earlier in the same hymn.

That is a false and ultimately inconsequential humanism that has little to do with Christianity and can very quickly turn into its opposite. The modern era gave us not only humanism but the most hideous of wars. Happily, the statement "We must love all human beings" as the kind of *universal intention* just described does not appear anywhere in the Bible, neither in the New nor in the Old Testament. The Bible is much too realistic to talk of such misty dreams.

The Bible says we are to love our *neighbors* and also that we should even love our *enemies*—but meaning those we really have something to do with and not some millions of people we can easily love because they are so beautifully distant from us. We only have to reread the corresponding texts in the Sermon on the Mount and elsewhere in the New Testament more carefully and we will see immediately that they are always about those nearest to us and not those farthest away:

- If someone strikes you on the right cheek

- If someone takes your shirt

- If someone begs from you (cf. Matt 5:39-42)

Letting oneself be struck, having one's shirt taken away, lending to some-one—all that supposes an immediate encounter and an unavoidable closeness. Such concrete encounters or confrontations are also presumed as a matter of course when Paul writes in Romans 12:17-18, "Do not repay anyone evil for evil, but take thought for what is noble in the sight of all. If it is possible, so far as it depends on you, live peaceably with all." In saying "all," Paul is obviously thinking not of all the people of the world but all those whom the members of the Roman community deal with every day. And that having-to-do-with is not about mere emotion but, as with Jesus, about real action:

- turn the other [cheek] also

- give your cloak as well

- give [what the person needs] (cf. Matt 5:39-42)

Saint Augustine once described the course of his day as follows:

> The turbulent have to be corrected, the faint-hearted cheered up, the weak supported; the gospel's opponents need to be refuted, its insidious enemies guarded against; the unlearned need to be taught, the indolent stirred up, the argumentative checked; the proud must be put in their place, the desperate set on their feet, those engaged in quarrels reconciled; the needy have to be helped, the oppressed to be liberated, the good to be given your backing, the bad to be tolerated; all must be loved.[5]

Here again it is clear what "all must be loved" means: all those who encountered Bishop Augustine from morning to night. So we have to drop the statement "Christians must love everyone" in a false *universal* sense from our repertoire. It is unbiblical because it does not understand that Christian love is always directed to a concrete person.

Jewish Down-to-Earthness

Let us go a step further, taking our starting point from a dialogue between Luise Rinser and Martin Buber. In her book, *Zölibat und Frau*,[6] Rinser writes:

> A few years ago Martin Buber asked me what I saw as the essential element of my Christianity. I said: "love." He wanted to know what I meant by that. I explained that I love all humanity because all are part of the mystical body of Christ. Buber thought for a while, and

then said: "Theory. Forced theory. You cannot love 'humanity.' One
may tolerate and even help 'humanity.' But one can love only a few,
and rightly so."

Apparently in what she said Luise Rinser had overlooked the fact that
the mystical Body of Christ is not by any means "all humanity" but the
church. To that extent her statement was revealingly self-contradictory,
and Martin Buber immediately detected the contradiction. What he said
is quite typical of how many Jews think of Christianity. It is an altogether
correct response—to Christianity falsely understood. It is a refutation of
what, alas, many Christians regard as distinctively Christian. At this
point Buber could have referred his Christian dialogue partner to what
Torah says about love of neighbor. He did not do so but argued in general
terms. Probably his silence had something to do with the dialogue
situation.

Torah and Love of Neighbor

In any case, Torah speaks very precisely about love of neighbor. We may
turn directly to the central passage in the Holiness Code in Leviticus:

> You shall not hate in your heart anyone of your kin; you shall reprove
> your neighbor, or you will incur guilt yourself. You shall not take
> vengeance or bear a grudge against any of your people, but you
> shall love your neighbor as yourself: I am the LORD. (Lev 19:17-18)

In this text we find four terms that all mean the same thing: "brother"
(rendered in NRSV as "your kin"), "kin," "neighbor," "your people."
These are the fellow citizens with whom the Israelite lives in the Land
and at the same time one's brothers and sisters in faith. Love of neighbor
is for them. Thus it has a definite place, and that place is Israel. But, of
course, it also applies to those foreigners who dwell in the Land:

> When an alien resides with you in your land, you shall not oppress
> the alien. The alien who resides with you shall be to you as the citizen
> among you; you shall love the alien as yourself, for you were aliens
> in the land of Egypt: I am the LORD your God. (Lev 19:33-34).

What is absent from the Holiness Code is the further extension of the
love commandment to foreigners whom the Israelites encounter as
"travelers" passing through the Land. The ethos of love does not apply

to them, but instead the ancient Near East's traditional and very high ethos of hospitality. One was to protect and defend one's guest, if necessary with one's own life.

And what about enemies? The Holiness Code includes them as a matter of course where it speaks of "neighbors" and "kin," for it says, "You shall not hate in your heart anyone of your kin. . . . You shall not take vengeance or bear a grudge against any of your people." The person against whom one bears hatred in one's heart and against whom one seeks revenge is none other than the person we call our "enemy." The "enemy" is also "brother" and "sister" and "kin" in Israel and therefore must not be hated. Such a one is included in the commandment to love the neighbor. But the very ancient Book of the Covenant contained in Exodus states very explicitly how one is to behave toward one's enemy:

> When you come upon your enemy's ox or donkey going astray, you shall bring it back. When you see the donkey of one who hates you lying under its burden and you would hold back from setting it free, you must help to set it free. (Exod 23:4-5)

The word "love" does not appear in this text, but its meaning is quite clearly there. In the Bible, love is not primarily a deep feeling and up-welling emotion but practical help, assistance, solidarity.

When we review all these texts from Torah it is clear that love of neighbor and of enemy has a fixed location in the Old Testament, a basis, a grounding, or whatever one wants to call it. That ground is Israel. Here Torah rules, and Torah commands the people of God to love neighbor and enemy; here people live in visible relationships; here people can tell the story of what God has done for God's people and allow themselves to be instructed to do the same.

So love is something very concrete. It does not fade away into a universal benevolence; it is tied to the real location of the "community of Israel." To that extent Martin Buber put his finger on the right place.

Christian Love of Neighbor

The last step can be kept very short, because our look at the Torah and Israel has revealed what is essential: Torah's demand for love of neighbor encompasses love of enemies as well, and the tying of love to a fixed location, a ground in which it is rooted, is not abandoned in the New Testament. On the contrary: that tie is only strengthened, because now the root and ground of love is the church, the eschatological Israel founded on the love of Christ. The basis of love is now the community in which baptized persons live.

Has anything of Torah changed in the New Testament, then? We should probably mention two points that, while they are not fundamental changes, still shift the perspective.

First, as a result of the Gentile mission the view within the church has expanded amazingly. Now the whole world does come into view. Acts 1:8 reads, "you will be my witnesses in Jerusalem, in all Judea and Samaria, and to the ends of the earth," and Matthew 28:19-20 says, "Go . . . and make disciples of all nations, baptizing them in the name of the Father and of the Son and of the Holy Spirit, and teaching them to obey everything that I have commanded you." But the universality of this command most certainly does not mean "universal" love. Instead, what is in view now is a network of communities of disciples throughout the whole world, in each of which love will be lived in a visible common life. This love constantly breaks out of the individual communities to embrace non-Christians, guests, strangers, the suffering (obviously including those in other countries), but it is always tied to the concrete experience of common life in the individual community.

Thus the universality of Christian love does not consist in the fact that we gather all the people of the world into our hearts in spirit. Instead, it is realized primarily in that, through our aid, more and more Christian communities come into existence throughout the world, communities in which fraternal and sororal love can be lived.

But the universality of Christian love also consists in the fact that the individual community has no borders that are permanently fixed. Each individual community constantly moves and expands its boundaries; it constantly adopts new people into the space of its common life, constantly brings into existence new "neighborly relationships," strives to attract more and more people into the sphere of its love. In this process it must repeatedly happen that enemies are transformed into friends because they are treated not as enemies but as people loved by God. In his interpretation of the first letter of John, Augustine expressed it this way: "Love all men, even your enemies, not because they are your brethren, but that they may be your brethren."[7]

So is this "universalizing" of love something new in contrast to the Old Testament? In a precise sense, no, because already in the Old Testament we read that someday all the nations will come to Zion, that is, to the eschatological Israel, in order to share in the peace and Torah-righteousness that are enkindled there. All that is new, since Jesus' death and resurrection, is that this incorporation of all nations into the salvation of Israel has really begun.

Love Based on Jesus' Self-Surrender

Another thing is new here in the sense of a shift in perspective: Israel's Torah has been bathed in a new light as a result of Jesus' death. That death was pure self-surrender for the sake of Israel and through Israel for the world. When, according to Luke's gospel, Jesus forgave his enemies while hanging on the cross (Luke 23:34), it is shown that in his death he overcame even the hatred that was concentrated against him. Out of this self-surrender even to death, even for the sake of enemies, the church came into being. It is the space for the love that Jesus lived and that he was, in person.

So in the church, in which Torah comes to its fulfillment, love moves to the center of the Law. Love, paradoxically speaking, becomes *agapē*, the surrender of life for the sake of others, and in light of that *agapē* the whole Torah is transformed, illumined by a new light, organized around the love commandment. The New Testament interprets and transforms all individual commandments in light of the love commandment. This centering was not yet so decidedly clear in the Old Testament. It gave the new communities an unbelievable impetus. "See how they love one another," it was said of them.[8]

When Sigmund Freud asserted in his book *Civilization and Its Discontents* that Jesus, in commanding nonviolent love of enemies, sought to bridle the aggressive drive by transforming it into guilt feelings—with the result, however, that it released all the more violent fantasies of revenge and intolerant absolutist claims in other parts of the psyche—he completely misunderstood Jesus. Love, for followers of Jesus, is something different. It is not meant to create guilt feelings; instead, it aims to bring the other person into the joy that has come into the world with the Gospel. In that joy it is possible to transform aggressions into passion for God and God's project. In that joy it even becomes possible to forgive one's enemy.

So, after all the distinctions that have to be made, we have finally arrived at what *agapē* really is. Its location is not primarily in the individual Christian, because it surpasses the individual. Nor is its primary place in the "natural" family, because that is the home of "natural" love, though that needs to be transformed by *agapē* as well. Nor is its location primarily in society, because the proper virtues of society are tolerance, solidarity, and justice.

Agapē is more. Its location is in the people of God, in the church, because Christ surrendered himself for it and it is his body, imbued with his Spirit. But the church exists for the sake of the whole world. If the selfless, self-surrendering *agapē* whose source is Jesus were truly lived within the countless Christian communities, the world would be unrecognizable.

Chapter 6

No Place for Warriors
in the Name of God

September 11, 2001, has rooted itself deeply in our consciousness. The pictures of the smoking and then collapsing towers of the World Trade Center are unforgettable. The events of that day changed history—also to the degree that, since that date, fear of terrorism has been misused to slander Christian faith.

The Great Accusation

The calumny that has been spread since September 11 tells us that faith is responsible for all of it. The religions have brought fanaticism into the world. Ultimately, the religions are responsible for terrorism and the constantly erupting violence on our planet. That is the message, and the fanaticism of Muslim terrorists is supposed to demonstrate its truth. Their grim determination offers the opportunity to toss Judaism and Christianity into the same pot of religious fanaticism. As so often happens, the German magazine *Der Spiegel* was the first to seize this favorable opportunity. Apparently it presumes such a dearth of information among its readers that it has no hesitation in quoting words of Jesus as witness to the danger posed by Christianity: "Do not think that I have come to bring peace to the earth; I have not come to bring peace, but a sword" (Matt 10:34).[1]

That the same Jesus calls the peacemakers blessed (Matt 5:9) and sends his disciples out without money or weapons, even without a staff or sandals (Luke 9:3; 10:4) so they cannot be confused with the Zealots, the fanatics of his time, that he thus permits no "warriors for God" in his ranks, and that the saying about the sword was *purely metaphorical*, namely, as an image for clarity in faith and the consequences such clarity had for Jesus' followers—none of that bothers *Der Spiegel* in the least. But the journalists at *Der Spiegel* are harmless in comparison to those who, in the letters to the editor, called for the death of the "dogmatic religions." Consider, for example, a letter in the daily paper *Die Welt* on October 5, 2001:

> People have to learn at last that the world is not divided among Jews, Christians, Muslims, and other religions. The convictions of the various religions that each is the only true one are the fundamental reason why there is no peace in so many parts of this world. . . . The world is full of human beings, and not of Jews, Christians, Muslims, etc. Only when human beings have overcome the dogmatic religions will there be peace on earth.

What this reader expresses as a great prophecy had long been thought by many educated people; they only expressed it more resourcefully and in more refined terms. They said: it is all the fault of monotheism.[2] Pagans were tolerant. If the world was full of gods anyway, a couple more (translated, this means a couple more truths) didn't matter. There was room for each and all. Every person had his or her god, and each had his or her own truth. It was only monotheism that insisted on *one* god and *one* truth. That is what brought intolerance and fanaticism into the world. Monotheism is the source of all violence, and Christianity, with its jealous God so eager to dominate everything, is a legacy that has poisoned the whole world.

As I have said, making monotheism the great scapegoat for all the evils in the world is nothing new. Arthur Schopenhauer had already accused the "monotheistic religions" of fanaticism in principle:

> Truly, it is the worst side of religions that the believers of one religion have allowed themselves every sin against those of another, and with the utmost ruffianism and cruelty persecuted them; the Mohammedans against the Christians and Hindoos; the Christians against the Hindoos, Mohammedans, American natives, Negroes, Jews, heretics, and others.

Perhaps I go too far in saying *all* religions. For the sake of truth, I must add that the fanatical enormities perpetrated in the name of religion are only to be put down to the adherents of monotheistic creeds, that is, the Jewish faith and its two branches, Christianity and Islamism. We hear of nothing of the kind in the case of Hindoos and Buddhists.[3]

So much for the slandering of monotheism. Accusations of this sort have smoldered for a long time, and since September 11 they have reignited. All of this presents a clear picture of the challenges to Christians. It is high time to think about those challenges and engage them. I will pose five questions and try to give an answer to each. To begin at the beginning: should religions be made the scapegoats for every kind of hatred and fanaticism in the world?

The Religions as Scapegoats

My answer to this question can be brief. Fanaticism—blind and aggressive pursuit of a goal, for the sake of which the fanatic will walk over corpses if necessary—does not exist solely in the sphere of religion. We only have to think of National Socialism and Stalinism. Hitler and his accomplices and Stalin and his abettors decimated many millions of people within a few years and brought about endless suffering. Hitler and Stalin were embodiments of fanaticism, and both of them had deliberately emancipated themselves from the Jewish-Christian tradition. Their goal was German or Soviet world domination, and in pursuit of that goal they trod underfoot every form of law and morality. Hitler and Stalin had predecessors; the way was prepared for them by the revolutionary anarchism in nineteenth-century Europe.

Alexander Solzhenitsyn, in his book *August 1914*, presents an insightful scene involving an elderly Russian anarchist who in her youth had fought against the rule of the czars. Her niece, Veronika, can scarcely understand the revolutionaries of that older generation:

> "But, aunts!" Veronika's fine eyes looked almost imploringly from under her delicately arched dark brows. "Does anyone have the right . . . to take the path of violence?" "We do!" Aunt Agnessa erupted like a smoke-wreathed volcano. . . . "Revolutionaries . . . want to bring down to earth an ideal already visible in the kingdom of God, which is within them. But what are they to do if that ideal is still beyond the grasp of the majority? The ground has to be cleared for

> the new world—so away with all the old garbage, beginning with the autocracy! Revolutionaries are not to be judged by the yardstick of old-fashioned morality. To a revolutionary, everything that contributes to the triumph of the revolution is moral, and everything that hinders it is immoral."[4]

But the anarchist aunt is not saying anything new. Robespierre had already proclaimed that "Justice is what serves the revolution," and Saint-Just had written, "Everything must be permitted to those who act on behalf of the revolution." We can drop the word "revolution" and read such statements in naked form; in that case they simply say, "the end justifies the means." And that statement is itself the basic presupposition of fanaticism.

Of course, at this point the objection is bound to come: anarchism, Stalinism, and National Socialism were all born from the womb of Christianity. They became secular religions, utopias of redemption, growing out of nothing other than monotheism's absolute claims, and therefore they had Christianity's fanaticist gene in their chromosomes. So the accusation remains.

But this objection is invalid. No matter how much Stalinism and National Socialism appeared as perverted religious salvation, in reality they were power-mad systems overblown to the utmost. There is an ancient obsession with power in humanity that acknowledges only the rule of one's own band, one's own clan, one's own tribe, or, later, one's own nation. This power obsession has demanded countless deaths since hominization occurred—long before the monotheism of Israel and the church.

The basic error of those who shove off all blame for fanaticism onto the monotheistic religions is that they do not reckon with the historical potency of evil. That potency is ancient, more ancient than the nations. It is much, much older than Israel and the church.

What Is Concealed

So I come to my second question: can anyone deny the hope and humanity the religions have brought to the world? The Nobel laureate José Saramago wrote not long ago in the *Frankfurter Allgemeine Zeitung*:

> We know that the religions, all of them without exception, have never served to bring people closer together and spread peace. Reli-

gions were and are the basis for endless suffering, mass murder, and monstrous physical and psychic violence that make up the darkest chapters of human misery.[5]

Saramago must be excused; he wrote those words in light of the events of September 11, 2001. We can even learn from him, because in his essay he distinguishes between the true God, about whose existence he, as an atheist, reserves judgment, and the "fabricated god," that is, the god people are continually making for themselves. But that Saramago has a mental censor that blindly obliterates every element of hope and humanity that Israel and the church have brought into the world is obvious enough.

One should also try a certain thought experiment: imagine yourself in a scenario in which the Ten Commandments do not exist. Never has it been said, "You shall not kill!" Never has there been a divine prohibition against despising old people; murder; theft; abduction; rape; betrayal; shameless exploitation of strangers, the weak, and the helpless—a divine prohibition that is not simply a traffic rule or a civil law but that says to people in the depths of their hearts, "You must not do that, because it is contrary to the will of God!" One need only imagine such a world, with its limitless inhuman chaos, for an instant to know how blind even a Nobel laureate can be. In fact, we lived quite palpably in a world without the Ten Commandments under Hitler. It was just like that.

Observe, Analyze, Evaluate

A third question necessarily follows. It is: may we place all religions on the same level? What drives the natural sciences, what makes them so convincing and effective, is precisely that natural scientists have to observe with precision. They cannot rely on vague guesses. They must observe, analyze, measure, weigh with the greatest exactitude.

The same must be true with regard to the religions. We should look closely at them and put them under the microscope. We should set them alongside one another and compare them as carefully as possible. And we should do so not primarily in light of what their adherents, their members, and their sympathizers *do*.

Human beings have many drives, and no one can say with ultimate certainty whether a person's actions flow only from his or her faith or perhaps from very different sources. If we want to arrive at clear results, we have to compare the normative documents of the religions. And here

I have long since arrived at some clear conclusions. I can compare, for example, Jesus' Sermon on the Mount in Matthew 5–7 with the Qu'ran, *Suras* 8–9. In *Sura* 9.5, I read:

> And when the sacred months have passed, then kill the polytheists wherever you find them and capture them and besiege them and sit in wait for them at every place of ambush. But if they should repent, establish prayer, and give [alms], let them [go] on their way. Indeed, Allah is Forgiving and Merciful.

In the Sermon on the Mount I read:

> You have heard that it was said, "You shall love your neighbor and hate your enemy." But I say to you, Love your enemies and pray for those who persecute you, so that you may be children of your Father in heaven, for he makes his sun rise on the evil and on the good, and sends rain on the righteous and on the unrighteous. (Matt 5:43-45)

Since I am not certain that I have understood the text of the Qur'an correctly, I consult interpretations by learned Muslims. I then learn that in the monumental commentary by Abu Ja'far Muhammad ibn Jarir at-Tabari (d. 923) the text is interpreted as follows: "The sacred months" are the four holy months when peace is commanded and there can be no fighting. Afterward, the battle against the heathen can be resumed—against heathens, that is, who have not made a treaty with the Muslims, or who had such an agreement but have broken it. If, however, they repent in sorrow, that is, no longer set other gods alongside the true God and accept the prophecy of Muhammad, they may freely go to their homes.

I also learn that in the classic medieval commentaries on the Qur'an the text I have cited from *Sura* 9 (which was called the "sword verse") was regarded as so central that it abrogates all the Qur'anic texts that appear more conciliatory and pacific; that is, it nullifies them. And I also learn from the media that at the present time quite a few fundamentalist representatives of Islam interpret *Sura* 9 as an authorization for violence against the godless West.

Finally, in contrast to such extreme interpretations, I learn that a great many Muslim authors at present regard wars and violent actions as legitimate only when undertaken for the defense of Islamic states or the freedom of Muslims. For the relationship between Muslims and non-Muslims, they say, *Sura* 8.61, to take one example, is much more important:

And if they incline to peace, then incline to it [also] and rely upon
Allah. Indeed, it is He who is the Hearing, the Knowing.

Thus, overall I learn that *Sura* 9.5 is disputed in Islam. Many modern
Islamic commentators do not cite that text for the present-day relationships of Muslims and non-Muslims, but the classic medieval commentaries certainly did. Many of those medieval commentaries even say that
it abrogates all the friendlier texts.

A non-Muslim nonexpert can scarcely say any more, but one must
affirm that all these interpretations, whether classic or modern, are about
war. In the text of the Sermon on the Mount, in contrast, the people of
God are forbidden, categorically and in principle, to engage in any war,
any violence, any aggression. That is the difference.

Obviously the comparison must be more extensive and consider many
other verses in the Qur'an, for it is imbued through and through with
commands to persecute, to strike, to kill, to destroy, to fight, to make
war. The comparison must also and above all observe the inclination of
the texts, their organic context, their basic tendency, their sense of direction, their former historical location. I would truly be happy if the Qur'an
could be absolved of commands to make war and religiously grounded
use of the sword, but so far no one has been able to show me such a thing.

I know that such comparisons nowadays clash with good taste, with
"political correctness," with the clouding of the massive differences
between the religions; they go against religious pluralism, which asserts
that all religions really worship the one God, the incomprehensible, hidden, highest Being. But I believe that such comparisons are urgently
needed, because they are the only way to make possible a realistic and
honest dialogue. They will also be a constant reminder to us Christians
of the lack of seriousness with which we approach our own foundational
texts.

Radicality and Fanaticism

But now comes the fourth question, the most vital of those to be posed
in this context. It has to come. It is: can we equate radicality with fanaticism? Or must we make a sharp distinction here?

I have already defined fanaticism: the blind, reckless, and aggressive
pursuit of one's own goal without regard to the whole of reality and
following the principle that "the end justifies the means." Radicality, on
the other hand—at least in theological usage—is something entirely

different from fanaticism. Radicality is not in itself either blind or aggressive. "Radical" comes from the Latin word *radix*, root. A radical's actions go to the root of his or her existence. A radical lives at depth, and for that very reason lives as undivided and whole.

Those who are radical in the biblical sense do not say, "I understand that I must change my life, but not just yet. There is always time for that later." Instead, they say, "Today! Now! This very hour!" Nor can a radical person say, "Part of my life belongs to God, but the rest of my life is mine. There, I'll do what pleases me."

So "radical" always means "today" and always undivided, whole, with body and soul, with everything we have, with all our passion. There is no better description of the radicality of biblical faith than the *Shema*: "Hear, O Israel! Yhwh is our God, Yhwh alone. You shall love Yhwh your God with all your heart, and with all your soul, and with all your might" (Deut 6:4-5). This radicality of surrender to God and God's project has not the least thing in common with fanaticism. Jesus, who lived wholly on the basis of the *Shema*, was radical, but his radicality was not fanaticism. Jesus was a radical, for example, when he said, "No one who puts a hand to the plow and looks back is fit for the reign of God" (Luke 9:62). He was radical when he warned, "if your eye causes you to stumble, tear it out; it is better for you to enter the reign of God with one eye than to have two eyes and to be thrown into hell" (Mark 9:47). He was radical when he challenged his disciples, "do not worry about tomorrow, for tomorrow will bring worries of its own" (Matt 6:34).

None of that is innocuous. It is radical to the highest degree. But the same Jesus, despite his passion and his shocking radicality, was not fanatical. Luke tells of an event that took place when Jesus was traveling through Samaria with his disciples; he had sent some of them ahead to find shelter. In this story the disciples reveal their own fanaticism; Jesus is altogether different.

> On their [the disciples'] way they entered a village of the Samaritans to make ready for him; but they did not receive him, because his face was set toward Jerusalem. When his disciples James and John saw it, they said, "Lord, do you want us to command fire to come down from heaven and consume them?" But he turned and rebuked them. Then they went on to another village. (Luke 9:52-56)

Some ancient manuscripts have an expanded version that interprets this: "rebuked them, and said, 'You do not know what spirit you are of, for the Son of Man has not come to destroy the lives of human beings but to save them.' "

We could cite any number of texts here. Anyone who searches the New Testament, and above all Jesus' message, will find radicality there, but not fanaticism.

Faith and Fanaticism

So I come to my fifth and last question: can fanaticism be equated with faith? I will not make the answer too easy for myself, because there is no denying that, alas, in the history of Israel and that of the church faith has all too often been turned into fanaticism. We only have to think of the Crusades, the burning of heretics, religious wars, and forced baptisms—the whole palette of Christian intolerance.

Nevertheless, we should be clear about the fact that all Christians who shouted, "God wills it!" and proceeded to torture and murder always had their own Sacred Scriptures against them. They had the Old Testament's visions of peace against them. They had Jesus' attitude against them. They had the Sermon on the Mount against them.

Still, the question is urgent: how is it that faith can so easily turn into fanaticism? It must somehow be connected with the totality and passion of faith, that is, with its radical nature. With faith, as with love, the highest and most beautiful spheres of human life are also the most perilous. Love is the greatest thing there is, but it can turn into hate, and perversions are always its nearest neighbors, even dwelling in the same house, in the soul's cellars. So also, faith is something very great; it directs human existence to the highest reality. But precisely because of its unconditional nature and its radicality it is deeply endangered and can turn into fanaticism.

Should we therefore forbid faith and get rid of it? In that case we would also have to get rid of love, because it is also always in danger. So it cannot be a question of banning faith from history; instead, we should work toward a true and enlightened faith. And precisely in that respect Jewish-Christian faith is an astonishing phenomenon, because ever since it entered the world this faith has been accompanied by a history of enlightenment that is unique in the world. That history of enlightenment, beginning with Abraham and culminating in Jesus, has worked like leaven in the world: it has made an essential contribution to the fundamental values of our Western civilization. The great slogan of the French Revolution, "liberty, equality, fraternity," ultimately rests on the book of Deuteronomy.

At this point we may mention three key points from that history of enlightenment that are irrevocably bound up with biblical faith: the exposure of violence, mission through fascination, and the self-critique of the people of God.

The Exposure of Violence

This theme pervades the whole Bible, starting at the very beginning, in the primeval history. Cain murders his own brother out of rivalry, and the murder is exposed for what it is. And in the last book of the Bible, the Revelation to John, we find two contrasting symbols—the "beast" in Revelation 13 as power-obsessed, brutal violence in which the forces of a God-hating society are distilled, and the lamb, an image of Christ, who knew no violence but held fast to his mission and therefore was killed.

It is true that there are texts in the Old Testament that at first glance seem to propagate violence and even to legitimate it. If we look closer, we see that these texts either uncover the reality of violence, thus exposing it for what it is, or they do not refer to revenge in the current sense, but advocate for the restoration of an order of law that has been destroyed. Or else they speak of real and unacceptable violence—and then those texts are themselves corrected, even within the Old Testament itself, but at the latest in the New Testament. That is to say, from a Christian point of view the Old and New Testaments must be read as a single book. At the very latest, the Sermon on the Mount neutralizes all the genuine texts of violence in the Old Testament and places them in the light of Jesus' message.

So the whole Bible, from beginning to end, is an exposure of violence and at the same time a tracing of the way by which violence can be transformed into reconciliation and peace.

Mission through Fascination

At the end of Matthew's gospel the risen Christ, exalted at God's right hand, speaks these words:

> Go therefore and make disciples of all nations, baptizing them in the name of the Father and of the Son and of the Holy Spirit, and teaching them to obey everything that I have commanded you. (Matt 28:19)

That means a mission to the whole world. The New Testament is thus convinced that there is only *one* truth and not many, that Christ is that truth, and that testimony to it must be given to all people. But it is not to be attested through violence, indoctrination, moral pressure, endless harangues; the testimony must come from the believing existence of communities of Christian disciples, so that those who are confronted with the truth of faith may remain altogether free.

The way this freedom can be made possible is evident already in the great vision of the pilgrimage of the nations in Isaiah 2: the nations see how peace is lived among the people of God, and they come to learn for themselves what peace is. They come in complete freedom, drawn only by the fascination that emanates from this different kind of society.

The Self-Critique of the People of God

Fanaticism is blind. It looks neither left nor right. It rages with closed eyes. Above all: it permits no critique. To that extent it is like delusive systems.

In contrast, it is characteristic of Israel and the church that there has always been critique within them. The critics of Israel were the prophets who pointed out, as clearly as could be, how much the people of God were disobeying God's will. In the church it is the saints who by their very existence unremittingly question the gentrification and self-centeredness of the people of God. And even better and more important than individual saints are communities that live according to the will of God. They are the true prophetic centers in the time after Jesus.

A great many such could be named. I think, for example, of the public confession of responsibility for the sins of Christians that John Paul II made at St. Peter's in Rome on March 12, 2000, or the great theme of fraternal and sororal correction that runs throughout the Bible. Faith requires self-critique of the people of God; it needs the others who again and again open our eyes. Faith can never be blind. It requires a history of true enlightenment that accompanies it unceasingly. Then it cannot turn into fanaticism. I know no religion, no ideology, no system of truth that treats its own history as critically as do Israel and the church.

Chapter 7

Did Jesus Die for "Many" or for "All"?

Bible translations have always contained explosive elements. This has been proven again recently in the case of a translation supported by the Lutheran state church in Hesse, the "Inclusive Language Bible."[1] In it, the Gospel of John no longer begins with the familiar sentence "In the beginning was the Word." The Bible reader has to adjust to "In the beginning was Wisdom," as it reads now. Pure whim? By no means! The author of the Johannine Prologue was working against the background of Old Testament wisdom theology, which was able to say that divine Wisdom existed before all things, was present at creation, was the standard and measure for it, and, finally, took up her dwelling in Israel as her home.

Still, the new translation is wrong. Insights of that kind belong in the interpretation of the text and not in the translation. The Gospel of John speaks of the *logos*, who was not only prior to all creation, but is "God" (John 1:1, 18). That is more than all wisdom theology could ever say. It rests, ultimately, on the experience of Jesus' disciples—on what they had heard and seen (1 John 1:1). To simply change the church's traditional translation at this point is a serious theological mistake. The translators should have listened to Martin Luther. In the last verse of his hymn, "A Mighty Fortress Is Our God," as we well know, he wrote: "That word above all earthly powers, no thanks to them, abideth."

Patching up the Words of Institution

But Catholics have translation problems of their own, and in particular with the eucharistic words of institution. For many centuries the priest said that Christ's blood was shed *pro vobis et pro multis*—"for you and for many." But when, in the 1970s, the official vernacular translations of the Latin Mass appeared, it was suddenly no longer "for many" but "for all." This new translation was an offense, not for all, but still for many church members. This was not an individual case: the English "for all" was echoed by the German "für alle," the Spanish "para todos," and even the Italian "per tutti." It seems, in fact, that this new translation began with Italy, through a special dispensation.

Then Pope Benedict XVI insisted that the vernacular Mass books must, where necessary, change "all" back to "many." That has created a new wave of annoyance—this time, of course, from the other side.

How did this correction of "many" to "all" happen in the first place? The culprit was the famous New Testament scholar Joachim Jeremias, who wrote a book on *The Eucharistic Words of Jesus* in 1935.[2] There he proposed that in Semitic usage "many" did not have an exclusive meaning, that is, "many, but not all," but an inclusive sense: the great, extensive multitude, that is, "all." Jeremias went on to offer support for his linguistic argument in a number of further publications, and apparently he impressed a great many people, above all because he added a theological argument: he spoke of the "boundlessness of the love of God."

Since the Roman directive, this "boundlessness of the love of God" has become the focal point of a heated discussion—among pastors who do not know how to explain the new/old translation to their parishioners but also in the letters to the editor in major dailies. One side says, "Jesus did, in fact, die for everyone and not for a limited number of people." "Obviously," says the other side, "but in fact he only redeemed those who permit themselves to be redeemed; therefore it has to be 'for [the] many.'"

What Jesus Was Really Saying

To put it bluntly: such arguments put the whole problem on a dangerously slippery slope. When Jesus, at the Last Supper, spoke of the "many" for whom he would give up his life, he was not addressing the question of whether "all" or maybe only "many" would be saved. He was thinking of something quite different.

Jesus was not naïve. He knew what was about to happen to him. He knew that people wanted to get rid of him. It was his goal to reassemble Israel, the people of God, in light of the coming reign of God, and to sanctify them. Now death was stalking him. In this situation he gathered the Twelve for a last meal together; it was probably the Passover supper. He did not celebrate it with his family, as was customary. He deliberately celebrated it with the twelve disciples. During the meal he interpreted the bread and wine in terms of his death. And by giving the bread and wine to the Twelve he gave them a share in his death, and so in himself. He gave himself to the Twelve in bread and wine.

We can really understand the words of interpretation he spoke only if Jesus was surrendering his life as "atonement" for the unbelief of the people of God. That is why in Luke 22:20 he says "for you." He addresses the participants in the meal, the Twelve, who represent the eschatological Israel, the people of the twelve tribes. Thus, as the words at the Last Supper show, Jesus died for Israel.

The same is utterly obvious for another reason. In the gospels of Mark and Matthew, Jesus speaks of the "blood of the covenant." The background here is the making of the covenant at Sinai (Exod 24:8), and the Sinai covenant (including the renewed Sinai covenant) was made, in the Bible, with the "house of Israel." Thus Jesus gave his life for Israel, for the people of God.

The "Many" Are the Nations

But that by no means says it all, for Jesus quite obviously interpreted his approaching death also against the background of Isaiah 52–53, which speaks of a "servant of God" against whom the "many"—meaning the nations—are conspiring. They strike and torture and kill him. In the book of Isaiah this servant of God is Israel, oppressed and beaten by the nations. Jesus saw himself as that servant of God; his fate was a distillation of the fate of Israel. In the situation of his death he was the only true representative of Israel. Thus it is clear that against the background of Isaiah the "many" in Mark 14:24 and Matthew 26:28 are the nations, the Gentiles. Jesus died not only for Israel but also for the Gentiles.

Is that a contradiction? The surrender of his life was for Israel but at the same time for the Gentile nations as well? No, it is not a contradiction. In Old Testament theology Israel is precisely God's sign for the Gentiles; it is to be a blessing for the nations. Its whole election was only for the sake of the nations. God cares about the whole world, but God can only reach out to the world if, within the world, there is a people in which God's salvation is visible.

Better to Clarify Than to Change

Thus the words of institution contain a comprehensive theology. It is present only in brief key phrases, but in Jesus' time everyone who lived from Sacred Scripture understood such "shorthand." These shorthand expressions compacted whole sections of the Old Testament. We cannot understand who the "many" are and what role Israel played for them if we do not keep Isaiah 52–53 in mind. To say it again and in somewhat banal terms: the question whether "all" or only "many" will get to heaven has nothing at all to do with the overall problem.

It is the great task of preaching and catechesis to lay out the Old Testament context in the book of Isaiah. The change from "many" to "all" did not clarify it but only obscured it, because then one could no longer perceive the play on Isaiah. It is theologically correct that we at last get to hear the original wording again—quite apart from reverence for a two-thousand-year-old tradition. Then we may be able to understand better that we ourselves, the little remnant God has found and assembled within the world, are responsible for *many*. "All" are a nameless, nebulous mass we can talk about in dogmatic and abstract terms. "Many"—those are many individuals who have faces and whom we meet every day. And from a biblical point of view they are also the nations, the vast number for whom Jesus died when he died for Israel.

Chapter 8

How Could an Individual Redeem the Whole World?

In 1969, Peter Handke wrote a piece about Jesus entitled "Biography (Jesus)."[1] It is just one page long. That is the first provocation: no one can describe the life of Jesus in a single page. The second provocation is the epigraph Handke placed at the head of that page, the rewriting of a saying of Jesus that previously was often translated: "what will it profit a person to gain the whole world and suffer the loss of his or her own soul?" (Matt 16:26). Handke makes it: "What will it profit a person to gain his or her soul but suffer the loss of the world?" That is: what good is it if the human soul is redeemed but that apparently redeemed soul is bloodless, divorced from reality, and unworldly? Incidentally, Handke could only twist Jesus' saying so elegantly because he was using a translation that was very common in the past but was wrong. In reality, Jesus said: "what will it profit a person to gain the whole world but forfeit his or her life?" Jesus is about the whole, the ample life, filled to the brim. And that is precisely what one loses when one tries greedily to have the world for oneself. Such a person destroys not only the self but the world as well.

Handke's third provocation is the way he describes Jesus' activity—as something innocuous, ineffectual, and profoundly inconsequential. His "biography" ends this way:

90

Without concern for the ban on assemblies, he often spoke in the open air. Thanks to the general boredom, he attracted some followers, but for the most part his preaching fell on deaf ears. As the charge later said, he tried to arouse the population against the authorities by pretending to be the longed-for redeemer. On the other hand, God [Handke means Jesus] was not inhuman. He didn't harm a fly. He couldn't even turn a hair on anyone.

He was not afraid of people. Apart from his somewhat boastful nature, he was basically harmless. Still, some people thought God [i.e., Jesus] was better than nothing; most, however, thought he was nothing at all. Consequently, his trial was short. He had little to say in his own defense. When he spoke, it was not to the point. He just stuck to saying that he was who he was, but mostly he was silent.

On Good Friday of the year 30 or 31 of the common era, after a not altogether proper trial, he was hanged on a cross. He spoke only seven words. Around three in the afternoon, in sunny weather, he gave up the ghost. At the same time there was a medium-strength earthquake in Jerusalem. There was only minor damage.

A blasphemy? No. In fact, it is not a text against Jesus, but against the innocuousness and complete inconsequentiality of an assimilated church. The text is more of a cry for help. It asks: where is the redemption the church is always talking about? Where did Jesus or the church change anything in this world? What is different, after the death on a cross of this strange Jesus, and after two thousand years of the church's history? "Minor damage!" Nothing else!

Now, in contrast, a church text—from *Gotteslob*, the current hymn and prayer book of the Catholic churches in German-speaking countries. At the beginning of the Way of the Cross, it reads: "Lord Jesus Christ . . . in gratitude we behold the great compassion with which you have atoned for our disobedience and wiped away our sins" (*Gotteslob* no. 775). At each of the fourteen stations, the prayer is: "Lord Jesus Christ, we praise you and we bless you, because by your holy cross you have redeemed the world."

Countless Christian prayers and hymns are similar. These texts, from the point of view of doctrine, are almost all correct. But are they clear? Or do they provoke the question: how can another atone for my disobedience? How does that work? And how can an individual take away the sins of all humanity? Still more, how can an individual redeem the whole world? That is just what Handke's text cannot believe. What changed with Jesus' death? What has the church altered by its proclamation of Jesus' death? Has anything in the world been made better?

That is precisely the Jewish objection to Jesus as well: for Jewish—and Old Testament—faith, redemption is always something real, palpable, bodily, public, worldly, something one can see and grasp. This is evident from the idea of the Messiah: when the Messiah comes, the Jews say, his coming will change the world completely. There is a Jewish story that illustrates this in impressive fashion:

> The students in the Shul were all highly excited. Instead of learning Torah, they were all chattering. When the rabbi entered the room, they shouted at him: "The Messiah has come!" The rabbi went to the window, looked down at the street, came back, sat down at his lectern, and continued from where he had left off. The students interrupted him: "What now? What shall we do?" "Nothing. Go on learning," said the Rabbi. "How can the Messiah have come if nothing in the world has changed?"

This little story is a genial formulation of Jews' primary objection to Christians: you say the Messiah has come. But where has anything in the world been made different? You say he has redeemed the world. But there should be some visible evidence of redemption. Friedrich Nietzsche made exactly the same objection, but more directly: "Better songs they will have to sing for me before I learn to believe in their redeemer; more redeemed his disciples would have to look!"[2] And elsewhere:

> But you, if your faith makes you happy, show yourselves to be happy. Your faces have always done more harm to your faith than our reasons! If that glad message of your Bible were written in your faces, you would not need to demand belief in the authority of that book in such stiff-necked fashion. Your words, your actions should continually make the Bible superfluous—in fact, through you a new Bible should continually come into being. As it is, your apologia for Christianity is rooted in your unchristianity, and with your defence you write your own condemnation. If you, however, should wish to emerge from your dissatisfaction with Christianity, you should ponder over the experience of two thousand years, which, clothed in the modest form of a question, may be voiced as follows: "If Christ really intended to redeem the world, may he not be said to have failed?"[3]

Christians have rightly defended themselves against such objections but not always in the right way, and often enough they have only succeeded in provoking new objections.

Invisible Redemption?

Some have responded, for example, to the accusation that the world has not changed in the least by saying that, indeed, nothing outward has changed. The world is still full of sickness, misery, and strife. But for those who believe, something has changed within. In themselves, in their hearts, people who believe are redeemed. God dwells in their souls. The justified person is filled with sanctifying grace.

What should we say about that? The concept of "sanctifying grace" is, of course, beyond question. It is correct, and even biblical. But where is that grace? Only in individuals? Not where two or three are gathered in his name (Matt 18:20)? And does redemption only dwell invisibly in the soul? Is it not also related to conditions in society, the whole social, legal, economic sphere, our homes, the things of the world in and with which we live? Woody Allen, New York's "urban neurotic," quipped, "There is no question that there is an unseen world. The problem is, how far is it from midtown and how late is it open?" Only a Jew can talk that way. Salvation is concrete or nothing at all. The same is true of the church: a purely invisible church banished to inwardness has betrayed the reality of redemption.

Against the response that declares redemption to be something unseen we have the whole biblical tradition. Jesus healed the sick, drove out demons, fed hungry people, gathered disciples, and lived with them as his new family. And he said, "Do not think I have come to abolish the law or the prophets. I have come not to abolish but to fulfill" (Matt 5:17). Jesus had no intention of abrogating the Torah; he wanted to bring it to fulfillment. But the goal of Torah is precisely this: to restore the world, create conditions of justice, and bring this stubborn, often chaotic world back to the glory and beauty in which it was created.

To say that salvation has already occurred, that Jesus has already redeemed us, but the redemption is only internal, invisible within souls, took place only within hearts, is an utterly invalid response. Its one-sidedness does justice neither to biblical tradition nor to the true tradition of the church.

Salvation beyond the Grave?

Another ineffectual attempt to deal with Jewish objections and Nietzsche's reproach runs this way: The redemption Jesus accomplished happens only after death. Earth is the place of testing, probation, decision, but salvation and liberation take place only beyond this world.

This response is likewise invalid; indeed, it is dogmatically false. Jesus never preached about the world beyond; he announced the reign of God, and said it "is among you" (Luke 17:21). He also said: "if it is by the finger of God that I cast out the demons, the kingdom of God has come to you" (Luke 11:20).

Moreover, during the Stations of the Cross we do not say "through your holy cross you will redeem the world," but "through your holy cross you have redeemed the world." The salvation of the world does not occur beyond the world, though that will be the time of its perfection. It begins here.

A Preprogrammed Redemption?

But how can we imagine that? How could a single individual redeem the whole world? Christians have always tried to answer this question through the Bible: it was the will of God that the "Son" become a human being in order to redeem the world through the sacrifice of the cross.

There are indeed many texts in the Bible that point in this direction. The Old Testament already speaks of the Servant of God, Israel, who must suffer for the salvation of the many, that is, the nations. When the nations look at this Servant, they say:

> Surely he has borne our infirmities
>> and carried our diseases;
> . . .
> . . . he was wounded for our transgressions,
>> crucified for our iniquities;
> upon him was the punishment that made us whole,
>> and by his bruises we are healed. (Isa 53:4-5)

The New Testament interprets the Servant of God as Jesus (cf. Acts 8:30-35). He represents and gathers all Israel into his own person. Jesus himself seems to have thought along those lines, as shown by his words at the Last Supper and by such sayings as "the Son of Man must undergo great suffering, and be rejected by the elders, the chief priests, and the scribes, and be killed, and after three days rise again" (Mark 8:31).

A good many other biblical texts make similar statements. We could misunderstand them all to say that God has a plan of salvation by which one must die for the sins of the world so that it can be redeemed. God desired and planned the death of the divine Son so that in this way atonement could be made for the guilt of all humanity. Then it starts to get dangerous: God wanted a bloody sacrifice for satisfaction, so that

God could be reconciled to humanity, and so the whole plan as described had to be carried out.

The notion sketched here underlies many pious texts; we encounter it in old hymns and even in devotional art. It seems to have the Bible in its favor, but in fact it is highly questionable. It distorts the biblical message and even poisons the image of God, because it suggests a God who insists on his own rights and requires a bloody sacrifice in order to be appeased. To sensible people, such a God can only appear shocking and cruel. Consequently many Christians take refuge in Mary, the mother of mercy. In his early book, *Introduction to Christianity*, Joseph Ratzinger wrote:

> To many Christians, and especially to those who only know the faith from a fair distance, it looks as if the cross is to be understood as part of a mechanism of injured and restored right. It is the form, so it seems, in which the infinitely offended righteousness of God was propitiated again by means of an infinite expiation. It thus appears to people as the expression of an attitude which insists on a precise balance between debit and credit . . . . The "infinite expiation" on which God seems to insist thus moves into a . . . sinister light. Many devotional texts actually force one to think that Christian faith in the cross visualizes a God whose unrelenting righteousness demanded a human sacrifice, the sacrifice of his own Son, and one turns away in horror from a righteousness whose sinister wrath makes the message of love incredible.
>
> This picture is as false as it is widespread. In the Bible the cross does not appear as part of a mechanism of injured right; on the contrary, in the Bible the cross is quite the reverse: it is the expression of the radical nature of the love which gives itself completely, of the process in which one is what one does, and does what one is; it is the expression of a life that is completely being for others.[4]

So we need to get ourselves away from false ideas that seem to be biblical but in fact are not based on the Bible at all. Therefore we have to ask simply: How did Jesus really appear? How did he begin his preaching? What was the center of his proclamation?

A Proclamation of Death?

Did Jesus appear in Galilee preaching the message, "I have come into the world to suffer and so to atone for the sins of the world; follow me and suffer with me?" Was the focus of his message "I have come into the world because God desires me as a sacrifice for the redemption of the world; death on the cross is the highest goal of my life"? If so, that would surely have been masochism, glorification of suffering, a culture of death.

The answer can only be no, that is not what Jesus was like. From the beginning, his preaching was called *evangelium*, good news. Mark, at the beginning of his gospel, summarizes Jesus' whole message as follows: "The time is fulfilled, and the kingdom of God has come near; repent, and believe in the good news!" (Mark 1:15). And later, when John the Baptizer in prison sent messengers to Jesus to ask him, "Are you the one who is to come, or are we to wait for another?" Jesus answered, "the blind receive their sight, the lame walk, the lepers are cleansed, the deaf hear, the dead are raised, and the poor have good news brought to them" (Matt 11:2-5). The blind, the lame, the lepers, the deaf, and the dead represent the suffering and misery in the world. Jesus attacks that situation. Misery and suffering are not what creation ought to be. Jesus' desire is that God be master of the world and thus creation become what it should be. That is the impetus of his message and his actions.

But how is that possible? It is so because Jesus trusts his heavenly Father absolutely. That trust tells him that God will act. God desires nothing but the happiness, the salvation, the liberation of the world. Anyone who says, "God will act at some point or other, but not today," lives in a state of mistrust. God gives all of salvation today, already now. We only have to allow it to happen. If anyone opens herself or himself to this salvation, the impossible becomes possible. Then the world begins to transform itself.

This transformation of the world does not, however, happen by magic. It happens through Jesus' surrender of himself to Israel, through his living for the people of God with his whole existence. This "for" is realized in multiple ways but above all in Jesus' gathering of disciples around himself. From him they learn to trust, to forgive, to care for one another, to turn their attention away from themselves and toward the people of God. They are to make God's care for the world their own.

Jesus gathers around him people who leave everything, not out of a sense of obligation, but out of their joy at having found the treasure of the reign of God; people who join their lives with one another, who forgive seventy-seven times a day, who serve one another and have no fear of death anymore.

But that would still not be enough. Beyond such disciples, Jesus needs many others who help from home with their joy, friendship, the aid they are able to offer, even if it is only a cup of cold water (Matt 10:42). Through Jesus and his group of disciples and the friends and sympathizers who look to him, Israel is to be made new, find liberation and peace, and by way of Israel the same is to be true for the whole world. That would be the remedy.

Imagine for a moment that Jesus had found such disciples and that they had grown more and more numerous, people who gave up everything and placed themselves entirely at his disposal so that there would be more and more places in Israel where God was master—more and more places where the *Shema* and the Our Father became lived reality. Then Israel would have transformed itself. Reconciliation and peace would have arrived. Then Jesus would not have died on the cross, and Israel would have become the shining city on the hill.

It Happened Differently

We all know that, alas, it did not happen that way. That is not how it turned out. Everything was different. Mark's gospel describes how Jesus began with his message of joy, how he gathered disciples, healed the sick, spread blessing around himself—but Mark also describes how from the beginning Jesus was attacked, how his opponents gathered, how he was deliberately slandered and his message twisted, how his disciples were not in agreement but instead fought among themselves over the places of honor. The gospels describe in positively nightmarish fashion how Jesus' loneliness grew: one of his closest disciples betrayed him, one denied him, and in the end they all fled. The one who had the remedy for the deep neediness of the world was to be silenced and his project eliminated from the world. But Jesus' death was not brought about by only the hatred of his opponents; it was due also to the fear and cowardliness of his followers and the indifference of the multitude.

One Alone?

So it seemed that Jesus had been successfully destroyed. His words and deeds appeared to have been refuted. But then came the miracle of Easter and Pentecost: the disciples, scattered to the four winds, reassembled. They saw the Risen One. They experienced their gathering as the place of forgiveness. They proclaimed Jesus as the one who had died for Israel and now is seated at the right hand of God—that is, they proclaimed him as the one who was right. They experienced their own repentance and their new, more profound view of Jesus as the work of God and the Easter gift of the Risen One.

Then they did exactly what they had learned from Jesus but had not understood before his death. They struggled for unanimity with one another and out of that unanimity they founded more and more new communities. Church arose on the earth of Israel. So Jesus' death proved not the end but a new beginning that continued in Israel what Jesus had begun. It was not a meaningless catastrophe but the seal set on Jesus' self-surrender and the fidelity with which he held fast to his task without ever turning aside. Through Jesus' death and resurrection the disciples' eyes were opened and they understood fully, for the first time, what their own duty was.

So the path to our redemption traces a wide arc. It began with Abraham. It reached its absolute pinnacle in Jesus Christ—but not primarily in his death. His death was only the ultimate and final culmination of what he had already lived: his complete surrender to his task, which was to be present for Israel and for the world. Jesus lived God's remedy for the world and so endowed the world forever with salvation. But that endowment of salvation for the world must from then on be lived in the church as transformative for the world so that it can reach all nations and cultures.

So were we redeemed by a single individual? Yes and no! Jesus was the only one who found God's remedy for the world and lived it in ultimate and absolute self-surrender. To that degree we are redeemed by him alone. And yet the long history of Israel's faith was needed in order to make Jesus possible at all. And Jesus needs a people so that what he lived may reach the whole world. The church is the sacramental sign that makes visible and mediates to the world the salvation of Jesus Christ, with which he has endowed it once and forever.

Both/And

This makes it possible for us to expand the questions we have been considering, so that our one-sided understanding becomes more nuanced and complete, encompassing the whole—in other words, becoming catholic. For the Greek words *kath' holon* (catholic) mean "containing the whole," "referring to the whole."

Redemption in the biblical sense always contains the world as both visible and invisible, this side and beyond, today and what is to come, our history of freedom and God's eternal plan, the proclamation of the life-giving reign of God and the preaching of the death of Jesus, the fact that Jesus alone has redeemed us and that he nevertheless needs the help of many in order for that salvation to reach the whole world.

We must now attempt to understand the great, ancient concepts of Christian tradition in light of this overall picture. These ideas are without exception proper and necessary, but they must be rightly interpreted on the basis of the whole of biblical thought. They cannot be distorted by fundamentalism, nor can they be made cheap and toothless. They certainly cannot be ignored or eliminated.

Representative Substitution

First let us consider the idea of representative substitution. Christian tradition says that Jesus took his suffering upon himself as our representative, and that he died in our place. This is precisely the neuralgic point in the European Enlightenment. How can another do for me what I must do for myself? How can I be redeemed by another? Must I not save myself? The autonomous human being is infinitely annoyed to hear, "You can't do it yourself." Therefore Immanuel Kant insisted, against all the theology of representative substitution, "You can because you should."[5]

But even such a great philosopher apparently knew little about human beings. From the beginning of our lives to their end we are dependent on other people. As children we needed our parents, who gave us food, clothed us, potty-trained us, wiped our noses, and tied our shoes, until we could do those things for ourselves. Then we needed teachers who with infinite patience instructed us in arithmetic and writing. And it went on and on: other people helped us, introduced us to new spheres of thought and action, preceded us with their own skills, showed us solutions. Even as adults we are constantly dependent on the competence and aid of others. And when we get old we most certainly need the care of others, conversation with relatives and friends, often even reminders about our surroundings when our own memory gets weaker and weaker.

And still more: when I drive across a high bridge I rely on the competence of the structural designers who built it and the diligence of the technicians who maintain it year after year. Every person and every society relies on an endless number of surrogates, representatives. Certainly the church lives out of the faith of its saints, and primarily and above all from the path Jesus chose. Kant's thesis, "you can because you should," is fundamentally false. It should read: "You can, if you are willing to be helped."[6]

In all this, representation or substitution never means dispensing the other from her or his own action, faith, and repentance. Rather, substitution is intended to make one's own action possible. True representative substitution does not incapacitate; it desires nothing more than that the other be free to act.

That is how we should also understand Jesus' representative substitution for us: he found the solution, building on the long history of Israel's experience, and he lived it unto death as being for others. *I* did not discover the solution for myself, but I can lay claim to it in freedom. By my own strength, alone and relying only on myself, I could never live it. But on the basis of what Jesus gave to the world I can enter into this solution with many, many others. That is what the words "representative substitution," which have become so incomprehensible, in fact mean for people today.

Perhaps the following thought process can also help us: It is obvious on the face of it that a solidary community in which each is there for the others would be the best of all societies. Just imagine a situation in which each stands in for the others and bears the others' burdens. Simply put: the ideal society! Paradise regained! Unfortunately, such a society can never be achieved simply on the basis of reason. It can function only if *all* are in solidarity. If I myself carry others' burdens without their helping to carry mine, I come off worse than the others. I will be shamelessly exploited, have no time left for myself; I will be ground down. So I won't do it in the first place.

So a solidary community only has a chance if someone who has no fear of drawing the short straw begins to live for others and if such a one finds many followers. Still, someone has to begin: with all her time, with all his strength, with all her property, with his whole existence. That is exactly what the Bible means by representative substitution. That One has begun, has given everything—not out of ascetic motives, not out of masochism, not out of a desire to suffer and sacrifice, but out of joy over the treasure found (Matt 13:44), out of delight in God and God's cause. Because he lived, because his joy and self-surrender existed, the church has become possible as the place of his enduring presence, and so our joy and self-surrender are possible as well.

Sacrifice

So we come to the concept of sacrifice. Here again it is necessary to see, first of all, that no human being can live without the "sacrifice" of others. Simply put: what have other people given for my sake, in terms of time and effort, to make me a more or less rational person! Today's parents experience not only the happiness children can bring but also, and often to a greater degree, the excessive demands imposed by raising children in the twenty-first century. For many parents, having children requires strenuous effort. They are exhausted; they lament the disappearance of any opportunity to withdraw and rest; they can scarcely combine work and family; often their only ambition is to survive. The mere fact that in the city parents can no longer simply send their children outside to play is an indication of the burdens on parents nowadays.

It was not, however, all that different in the past. Then there were rampant diseases that took the lives of many children and filled their parents with sorrow. Bringing children into the world, however joyous it is, has always been associated with sacrifice. We all live from the fact that our parents did not refuse to make those sacrifices. Anyone who longs for a life without sacrifice is simply blind to reality.

But instead of "sacrifice," maybe we should speak of sympathy and self-surrender. Then it may be clearer that we are talking about something without which no one can exist. In fact, every genuine love demands sacrifice, because I cannot bend the other to my will, cannot accommodate the other to my own wishes or shape him or her in my image. Benedict XVI wrote in his encyclical *Spe salvi*:

> In the end, even the "yes" to love is a source of suffering, because love always requires expropriations of my "I," in which I allow myself to be pruned and wounded. Love simply cannot exist without this painful renunciation of myself, for otherwise it becomes pure selfishness and thereby ceases to be love.[7]

When we speak of Jesus Christ's *sacrifice* on the cross, then, it means that with his ultimate self-surrender he chose to exist not for himself but for God and all human beings.

In speaking of Christ's sacrifice, we have to free ourselves of the ideas associated with religious sacrifices. Those may also be about surrender to the Holy, submission to the Wholly Other, even worship and adoration. We cannot exclude any of that. But on the whole, pagan sacrifices present another picture: they seek to influence invisible forces, neutralize evil influences, appease dangerous powers. It was all very concrete: the gods smelled the smoke from the oxen and sheep and were mollified. Or people put on sackcloth, smeared ashes on their faces, cut themselves so they bled, and believed that would change the gods' minds. Or they offered the dearest things they had, even their own children, to appease the gods and rescue the city from its enemies. Or they made pilgrimages with rocks in their shoes, traveling the last part of the way on their knees, to get what they wanted from God.

All these kinds of sacrifice run the risk of doing service to a god in order to fulfill human interests. Sacrifice in the biblical sense means something different: it signifies self-surrender, listening with one's whole existence to what God wills. Then it is no longer about one's own cause but about God's.

Atonement

In the same way, atonement in the biblical sense means something different from atonement in the various religions. Biblical atonement begins with the fact that a human being has caused harm, to himself or herself and to what lies around him or her. This self-created damage expands, produces new damage, destroys lives, begets a wave of death. Then God offers new life, a new beginning—but not in the form of a voice from heaven that says, "Oh, well, it wasn't so bad," or, "Now we are all in harmony again and everything is okay." It is by no means okay. What the human being has wrought is disastrous and has ruinous consequences that can take on exponential dimensions.

Atonement in the biblical sense means that God produces atonement within this situation. *God* creates atonement, that is, creates a new beginning to enable human beings to get out of their hopeless entanglement. God gives new life. No one has to earn it. That is what the Bible means by atonement. And in that sense God made the death of Jesus, which God in no way desired or willed but that human beings brought about, into a new beginning that revolutionizes everything.

If at this point we look at Aristotle's theology we can take this somewhat deeper. For Aristotle, God is infinite and perfect spirit, existing from eternity from and through God's self. God is pure spirit, pure thought. "But what does he really think?" Aristotle asks in the twelfth book of his *Metaphysics* (1074b). He answers: God thinks God's self, because God is the highest and best that exists. What else, in Aristotle's logic, could God think? God is perfect existence in God's self; if God were to think anything other than God's self, such as human beings or any individual thing, God would no longer be thinking the highest thought and so would turn away from God's self and lose the divine perfection.

Christian theology has been glad to make use of Greek philosophy and has thought about God in Aristotelian categories. But it has gone far beyond Aristotle because from the beginning it has known that God is not only self-possession but also self-gift, so that Jesus can say, "all things have been handed over to me by my Father" (Matt 11:27). The Father's self-gift is continued in the Son's self-surrender and the Holy Spirit's self-outpouring. It is precisely in this self-gift that God possesses and thinks God's self. Out of his love, in his self-gift to the Son and the Holy Spirit, the Father thinks the world and calls it into being so that it may share in God's eternal life. It is from this perspective, from this primal trinitarian movement, that redemption must be conceived.

Jesus' death was not willed by God. Human beings caused it. Jesus' opponents wanted to eliminate someone they profoundly hated. But Jesus retained his absolute self-surrender to his people, and thus to the world, and in that way he endowed the world at enmity with God with divine self-gift.

A Nearly Unavoidable Death

To conclude, let us ask again: how could Jesus' death, the death of an individual, redeem us all? The answer is: because he found the solution, the solution of the reign of God, the solution of the new life together in which each is there for the others. He not only found it; he lived it. He not only lived it; he died for that solution and so expressed his self-surrender for others in this ultimate, unmistakable way.

We need to repeat it again and again: God did not will his death. People brought it about. But that death was almost unavoidable because people do not want what God wants. Human beings want themselves. Anyone who speaks and acts entirely in the name of God and desires nothing for herself or himself but only what God wills, such a one will be hated.

Plato, the great Greek philosopher, spoke almost prophetically, some four hundred years before Christ, in his *Republic*. He said that the completely just person, one who desires not only to appear just but really to *be* just, if such a person existed, would be whipped, racked, and bound. That person's eyes would be burned out, and after all that mistreatment, she or he would be crucified (*Rep.* 361e–62a). This gives another and deeper meaning to the question "was it not necessary that the Messiah should suffer these things?" (Luke 24:26). The Bible speaks again and again of this "necessity." We no longer understand it to mean that Jesus had to die because God had planned it that way; rather, he had to die because he collided with embittered hatred. Human beings desire not what God desires but themselves. That is the deepest reason for Jesus' death, and in that sense his death was unavoidable. But out of that very catastrophe God fashioned salvation for Israel and the world, salvation reaching to the roots of the world, because there was one person who understood God utterly and who lived and died entirely for God and for the world.

Let me conclude with a passage by Günther Krasnitzky. He was a member of the Catholic Integrierte Gemeinde and a pastor in the village of Walchensee in Upper Bavaria:

> It has often happened that someone is unjustly condemned and brutally executed. Injustice and cruelty are nothing unique. But what was unique was that you, God, found a human being who knew your path utterly, who kept back nothing for himself, who was united with your will and gave everything in order to gather your people and lead them to the liberating knowledge of your will. So you reached the goal of your creation. And since then we celebrate Easter as the festival of completion, because in Jesus' dying and rising the new creation has already begun. Now the work is placed in our hands, the work that you began in him, and we must carry it on. For none will believe that he, and what he did, are the solution if that solution is not visible and tangible today—in our midst.

Chapter 9

Jesus and the Shattered People of God

We all suffer from the division of the church—its shattering into confessions, free churches, and countless denominations. In mixed marriages, to the extent that the marriage partners are believers, that division is experienced as especially hard. Many Christians suffer from the absence of eucharistic community, and we are all injured by that, especially if we believe that at the present time there cannot be a common Eucharist.

I myself find it a shocking deficiency that in Germany we do not even have a common translation of the Bible. There could be one, just as there could long since have been many things we hold in common. Since the ecumenical movement began to bloom in the twentieth century we have said again and again that the division of the church is a scandal, a deep wound in the Body of Christ. And then we rightly refer to Jesus' prayer of farewell in John 17:1-26, in which he prays again and again for the unity of his disciples and thus of the church (John 17:11, 21-23).

The Axiom of the Flowery Meadow

And yet we increasingly hear quite different ideas. For example, the image of the blooming field of flowers recurs frequently. The question is raised: what is it that makes a flowering meadow so lovely—one, that is, that is not over-fertilized and is not mowed every week like an English lawn? Well, we say, what makes a real meadow so beautiful is that the greatest variety of flowers and herbs grows there: daisies, red clover, milfoil, chervil, soft-grass, columbine, pasqueflowers, buttercups, pheasant's eye, shepherd's purse, lady's smock, rock roses, wild pansies, chickweed, sweet william—the list could go on and on to unbelievable lengths. And it is precisely this variety and multiplicity, this bewildering wealth of forms and colors, that makes a meadow lovely and draws countless butterflies to it.

So also with the church, not a few theologians say today. The church always has to do with Jesus, but it is the many different ways in which Christians follow Jesus that make the church a living thing—from strictly orthodox monks on Mount Athos to American sects that bring hope and material aid to people in the *favelas* of Latin America. Multiplicity and variegated forms in Christianity are nothing negative, it is said, but are in fact signs of its abundance, its constant growth, and its repeated return to the Gospel.

What should we say to that? Are those voices correct? The answer must come from Jesus, the Word made flesh. Did Jesus' own work produce a multiplicity of churches? Did the basis Jesus laid necessarily point to plurality? Did Jesus ultimately desire such a variety? Does the New Testament itself furnish a basis for the confessional diversity of churches?

The Lutheran theologian Ernst Käsemann tried to demonstrate just that, some decades ago, in an important essay.[1] He asserted that the numerous theological positions found in the New Testament itself were the basis for the multiplicity of confessions. Did Käsemann have the right view of things? Or must we say that Jesus desired the unity of the people of God and that the whole of the New Testament remained true to him? That its authors and those who created the canon of the New Testament understood what Jesus' purpose was, and they did not desire divisions, separated churches, and isolated communities?

My primary interest is in the question of what Jesus himself wanted. We must face this question directly, because it is fundamental. At this very point we run the risk of making Jesus unbearably tame and irrelevant. But the question of unity is also conclusive for our understanding of the nature of the church. We can be aided in the whole question by the fact that Jesus faced a problem very similar to our own: he stood face-to-face with a divided and fragmented people of God that had split into the widest variety of groups—factions that no longer understood each other and sometimes were violently at odds.

In the first part below I will describe this fragmentation of the people of God. Then, in a second part, I will ask how Jesus acted in the face of this fragmentation. Finally, I will take a look at our situation today.

The Fragmentation of the People of God

1. For Jesus, the fragmentation of the people of God was probably most crassly evident in the division between Jews and *Samaritans*. The prologue and beginning of that division was the separation of the Northern and Southern Kingdoms during the royal period. The people of the twelve tribes suddenly had *two* foci: Samaria and Jerusalem.

Then, probably in the year 721 BCE, Samaria, the capital of the Northern Kingdom, was seized by the Assyrians. The upper classes of the population and many who exercised important professions were deported. All in all, some thirty thousand Jews were removed to the East at that time and replaced by Assyrian colonists. The result was a mixed population that was viewed in Jerusalem and Judea with increasing mistrust.

But the Samaritan Jews still considered themselves genuine Jews; in fact, they were largely of a conservative type, for they accepted only the Pentateuch, the first five "books of Moses," as Sacred Scripture. The more recent prophetic books were not Scripture for them. They had a sanctuary on Mount Gerizim with its own sacrificial cult. There sacrifices were offered to Yhwh in accordance with the prescriptions of Exodus and Leviticus. The Samaritans called themselves Israelites, who brought offerings to the holy temple on Mount Gerizim.

To the Maccabeans and Hasmoneans, that temple was a horror. They acknowledged only the Jerusalem temple. In about 110 BCE the sanctuary on Gerizim was destroyed by the Hasmonean John Hyrcanus I; thus the Samaritan Jews were deprived of their cultic center. That only deepened the division and created greater hostility. In Jesus' time Galileans and Jews from Judea used the word "Samaritan" as a term of abuse. In contrast, the Samaritans regarded themselves as the true Israel.

Galileans who traveled through the Samaritan highlands on their pilgrimages to Jerusalem were not welcome there; often they were refused shelter. As we know from Luke's gospel, Jesus and his disciples had the same experience on one occasion. They were not received "because his face was set toward Jerusalem" (Luke 9:53). At one time a Galilean (or a whole group of them) was murdered by Samaritans while on the way to the festival. So the Jewish historian Josephus reports.[2] He also writes that once, during a Passover, Samaritans had scattered the bones of the dead within the Jerusalem temple precincts and so made the temple cultishly impure[3]—which, from the point of view of the Galileans and Jerusalemites, was an abominable sacrilege. That event exemplified the two groups' mutual hatred.

2. Another group in Israel at the time of Jesus was made up of the *Sadducees*. According to Josephus they were a separate "religious party" in Israel. If we want to use the dubious label "conservative," we can say that the Sadducees, as far as their faith was concerned, were conservative. In contrast to the convictions of the Pharisees, for the Sadducees the oral and written traditions had no place *alongside the Torah*. What was essential to their faith was the connection of the people of God to the temple and the land. The true Israel was for them a kind of "temple state."

As regards the law, they held strictly to the Torah, that is, the books of the Pentateuch. Apart from that they permitted everything that seemed reasonable to them, including a full cultural accommodation to the Hellenistic-Roman world. They rejected belief in the resurrection of the dead because it played no part in Torah.

From a sociological point of view their basis was in the upper levels of society in and around Jerusalem. There were Sadducees especially in the lay nobility of large landowners and the priestly nobility in Jerusalem. They attained the pinnacle of their power when Judea came under the rule of the Roman prefects. In Judea's delicate political situation, the Sadducees wanted to avoid any kind of disturbance, because otherwise there was danger that the last remnant of Jewish freedom would be lost. This was also about their own retention of power, however, because that power was not anchored in the people but derived from the favor of the Roman occupying power.

3. The *Zealots* were altogether different. Their goal was not at all to maintain the status quo but to lead a grim war for freedom from Rome.

How long had the Zealot movement been in existence? In the year 6 CE Archelaus, a son of Herod the Great, was deposed by the emperor Augustus for misfeasance in office. Judea, Idumea, and Samaria became a Roman province. The Romans then conducted a census in order to create the basis for a comprehensive system of taxation. In that situation a Galilean named Judas called on the people to refuse to pay any more taxes to the Romans.

But Judas Galilaeus and his fellow fighters were not only politically and socially motivated. They agitated primarily on a theological basis. They said: if God is our Lord, the Romans cannot be our masters. Therefore we must fight them. The action continued for years in the form of ambushes and lesser attacks, that is to say, through guerilla tactics, until in the year 66 it became a revolt of wide dimensions. The Jewish-Roman war then began; it ended with the destruction of Jerusalem in the year 70.

The Zealots were religious fanatics. They were convinced that the time had come when all Israel had to carry out the eschatological battle against

foreign domination. They wanted a theocratic state with rigorous observation of the law. They saw themselves as God's warriors, permitted to
act violently in the name of God—to use brutal violence to set up the
reign of God. They tried to draw the whole people of God into their
struggle. They too were convinced that they represented the true eschatological Israel.

4. So I come to a further group: the *Pharisees*. These were the people
Jesus had the most dealings with, and they are most frequently mentioned in the gospels. The Pharisees were also convinced that they were
the true Israel. They were an influential lay movement organized in
"communities" or "associations" (Hebrew *haburot*). They had establish-
ments throughout the land. The leaders and most important members
of these associations were the scribes, though by no means were all
scribes Pharisees.

The close association among Pharisees had developed when, after the
Maccabean wars of liberation, the "liberators," though themselves Jews,
built up a system of rule that was just as corrupt as the previous Jewish
collaboration with the great Hellenistic powers. The Pharisees wanted
to resist this falling away from the faith of the ancestors. So they were a
kind of conservative protest movement. Nevertheless, we should avoid
taking a one-sided view of their conservatism. The Pharisees wanted to
make it possible for Israel to be the "holy people" chosen by God. Therefore, beyond the Mosaic law, the Pharisees cultivated an oral tradition
of interpretation.

The Pharisees' traditions were intended to make the ancient biblical
legal prescriptions understandable and practical in the present time.
Rules for purity that in the Old Testament were only for the priests were
to be applied to all Israel (in a reduced form) so that the whole of life
would be made holy. Still, the rules had to be practicable and not impossible to carry out.

In contrast to the Essenes, of whom I will speak next, the Pharisees
did not separate themselves from the people as a whole. They tried to
educate people to a reasonable devotion to the law and so to a holy life.
Because, in addition, they again and again protected the people from the
powerful overlords, they had ordinary people on their side and were
highly regarded. On the whole, their religious zeal was deep and genuine.
Only in this light can we understand their sharp confrontations with
Jesus.

5. So, finally, we come to the *Essenes*. Oddly enough, they are not mentioned in the gospels, but Josephus speaks of them, and since 1947 we
have been in possession of some of their original writings, thanks to the

discoveries in the ruins of Kirbet Qumran on the Dead Sea. I will not go into the full history of the Essenes' origins; that would take us too far afield. What is important for us is to know that the Essenes also lived in communities, as did the Pharisees, but they separated themselves much more fully from the rest of the population. The conviction that they alone were the true Israel willed by God was truly constitutive for their movement. Both the Pharisees and the Sadducees were categorically rejected by the Essenes.

In one of their writings, the so-called Community Rule, we read that members of the community must love all those whom God has chosen and hate all those whom God has rejected (1QS 1.3–4). A little later the dictum is much harsher:

> . . . to love all the sons of light, each one according to his place in God's plan, and to hate all the sons of darkness, each one in accordance with his blame in God's vindication.

The sons of light are the members of their own community. The sons of darkness are those outside. There were correspondingly rigorous rules for admission and for the behavior of those who wanted to live in their "covenant." The segregated nature of their life included a distancing of themselves from the temple and its worship. They regarded the sacrificial cult then being practiced in the Jerusalem temple as invalid and saw their own community as the "sanctuary for Israel."

When we survey these various social classes, groups, and parties within Israel—the Samaritans, Sadducees, Zealots, Pharisees, and Essenes—we cannot avoid the conclusion that in Jesus' time (and for centuries previously) the people of God were deeply divided. In practice, each of the groups we have named claimed to be the only true Israel living according to God's will. Each group kept apart from the other groups and fenced them out. They were judged not to be living according to God's will and not matching up to it. And for the most part the others were not only excluded but also despised and challenged to adopt the self-concept of one's own group.

In all this, questions of purity according to the law, cultic practice, the calendar, and the interpretation of Scripture played a crucial role. On the whole, the observer is confronted with an extraordinarily gloomy picture! What is so tragic is that all these groups wanted to live according to the will of God and see themselves as the true Israel.

The picture I have just sketched so briefly is what presented itself to the eyes of Jesus: a disunited, divided, profoundly damaged people of

God. How did Jesus react to the division of Israel? How did he deal with it? What did he do? That brings me to my second section.

Jesus and the Gathering of the People of God

In what follows I will maintain that a decisive part of what Jesus did consisted precisely in healing that state of division. Jesus did not regard the picture presented by the people of God as a pleasant and attractive "meadow of flowers." He did not see Israel's divisions as simply a given or accept them as inalterable. He saw them as a profound evil. He tried to heal them. No, he did not just try to heal them: he *did* heal them.

In our context, of course, the crucial question is: How did he do that? What exactly did he do? Was it even possible to heal these divisions?

To begin with, Jesus did not try to build institutional bridges between the groups in Israel that were thus drifting apart. He did not make an effort to create mediating structures. He did not set up group meetings on faith questions. He did not—to speak somewhat anachronistically— invite people to a dialogue process. He most certainly did not try to create formulas of compromise or consensus papers. No, he began much more basically and much more radically. In an elemental and profoundly based sign-action, Jesus chose twelve men from among his disciples and set them before the others. He would have explained this sign-action with a prophetic saying, but it may well have been that the meaning was clear to all the eyewitnesses anyway: these Twelve here—they are the beginning and the center of the eschatological Israel!

We have to take care not to underestimate the enormous weight of Jesus' sign-action, for at that time the twelve tribes of Israel's early time no longer existed and had not for many, many years. In the eyes of Jesus' contemporaries, all that was left of the twelve tribes were two and a half: Judah, Benjamin, and half of Levi. When Jesus chose twelve men and made them a sign and a symbol for all Israel, it meant that God was thereby creating God's people anew. Now the promises of the prophets, that in the end time God would again gather Israel, unite and renew it—the whole people, all twelve tribes—were being fulfilled. Now the promises that at that time all strife within Israel would be buried and all rivalries brought to an end were coming to their fulfillment.

The choice and establishment of the Twelve was the central event of Jesus' public appearance. It is no accident that a list of the names of the Twelve appears in several places in the New Testament. The Twelve were not only important to the early church; they were fundamental. Everyone knew that they were foundational for the gathering and uniting of the people of God. This position expressed in the New Testament corresponded exactly to Jesus' will: for him, the establishment of the Twelve was the visible, tangible side of his proclamation of the present coming of the reign of God.

Everything else Jesus did was a concretization, a realization of this basic action. I will only list a few of these concrete events, without describing them in detail.

1. When Jesus included among the Twelve a toll collector named Levi (Mark 2:14) and a Zealot named Simon (Luke 6:15), that indicated that he paid no attention to party divisions within Israel. A greater distance than between a toll collector who collaborated with the Romans and a Zealot who was promoting revolt against Rome is unimaginable. The Twelve were a crazy quilt mixture. I would even say they were a highly explosive combination. The establishment of the Twelve was meant to demonstrate that everyone, without exception, is part of this new thing. There are no more differences, no more rifts.

2. When Jesus turned to the outsiders and the socially stigmatized, the sinners and prostitutes, the toll collectors and collaborators, the lepers and the sick—in sum, the despised and the shunned—he showed by it that his concern was with the whole people of God and that he desired no separations and most certainly no ostracism in Israel.

3. When Jesus repeatedly healed sick people and cast out demons, he did so not *only* out of sympathy and compassion for the suffering. It was a fulfillment of the prophetic promises that God would finally make all Israel whole and healthy—heal it also from its demonic hardening and compulsions. In his many healings of the sick Jesus was concerned not only for physical illnesses (although, of course, he was disturbed by those too) but for the healing of the people of God.

4. When, in the parable of the merciful Samaritan (Luke 10:25-37), Jesus portrayed, of all people, a man from among the hated Samaritans in bright and brilliant colors—the man from Samaria lives God's mercy, while the priest and Levite look away and leave the battered man lying in his own blood—when, that is, Jesus depicted a man of the despised Samaritans as a model, it was a sign to everyone who heard him that he would not stand for the mutual contempt and demonizations that existed in Israel. Jesus saw more deeply—not only the evil in the people of God, but also the good, and he wanted the Samaritans to belong to Israel.

5. When Jesus did not go to the Gentiles, when he avoided the Hellenistic cities in Palestine and concentrated entirely on Jewish territory, he was saying: now, for the present, it is all about the gathering, the healing, and the renewal of the people of God. Now it is about the children of

Israel. Obviously he was also concerned for the Gentiles, but the Gentile people can only find the true God if first the people of God, Israel, finds its way to unity and salvation.

6. When Jesus, in the very first petition of the Our Father, has his disciples pray "hallowed be your Name," he is alluding to a central text of the prophet Ezekiel, in the thirty-sixth chapter. There God promises personally to make scattered and divided Israel whole again. God will heal it by gathering it, cleansing it of its idols, giving it a new heart and a new spirit. So the first petition of the Our Father is a plea for the gathering and healing of the people of God. For Jesus, that was so central that he tells his disciples to pray for it—in the *first* petition of the Lord's Prayer.

7. When one day, we do not know when and where, Jesus was moved to utter his "call for decision" (whoever is not with me is against me, and whoever does not gather with me scatters [Matt 12:30 // Luke 11:23]), he showed that the gathering of the people of God was the fundamental event of his whole public life. Jesus wanted to deliver Israel from its divisions and lead it to unity. Anyone who, in this eschatologically crucial situation, did not join Jesus in gathering the people of God made herself or himself complicit in its division. More even than that: such a one is guilty if the people of God finds no healing.

8. When, beyond the group of the Twelve, Jesus gathered disciples around him, he did so not only to have more helpers for his work in Israel. The group of disciples who accompanied Jesus in his travels through Israel, and to whom he devoted so much instruction, had another and probably a much more important function. The disciples were not only to help Jesus in his gathering of the people of God; they themselves were to represent a bit of that gathering and uniting of Israel, already made real. They were the center, in fact the nerve center of the people of God in renewal. Therefore Jesus taught them that none among them was to "rule" over the other disciples and that they must forgive one another not seven times a day but seventy-seven times, that is, constantly.

To sum up: Jesus' whole activity was directed to the gathering and uniting of Israel, to overcoming the internal barriers between groups, and to creating reconciliation and peace among the people of God.

Jesus' Clarity

Certainly at this point I should emphasize something without which everything I have just said would be one sided: Jesus was not only someone who reconciled, brought people together, unified them, made peace.

He was, by his own claim, the absolute center of Israel in person, and he was by no means so as a figure of compromise, so smooth edged and without contour that everyone could recognize themselves in him in full harmony. That is another concept that often tames Jesus and flattens him out.

It is true that Jesus collected Israel's best traditions in his message and his actions, but with him that most certainly did not result in the kind of religious supermarket so typical of national church gatherings in Germany, where one can find anything imaginable. Each visitor puts what is to her or his personal taste in her or his religious shopping cart, leading to a random collection of almost unimaginable scope.

With Jesus, in contrast, nothing was random. His was such a radical unambiguity, decision, and clarity that one had to be either for him or against him. Take, for example, his absolute nonviolence; that put the Zealots against him. His critique of the temple brought out the Sadducees against him, and his attention to sinners and the lost was a positive scandal to the Pharisees and Essenes. Indeed, what the ancient Simeon had prophesied about him was precisely true: "This child is destined for the falling and the rising of many in Israel, and to be a sign that will be opposed" (Luke 2:34-35). What hatred was directed against him! He not only gathered Israel; he brought about separations, new divisions, because everyone had to decide for or against him. That was just what he meant when he said of himself: "Do not think that I have come to bring peace to the earth; I have not come to bring peace, but a sword" (Matt 10:34). So we must not clean up the Jesus who unites and reconciles in such a way that we scrub out his clarity and lack of ambiguity. On this point, once again, we must not make Jesus irrelevant.

All that needs to be said at this point so that there can be no misunderstanding. But to return to our real subject: it should be clear by now that Jesus by no means abolished the bitter separations within Israel. He would have laughed out loud at the theory of the flowery meadow. Reality was altogether different. Israel was not a flowering meadow. The discords within the people of God were deadly. They had darkened the brilliance that was supposed to emanate from Israel, and they brought the Gatherer of Israel to his death.

Was Jesus Successful?

So was Jesus successful in gathering the people of God? Was he in any way able to bring Israel together and unite it? Evidently not. Did everything go awry for Jesus?

The lack of success began in the group of the Twelve itself—the group who were supposed to be the signal, the sign for the eschatological, gathered people of Israel. Judas, one of the Twelve, made Jesus' capture possible through his betrayal (Mark 14:10-11). Peter, who rightly stands first in every list of the Twelve, denied him three times: "I do not know the man!" (Mark 14:66-72). And they all fled and hid when things started to get serious (Mark 14:50).

But Jesus' apparent lack of success began much earlier. It came to his ears one day that the Twelve had been arguing among themselves on the road. Why? They were disputing about which of them was the greatest (Mark 9:33-37). So the later divisions in the Jesus movement were preprogrammed. In Corinth some would say, "I belong to Paul," others, "I belong to Apollos," and still others, "I belong to Cephas." And then Paul even posits hypothetically the claim, "I belong to Christ." He had to ask the community in Corinth acerbically: "Has Christ been divided?" (1 Cor 1:10-13).

It looks as if Jesus' gathering of Israel was a failure. Not long ago a young American whom I had informed of my intention to give this lecture wrote to me, in a mood of sorrow and fatalism: "Churches or communities that believe in Jesus necessarily split up, sooner or later. That is an iron law. It was always that way. It will always be that way." Then he listed example after example from church history. Wasn't he right? Did Jesus fail? Was all his work for nothing? Didn't he attempt too much? It is not presumptuous to ask such questions; we are positively forced to think in that direction.

And for that very reason we are compelled to dig deeper. What I have said above in eight points about Jesus' gathering of Israel is not everything. Something crucial is missing.

What Truly Unites

That decisive moment took place in the upper room, at the Last Supper. By this time Jesus had long known what would happen to him. He was aware of the bitter hatred of the Sadducees. He knew they could not endure the fact that he called the administration of the temple into question. He also knew the fear of his disciples, who would have preferred to avoid the sharpening conflict. He was clear about the shifting moods of the crowds. He sensed that the temple police would hunt him down, because one of his circle of Twelve had told them where he was staying. So in this situation he gathered the Twelve around him once again, for the solemn Passover meal.

And during this solemn and festive meal he again performed a sign-action, this one the most profound and fundamental of all his many sign-actions, beginning with the establishment of the Twelve. At the point when the opening table prayer was spoken, he handed the broken loaf of bread to those gathered around him and said, "This is my body." That is, "This is my life, and it will be torn apart like this bread." After the meal he handed them the cup filled with red wine and interpreted it, like the broken bread, in terms of his death.

But what is crucial about the course of this sign-action is that in doing it Jesus interpreted his death as *dying for Israel*, because the participants in this meal to whom he gave the bread and wine with the solemn "for you" represent the eschatological Israel. That had always been the meaning of the Twelve. So Jesus dies *for Israel* and gives the Twelve a share in his death and its fruits. Apparently in this climactic situation at the Passover feast Jesus was deeply convinced that his death was not for nothing. Everything he had taught, everything he had proclaimed, all the healings of the sick, all the solidarity with the excluded, all his efforts to gather Israel, even the establishment of the Twelve were not the ultimate. It was only with his dying for Israel, his self-surrender even unto death, that the gathering of the people of God would be completed; his death would constitute the unity of God's people.

That is how the church always saw it after Easter. It was convinced of it, and numerous texts of the New Testament reflect that conviction: it was not just Jesus' preaching, not his mighty deeds, but only his death, that *definitively* gathered and unified the many, creating the people of God as an eschatological people. In the crucified and risen Christ, the New Testament teaches us, the unity of the people of God has been achieved, and all who believe in him already have a share in that union. This is the teaching of the farewell discourses in John's gospel, the teaching of Paul, and the teaching above all of the letters to the communities in Ephesus and Colossae; it is the teaching of the whole New Testament.

This brings me to my final section, because obviously the problems are not all taken care of. On the contrary: now they really begin.

The Axiom of the Invisible Church

I think all Christians are united in the belief that the Crucified and Risen One *is* himself the church's unity; he himself is its healing; only he can give unity, and he gives it to those who surrender themselves to him, listen to him, believe in him, and follow him. We ourselves cannot create the unity or establish it. It can only be given to us. We can only find it in the Crucified and Risen One and in the Holy Spirit who unites us with him. As I have said: there is consensus about that; all Christians would agree.

But at precisely this point we are again confronted with a theory that needs testing in the brilliant light of the Bible. It is more sublime than the one about the beautiful, flowery meadow; above all, it is more theological. As the theory of the flowery meadow appeals to the *eyes*, this one speaks to the *spirit*. It proceeds, very realistically, from the fact that there is no unity within Christianity as it really exists. But it also assumes what I said at the end of my second section: that in the room at the Last Supper and on the cross Jesus has already created the unity of the people of God. The spirit-theory then seeks to link the two. It can be summarized as follows.

There are any number of confessions, many independent churches, countless denominations. That is the indisputable reality. From that point of view there is no unity in the Church Visible. But then there is the Gospel, the good news of the justification of sinners, and that Gospel is proclaimed everywhere in Christianity. Many Christians believe in that Gospel and accept it in faith. Wherever this Gospel is rightly preached, and wherever Christians remember in the Lord's Supper Jesus' death on the cross and his resurrection, and so allow themselves to be received into his death and resurrection—*there church happens.*

From an external point of view the church continues to be divided into many churches. Externally regarded, separation reigns. But wherever the Gospel is believed, here and there, the *one* church of Jesus Christ is happening, through the Holy Spirit, in the inner lives of the faithful. The Holy Spirit makes the many believers one and joins them together.

Conclusion: there is an *invisible, hidden* church that is given through the death and resurrection of Jesus. Within this invisible church all are already united in spirit, *if* they only believe in the Gospel and open themselves to the Spirit of Jesus. Unity is thus already invisibly present. It is *within* the many, many believers.

You can surely sense that all this sounds good. And this theory has some major advantages: it can take seriously the condition of Christianity as it really exists—the many divisions, the many ecclesial communities. At the same time it can take redemption seriously, the power of Jesus' death and resurrection and of the Holy Spirit. This theory can even say: we can make the invisible unity of the church a reality even now, and again and again—for example, in eucharistic sharing—for where the Gospel of Christ is believed and his sacraments rightly administered and worthily received, the one church is already happening, bit by bit.

As I have said, that all sounds very good and very beautiful. It is a finely wrought theory, exquisitely accommodated to reality. In a certain sense it even justifies the separation of churches, for then—we may assume this in advance—they are seeking the "true Gospel."

The Bodily Nature of the Church

But as lovely as this theory is and as inviting as it sounds, it has a serious defect: Scripture is against it—in fact, a central aspect of Scripture that is constitutive for it and runs throughout. The fundamental aspect I refer to appears at the very beginning of Sacred Scripture: while it is true that the creation of the world takes place through the word alone—the simple word of God—and creation is saturated with the Spirit of God that moves over the waters, still, this creation is real. It is visible. One can grasp it. It is resistant. It is physical and material in a positively obnoxious way.

In the same way, salvation history is also real. Abraham leaves his home country, taking his flocks with him. Israel is liberated by departing from Egypt with all its property. The Israelites have to get on the road again to attend Israel's great festivals—along with their sons and daughters, their slave men and slave women, the aliens, orphans, and widows who live among them, to celebrate before the Lord, in the real place that is Jerusalem (Deut 16:9-12).

Or we may consider the Torah, Israel's social order intended to create a holy people for God. Gerhard von Rad, in his magnificent *Old Testament Theology*, emphasized that Israel's experiences of the Holy were indeed of the most exalted spiritual nature and extended their influence deep within each person's inmost being, but at the same time they touched radically what is physical and material. In this very context he speaks of how "[YHWH's] holiness wants to penetrate the whole of [the human person], and is not satisfied merely with [the] soul."[4]

This irreversible law of creation and salvation history, the worldliness and materiality of the event of salvation, is perfected in Jesus. In him the hidden Logos of God became truly human. He did not assume the appearance of a body, as many Hellenistic-minded false teachers in the ancient church repeatedly asserted; nor did Jesus float six inches above the ground as a kind of "spirit." The Logos, the Word of God, became, in a positively offensive way, "flesh" (John 1:14).

Certainly, everything Jesus did was swayed and supported by the Holy Spirit, but it was visible, tangible, obnoxiously material reality. Jesus laid hands on sick people, smeared mud on blind people's eyes, stuck his fingers in deaf people's ears. He embraced children. He ate and drank with sinners.

There is no creation or redemption in the Bible apart from this persistent "here"ness. The mystery of creation and the history of salvation consist precisely in this: that the invisible is bound up with the visible, and it is only in what is visible that the invisible lets its light shine. The Word became flesh; indeed, in a thoroughly annoying way, it became a Jew. Jesus is true God but just as much true human being. Only when we look at the man Jesus do we see the Father (cf. John 14:9).

And this is likewise the mystery of the church. Like the whole creation, the church is filled with the Holy Spirit, is "the creation of the word," but at the same time it is worldly, world-bound, and therefore offensive reality.

It is on the basis of the fundamental biblical law sketched here that the Catholic Church sees itself. This is its self-understanding: the church, by its very nature, is *sacramental*, that is, it effects the invisible in the visible and only in and through what is visible. Therefore, in a catholic conception of the church, a *purely* invisible church that happens only now and then is unbiblical. To anchor the unity of the church in its invisibility *alone* is, in a catholic understanding, contrary to the Bible's salvation-historical realism. Therefore, for many Christians, the solution to the ecumenical problem and the hideous distress of the church cannot lie here.

The solution can be found only where the unity of the people of God that Jesus Christ handed on to us is tangible in the visible, resistant sphere of history. This visible side of the church includes the canon of Sacred Scripture, the episcopal office that continues the mission of the apostles, the sacraments as the realization of the church's very essence, and the church's traditional teaching, condensed in its creeds.

Obviously the crucified and risen Christ, as the innermost center of the church, is not visible. But the church, as his body, *is* visible, just as he himself once was: flesh, obnoxious history, materiality, world. Therefore the unity of the church cannot remain *only* invisible. And so there must be a struggle toward this visible unity that is not yet full reality. Above all, it must be longed for and prayed for.

And the search for this unity cannot avoid the fact that Jesus tied the unity of the eschatological people of God he gathered around him to the group of the Twelve. Therefore the Nicene Creed, the great confession of faith, speaks of the "one, holy, catholic, and *apostolic* church." The church is "apostolic" because it is built on the foundation of the apostles (Eph 2:20) and therefore is a visible structure. And it is "catholic" in the sense that it has expanded universally in unity—and that too is a visible, tangible reality.

The catholic understanding is thus that the *one* church already exists, not only in Jesus Christ, but visibly in the world as his "Body." And we must immediately add: it is not yet the whole people of God as Jesus wanted it to be. What, then, is our task?

We will arrive at the church *in the fullest sense* when we all—all church communities without exception—repent and return to Jesus Christ, driven by deep longing, sustained by the spirit of reconciliation and by the infallible hope that God will give us full unity. We must not suppress the fact of the church's real divisions and create a substitute unity as something internal or invisible. True unity can only be physical, visible, tangible, graspable. Otherwise it would not correspond to the fundamental law of creation and salvation history.

That within this visible unity there must still be multiplicity, variety, and constant new movements is clear. On that point the idea of the flowering meadow has something right about it. But visible unity is the precondition for legitimate multiplicity. In order for that to come about, we must all repent and turn back—not only the Protestant side, but the Catholic as well. We must all confess our guilt and return to Jesus Christ. Then God will give us the unity we long for. And the many signs of respect for the dignity and faith of the others that we can already give one another even now are profoundly hopeful and consoling.

Chapter 10

The Canon and the Many Confessions

In the previous chapter I referred to Ernst Käsemann's 1952 essay, "The Canon of the New Testament and the Unity of the Church,"[1] in which he examined the question whether the New Testament canon is the foundation of the church's unity and concluded that it is not. On the contrary: the canon is the basis for the variety of confessions because in the New Testament itself, according to Käsemann, there are "irreconcilable theological contradictions" and quite a variety of community structures in conflict with one another. The New Testament itself, he says, contains the voices of numerous confessions.

I will summarize quite baldly what Käsemann says with a wealth of words and sometimes not so directly: some parts of the New Testament are evidence of "early Catholicism," and others—at least this is how one must interpret his appeal to Paul—are Protestant. Therefore each of these confessions is somehow in the right and can appeal to the canon. Of course, it is not hard to hear the subtext: the ones that appeal to Paul are more likely to be right.

With that view of things, at the end of his essay Käsemann could only offer the consolation that the canon is not identical with "the Gospel." Behind this statement, quite clearly, is the Pauline Gospel. "The Gospel" is said to be more than the canon, and only a canon that is continually becoming "Gospel" is the basis for "the one church in all times and places." Therefore the unity of the church never exists in perceptible form but "only for faith."

This sets over against the traditional canon of Sacred Scripture an inner canon, namely, "the Gospel," about which the believer, who is "led by the Spirit and [listens] obediently to the Scripture," must continually decide. Correspondingly, the unity of the church, like the canon and the Gospel, is something that must be rediscovered again and again "among the confessions and in spite of their multiplicity."[2]

With this thesis Käsemann has given an elegant historical justification for the actual multiplicity of confessions and therefore for the great divisions within the church. But the price he had to pay was enormous. Factually, he had to relativize the traditional concept of the canon in favor of an inner canon, a canon within the canon. And he had to relativize the visibility and legal composition of the church in favor of an invisible church that appears anew to each believer who listens to the Gospel. For this position, common eucharistic celebrations between Protestants and Catholics pose no problem: one can always appeal to the fact that in such celebrations the invisible unity of the churches expands and manifests itself.

This essay by Käsemann, which is now sixty years old, shows that the roots of current problems about common celebrations of the Eucharist are longstanding and deeply rooted. It is the old problem of a correct understanding of canon and office.

Käsemann was by no means alone in holding this view of the New Testament, but was he right? Ultimately it all depends on whether Sacred Scripture is received as *the church's book* or not. More precisely: ultimately it all depends on whether Sacred Scripture is received as a *single book*. If so, it has a clear authorial intent behind it. Certainly, I will have to explain in what follows what I mean by "authorial intent," and so it will be necessary to speak at least briefly about the origins of the New Testament.

How the New Testament Came to Be

We could imagine its origins this way: the Great Church had twenty-seven individual writings that were especially important to it and that it therefore wanted to keep together. So it gathered all of them into a single volume and said, "Each of these individual writings is valuable to us in its own way. Therefore we have bound them together and we call the whole thing 'the New Testament.'" Then the individual writings would have constituted something like a small library, with quite different positions, as is inevitably the case with books in a library. But for practical reasons the individual books were all incorporated in a single collected volume. As we have said: one could imagine it that way. But it was not that way at all.

After Easter, Sacred Scripture consisted at first only of what we, for centuries now, on the basis of 2 Corinthians 3:14, have called "the Old Testament." Of course, at first it was simply *graphē*, "Scripture." But the early Christian communities did not let things rest there. Even in Paul's lifetime his letters were preserved and read at worship, after the reading of "Scripture." After his death there was an effort to collect whatever writings of his remained, and they were put together into a collection of Pauline letters. It was at that time, after Paul's death, that Colossians, Ephesians, 2 Thessalonians, and at a later period the "Pastoral Letters" (1 and 2 Timothy and Titus) were written, by students of Paul and in the name and spirit of Paul, to fill the gaps that appeared in his communities after his death. These post-Pauline letters were apparently added quite soon to collections of genuine letters of Paul, and so the *Corpus Paulinum* was created. There was reading from this collection at worship, and so it became itself "Sacred Scripture."

But that was only the beginning of what would later be called "the New Testament," for not only Pauline letters but also other writings, especially the gospels, were read in the worship services of the early Christian communities. A selection was made from this whole range of writings and, with great compositional care, was joined to what was then called "the New Testament." I have been fairly vague in what I have said here because the exact time at which all this happened can no longer be determined; nor do we know anything about the group of people who undertook the compositional task.

Four gospels were chosen as a basis for the collection: our present Gospel of Matthew and those of Mark, Luke, and John. Luke's gospel, however, was constructed differently from the other three; it had a continuation, a second book, namely, what we now know as the *Acta Apostolorum*, the Acts of the Apostles. In order to establish a gospel canon, the compositors separated Luke's gospel from its second book, placed the four gospels together, and added the second volume of Luke's double work at the end, to produce the sequence of "four gospels and Acts." That was a drastic alteration of Luke's twofold work.

The *Corpus Paulinum* was, however, not placed directly after Acts, as we have it in our New Testaments today. Instead, another collection of letters, the so-called Catholic Letters, was inserted there.[3] They were called "catholic letters" at a very early period, because they (at least

James, 1 Peter, 2 Peter, 1 John, and Jude) were addressed not to individual communities but to regional churches or even to the church as a whole.

One reason for the sequence "Acts–Catholic Letters," so unfamiliar to us today, must have been that in Acts both Peter and John, as well as James, the Lord's brother, played important parts. The desire was, so to speak, to augment what was related in Acts and enrich it with writings from the three "pillars" of the original community (Gal 2:9)—namely, Peter, John, and James. But Paul also played a significant part in Acts, after the author had described the life of the original community in Jerusalem. In fact, Paul's role in that book is much more important than that of James. Hence a collection of Paul's letters was added after the Catholic Letters. The two letter collections were of equal weight. Finally, the whole composition was rounded off by the addition of Revelation.

This process produced a well-ordered composition of New Testament writings. The individual documents followed the course of history: first come the gospels, with the life and work of Jesus. At the end of the whole book stands Jesus' return at the end of time. In between we read of the development of the church, in the way Luke depicts it in Acts: Peter and the original community, James at the "Apostolic Council" (Acts 15:13-21), Paul. Following 2 Corinthians 3:6, the whole collection received the title "the New Testament." It was also characterized by some special techniques of book composition, for example, the consistent naming of authors at the head of each individual writing and the abbreviation of the *nomina sacra* "God," "Lord," "Jesus," and "Christ." The abbreviations normally consisted of writing the corresponding Greek word forms with only the first and last letter and a horizontal line above them.

To repeat: all that can only be understood as a carefully worked out process of redaction, done by highly competent, believing Christians with the goal of creating a single homogeneous book. So the New Testament is not a more or less accidental collection of writings important to the early church; it is a single book, a well-thought-out theological composition that reveals a clear authorial intent. We should, of course, note that the New Testament deliberately attaches itself to the "Scriptures" (the Old Testament). "Scripture" is the foundation of the whole. The New Testament was incorporated into "Scripture" and shaped, with the Old Testament, into a single larger book. It is, we might say, the last level of interpretation of the Old Testament. And like the Torah in the Old Testament, the basis for the New Testament is the four-gospel canon.

Accordingly, the compositional intent that underlies the New Testament is unmistakable. The authors who created this organically conceived work wanted it to be read as a unified book. The early Christian theologian Origen wrote correctly, in his commentary on the Gospel of John:

> We must approach the whole of Scripture as one body, we must not lacerate nor break through the strong and well-knit connections which exist in the harmony of its whole composition, as those do who lacerate, so far as they can, the unity of the Spirit that is in all the Scriptures.[4]

All this should make it clear that creating a standard for oneself according to which the canon has to be reworked is a clear violation of the authorial intent behind it. To speak of "authorial intent" here is not, of course, to say that a single theologian or bishop created the New Testament canon. There may certainly have been an authorial collective. Moreover, there is a successive side to the creation of the New Testament canon: what was created by an act of genius had to be accepted by all the churches if it were really to become the canon of the Great Church. That was, obviously, a long process. But because this process of acceptance was necessary and did in fact happen, we can rightly call the church the author of the canon.

The Exclusion of Apocryphal Writings

In fact, this authorial intent of which I have repeatedly spoken is evident not only in the *composition* of the New Testament but in the end also in another phenomenon. The church's ultimate agreement to the New Testament canon as we now have it amounted to a serious process of *selection*, because in the ancient church there were decisively more gospels, revelatory writings, letters, and acts of apostles than were accepted as "canonical" in the New Testament.

The criterion of selection was clearly "apostolic," that is, the original, unfalsified tradition that people were convinced went back to the apostles. There was an urgent reason why this criterion was so important and why a canon of authoritative "apostolic" writings was created: heresies were spreading, divisions mounting, and the continuity to the apostolic period was in danger of interruption. The choice of the New Testament writings and their composition was intended from the beginning to serve the unity of the church and preserve it from a break in continuity.

The Unity of the New Testament

If we look more closely at the individual writings of the New Testament and compare them we can only be astonished at the degree to which they testify to the unified faith of the church. Certainly it has been common in New Testament scholarship for a long time to emphasize the differences, divergences, tensions, and contradictions among the "theologies" of the individual New Testament writings. And there can be no question that these writings contain accents that deviate from one another and the greatest variety of forms of speech, turns of phrase, and systems of thought. But if we take into account this disparity in speech and forms, it is still difficult to locate creedal contradictions. The variety of the New Testament by no means requires a variety of Christian confessions: quite the contrary!

Despite all its variety, the New Testament reveals a truly fascinating unity that defies all our common experience. The tendency of society is centrifugal, that is, society is inclined, over and over again, to produce profound differences in thought, rivalries, and divisions. That the New Testament, despite all the divisions that did exist in the early Christian communities, represents such a unity seems to me a miracle.

We also have to take into account the poor communication facilities in antiquity. If an exchange of information between communities was necessary, the messengers could be on the road for weeks. Those messengers brought letters with them in which no one could ever explain everything, and in the exchanges it was all too easy for the parties to be talking past one another.

In light of this miserable starting point, the fact that there arose a unified faith in the communities around the Mediterranean, despite all their divisions and heresies, is an almost unimaginable phenomenon. For me it is only to be grasped in terms of the historical power of the person of Jesus Christ.

But let us suppose for a moment that there are contradictions between the individual New Testament writings on the level of faith, that is, in the creed itself. Then it would indeed be a serious matter to say that Sacred Scripture does not consist of a bundle of different writings that can be played off against one another but is a single book, willed as such by its author. In recent decades the historical-critical method, using newer literary-critical techniques (synchronic analysis, the "canonical approach"), has by itself approached an affirmation of that unity. It has acknowledged with increasing clarity that in fact its task is to interpret the canonical "final text" of the Bible and not just some of its parts or even previous layers.

If the authorial intent of the church created the final text of the Bible, namely, the canon, the church can only have understood its own book in such a way that within it all the divergent tendencies possible within the faith of different communities or different church regions are brought together in unity. Certainly the task of exegesis is to apply its historical-critical methods in seeking out the different traditions and layers within the Bible. Simply for the sake of interpretation it cannot avoid doing so. But as soon as it begins to interpret the Bible theologically—and that is its main task—it is required to interpret the *final text*, and to do so *in terms of its unity*. Whoever does that is by no means engaging in falsification, forcefully creating a harmonic concord out of disparity. Instead, such an exegete takes the canon seriously as canon. From this point of view also it is impossible for the canon itself to form a basis for the differences among the confessions. Rather, the canon, or its authors, deliberately brought together into one the gospels and letters, Petrine and Pauline texts, Pauline and Johannine texts, official and charismatic writings.

The Purpose of the Later Writings

Another observation belongs in this context: the "late writings" of the New Testament in particular emphatically develop the theme of the apostolic tradition and church office. This is perceptible especially in the letter to the Ephesians, the Pastorals, and Luke's two-volume work. For the New Testament as a whole, continuity with apostolic tradition and service to the unity of the church demand an emphasis on church office. This is especially clear in Ephesians 4:7-16, which speaks first of the exaltation of Christ and then, reflecting on the gifts of the Holy Spirit, which the Exalted One has bestowed on the church, proceeds directly to church offices:

> The gifts he [the exalted Christ] gave were that some would be apostles, some prophets, some evangelists, some pastors and teachers, to equip the saints for the work of ministry, for building up the body of Christ, until all of us come to the unity of the faith and of the knowledge of the Son of God, to maturity, to the measure of the full stature of Christ. (Eph 4:11-13)

The offices and charismatic services, according to this text, can be traced to Christ himself. They are gifts of Christ to the church in order that it may be built up as his Body.

The link between church office and the unity of the church is just as clear in the theology of the two-volume Lukan work. For Luke, the Twelve secure the continuity between the time of Jesus and that of the church. Like every living organism, the people of God also requires "genetic information." The Twelve are for Luke, we might say, the enduring memory of what Jesus did and taught. They represent the non-corruption of the Jesus tradition. Luke emphatically states that they were present throughout the whole time during which Jesus came and went among his own (Acts 1:21-22).

Then, in the great missionary discourses in Acts, Luke shows what the apostles taught. For him, in the time after the Twelve, Paul became the vessel of continuity. On leaving his mission field in the East he gives a farewell speech before the presbyters of the community in Ephesus that is intended, in turn, to indicate continuity with the time to come. This is the only speech in Acts that is addressed exclusively to church officials. For Luke it is Paul's testament to the later church. There we read:

> Keep watch over yourselves and over all the flock, of which the Holy Spirit has made you overseers, to shepherd the church of God that he obtained with the blood of his own Son. I know that after I have gone, savage wolves will come in among you, not sparing the flock. Some even from your own group will come distorting the truth in order to entice the disciples to follow them. Therefore be alert, remembering that for three years I did not cease night or day to warn everyone with tears. And now I commend you to God and to the message of his grace, a message that is able to build you up and to give you the inheritance among all who are sanctified. (Acts 20:28-32)

Luke here writes clearly in terms of the distresses of his own church situation. There are already heresies and divisions, and the heretics come partly from outside and partly from within the communities themselves. In view of this situation in the church, there are two primary things that offer security: first, the Gospel, here called "the message of his grace," which has the power to build up the church. Second is church office, which plays an important role in this speech. The officeholders are to pasture the church of God, that is, like shepherds they should continually gather their flocks so that they will not be scattered or confused by heretics. So Luke sees church office and holding fast to the Gospel as the guarantees of church unity. Something similar can be found in the Pastorals.

Early Catholicism?

It is not appropriate to disqualify all these texts, which constitute a significant portion of the New Testament, by simply calling them "early catholic" and contrasting them with the supposedly pure charismatic structure of the Pauline communities. If the New Testament is to be interpreted as a single book, and if it was created precisely for the sake of the church's unity and the preservation of the apostolic tradition, those kinds of criteria for selection are mistaken and inappropriate. Besides, it is a scholarly fable that the Pauline communities had a purely charismatic structure, though that structure seemed obvious to Käsemann:

> Characteristically, the genuine letters of Paul mention neither ordination nor the presbytery, but leave the functions of the Church to charismatics and address every Christian as a charismatic. That is not to say that certain duties were not more or less firmly bound to persons suited for them. Nonetheless, in their positions these people counted as special representatives of the universal priesthood, to which baptism with the gift of the Spirit calls the Christian and for which the Spirit qualifies him ever anew. To put it pointedly, but without exaggeration, the Pauline church is composed of nothing but laymen, all of whom nevertheless are all, within their possibilities, at the same time priests and officeholders, that is, instruments of the Spirit for the enactment of the Gospel in the everyday world.[5]

That may well be true in general, although one should not overlook the role assigned to Timothy by Paul himself (cf., e.g., 1 Cor 4:16-21). But Käsemann distorts the crucial element, namely, the function Paul himself assumed for his communities. The very beginnings of his letters show that he related to the communities in his missionary sphere as an apostle who ordered, regulated, and led them, and this is evident not only from the prescripts but also from the letters themselves. To regard Paul simply as one charismatic among many by no means does him justice. Paul was altogether aware of his mission and his apostolic responsibility for his communities. This structure of offices, which he himself valued to the utmost, had to be taken up after his death and continued in an appropriate form.

It is a strange thing: within the New Testament tradition itself (and not first of all from outside it) there is an unmistakable and increasing reflection on what is apostolic and, within that, on church office—precisely for the sake of the church's unity. Today, by contrast, office is regarded by many critics as an obstacle to church unity. Such critics are not thinking biblically; they have the New Testament against them. The major objection today to Käsemann's theses mentioned at the beginning of this essay has to be that they do not take the New Testament seriously *as a text*.

Käsemann and the Final Text

If we suppose that there really are unbridgeable differences in doctrine within the New Testament (something that seems highly questionable to me), we would have to inquire in particular about the intent of the *late* New Testament authors, because they were much closer to its final redaction. Their writings are an essential component of the "final text" of the New Testament. In principle such a method for interpreting any text (above all, those of a juridical nature) is a matter of course. When a varied group of texts is redactionally linked and liturgically bracketed together it is insufficient for interpretation that I simply read individual parts of the text separately and isolated from one another. Instead, I must take into account the whole and its sense of direction.

Still more, the redactional parts or brackets demand my particular attention, because they directly reflect the shaping intent of the final redactors. In principle this method is not merely obvious to modern textual criticism; it is positively banal. Oddly enough, Käsemann could not see that, even though redaction-critical methods already existed in his time. His mistake was that he apparently regarded the whole New Testament as a loosely assembled packet of individual writings. In that he was far removed from the textual criticism of his time, and also from the ancient church's attitude toward the text.

The canon is not a bundle of individual books placed alongside one another, nor did it simply fall from heaven. The church created the canon, that is, it fashioned the New Testament (as the final redaction of the Old Testament) as a unified book, and it did so with the fundamental intent of serving the unfalsified transmission of Jesus' message and the unity of the church. Obviously it intended to collect the apostolic tradition within this book, and to preserve and secure it. But at the same time it built protection for that tradition into its book by giving plenty of space to the so-called late writings, and thereby to church office.

Chapter 11

Some Irenic Thoughts on the Episcopacy and the Primacy

The bishop as known and understood in the catholic churches today does not appear in the New Testament. The Pastorals come closest to our idea of a bishop, for example, in the "episcopal code" in 1 Timothy 3:1-7. But the *episkopos* of that text is in all probability not yet a monarchical bishop; he is probably part of a group that leads the community. Besides, the text says that he should be a good "head of his household" who raises his children in orderly fashion so that one can see whether he is also able to be a good leader for the ecclesial "household." So the bishops in the Pastoral Letters were married, probably each led a single community, and they were associated in a college of *episkopoi*.

The bishop in the modern sense first appears in the letters of Ignatius of Antioch (in the early second century CE). So we cannot say that the episcopal office as we know it today already exists in the New Testament; it is on the way there, but a good deal is not yet settled.

Organic Developments

In the past there were quite a few Catholic theologians who, in light of this situation, got themselves entangled in an almost despairing apologetic. They gathered up everything in the Pastorals and elsewhere in the New Testament that seemed to have anything to do with the later development of the episcopate. They laid mosaic tile after mosaic tile in an effort to demonstrate that the episcopal office of the second and third centuries could already be found in the New Testament texts. The result was a construct that, while it corresponded to the episcopal office as it is today, was simply nonexistent *in that form* in the New Testament period.

That kind of artificial reconstruction has since, and rightly, been rejected. We may quite freely accept the texts as they are. We may calmly assume that church office, like any living organism, had to undergo development. How else would there be room for the power of the Holy Spirit, who, in the sense of John 16:13, gradually leads the church into all truth?

I say "gradually" not because the Holy Spirit is by nature slow but because it is usually historical necessity to which the church opens its eyes and that compels it to recognize and develop what it has long possessed. Isn't it a rather naïve idea that everything in the church must have been complete and finished from the very beginning? That the young church in particular was extraordinarily vital and world altering is another matter. And yet it is true that every newborn requires a good deal of time to grow up. That distinguishes human beings from most animals, despite the fact that in the human genome a lot is already preformed and established.

The case with the episcopal office and papal primacy is the same. The two had to develop successively but according to a rule that basic structures with which the church was endowed from the beginning gradually found their appropriate form. With regard to episcopal office, for example, I would certainly not try to establish identity between the *episkopoi* in the Pastorals and the monarchical bishop of the letters of Ignatius. Instead, I would look to Paul's apostolic office and that of the Twelve. Here we have the real New Testament models, the proper basis for the later episcopal office.

In what follows I will present some aspects that are characteristic of Paul's notion of apostolicity and that we later find in the episcopacy. That, in my opinion, is the only way to get a picture of the New Testament basis for episcopal service.

"Not from Human Authority"

To begin with, Paul is "an apostle—neither by human commission nor from human authorities, but through Jesus Christ and God the Father"

(Gal 1:1). In the same way the later bishops did not receive their office by delegation from the people of the church, as in a democracy all the power to govern emanates from the people and is delegated to elected representatives. No, the bishop receives authority from God, or rather from Christ, just as Paul is an apostle "through Jesus Christ and not by human commission." The Bible expresses this in the concept of "sending," but it is not the people who send; it is God who sends through Jesus Christ.

This process is founded on the sending through election and the sending out of the Twelve by Jesus. The gospels are clear on this point. No one became a disciple, student, or follower of Jesus by seeking out Jesus as teacher and master, but by being sought out by him. Indeed, Jesus called to the circle of the Twelve only those "whom he wanted" (Mark 3:13), and he himself sent them on their mission to proclaim the reign of God and gather the people of God (Mark 6:7). This mission was something the disciples could not do on their own authority, nor could the people of God empower them to do it.

This is put into words in exemplary fashion in Mark 5:18-20, when a man healed by Jesus asks to "be with him." Those are the exact words Mark uses in 3:14 to express the common life of Jesus and the Twelve. Jesus does not offer it to the healed man but sends him home to tell what Jesus had done for him. That would become extremely important for spreading the word about Jesus and for the expansion of the Gospel in the Decapolis (Mark 5:20). But the healed man is not sent as the Twelve are. Later, the Gospel of John would reflect this specific mission given the disciples by Jesus in the words: "As the Father has sent me, so I send you" (John 20:21).

So at a very early period the church had the task of finding symbols and structures that could express outwardly this fundamental event of the sending of its bishops, or, in other words, the origins of episcopal authority.

Office as Confrontation

A second observation: it happened from time to time that Paul "stood against" one of his communities as one sent by Christ. This is especially clear in the conflicts with the community in Corinth: Paul uses his apostolic authority to pass judgment, for example, on a case of incest (1 Cor 5:1-5). Some in the congregation he describes as having become "arrogant" (5:2)—that is, apparently they had an opinion very different from

Paul's. Paul insists on the church's position, against the ideas of the Corinthian Christians. It is true that the community has to participate in the judgment on those concerned (5:4). They are to assemble and pass their own judgment, but that does not detract from Paul's official intervention.

In the same way, a bishop today must represent the will of God, "whether the time is favorable or unfavorable" (2 Tim 4:2), even against resistance in the local church itself. An official structure that is set up in such a way that the majority can decide the truth by vote is absolutely unbiblical. That is why in the Roman Catholic Church the synodal principle, which plays an important role (consider, for example, the election of a pope), is always augmented by the personal principle. The final assent to or dissent from decisions reached by a synod belongs to the pastor or the bishop or the pope. They are obligated to uphold the truth of the Gospel, the truth of the tradition, but they must listen with the greatest intensity to the "counsel" they receive.

Communio

A third observation: although Paul's authority comes from God and cannot be derived from humans, he does not represent only himself. He knows that he is bound to the rest of the church, especially the congregation in Jerusalem. He explicitly cites creedal formulae he has received (1 Cor 15:3), or he maintains moral principles that are valid throughout the church (1 Cor 11:16). In 1 Corinthians 15:5-7, Paul lists the appearances of the risen Christ to Peter, the Twelve, more than five hundred sisters and brothers, James, and all the apostles before finally speaking of the appearance afforded to him also, as an apostle. So he knows himself to be joined to all the apostles.

A passage in Galatians 2 is important in this connection. There Paul first gives reasons for the independence of his apostolic office. He wants to demonstrate the "not from humans" in terms of the historical course of events. But then, again through historical sequence, he emphasizes his *koinōnia*, his communion with Jerusalem and the "acknowledged leaders."

> Then after fourteen years I went up again to Jerusalem with Barnabas, taking Titus along with me. I went up in response to a revelation. Then I laid before them (though only in a private meeting with the acknowledged leaders) the gospel that I proclaim among the Gentiles

> [for their judgment], in order to make sure that I was not running,
> or had not run, in vain. (Gal 2:1-2)

The "acknowledged leaders" are the apostles, and perhaps the presbyters of the Jerusalem community as well. Thus Paul emphasizes the direct reception of his apostolic office from Christ and at the same time the necessity of *communio* with the rest of the church.

Vatican Council II stated that it is essential that a bishop have his office from God through Christ (*LG* 20) but at the same time that he is joined with the *collegium* of all bishops (*LG* 19). All that is clearly modeled by Paul.

Succession

A fourth observation: bishops install other bishops, so that the line of succession remains intact. Certainly we should not misunderstand this succession in a purely external and mechanical fashion. The external gesture of laying on of hands, which undoubtedly is important, means something deeper: the link to the tradition, handing it on, and remaining in continuity with the apostles.

Nevertheless, we find that already in the case of Paul, namely, in the way in which he introduces his numerous coworkers, especially Timothy. Look at what he writes to the community at Corinth in 1 Corinthians 4:16-21:

> I appeal to you, then, be imitators of me. For this reason I sent you Timothy, who is my beloved and faithful child in the Lord, to remind you of my ways in Christ Jesus, as I teach them everywhere in every church. But some of you, thinking that I am not coming to you, have become arrogant. But I will come to you soon, if the Lord wills, and I will find out not the talk of these arrogant people but their power. For the kingdom of God depends not on talk but on power. What would you prefer? Am I to come to you with a stick, or with love in a spirit of gentleness?

Why is this Pauline text so telling? It presumes that the apostle is absent; he is not with his community. Although it is urgently necessary, he cannot embody either his teaching or his apostolic existence for the congregation in Corinth. But he can mediate his own presence by sending, for the time being, his "beloved and faithful child in the Lord," Timothy, who in Paul's absence constitutes the living "reminder" of Paul and his teaching. In principle the succession is already implicit in this event: a coworker of Paul's who represents the next generation conveys Paul's intent, extends his teaching and existence, makes possible Paul's "apostolic presence."

In a time when Paul was already dead and could no longer come to his communities, the Pastorals took up this precise schema and made it concrete. So the succession already existed in the days of the historical Paul as an ecclesial "heritage."

I hope these four observations have made it clear that the essential elements of the later episcopal office already exist in the New Testament, not in some superficial way but in their basic structure—namely, in the office of the apostles, especially palpable for us in the office of Paul. Therefore the church very soon began to call its bishops, rightly, the "successors to the apostles." It thus expressed the fact that if we are to find a basis for episcopal office in the New Testament we must look to the apostles and what the New Testament says about them.

This concludes the first section of this chapter. The second presents more difficulty: can the basis for the papacy also be found in the New Testament?

Three Texts on Papal Primacy

The Roman Catholic Church grounds the primacy of the pope in his succession to Peter, externally manifested by the existence of Peter's tomb in Rome. Regarding the office of Peter and his successors, it rests its case primarily on two New Testament texts. Most frequently cited is the promise Jesus gives Peter in Matthew's gospel, which is inscribed in huge letters in the cupola of St. Peter's in Rome:

> Blessed are you, Simon son of Jonah! For flesh and blood has not revealed this to you, but my Father in heaven. And I tell you, you are Peter, and on this rock I will build my church, and the gates of Hades will not prevail against it. I will give you the keys of the kingdom of heaven, and whatever you bind on earth will be bound in heaven, and whatever you loose on earth will be loosed in heaven. (Matt 16:17-19)

Equally important is a conversation between the Risen One and Peter in the so-called postscript to the Fourth Gospel. While it is not part of the earliest form of that gospel, John 21 is certainly part of the canon.

> When they had finished breakfast, Jesus said to Simon Peter, "Simon, son of John, do you love me more than these?" He said to him, "Yes, Lord; you know that I love you." Jesus said to him, "Feed my lambs." A second time he said to him, "Simon, son of John, do you love me?" He said to him, "Yes, Lord; you know that I love you." Jesus said to him, "Tend my sheep." He said to him the third time, "Simon, son of John, do you love me?" Peter felt hurt because he said to him the third time, "Do you love me?" And he said to him, "Lord, you know everything; you know that I love you." Jesus said to him, "Feed my sheep." (John 21:15-17)

Jesus' threefold question refers to Peter's threefold denial of him. Thus the guilt of his denial is forgiven. At the same time he is entrusted with the office of shepherding the flock, the same office Christ himself exercises (John 10:14). It is impossible that the sheep here represent individual congregations. They are an image of the church as a whole.

A third text that is important for Peter's primacy is in Luke's gospel, part of the conversation at the Last Supper. Jesus announces to Peter that Peter is about to betray him: "Simon, Simon, listen! Satan has demanded to sift all of you like wheat, but I have prayed for you that your own faith may not fail; and you, when once you have turned back, strengthen your brothers" (Luke 22:31-32). So after his repentance Peter is to assume responsibility for the Twelve, and beyond them for the church that will gather around the Twelve.

It is important to note that these three texts are by no means isolated instances within the gospels and Acts. They are interwoven in a fabric of passages that show Peter as the speaker for and representative of the disciples. There is no dissension within contemporary biblical scholarship about this prominent placement of Peter within the gospels or about the post-Easter office assigned to him by Christ in the gospels.

Two Different Interpretations

You may say, "Well, that is wonderful. It seems we have at least three texts in the New Testament that quite clearly emphasize the special role of the Petrine office. And when in addition Matthew 16:18 says that Jesus intends to build his church on the rock that is Peter, then everything is clear and the papal primacy is exegetically secure." If only it were that easy!

Protestant exegesis by no means accepts Matthew 16:18 as proof of papal primacy. It sees no foundation in the text for the current worldwide authority of the bishop of Rome. This different interpretation is one of the reasons for the still-existing gulf between Catholics and Protestants. On the Protestant side it is argued that Matthew 16:18, as well as the other texts that emphasize the role of Peter, refer only to the *historical* Peter, who had a unique function for the church. He was indeed its rock, but that function was his alone, and it vanished with his death. The church is built on his faith and his confession of Jesus as Messiah, as if on a rock, but one cannot conclude from these texts to an enduring Petrine office.

Then follows a serious and profound argument that cannot simply be swept aside: if the three texts mentioned did in fact refer, within the meaning of the New Testament, to the primacy of Peter's successors, then such a Petrine office would have to have been established in the first century. Concretely: Peter or the existing communities at that time would have had to designate a successor to his office. But in fact that did not happen. It is true that later the church tried to construct such a list of Roman bishops in succession. Around the year 185, Irenaeus of Lyons listed the following men as Peter's successors in Rome: Linus, Anacletus, Clement, Evaristus, Alexander, Sixtus, Telephorus, Hyginus, Pius, Anicetus, Soter, and Eleutherius.[1]

But that is surely a reconstruction. In reality the Roman community was very conservative, in this matter as in others. While the monarchical episcopate had already established itself in the East, the Roman community maintained a collegial constitution on the Jewish model well into the mid-second century. The persons named, at least in the first part of the list, are probably members of a *collegium* (or several *collegia*) of presbyters. There can be no argument on historical grounds for a claim of these early Roman presbyters to jurisdiction over the whole church. The primacy was established only in the course of centuries, very slowly—and only in the West. The word "pope" was first used as a self-designation by the Patriarch of Alexandria and is attested for a Roman bishop only in the second half of the fourth century.

When do the surviving sources first recognize a claim to primacy on the part of the bishop of Rome? Only under Victor I, toward the end of the second century, in a dispute about a unified date for the celebration of Easter throughout the church. And under Pope Stephen I we encounter for the first time the argument that the bishop of Rome, as successor to Peter *according to Matthew 16:18*, also possesses his full authority. Stephen I was bishop of Rome from 254 to 257.[2]

So is it nothing but ideology to speak of the Petrine office as divinely instituted, and can no real ground for it be found in the New Testament? Protestants and Orthodox believers say there can be no question of an institution by divine will, that is, derived from Sacred Scripture. The papacy is purely a human institution. Can we get beyond this discrepancy of opinion?

Peter as Model of the True Disciple

An interesting development in this regard has made its appearance in recent Protestant exegesis. A series of works whose primary focus is no longer on the reconstruction of preliminary layers of the text but on the statement of the *end text* agrees that Peter is deliberately portrayed in the gospels as the "type of the true disciple." For example, the Lutheran New Testament scholar Jürgen Roloff describes Peter as the "model of the true disciple" in his book, *Die Kirche im Neuen Testament*.[3] That is to say: Peter is *the* type and model of a disciple, and in later times the church is to read in him how a disciple confesses Jesus as Messiah and Son of God, joins oneself to him, and despite all one's failures remains Jesus' disciple. The church's enduring tie to Jesus is concretized in Peter.

This insight is of signal importance because it shows that the authors of the four gospels did not think one-dimensionally. On the one hand they wanted to describe what had happened in the life of Jesus that was unique and unrepeatable. But beyond that they wanted to make those events transparent for their own ecclesial present. As Peter believed with all his heart, so also must every disciple in the time to come. As Peter repented and thereafter made himself available without reservation, so every later disciple must repeatedly repent and devote his or her life to Jesus' mission. That is the new exegetical insight of both Catholic and Protestant exegetes, and it is foundational, because it can be built upon.

Peter as Model Official

In the gospels, Peter is not only the type of a *disciple* but also, and still more, the type of the *apostle* and therefore of a church official as such. This is more than mere disciple-typology. For example, Peter represents for Matthew the model apostle. He comes first in the list of the apostles (Matt 10:2) and is said to be the foundation of the future church (Matt 16:18).

What does it mean that Peter is depicted as the "type" of a church official? We need to think for a moment about what a "type" or "model" or *figura* is.

Type, Model, *Figura*

It is of the essence of a model that it be reproduced and emulated. In Greek the *typos* is first of all the "mark," the "imprint," the "copy." But it is also the thing itself that leaves the mark, and so the "model," the "sample," the "original image" that shapes the copy. Our concept of a "type" derives from this second meaning. Every type exists as a model that will shape and form later reality.

This is easily illustrated, as a theological process, in the exodus narratives of the Old Testament. They have become a "type," and in their written form they were intended from the start to be just that. The narration of the unique event is made transparent for later events in the history of Israel. Later Israel not only sees itself reflected in the exodus texts—which would be too little—but later experiences are shaped by this model into new exodus narratives. Thus the exodus texts are typological to the extent that they are open to later realizations of exodus, indeed, to the point that they positively demand them.

The Church's Embodiment of the Peter Typology

When we apply what I have described as the essence of the type or model to the primacy texts in Matthew, we can say that as soon as the figure of Peter, as Matthew paints it, is understood as a type it necessarily follows that, according to the evangelist's intention, it is meant to be a model, indeed, a figure for imitation in the future church.[4] It is to be a model, a figure for imitation not only for *disciples* but also for *officials*. From this point of view it is clear that the Protestant position whereby the founding rock that Peter represents for the church is something historically unique and unrepeatable must be called into question. The sense of Matthew 16:18 is not fully embodied in the current Protestant position.

As we have seen, the thesis of the uniqueness of Peter's function as foundation stone rests on the fact that after Peter's death there was no immediate establishment of a Petrine office. Matthew, at any rate, was unaware of such an office for the entire church, and it was a relatively long time before it developed in Rome, in the place where Peter died a martyr and his tomb was revered. But this only establishes that the type projected in the image of Peter in Matthew's gospel needed some time to take shape. That generally characterizes any type: namely, that it reveals its historical power only at a later time. Consider the exodus narratives! Rudolf Pesch was correct when he wrote:

> That Matthew did not yet see how Peter's office as rock would be concretely realized and developed in the church does not alter the fact that he was able to present it as something indispensable and essential for the church. If Peter is the "model," then so is his function as foundation stone, and that, too, must then take shape within the church.[5]

Something similar is true for Luke and the author of John 21. Neither of them defines a later Petrine office. They present us only with images: that of an official who sustains his brothers in their apostolic office and that of a shepherd who pastures the whole church.

The church itself had to try to give that image some concrete form, with all the conditions that are part of a historical realization. The shape of the Petrine office first appeared within a process of becoming, unfolding, gradual discovery, stimulated primarily by the church's needs. Can we not also say: stimulated by the Holy Spirit, who is to lead the church "into all truth" (John 16:13)?

And because the complete form of the people of God presupposes a long path of discovery, and because the church had first to discover all its offices, even though it had been endowed with them from the start, we may suppose that the office of the papacy can also be further developed. In light of the New Testament it must understand itself primarily as in service to the unity of the church. The successors to Peter's office are to strengthen their sisters and brothers and never forget that they are only the first among brothers and sisters and the servants of all. That is particularly stressed in Matthew's gospel. There could be a great deal more said about the Roman primacy, but in any case it is much more biblical than often appears.

But what is equally important is that the slow development of that office in the church and its transformations through the centuries show that the church is a living thing. According to the Bible it is not only a structure and a temple but the people of God, God's planting, God's only spouse, the Body of Christ—and even the building is made up of living stones. The church did not enter the world as a finished entity. Although it has been endowed with everything, it must still grow and develop toward and into Christ.

Chapter 12

Must the Pope Be Conservative?

No matter whether it is Paul VI, John Paul II, or Benedict XVI, no pope today can escape the censure of being conservative. The word "conservative" is mild in the extreme. More and more often the current pope is characterized in terms such as "inflexible," "antimodern," "antiquated," or even "fossilized." The pope is said to build barriers, fight desperately against the currents of the age, set models, norms, and institutions in stone in ways that no one today can understand. The reproach of conservatism is so notorious that it is worth thinking twice about the word itself. What does "conservative" really mean, and why do the popes and the church as a whole appear to have this ineradicable love for conservatism?

Conservative

Often in the case of such problems a look at the dictionary can be a good first step. "Conservative" comes from Latin by way of French. The verb *conservare* meant for the Romans to "preserve unsullied," "protect against decay," "keep alive," "rescue." That gives us a preliminary insight. *Conservare* is not about marginal issues, things one may do or not do. It is about the whole thing, about existence, naked life. *Conservare* says that something crucially important is in extreme danger and absolutely must be rescued.

Of course, I understand that the concept of "conservative" has acquired a number of different nuances in the climate of modern political parties, not all of them congenial. But that should not dissuade us from uncovering the core concept. No one can stop us from considering it theologically, indeed, seeing it in the light of the Gospel and the church.

What does the church care about? What does it have to keep alive, protect, hand on undamaged—even rescue? At the center of the church's faith stands Jesus Christ. The New Testament and, with it, the whole Christian tradition confesses that he is the final, definitive Word of God. More than this God cannot say, to all eternity. In Jesus Christ, the Son, God has *said* everything. In him God has fully and finally spoken the innermost divine essence.

But God has also *done* everything in Jesus. In him God has given God's own self to the world in the ultimate act of love. In the risen and exalted Christ, therefore, the world has already reached its perfection. More than the creation perfected in Christ the world cannot receive. But that means that what is decisive in world history has already happened. It is given to us. It comes to us as something that has already come to pass. Therefore that event must be preached as Gospel, mediated through sacrament, preserved unsullied, and so again and ever again be brought into the present in order that the world may be changed toward its future, which has already come into being.

Precisely that is the church's task, and within the church it is the particular task of the ordained ministry. The church must be conservative from its heart to the tips of its hair—precisely because what is decisive has already happened and has been entrusted to it by God. Those who hold office in the church can only preserve and hand on the "good treasure entrusted" to them (2 Tim 1:12, 14). The church, and its popes, must therefore be conservative. It is not an option for them not to be conservative.

Progressive

But—if Jesus Christ is really the final, irrevocable Word of God, and if in him the whole of evolution has already reached its goal, then what has been given to the world in him surpasses all our concepts and notions. Then Christ is always far in advance of advancing history. Then what he said and did is new wine that bursts all the old skins (Matt 9:17). Then the church is constantly an experience of the new. Then Christian communities, whenever they apply themselves to the task of *conservare* that has been entrusted to them, are an explosive force within the old society.

If we apply this to recent popes, then precisely to the degree that they have been radically conservative, that is, served with their whole existence what was entrusted to them in the Gospel of Jesus Christ as a precious treasure, they were progressive. We can readily envision this in the context of the church's relationship to the Jews. Over centuries the church, and the papacy with it, had a broken relationship to the Jews. It is true that the church states did not participate in the major persecutions of the Jews; those raged elsewhere. But since the second century the church has been unable to understand what Israel means for it. Its theologians increasingly suppressed the idea that God has not abrogated the covenant with Israel, and that the church is only church to the degree that it participates in the "privilege of Israel" (to quote the third prayer of the Easter Vigil).

It is only the most recent popes who have again understood this to the full extent, and in that they were and proved themselves to be altogether progressive. But with this progressivity they were only reclaiming what Paul had long ago said in Romans 9–11. To that extent they were in this instance not only progressive but conservative at the same time. John Paul II was a conservative revolutionary, and that is not an oxymoron.

Is this not true in many other cases? Was John Paul II perhaps, in seeming to live in the past, actually far in advance of his time? And Benedict XVI, when he (from the point of view of his opponents) became a crusty conservative—was he not in fact shielding the church from postmodern arbitrariness?

Regressive

Moreover, the opposite of "progressive" is not "conservative" but "regressive." And "regressive" can mean "falling back to earlier, more primitive levels of spiritual development," according to the dictionaries! Are not the professional critics of Pope Benedict XVI, who claimed he was not progressive enough, perhaps themselves regressive? The church will only survive if it accommodates itself to society, so they decree as they loudly lament the church's dramatic loss of "ability to relate to society"—and then inevitably there follows the long list of necessary accommodations. They do not take into account that for the people of God, from Abraham through the prophets to Jesus, and then through the saints (despite all their respect for and internalization of the true values of society) there has been a continuity of "non-accommodation." This last was by no means innocuous. It could be dangerous, for it was always an irritation to those who did accommodate themselves.

Those who hold to the Gospel and the church's tradition of interpreting it are conservative in the best sense of the word: they rescue and preserve God's project in the world. And God's project is always progressive. Could it be that those who refuse to see that are the real nonprogressives?

Chapter 13

What Constitutes the Church's "Newness"?

The early church lived, to a degree we can scarcely appreciate, in an awareness of being something completely new within the ancient world. In 1939 the theologian and historian of religion Karl Prümm, SJ, published a book with the appropriate title, *Christentum als Neuheitserlebnis.*[1] In it, this specialist in the study of antiquity and Christianity described the newness of Christianity in detail, and thus at the same time portrayed the thrilling sense of newness enjoyed by the early Christians. Adolf von Harnack had already indicated something similar in 1902 in his great two-volume reference work, *The Mission and Expansion of Christianity in the First Three Centuries*. He was able to show that Christians were regarded by their pagan opponents as a "new people," and that corresponded wholly to the consciousness of the Christians themselves.[2]

The Inbreaking of the New

This self-concept on the part of the early Christians is all the more striking because in antiquity something new was not necessarily regarded as something better—quite the contrary! New things were suspect; they counted as disturbing and of lesser value. Only what is ancient and original was accorded respect and considered reasonable. In fact, Christianity's pagan opponents accused it of having introduced absurd and criminal novelties into the world and of despising old and tried ways of life.

In view of this widespread mentality the Christian awareness of representing something entirely new, and of themselves being new creatures in the world, was positively revolutionary. We find this conviction already fully developed in Paul, for example, when in 2 Corinthians, in connection with the Christian experience of baptism, he writes, "if anyone is in Christ, there is a new creation; everything old has passed away; see, everything has become new!" (2 Cor 5:17). Baptism was experienced as a step from the old, sick world of paganism into a new society. Not only in 2 Corinthians, but also in Galatians 6:15 Paul refers to the baptized as a "new creation." The letter to the Ephesians speaks of the "new person" (2:15; cf. 4:24), and its author means not only individual baptized persons but the church made up of Jews and Gentiles that has come into the world as something incomparably new.

Within the ancient world, the early church was the truly modern event. At any rate, that is how the Christians themselves saw it, and so increasingly did the Gentiles as well. The Christians of the time had no such thing as that peculiar inferiority complex from which today's church suffers in its relationship to society.

The fact that Christians were the vanguard of society, and not its limping stragglers, in the course of time changed history. In the fourth century the Roman emperors first made Christianity a civilly permitted religion (*religio licita*) and later the official state church. It is an erroneous belief that the coolly calculating emperors only did so because of miraculous appearances from heaven. They saw how the old empire was breaking up before their eyes; they sought a new cement to hold the empire together and found it in the church—in the 8 percent of Christians then living throughout the Roman Empire. The church could never have appeared to be such a binding force if its modernity had consisted in its *accommodation* to the society of the time. Its modernity, its newness, its promise was nourished from other sources.

Let us listen to a witness above suspicion, not a theologian or a bishop of those times, but the Roman emperor Julian, who later received the epithet "the Apostate." Julian, although he was brought up a Christian, desired to restore the ancient pagan religion, and so he abjured the Christian faith. He knew for a fact, however, that he would have no chance of restoring pagan religion unless he retained what was new and modern in Christianity: *agapē*, the profound solidarity of Christians that extended far beyond the limits of their own communities. Therefore Julian wrote:

Why do we not observe that it is their benevolence to strangers, their care for the graves of the dead and the pretended holiness of their lives that have done most to increase atheism? . . . when . . . the impious Galilaeans support not only their own poor but ours as well, all men see that our people lack aid from us.[3]

This extract from Julian's letter to the pagan high priest in Galatia shows that the Christians' way of life must have made a deep impression on Gentile society. No one wanted to eliminate this new thing that had appeared in history and go back to the time before. Nevertheless, the emperor could not quite understand what this new, modern thing really was. From his pagan point of view he calls it the "benevolence" of the impious Galileans. It was indeed their benevolence, but it was much more.

I will only ask: what then and what today constitutes the "newness" of the church, the modernity in it that erupts into history again and again? Or, still more briefly: what makes the church so constantly new? Of course, a great deal could be said about that; we could talk a long time about the content of what it means to be a Christian. But in the following pages I am not going to describe content, in the main, but something that has more to do with form.

I will proceed in two steps. In a first one I will assert that the church derives its newness precisely from the fact that it constantly looks back to its past, that it "remembers" unceasingly. In other words, the church is more modern than any other society because it has a better memory. (Clearly, if this thesis is correct, then antiquity's reverence for the old is validated, though in a somewhat different sense.)

In a second step I will try to show that the church is also unceasingly new because God himself is acting in it, and there is nothing newer or better than the action of God. But now to the matter itself.

First: the church, or the people of God, is more modern than any other society because it constantly recalls what is long past. I need to give reasons for this shocking paradox, and to do so I have to expand my remarks.

Technical and Social Memory

There are a great many different forms of memory: technical, social, and also the memory of the people of God, which, of course, is also a social memory, but that of a unique society. Technical memory appears at first sight to be by far the most effective kind. It is the cause of social revolutions at shorter and shorter intervals. We are all contemporaries of one of the major technical revolutions, brought about by the invention of microchips.

But the microchip had to be preceded by countless other inventions. At some point people invented the wheel, at some other time the working of metals, some time or other the microscope—I have no need to go on describing these developments. Each of them changed society. But what is decisive is that none of these inventions—apart from a few marginal phenomena—was lost. Once the wheel had been invented it was never forgotten. The art of smithing iron never vanished. Technical memory is extraordinarily efficient. It works. It works all too well.

Likewise, what I have simply called social memory seems to do its work efficiently. Nowadays every new year brings with it a wave of jubilees and anniversaries, *Festschrifts* and exhibitions. Every day the online encyclopedia, Wikipedia, offers a long list of what has happened on that particular day in decades and centuries past. The list makes it obvious that everything, even the tiniest detail, has been archived. Everything is stored. Modern data processing makes it possible to retain every detail and, when needed, to retrieve it.

Of course the big question is whether the memories that are really significant are retained and can be retrieved at the right moment. Will society remember, at the right time, what neopagan ideologies like communism or Nazism have cost humanity? Or is the next ideology that will drive millions of people to their deaths or into a state of misery already lurking in the bushes?

We can also ask, much more simply and to the point: are parents in a position to hand on to their children the good and bad experiences they have had in their marriage so that the children need not start at zero and have to deal with exactly the same problems? The French cultural critic Hippolyte Taine wrote a nearly fatalistic work on marriage in which he asserted that we should not expect such a handing on of experiences within the family: "We get acquainted over three weeks, we love each other three months, we squabble three years, we tolerate each other thirty years, and then the children start all over again."[4]

We may certainly hope that not every marriage that appears to hold together and lasts many years is merely a matter of exhaustion, as Taine asserts. But he is right about one thing: the children—at least by the third or fourth generation—start all over from the beginning. Still worse: often they cannot even begin at the beginning because they are far from living in a neutral space in which one can simply start over. They are shouldering all the old burdens their mothers and fathers have left them. Their starting point has not improved; instead, it has gotten worse.

As marvelously as human technical memory functions, its social memory is deficient to the same degree. How does that happen? The main reason may be that social memory is self-censoring: it stubbornly suppresses its own failures and exalts the past. This self-censoring leads to the constant repetition of the failures of the past, and not only in family life. Otherwise a profound evolution in humanity would have taken place, and the world would have been transformed into a paradise.

Israel's Memory

But now for the crucial question: does the people of God (and here we must think primarily of Israel) have a better memory? That is a question of fact, and here I would assert that I know of no other people that has looked so intensely, so soberly, and so self-critically at its own past as Israel. This is evident simply on the level of language: ancient Israel did not look to the future as modern people do. Israel always regarded its future as *behind it*. It had the future at its back. The Hebrew word for "future" means "what is behind." The past, on the other hand, means something like "what is ahead." The Israelites would not have said, "Auschwitz is behind us," but, "It lies before us; it lies before our eyes." And so even when it was moving into the future Israel looked not forward but back to what had already happened, and thus turned backward, it took a step farther into the future.

Israel's forward progress was therefore not steered by assumptions about what is future but by memory of what has already happened. Insofar as the past appeared like a connected series of traces that showed the right and wrong steps, the detours and false directions, the next step was made possible. We could compare the whole thing with the progress of someone rowing a boat, always seated with her or his back to the direction of movement and oriented to points long left behind. Israel went its way in the same fashion. It moved into the future by constantly looking back to its past.

Every feast, Passover above all, is a remembrance of the past, a sacred memory. The Mishnah prescribes for the celebration of Passover: "It is . . . incumbent on every person, in all ages, that [he or she] should consider it as though [he or she] had personally gone forth from Egypt" (*Pesaḥ* 10.5). Thus participants in the feast are not only required to cast a glance back to Israel's past. No, the feast demands of them that they place themselves, their whole persons, back in what happened then and in this very way permit God's ancient deeds to be renewed in them.

Israel constantly looked backward. It is true that other nations did the same thing, but Israel, unlike its neighbors, did so with relentless soberness. All the peoples of the ancient Near East glorified their own past in their "cultural memory" and told bombastic myths of their origins: how their kings descended directly from the gods and the state was therefore untouchable and sacrosanct. Israel, on the contrary, said in its most ancient creed: "A wandering Aramaean was my ancestor" (Deut 26:5). You can't get more realistic and sober than that. Israel analyzed its historical failures with the same lack of illusion. There is no nation in the world that has interpreted its history, as Israel did, as an unending series of complaints, resistance, and rebellion against its God. There is no people that has so unsparingly revealed its own lack of faith and lack of fidelity to its God.

This critical retrospection culminated in the time of the Babylonian exile. At first it seemed as if, with Israel's being driven out of its land, everything had come to an end, as if the thread of history with God had been finally and utterly broken. But in fact it was out of the catastrophe of the exile that Israel drew a decisive new beginning, for the most extensive parts of the Old Testament arose out of reflection on the cause of the exile, out of a look back, out of repentance, out of an understanding of their own failure as a "happy fault." The exile effected a qualitative leap in Israel's ability to perceive and understand. A good deal of what we take as a matter of course as part of the faith of the Old Testament people of God became clear to Israel's consciousness only through the exile.

It is important to note that the penetrating look backward to their own past did not make biblical Israel incapable of action. That constant retrospect, especially on the exodus from Egypt, instead set a new history free, and one with an incomprehensible dynamism. It is like a chain of explosive charges, a constant field of experimentation. Their history is revised again and again, is critiqued by the prophets in the most radical fashion, takes utterly unexpected turns, and is altogether oriented to the future.

We would not be wrong to suppose that the breathtaking development of our Western society ultimately goes back to Israel's impetus, the critical and enlightened historical awareness of that tiny nation. The American author Walker Percy illuminated this situation in some simple but accurate reflections:

Why does no one find it remarkable that in most world cities today there are Jews but not one single Hittite, even though the Hittites had a great flourishing civilization while the Jews nearby were a weak and obscure people?

When one meets a Jew in New York or New Orleans or Paris or Melbourne, it is remarkable that no one considers the event remarkable. What are they doing here? But it is even more remarkable to wonder, if there are Jews here, why are there not Hittites here?

Where are the Hittites? Show me one Hittite in New York City.[5]

The Church's Memory

In Jesus and the church grounded in him, the history of Israel again took a turn that overturned all expectations. For the most part we forget that what happened then in Galilee and in Jerusalem was not something foreign or alien to Israel; it was Jewish history. The actors were all Jews without exception. Jesus was a Jew, Mary was a Jew, and all the apostles were Jews. It seems banal to say all this, but unfortunately there is still reason to do so. The church arose in Israel and sees itself as the eschatological Israel gathered by Jesus; it is therefore irrevocably and forever bound up with the whole of Israel.

The exodus of the people of God out of Egypt is also our exodus, the ancestors of Israel are our ancestors, Israel's memory is also our own. Jesus pressed forward Israel's history, with its constant and unique view to the past, and did so in radical fashion. He lived from the Old Testament and focused on its essential points—for example, the double commandment of love of God and neighbor.

When the church looks back it uses the same book with whose aid Israel likewise looks backward; it has only expanded it with its own experiences. The Bible is nothing but collected experience—condensed, thousandfold tested, and repeatedly considered experience from more than a thousand years, growing out of the soil of the people of God. The Bible enables every generation to compare its own experiences of faith with the previous experiences of God's people.

Those who only read the Bible for personal improvement or to find consolation and help in their individual crises do not plumb its whole depth. It is true that there are many ways to read the Bible, and in any case it is good to read it. But it exists primarily to interpret for the gathered community, to clarify its current situation in light of the long history of the people of God. Therefore the Bible's proper *Sitz im Leben* is the worshiping assembly. There the church looks back, so to speak officially, and with excited attention, to its past. In the Liturgy of the Word, God's deeds are told and interpreted, and in the eucharistic prayer God's final and ultimate act of redemption is remembered: in sacred memory the church recalls Jesus' death and rescue from death, and this *memoria* is so deep-seated that faith can say: God's saving deeds in the past, above all, the great saving act in Jesus Christ—all is here present.

Have I gradually wandered away from my subject? Not at all! The thesis was that the church, that is to say, the people of God, is more modern than any other society because it has a better memory. On the basis of its biblical tradition it has a memory that retains all the experiences of the past, and it has an assembly in which its saving knowledge is handed on from generation to generation and constantly becomes new.

No solutions already discovered thus need to be lost; nothing need disappear. It is not necessary for every generation constantly to begin at zero. And for that very reason the church is in a position to be always new, always younger and more modern than any other society, because radical memory gives a future and causes the church, insofar as it takes its own experiences seriously, always to be ahead of its time. The Jewish saying is also true of the church: "The secret of redemption is remembering."

The Easter Vigil

All this is concentrated in the Easter Vigil, the central place of all the church's remembering and renewal, and the standard for every church gathering.[6] In the long night of this vigil the church tells, in more stories than at any other time, the one history of how God's people were led out of the darkness of the beginning into the light of Easter dawn. It looks back to its own beginning with Abraham and even further back to the roots of humanity. It traces the whole path once again: the creation of humans, the call of Abraham, the binding of Isaac, the passage through the Reed Sea, the rescue from Pharaoh and his army, being led back out of exile, the raising of its Messiah from the darkness of the grave, and it is not afraid to say: All this is happening today! This is the night of the exodus and the liberation! This water of baptism is the same water through which our ancestors were rescued from the power of the Egyptians, and it is also the water over which the Spirit of God swept at the beginning of all things!

In this night, as on the first day of creation, the church kindles light, knowing that the true light of the world is Christ, and the eighth day, the day of the new creation of the world, has already begun. In all this the church confidently surpasses the awareness not only of most contemporaries but also of the majority of Christians and revolutionizes all factuality by announcing the revision of all things as the logic of its remembering. In the great liturgy of the Easter Vigil the church conducts its believers into God's "now." It views the history of the world through its own eyes, and in doing so it sees what is evident only through familiarity with its thought and the constant experience of its action, what is visible to no one else. But to the church, in this night, it gives its light.

This night, the church therefore says, is as bright as day and snatches the people of God from the darkness of sin. In it heaven and earth are joined, in it what is cast down is raised up, what has grown old has been made new, and the broken world is restored to its original beauty. Anyone who takes the Easter Vigil even a little seriously can never again say that the church is old-fashioned. Such a one can only say that the church is far ahead of its time. It is already the beginning of God's new creation.

Buried Memory

Having said all that, we must also add, and with the same clarity, that the church is far from being always on the exalted level of what it celebrates. Just like Israel, it has very often corrupted its own memory through unbelief and hardness of heart, through forgetting and suppression. It contains a bad, a rotten memory as well. When the church joined itself to the governing authority and permitted itself to become a state church, it had simply forgotten the dangerous experiment Israel had made with the state in its royal period, and at the cost of fearful sacrifices. When, a little later, it called upon the state to extirpate heretics from its midst with physical force, it sinned most grievously against one of its biblical founding documents, namely, the Sermon on the Mount.

When it did not resist increasing anti-Judaism within its own ranks, but instead deepened it by asserting that Israel had lost its place as God's elect and the church itself had taken Israel's place, it forgot that the church owes its existence to Israel and through God's grace has been grafted into the ancient olive tree (Rom 11:13-24). The real consequences of that loss of memory were fearful.

I could continue the list for a long time, but I have selected these few points to make it clear that the church is, alas, not "pure memory." It also contains bad memory, concealed, buried, even false. Therefore one of its most important duties—and this concerns all of us—is to continually test, purify, and renew its memory. It cannot do so by its own power, but Jesus has promised it the Holy Spirit, who reminds it and leads it into all truth. That has nothing to do with accommodation to society. It means, rather, abandoning the false models in society, turning to the "dangerous memory" of the people of God, daring the exodus again and again, and in that way remaining ahead of the times.

Did God Act Only in the Past?

I have tried to show that the church is continually new; no matter how often it lags behind its possibilities it is never really out of date. It is even ahead of its time because it has a "better memory." But that is not enough. I have to add—and this is the *second step* I want to take with you: the church is also continually new because God acts through it.

The whole celebration of the Easter Vigil would be meaningless, a mere staging, a liturgical glass-bead game and nothing more were it not that in it we celebrate that God really acted, really led God's people out of Egypt and at Sinai gave it a new social order, that God really rescued Jesus from death and in him restored the people of God to life. The church celebrates in the Easter Vigil and in all its festivals the mighty acts of God, always far beyond our human actions; it celebrates God's miracles in the world.

Precisely here, of course, the question arises that may be the most important of all in regard to church reform: why do our worship services always tell only of God's deeds *in the past*? "Tell" is not even the right word. We just read about them. So I have to ask: why do we always read in our worship about God's former deeds? The exodus from Egypt, the giving of the law at Sinai, Jesus' death for his people—all that is long past. Can we really expect people to believe something that happened once upon a time in a misty past but apparently never happens nowadays? Why did God only act from about two thousand years before Christ till 70 CE? That is the only period in which God's deeds, God's miracles in the world, are told of when we are at worship.

There was a joke circulating in antiquity about a pentathlete from the island of Rhodes who boasted that the men in his home island could all jump much farther than athletes from the continent. People shouted at the braggart: "*Hic Rhodus hic salta!* [Here is Rhodes; jump here!]" Would we not have to say, similarly: here is the Reed Sea; here is Sinai, here is Galilee? Here we leap and dance; here is the wedding feast! If I am to believe that God once acted, then there have to be new miracles among us; otherwise I cannot believe in the ancient miracles.

You surely know what theologians say in answer to this problem, which bothered even Augustine.[7] They say that the era of revelation that began with Abraham concluded with Jesus and the death of the last apostle. In Jesus, God is self-revealed entirely and forever. In him, God has said everything, done everything. God's *logos* has become flesh; God could do no more.

All that is true, and it is an infinite amount. And yet it is only half the truth. While revelation closed with the death of the apostles, while in Jesus God has really acted entirely and with finality, still that "entirety" is so great that it has to unfold itself in the history of the church and the world. In the farewell discourses in the Fourth Gospel, Jesus speaks of God's "work." He says that he himself has desired nothing but to complete God's work in the world. Then on the cross he says, "It is finished" (John 19:30). By this the evangelist means the great, definitive work of God about which Jesus spoke repeatedly in the farewell discourses. And yet the same Jesus says to his disciples in those discourses: "the one who believes in me will also do the works that I do and, in fact, will do greater works than these" (John 14:12).

That means, however, that what happens in the hour of the Son of Man is so abundant, so comprehensive, so surprising, and so new that it can only be realized slowly, over time. It will be taken up by many, it will mingle with the world's history like yeast, and it will happen again and again by becoming present in every generation. Otherwise it cannot be grasped in its all-surpassing power. In that sense Jesus' disciples will do "greater works than these." Israel's psalms urge again and again: "Sing to the LORD a new song!" (Pss 96:1; 98:1; 149:1)—a new song because there are new things to tell. It is not only that God's ancient deeds have to be told over and over again. They have to be told *anew* because they happen anew today. God acts in the world even today. Not to believe that means no longer believing in the Holy Spirit, who renews the face of the earth.

The True Miracles

But how does God act? By issuing a secret message? Does God act by causing statues of Mary to weep bloody tears? Does God act by—no, never mind, I won't go on. All these "miracles" we hear about over and over again, that are so precious and important to quite a few Roman Catholics, really indicate only one thing: that a great many people have a fully justified longing for miracles in the church that they do not find and therefore look for in the wrong places, in the shady realm of the "miraculous."

The real miracles we must all long for are repentance, faith, and unanimity in the church. Here is the realm of real miracles, because none of that is possible for human beings on their own. That people turn from their false and faithless life projects; we could also say: from the gods of society to the true God, even though in reality we would all prefer to continue as we have been doing—that is the real miracle in the church. That people believe and trust in the ancient experiences of the people of God that are handed on in the church—that is the real miracle in the church.

I need to explain this more clearly. Faith is more than an intellectual acceptance of something as true. It is also more than a spiritual wallowing in the world of religion. Every esoteric today does that. Faith in the biblical sense means entrusting oneself, with one's whole existence, one's whole life, to *the history* that began with Abraham.

Finally, that people permit themselves to be gathered and interweave their lives with those of others to form genuine community and that this happens over and over again in the history of the church even though in reality each of us wants to be her or his own master and although we would each prefer to shut ourselves up within our own four walls—that is the real miracle in the church. Where all that happens, God is at work. God cannot work in the world at all unless God finds people who open their hearts, place their lives at God's service, and allow themselves to be gathered into what God wants to bring about in the world. But when such people are found, then God's miracles happen in the world and God's ancient wonders recur anew.

For all that to happen, Christians' primary requirements are not pastoral strategies and plans. Basically they only have to take seriously what is told at the Easter Vigil. They only have to surrender themselves to what happens there. The celebration of the Easter Vigil is the best and most fundamental pastoral program the church has ever known.

Those who have experienced the liturgy of the Easter Vigil in all its depth and then try to live it find the critique of the church that has become such a popular sport today sticks in their craw. Please do not misunderstand me. I know that critique of the church is bitterly necessary, but a true critique must begin with me myself, and it cannot consist of making scapegoats of the pope and bishops. A true critique of the church must be: am I myself living the Gospel, am I living the Sermon on the Mount?

A true critique of the church must not constantly demand a transformation of structures and institutions in the comical hope that this alone will renew the church. Rather, it must begin at the point where all repentance and renewal begins, at the point where Jesus says that here one will lose one's old life but find a new one, and that will happen today. This kind of repentance and renewal always begins with oneself. Where Christians repent in this radical sense the church is new—and there it is far ahead of society.

Chapter 14

The Church's Proper Name Is "Assembly"

Let us travel backward in time to the days after Jesus' execution. A community of his disciples has assembled in Jerusalem, and soon it grows beyond the city itself. Part of the community speaks Aramaic; these are the ones Luke calls "Hebrews" (Acts 6:1). Another group within the community speaks Greek; these Luke speaks of in the same context as "Hellenists."

Church as "God's Assembly"

Very soon, beginning just after the first Pentecost, the Hellenists must have referred to their community as *ekklēsia tou theou*, literally, "God's assembly" (or: "people's assembly," equivalent to the New England "town meeting" of today). None of our Bible translations uses "assembly" or "people's assembly," however, for the word *ekklēsia* in its specific theological sense. *Ekklēsia* is rightly translated either as "church" or as "community/congregation." But we need to know that in its proper sense the word means "assembly."

How do we know that the original Jerusalem community called itself "God's assembly" or "God's popular assembly" (or even: "God's town meeting")? The expression *"ekklēsia* of God" appears in the New Testament only in Paul and the writings of his close associates, namely, in

Acts 20:28; 1 Corinthians 1:2; 10:32; 11:16, 22; 15:9; 2 Corinthians 1:1; Galatians 1:13; 1 Thessalonians 2:14; 2 Thessalonians 1:4; 1 Timothy 3:5; cf. 1 Timothy 3:15. Of these, those that come first to mind are 1 Corinthians 15:9; Galatians 1:13; and 1 Thessalonians 2:14. In this last passage Paul speaks expressly about the "churches of God . . . that are in Judea," and in 1 Corinthians 15:9 and Galatians 1:13 he tells of his own persecution of the Jerusalem community and the Jewish congregations around Jerusalem: "You have heard, no doubt, of my earlier life in Judaism. I was violently persecuting the church of God and was trying to destroy it" (Gal 1:13; cf. 1:22-23).

If Paul describes the local church or the church as a whole as "the *ekklēsia* of God," that expression may well have had its origin in Jerusalem. The Greek-speaking followers of Jesus in Jerusalem thus called themselves the *ekklēsia tou theou*, God's assembly. But it may be that the Aramaic-speaking part of the early community also used this concept, in which case the Hebrew *qahal* or Jewish-Aramaic *qehalaʾ* would have been used.

It is true that the Hellenists in Jerusalem could have chosen the Greek word *synagogē*, which also means assembly. But that word was already taken, for in parts of Hellenistic Judaism *synagogē* was the word used for Jewish houses of prayer, or more often for Jewish community centers. So *ekklēsia*, which was as biblically well qualified, was used instead.

The usage would then have been adopted, starting from Jerusalem, by all the congregations surrounding the Mediterranean. Those in the West who spoke Latin adopted Greek *ekklēsia* as a foreign expression, spelling it *ecclesia*. The Latin word for a popular assembly would have been *contio* (= *convocatio*; cf. Deut 9:10 in the Vulgate). But in the West the foreign word *ekklēsia* was retained; it already had a dignified and sacred sound. The later Romantic languages developed their words for "church" from Latin *ecclesia*, for example, Italian *chiesa* and French *église*. The German word *Kirche*, the Dutch *kerk*, and the English *church* have a different root; they are derived not from *ecclesia* but from the Greek *kyriakē* (*oikia*), "(house of) the Lord."

So in Greek, *ekklēsia* describes the assembly, and more precisely the lawful assembly of all eligible citizens of the *polis*, the city-state. The *ekklēsia* is the legitimate popular assembly called together by a herald's proclamation. Thus in a derived sense *ekklēsia* is any kind of assembly. Thus, for example, in Acts 19:32 even the tumultuous mob in the theater at Ephesus is called an *ekklēsia*. I say all this as a purely linguistic preliminary, and it may be rather boring for some people, but it is necessary if we are to approach two much more important questions:

1. Why did the primitive community call itself "assembly"? Why was it that some other appellation did not take hold, for example, "the brothers and sisters" (Acts 1:15 and elsewhere), or "the saints" (Acts 9:13 and elsewhere), or "the disciples" (Acts 6:1-2 and elsewhere), or "the way"? According to Acts, this last name, "the way," played a far from unimportant part in the time of the church's beginnings (cf. Acts 9:2; 19:9, 23; 22:4; 24:14, 22).

2. Why is the question important at all?

Let me begin with the second point: why is it so important for us to look back to the original meaning of *ekklēsia*? I will take a broad approach here and first pose a very basic question: what should the process of formation of a religious community look like? In other words, what are the possibilities for living religion in common? I will now describe five models that have existed in real historical time, and will then put forward a sixth model that is fundamentally different from those five.

1. The Eleusis Model

In 395 CE the cultic shrine at Eleusis near Athens was destroyed by christianized Goths under King Alaric, who thus put an end to a history that stretched over more than a thousand years. Countless people had come to this place to be inducted into the mysteries of Eleusis—not only Athenians, but increasingly men and women from all Greece, in the late phase Romans as well, and even Roman emperors. The cultic shrine at Eleusis promised those who allowed themselves to be initiated into the mysteries that they would have well-being in their earthly lives and an eternal, happy life after death.

The celebrations of the mysteries at Eleusis could serve as a model for the personal, individual quest to achieve salvation. They are, in themselves, nearly the opposite of creation of religious community. The individual alone receives salvation. It is true that people traveled in a common procession along the "holy road" from Athens to Eleusis to receive the principal levels of dedication, and the night of induction, with its mysterious and secret rituals over which a severe requirement of silence was invoked, was likewise celebrated in common. But then the "mystics," that is, the "initiates," returned to their daily lives without any new ties or restrictions. Eleusis knew nothing of the building up of congregations or churches. The initiates did not even gather in cultic associations, as was often the case with later mystery cults.

The Eleusinian Mysteries are extraordinarily instructive for us, for they reveal the human need for a "personal religion." At the same time

they signify the deep longing to go beyond the limits of banal daily existence and enter into mystery. We see today how Christianity is diminishing in Europe; the numbers of the baptized, and even more of practicing
Christians, are rapidly declining. At the same time we find that religion
is not disappearing; instead, there is an increase in esoteric and wellness-
oriented forms of religion.

In these forms of ersatz Christianity everything is directed toward the
individual; she or he alone strives for the supposed "salvation," altogether for herself or himself. There may be others nearby who are following a similar path, but everything focuses on what happens for and
within the one self. This is a form of religion in which feeling and personal experience play a crucial role. The individual tries to surrender to
the moment, seeking the religious event, something like a primal religious experience—and yet the individual shrinks from any kind of
commitment.

One need only read the programs of the esoteric sessions that happen
every year in Munich. There are lectures and practical exercises in astrol-
ogy and hypnosis, spiritual healing and tea-tree oil, lunar oracles and
the Mayan calendar, clairvoyance and reincarnation, aromatherapy and
healing with crystals and precious stones. For example, the "advanced
life-counselor" Jutta Coblenz regularly speaks about "Angels and Other
Beings of Light: How Can I Contact Them?" If one looks at the advertising flyers that appear in the mailbox every time an esoteric fair takes
place in Munich it is clear how people today envision their own healing,
liberation, and salvation. There is no need even to visit the esoteric fair;
we can go to Catholic retreat houses and participate in similar courses
on "self-discovery." Let me quote directly from the description of one of
the many courses offered in the annual program of such a Catholic retreat
center for 1998:

> Letting go of everyday things—coming to oneself and thus to the
> deepest inner divine center of one's own person—then returning to
> everyday life strengthened from the center. Gentle, meditative
> dances and sitting in the stillness of Zen. Days of silence and vegetar-
> ian meals are part of this path.

I have nothing in principle against dancing, meditation, silence, or
vegetarian food. But a retreat house is surely not about "coming to oneself" but about attaining the will of God. In general, the "self" and the
"will of God" are rather widely separated. God's will is tied to a concrete
history extending from Abraham to Jesus and beyond, through the history

of the church to us today. That history cannot be replaced by a "divine center" in ourselves. The life of the triune God in which we share through baptism, and through our existence in the church, is something given to us. We do not possess it by nature. Talk about the "divine center" or "divine core" of human beings is highly questionable. Human beings of themselves possess nothing. Apparently, however, the search for the religious self is extremely attractive. It is fun, and it costs nothing. It entails no obligation and is absolutely without consequences.

Do I need to go on? None of this—from Eleusis through spiritual healing and Zen meditation to wellness baths—is the model for Christian faith or for Christian community.

2. The "Invisible Church" Model

In the winter semester of 1899–1900 Adolf von Harnack gave sixteen lectures for students from all departments of the University of Berlin, entitled "Das Wesen des Christentums" [The Essence of Christianity]. More than six hundred students heard them. The book Harnack published a few months later, based on his lecture manuscripts and bearing the same title, was an even greater public event.[1] At the end of his third lecture Harnack spoke the now-famous sentences:

> If anyone wants to know what the kingdom of God and the coming of it meant in Jesus' message, he must read and study his parables. He will then see what it is that is meant. The kingdom of God comes by coming to the individual, by entering into his soul and laying hold of it. True, the kingdom of God is the rule of God; but it is the rule of the holy God in the hearts of individuals; it is God Himself in His power. From this point of view everything that is dramatic in the external and historical sense has vanished; and gone, too, are all the external hopes for the future. Take whatever parable you will, the parable of the sower, of the pearl of great price, of the treasure buried in the field—the word of God, God Himself, is the kingdom. It is not a question of angels and devils, thrones and principalities, but of God and the soul, the soul and its God.[2]

When I read this text to a highly educated Catholic woman a few years ago, she interrupted me, saying: "How lovely! How appropriate!" Here Harnack apparently struck on a religious mood that was not only widespread at the end of the nineteenth century but still is: religious individualism.

According to Harnack, the reign of God has no history; it is ahistorical. It does not enter into a historical drama; it arrives gradually with individuals. We may choose another text from his lecture: "The individual is called upon to listen to the glad message of mercy and the Fatherhood of God, and to make up his mind whether he will be on God's side and the Eternal's, or on the side of the world and of time."[3] Or consider: "Here for the first time everything that is external and merely future is abandoned; it is the individual, not the nation or the state, which is redeemed."[4]

As the reign of God happens not in the world and in community but only within the individual, so also it does not affect what is external but only what is internal, the inner human being, the soul. So one final quotation: "The Gospel is above all questions of mundane development; it is concerned, not with material things but with the souls of men."[5] Accordingly, the church is a *societas in cordibus*, a spiritual organization of many individuals. Its true place is in human hearts. These many individuals are redeemed, singly, by their faith in the Good News—that is, the good news of their immediate link with God. Thus the true church is invisible, hidden, spiritual. It cannot be identified with any concrete church. Everything that has to do with church tradition, church dogmas, church rituals, and church authority shackles religious freedom and sets obstacles to a true encounter with the Gospel of Jesus.

I will say that this model of the invisible church also plays a role in Christianity today, and indeed an extraordinarily powerful one. I encountered it for the first time tangibly and directly in Tübingen, when the famed Lutheran New Testament scholar Ernst Käsemann publicly threatened that if the Lutheran Church of Baden-Württemberg did not change he would leave the church.

At the time I was slightly confused. Käsemann had no intention of becoming a Catholic, nor did he want to join any other church community. What church would he belong to, after his departure? Only gradually did I comprehend that for him church was not at all that common life, that Body of Christ that is necessarily tangible, palpable, and socially definable. Church for him was a reality that can appear anywhere but always surfaces only fleetingly in the real church entities and therefore is not bound to any visible church body.

3. The Club Model

Private clubs and associations played a major role in ancient society, especially after the advent of Hellenism. Formally, they were almost all "cultic associations," that is, the purpose stated in their statutes was the worship of a particular divinity or the annual remembrance of a person who had died. In fact, though, they were more and more inclined to be groups based on common interests, and very often merely societies for feasting and fellowship, what we would call "clubs" today. The real purpose of the association was then frequently nothing but holding an annual banquet or a monthly drinking party.

It is clear from this what an association or club is. Individuals join together for a particular purpose. They remain individuals, but they are united by a common interest—whether it be the cultivation of blue roses, the breeding of crocodiles for competition, or the construction of vintage locomotives. I can join with others to form a club for any purpose, and what links the members of a club or association is a common interest. In general, the others are not interested in the private lives of individual members unless they cause significant damage to the club.

For many people today the church is a kind of club or association. It is no longer an integrated sphere of salvation but more of an arena for religious activities. Many regard and use it also as a "service center." The church embellishes the rituals of transition for them. Baptism adorns entry into childhood, while confirmation announces that one has arrived at puberty. A church wedding ornaments—though less and less frequently—the entrance into adulthood. A church burial gives dignity and shape to one's departure from this life. People in Germany pay their church taxes in order to be able to lay claim to these services. I have spoken very harshly and one-sidedly, but any pastor can confirm the crisis in the church that is involved here.

The church covers a particular sphere of life, but there are many other areas in which the church is not to be mentioned. This corresponds precisely to the segmentation of our society. There is the sphere of employment, that of the economy, of education, of family, of free time—and somewhere or other the sphere of the religious as well. But all these areas have little or nothing to do with each other. They have their own rules, their own personnel, their own different places.

In the United States, which is always a little ahead of Europe, this can be observed in model fashion. There we find a new kind of church: its location is outside the city, precisely where the big box stores are found and there is room for gigantic parking lots. One enters a huge church space; a professional choir is singing up front, a professional orchestra or band is playing, and a rhetorically cultivated preacher is speaking; one can also watch him or her on television. Simultaneously with the service for adults there is professional childcare and a well-organized Sunday school or children's service. Afterward there is a big coffee hour with pleasant conversation where there is also opportunity to make new acquaintances.

I don't want to run all that down. After all, more than half of Sunday is given over to it, and the Christians who are involved make major contributions and get involved so that their free Christian community can flourish. Somehow or other it is an attempt to make faith a part of life. But then come the weekdays, and on those days there is a quite different life to be lived, with other centers of attention, other interests, and other rules of behavior. Life proceeds in segments, and one segment is called "religion."

4. The Theocratic Model

This model is probably the oldest: religion and life constitute an organic whole and interpenetrate. We can consider ancient Egypt: society, state, culture, nature, cosmos, religion, rulership, and well-being were melded together in Egypt to form a grandiose unity, palpably present in the person of the pharaoh. He was the center of meaning for the whole land. He was the god-king, the real image of the sun god. He ensured fullness of life for the whole land and all its inhabitants.

Ancient Egypt may be far removed from our conscious awareness, but those to whom it seems too distant can substitute Germany's National Socialism or Stalinism in the USSR. Obviously there are profound differences between the religion of ancient Egypt and Nazism or Soviet communism, and yet they have much in common. The "Third Reich" and the Soviet Union were also closed systems with quasi-religious claims. Here too society and state, work and culture, private life and faith were to be melted into a complete unity, and faith was to be faith in Josef Stalin or Adolf Hitler. The following poem illustrates how far that went. It was circulated for use in youth celebrations honoring Hitler. It is not exactly a prayer to Hitler, but it is very close to the genre of "prayer." Here Hitler's presence as the "figure of light and salvation" is celebrated in the style of Rainer Maria Rilke's poetry:

> In many nights it may be so:
> We sleep, while you watch with anxious care,
> For you will pass those many nights in thought
> In order then, at dawn, to look clear-eyed into the light.[6]

Then, in the following table prayer, the Hitler cult truly became prayer:

> Leader, my Leader, given me by God,
> Protect and sustain my life for long years!
> You have rescued Germany from the depths of its need.
> I thank you today for my daily bread.
> Remain by me, do not leave me,
> Leader, my Leader, my faith, my light![7]

Other examples of the interweaving of religion, society, culture, and state are provided today by fundamentalist Islamic states, though again the profound differences between these and Stalinism or Nazism must be kept in mind. The state belongs to God, inasmuch as the worship of the one God should saturate everything in it. Public laws and religious laws are identical in particular areas. I am referring to the phenomenon of *sharia*, a type of Islamic religious law concerning property rights, penal law, family law, inheritance law, and other legal matters as well.

Precisely here, of course, we must try to understand. Here we find signs of the longing for the "wholeness" of faith. It should not be merely a segment of life but should penetrate all areas, shaping life as a whole. Islamic believers' feeling of superiority toward the West can be understood from this perspective. They get nothing from our segmented, isolated faith, threatening to drown in a libertinistic society. They fundamentally despise it. They say proudly: "Our faith shapes our whole life. We have our fixed times of prayer, the call to prayer from our muezzins, five times a day. We have the month-long fast of Ramadan in which all participate. We make our pilgrimage to Mecca. Above all: we do not permit anyone to insult our religion. We stand up for our faith. We are a worldwide community [*umma*] in solidarity. Christians, by contrast, put up with anything."

For many Muslims, faith and life are a single thing. Faith can likewise be culture; it is meant to shape society and the state. In a truly fundamentalist Islamic state no one may abandon the Islamic faith in favor of another religion. Anyone who does so can be punished by death. In such a fundamentalist Islamic state I am not free to accept another faith. The "wholeness" of faith is thus purchased very dearly there, at the expense of freedom. It can give way to fanaticism, which produces warriors for God.

That same lack of freedom prevailed in Christianity for a long time, over many centuries after Christianity became the imperial religion. But even in the centuries of its symbiosis with the state, the church constantly sought models of freedom. This is evident in the fifth model.

5. The Monastic Model

It is no accident that almost precisely from the moment when the church was united with the empire, monastic communities began to play a greater and greater role within it. Beginning with the years 311 and 313, Christianity became a *religio licita*, a permitted religion, within the Roman Empire. From that time forward Christianity steadily acquired more privileges as older religions were gradually suppressed. Ultimately, beginning with Emperor Theodosius I in 380, Christianity became more and more firmly established as the official religion.

It is significant that the first monastic communities were founded, under Pachomius, around the year 325, in the midst of this process of wedding the church to the state. Underlying the growth in the numbers of monastic communities was the longing for a "complete" discipleship. Faith ought not to belong merely to a segment of life but should encompass the whole of it, including work. From this came the idea of Western (and, with alterations, also of Orthodox) monasticism, in which the monastery is a world unto itself in which both time and space are sanctified. Prayer and work alternate and fill the days. At the center of the monastery is the common table given us by Jesus: the table of the Eucharist and the table in the refectory, the dining hall.

This form of life had an extraordinary effect on the cloister's surroundings and on the whole church. Once again there was a profound unity of world, life, culture, and faith. But—and this was a significant difference from the theocratic model previously described—entry into the monastic community was chosen in complete freedom. Discipleship cannot be compulsory.

The creation within the post-Constantinian church of monastic communities as strictly defined spheres of discipleship and the "evangelical counsels" was an almost necessary development because the community churches of the early days had become a church of the masses and because freedom of belief was no longer discernible and in fact very soon became nonexistent. Monasteries of women and men sustained the ideas of discipleship and freedom to follow and to believe through the centuries in the church.

Certainly, these models had new deficiencies, because through them discipleship developed in the church as a special form of life, the only form in which it was thought possible to live as a disciple of Christ. For the rest of the baptized (that is, for families or married couples) there was scarcely any opportunity to live a life of discipleship and to make visible what faith really is. To do that, one had to enter a monastery.

6. The Community Model

After Jesus' death, the first Christian community was created in Jerusalem. It was, so to speak, the primal model for church as community. But where did the model of "community" come from? Was it an invention of the apostles? Of the first disciples?

No, in fact the model of "community" or "congregation" had been invented in Israel long before, possibly in the Diaspora, where there was no temple to which one could make pilgrimage, and where people could no longer assemble at the gates in the city wall. So they gathered in private houses, in small communities the eye could readily take in. A single house could not contain more than 70 to 120 people. Even when separate synagogue buildings were constructed they were at first only expanded private houses, and at the beginning they retained the character of private homes.

What was essential was therefore, *first*, the Diaspora situation. The surrounding society did not share the same faith, and the contrast was significant. The *second* essential was the relatively small size of the synagogue communities. And because their existence as visible communities depended on their contrast with the larger society, the houses in which they gathered were also the centers of their common life. The synagogue existed for worship, of course, but beyond that it served a number of other functions. There people gathered for meetings of the council and for judicial matters; there official documents were prepared; there found objects were advertised, witnesses sought, acquaintances made, business deals developed, wakes held for the dead, and public mourning conducted. Most synagogues contained a community archive as well as a kitchen so that the poor could be served. Often there was even a facility for bathing so that people did not have to go to the pagan baths. Finally, the synagogue building served as a shelter for traveling fellow Jews and for school classes. The oldest surviving inscription for a synagogue in Jerusalem, the famous Theodotus inscription, reads:

> Theodotus, son of Vettanos, a priest and an *archisynagogos*, son of an *archisynagogos*, grandson of an *archisynagogos*, built the synagogue

for the reading of Torah and for teaching the commandments; furthermore, the hostel, and the rooms, and the water installation for lodging needy strangers. Its foundation stone was laid by his ancestors, the elders, and Simonides.[8]

So the Jewish synagogue was more than a house of prayer. It was a community center belonging to a congregation that gathered regularly and shared a common life. This form, the synagogue community, is a Jewish invention, and it was adopted by the original Christian community, which, after all, was entirely Jewish. It was not only adopted but intensified: Jesus had gathered his disciples at table; at his last meal he grounded community in his own death. Out of his sacrificed and risen body grew the Body that is the community. Paul was able to say: we, though many, are one body (cf. 1 Cor 12:12, 20).

Thus, beginning with the model of the synagogue community and deepened by Jesus' action, there arose what we call a community or congregational church. It is essential to this kind of church community that people freely join their lives together. Their community has an origin and a center: the risen Christ. This center is evident at the common table, around which a visible community assembles. It lives in a Diaspora situation, that is, in a world that thinks differently. There is opportunity for all to be disciples, but at the same time there are many kinds of callings and many forms of participation in the community's task. And finally, the individual community does not exist for itself but makes present in itself the church universal with which it is visibly united.

Consequences

Conclusion: we have looked at five different models of religious community formation, although the first is practically a counter-model to community. None of them is entirely absurd or false; each contains a morsel of reality. The Eleusis model shows the importance of the individual and her or his free decision. The model of the "invisible church" is correct in saying that the church really does have an invisible dimension, just as there cannot be a body without a soul. Likewise, the club model contains some truth in its emphasis on common interest in something. So with the theocratic model: it rightly emphasizes the necessity of "totality." The monastic model shows how necessary discipleship is for the church, a discipleship lived in freedom.

Then at the end was a sixth model: the concept of the church as community or congregation. It is the truly biblical model, developed in the time before Christianity. Jesus adopted it in calling disciples to a common table. After Easter it became the definitive form of the church, which is a network of communities or congregations.

The Public Assembly of the Whole

Now, after this first part, I can turn to our particular question: why did the original community call itself "assembly"? After all I have been saying, I can answer the question much more quickly and far better.

First, to recall the crucial linguistic phenomenon: the young community in Jerusalem called itself the *"ekklēsia* of God," and we have seen that *ekklēsia* in Greek is the popular assembly, the coming together of all free, enfranchised citizens. The community in Jerusalem, in applying to itself this politico-legal concept from the life of the *polis*, the city-state, raised an extraordinary claim. It thereby showed that it did not see itself as a gathering of many individuals who had in common only that they had received the same initiation into the mystery, namely, baptism. It further showed that it did not understand itself to be a circle of like-minded friends or a private club of people who had joined together because of particular interests. Instead, it saw itself as an assembly, indeed, a society, in which everything was on the agenda and was "public." In this context "public" means that what is at stake is the world, the public good, what matters to everything and everyone.

So the *ekklēsia* is not a private matter, a mere section or sector of life. It is about the whole of life. Accordingly, even in later times the church avoided applying the multifaceted terminology of the ancient club world to itself. The Christian community was neither *thiasos* nor *eranos* nor *koinōn* nor *sissitia* nor *hetaireia* nor *synodos* nor *syllogos* nor *collegium*. All those are ancient words for what we would call a "club" or "association," or rather they are technical terms from the world of the clubs.

We can see from the very multiplicity of these terms what a significant role club life played in the ancient world. The early Christians did not adopt any of these terms for themselves—probably, among other reasons, because they were to a degree associated with pagan worship. But above all the choice of the word "assembly" was meant to show that the church is neither an esoteric circle nor an association of friends nor a cultic fellowship nor a selective group nor a faction within the state nor a club. It is, as Joseph Ratzinger wrote in his *Principles of Catholic Theology*, "a public assembly of the whole."[9]

But what is this "whole"? Not, of course, the state, the *polis*, and most certainly not the Roman state. The "whole" is the people of God. The word *ekklēsia*, that is, betrays something still more. As a designation for the church it is most certainly not derived directly from the popular assemblies of the Hellenistic cities, if only because the whole people of a *polis* were not admitted to those assemblies. For example, the mass of slaves was excluded, as were women and foreigners. If we look at it closely, the *ekklēsia* of the Hellenistic *polis* was not the "whole" at all.

Origins at Sinai

So besides the general Greek linguistic background there must be a more specific basis for the original Jerusalem community's choice of *ekklēsia* as its designation, and it is easy to find. The real origin of the "*ekklēsia* of God" is in the Old Testament. Ultimately, *ekklēsia* refers to the people of God assembled at Sinai, the whole community of Israel.

The book of Deuteronomy uses a fixed formula for the day on which "the whole number of" Israel was assembled around the mountain of Horeb (= Sinai) and received the Ten Commandments "out of the fire, the cloud, and the thick darkness" (Deut 5:22). That day was called "the day of the assembly," in Hebrew *yom haqqahal* and in Greek *hēmera [tēs] ekklēsias*. This formula appears in Deuteronomy 9:10; 10:4; 18:16. According to the book of Deuteronomy, the founding assembly of Israel that constituted them as a people occurred at Sinai.

When the young community in Jerusalem adopted the term *ekklēsia* it thereby showed that it saw itself as the eschatological fulfillment of this assembly at Sinai. It understood itself to represent the true, eschatological Israel. The War Scroll from Qumran (1QM 4.10) gives us the first evidence of the use of *qahal ʾel*, the Hebrew equivalent of *ekklēsia tou theou*.

It may be that the followers of Jesus even called themselves by this name on that first Pentecost, which Luke portrays as having a church-founding character, since Pentecost was the Jewish feast of Weeks. This was at first purely a celebration of the harvest, but as early as New Testament times it must already have been celebrated as a commemoration and making-present of the event at Sinai.

But whatever may have been the connection between the origin of the concept and the feast of Pentecost, the word *ekklēsia* shows that the church saw itself as the eschatological Israel, the perfection and completion of Israel's great assemblies that began at Sinai. And the gathering of Israel at Sinai, as Scripture describes it, did not include only the men; it was the "whole people" (Exod 19:8, 11, 16; 20:18), that is, all the women and children as well.

But the word *ekklēsia* shows us still more. We have seen that the word always includes the image of concrete assemblies: of those who had the franchise in the ancient *polis* and of the whole people of Israel at Sinai. But this means that the church lives out of its concrete assemblies. They are the implementation of its existence, in which it makes itself present. In them it is most clearly obvious what it is and what God wants of it.

So the church's proper place of being is the assembly—namely, the assembly in which the whole community comes together, recalls God's saving deeds, and receives from God its mission for the world. So the concept of *ekklēsia* makes it clear that this is not about a piece, a segment, of society; it is about the whole. Thus the concept of the *ekklēsia* includes an enormous claim: this is about the world in all its dimensions. It is about society, *societas*. This could, of course, lead to the false conclusion that the church, like Islam, sees itself as a theocracy, a situation in which church and society, state and religion are as identical as possible. But that is not at all the case. The church must be nonidentical with the state and the rest of society so that each person may be free to be a member of the people of God or not.

So *ekklēsia* means being called out by God—called out from the overall society—and for that very reason contains the freedom to accept or reject that calling by one's own decision. Church is world, again and again healed, saved, redeemed world, but precisely *not* a totalitarian system to which one must belong. Life in the church is pure grace, and for that very reason pure freedom.

Chapter 15

The Unknown Paul

There are very few people of antiquity about whom we know as much as we do about Paul. I am not referring to the fact that we have some very ancient copies of his authentic letters—letters he once dictated himself, and signed. I am thinking of something else: namely, that Paul wrote with a frank directness unlike that of any other author before his time. It was simply not customary in antiquity to open one's heart as boldly as he did.

Certainly Paul had none of the compulsion of today's bloggers to reveal his own life without restraint. He was writing to Christian communities and speaking within the context of *agapē*, therefore within a secure and well-guarded space. Within that context, though, he spoke openly and clearly and with his whole self.

The chances for an immediate encounter with Paul are thus very favorable in themselves, and yet it is with him as with all great figures in history: the image we have of Paul is an inherited one, fixed, predetermined, and often concealing the contours of his work. We might do better to say that it is like an image covered with a thick layer of varnish. What I would like to do here is to remove a little of the varnish so that the real world of Paul, with its unbelievably bright colors, may come to the fore.

The Synagogue: Catechumenate for the Gentiles

Let me begin right away with the title most often applied to Paul: "apostle to the Gentiles." In itself this idea is entirely correct. After all,

Paul applied it to himself in Romans 11:13. He was really the great missionary to the Gentiles. And yet the title "apostle to the Gentiles" became fuzzy and vague at a very early time; it was far too laden with false preconceptions. Who were the Gentiles whom Paul won for Christ in such great numbers? They were, almost without exception, Gentiles who lived in the physical and spiritual environment of Jewish synagogue communities, people fascinated by Jewish monotheism, the blessing of the Sabbath, and the synagogues' care for the poor. Those Gentiles were known as "God-fearers" (cf. Acts 16:14; 17:17; 18:7).

These God-fearers were friends and sympathizers toward Israel who simply had not taken the last step into Judaism: they (that is, the men) had not been circumcised. They did not keep the Torah fully, and yet they already lived in the light of Israel. They attended the synagogues and believed in the one God; they kept their distance from pagan customs.

The Gentiles whom Paul won for Christ came almost entirely from among these "God-fearers." Where he attempted a purely Gentile mission, distant from the Jewish environment, he apparently failed for the most part. We need only to reflect on how things went for him in Athens (cf. Acts 17:16-34). So Paul did not simply convert Gentiles; he gathered Gentiles from the synagogue environment. It was only for that reason that he was able to found so many communities so rapidly: his audience was already prepared for the message of Jesus Christ. They already knew that turning from the rule of the many gods to the one true God was essential to faith. They did not have to be taught what worship of God in spirit and truth is. They did not need to learn the right way to pray; they knew some early forms of the *tefillah*, the Jewish Eighteen Benedictions. They knew that this basic Jewish prayer appealed for the coming of the Messiah—and not only the Messiah's coming, but also the eschatological gathering of Israel. In the synagogues they heard the reading of the Torah and the promises of the prophets. They knew the history of God with God's people since Abraham. But above all, they did not need to learn what community life was, for the form of "community," one of Israel's most fortunate and important inventions, was already familiar to them.

All they still needed to learn was simply that Israel's history had now finally entered the stage of fulfillment. Concretely, they had to learn that, in the crucified and risen Jesus, Israel's messiah had already come and that the eschatological gathering of the people of God, and with it the messianic transformation of the world, had also begun. As soon as they believed that and publicly confessed it, they were admitted to baptism.

These God-fearing Gentiles had thus been living *de facto* in a basic catechumenate for a long time. Judaism was the catechumenate of the early church, and it was the catechumenate of the Gentile Christians. Only when the church, beginning in the fourth century, gradually lost its roots in Judaism was there a need for a catechumenate as a separate church institution.

What does all that mean for us today? Well, once again we are living among Gentiles. Still more: we are living scattered throughout a society that is much more pagan, much more foreign to and hostile to God than ancient paganism ever was. Where is there among us a comparable vestibule for Christian faith, a preparation for the Christian way of life like the one Paul found in the environment of the synagogue?

Is it an exaggeration to say that there is nothing comparable to this preparation nowadays? But it is urgent that there should be, because in the future we will encounter more and more neopagans seeking the truth about the world and, above all, in search of a different way of life. Where will they find among us an introduction to a new and better form of life, something the synagogue provided for the Gentiles back then?

It is surely not enough to offer such a seeker a beautiful book on Christianity or invite her or him to a week's retreat at a Christian center (apart from the fact that in such places they are more likely to learn something about Eastern meditation techniques than anything specifically Christian). Isn't it necessary that they find Christians who can not only tell them about their life of faith but steadily introduce them to the way Christians live? The great John Chrysostom, who lived in the fourth century, said, "If you want someone to become a Christian, let the person live with you for a year." That involves a terrifying demand, but I believe the principle is entirely correct. In the United States there are already Christians in many parishes who make themselves available for such a task, that is, who are prepared to introduce seekers to the church not only through words but by becoming their companions on the way and so introducing them to the way of life that is faith.

That is a heavy task, it is true, almost too heavy for individuals, and yet at the same time it is an extraordinary opportunity to win people to Christ and at the same time to deepen one's own faith. Those who do such things need not stand alone.

The Role of the Christian Household

This brings me to a second point that can also help us to understand Paul better and clarify our image of the "heroic" missionary to the Gentiles.

For Paul was not alone, either. He had the support of Christian houses and Christian families.

It is astonishing how many households we know by name, just in connection with Paul's apostolic work: for example, the house of Lydia, the dealer in purple, in Philippi (Acts 16:15); the house of Jason in Thessalonica (Acts 17:5-9); in Corinth the houses of Titius Justus (Acts 18:7) and of Gaius (Rom 16:23); the household of Nympha in Laodicea (Col 4:15); that of Philemon in Colossae (Phlm 2); as well as the houses of Prisca and Aquila in Corinth, Ephesus, and Rome (Acts 18:1-3; 1 Cor 16:19; Rom 16:5). The life of the communities in the early period of Christianity developed in these and many other houses. The natural family, the center of the household, was opened to and bound into a much broader context: the "new family" of the church. And still the church drew its life from families such as those I have listed.

In these households catechumens were instructed, traveling members of the faith were housed, and the community met for its gatherings and the celebration of the Lord's Supper. Here unemployed Christians found work, and here as a rule the first contacts were made with those who wanted to get to know a Christian community. There they learned not only abstract principles of faith but Christian life, a life that had to present a contrast in a Gentile society. Peter Stuhlmacher writes, quite correctly, in his commentary on the letter to Philemon:

> Paul himself lived and taught in house churches and founded them as well. For him not only the larger community but also the house church was the place where the sociological and ethnic-religious barriers between Jews and Gentiles, free and unfree, men and women, high and low, educated and uneducated, which were especially serious matters in antiquity, were broken and leveled in favor of the new bond of all to Christ as Lord.[1]

We should add something else as well: the houses in which Paul lived were often those of the first converts in a given city. This was the case with Lydia's house in Philippi, Jason's in Thessalonica, and probably also Gaius's in Corinth. It was usually in the homes of the first converts that the community also gathered. But those houses in themselves embodied a living piece of community history that was made present in every gathering—not only in the spaces, but, above all, in the persons present.

In this context we should also consider that the ancient house cannot simply be equated with our houses of today. For us, houses are primarily dwellings, but in antiquity, and for a long time afterward, the household was a larger and highly complex social unit, at least among those with means. Their households contained not only their families in the strict sense but also a good many other people who lived and worked there, since the house was often a production center as well. More extensive factories separated from the house were rare. This meant that in Christian households, for example, that of Prisca and Aquila, faith and life—or faith and work—were firmly united. This repeated mention of two of Paul's most important coworkers, Prisca and Aquila, brings me to a third point.

A Leatherworking Shop

Obviously the couple, Prisca and Aquila, are already known to us. Prisca, Aquila's wife, is mentioned relatively often in the New Testament—sometimes with the familiar form, "Priscilla," or "little Prisca." As I have said: this couple is not unknown to us. But we have to be clear about what Prisca and Aquila meant to Paul's missionary work.

Paul had met the couple in Corinth. They were tentmakers by trade and had their own shop. At that time smaller tents might be made of linen, but big ones were fabricated out of woven goat hair or were constructed of skins. For that reason tentmakers also worked in leather. In all probability Aquila and Prisca's shop was not only a tentmaking business but also manufactured leather goods including tents, bags, sandals, belts, saddles, and tack.

We know from the book of Acts that the Roman emperor Claudius had driven Prisca and Aquila out of Rome, along with many other Jews. When Paul met them they were already Christians. They took him into their family in Corinth. At first Paul worked in their business with them and at the same time used their house and shop as the base for his missionary work (Acts 18:1-5). Prisca and Aquila, with their family and their tentmaking shop, would prove to be of the utmost importance for the Pauline mission.

After many months of fruitful work in cooperation with Paul in Corinth, the couple moved to Ephesus, probably not least in order to prepare a base for Paul in Asia Minor (Acts 18:18-19). Paul would have lived and worked in their house when he was in Ephesus. It was also the gathering place for the community at Ephesus, or at least part of it. This we know from 1 Corinthians, which Paul wrote in Ephesus. In it he sends warm greetings to the community at Corinth from "Aquila and Prisca, together with the church in their house" (1 Cor 16:19).

In Ephesus, at a time when Paul was absent, a highly gifted Jew from Alexandria named Apollos came to Prisca and Aquila. They took him in also and introduced him to the course the history of salvation had taken (Acts 18:24-28). Years later, when Paul wrote the letter to the Romans as preparation for a missionary journey to Spain, he asked the Roman community to give very special greetings to the couple: "Greet Prisca and Aquila, who work with me in Christ Jesus, and who risked their necks for my life, to whom not only I give thanks, but also all the churches of the Gentiles. Greet also the church in their house" (Rom 16:3-5). This shows that in the meantime Prisca and Aquila had returned to Rome, where their original shop had been located. Possibly during the time when they were forced to leave Rome a non-Jewish manager had continued their business there. After their return there was again a community in their house. That would have been their extended family on the one hand, but on the other hand also Roman Christians who regularly assembled in their spacious house.

So the household of Prisca and Aquila gives us a vivid picture of the "new family" Jesus had begun: a normal family that, however, did not live only for themselves and their private interests but put their house wholly at the service of the Gospel. It became a base for Paul's mission, first in Greece and then in Asia Minor, and probably their resettlement in Rome was intended to create a staging point for Paul's planned mission to Spain.

At the same time, the home of Prisca and Aquila became a crystallization point for new communities that grew up around it. They found there the space necessary for their meetings, but not merely space. There was much more: a couple who placed themselves and all that was theirs at the service of the communities. They instructed Apollos in the faith and most certainly many others as well. They stuck out their necks for Paul in Ephesus. All Gentile Christian communities owe them thanks, as Paul says.

In the early days of the church the founding of new communities always depended on whether there were families like that of Prisca and Aquila who were prepared to move from city to city for the sake of the Gospel and in each place to make their home a center for a new community. There was not yet the principle of territorial parishes at any price. The concept of "pastoral care" in the sense of ordained *cura animarum* has existed since only the early Middle Ages. It was marginal to what Paul desired. His first concern was to build up living, easily manageable communities, and those were not laid out on a map. Rather, they depended on people, on believers. The former Cardinal Joseph Ratzinger put it so well: "God did not build his church on principles, but on people."

Paul and His Coworkers

From this point of view in particular—the gathering of people and coworkers—Paul was a genius. This brings me to my fourth point. One need only read the sixteenth chapter of the letter to the Romans to get an impression of how Paul was accustomed to speak of his coworkers: perceptively, lovingly, gratefully, the way one speaks of one's very best friends. He writes:

> Greet my beloved Epaenetus, who was the first convert in [the province of] Asia for Christ. Greet Mary, who has worked very hard among you. Greet Andronicus and Junia, my relatives who were in prison with me; they are [distinguished] apostles, and they were in Christ before I was. Greet Ampliatus, my beloved in the Lord. Greet Urbanus, our coworker in Christ, and my beloved Stachys. Greet Apelles, who is approved in Christ. Greet those who belong to the family of Aristobulus. Greet my relative Herodion. Greet those in the Lord who belong to the family of Narcissus. Greet those workers in the Lord, Tryphaena and Tryphosa. Greet the beloved Persis, who has worked hard in the Lord. Greet Rufus, chosen in the Lord; and greet his mother—a mother to me also. (Rom 16:5-13)

That is only a selection from this closing chapter of the letter to the Romans. If you have paid careful attention you will notice that the number of women mentioned is rather high. It is too bad that this magnificent chapter of greetings is not included in our three-year Sunday lectionary. It is simply suppressed, and so our congregations are deprived of the knowledge of how Paul constantly gathered coworkers around him and how devotedly he speaks of them, from the heart. What a lot of good the spirit of Romans 16 would do our pastors, parish councils, parishes, and parish groups!

The Weak and the Poor

If you have gotten the impression that I am trying to paint a glorified picture of healthy communities free from conflict and a marvelously successful Paul, you have misunderstood. Paul bore heavy burdens; he suffered to the depths of his existence not only from the resistance of Gentile society, not only from ruthless opponents within the church who literally followed him around, trying to turn his communities against him. No, he also suffered because of his communities themselves. After all, Christian community is not a happy ghetto of like-minded people; it is not a cozy corner for ecstatic souls. It is a gathering of people from the widest variety of social origins and almost always with the utmost variety of points of view.

As a matter of course, in the intimate space of the earliest Christian communities gathered in houses, conflicts were much more bitterly obvious than in our parishes, where people all too often take care to insulate themselves from each other and prevent any interference in their private lives. So in the early Christian communities mutual correction, *correctio fraterna*, was something quite familiar. It shows up again and again in Paul's letters. People simply did not live in isolation from one another.

The quarrel between Paul and Peter in Antioch over the question of table companionship of Jewish and Gentile Christians took place, according to the letter to the Galatians (Gal 2:14), "before them all." And what Paul wrote to the community in Corinth about the miserable situation at the Lord's Supper there was certainly read out loud to the assembly, probably before the eucharistic celebration (see 1 Cor 11:17-34). Unfortunately, we do not know how these gatherings were conducted. We would like to have many more details about the concrete lives of the early communities and about Paul's real life, but the available sources offer only limited material to satisfy our curiosity. And yet they do tell us a great deal.

In any case, we know enough that we are in no danger of glorifying community life back then. The Corinthian letters in particular show us a community filled with insecurity, pride, peculiar theological trends, and serious social conflicts. Things would not have been different in other places.

What distinguishes these communities is not their moral integrity or the strength of their faith, still less their unanimity. Nevertheless, Paul speaks of them in the introductions to his letters as "the saints," that is, those "sanctified in Christ Jesus," those "called," those "beloved of God," the *ekklēsia tou theou*, that is, "God's assembly." He thus expresses the fact that what is decisive is not the mistakes that are made; those will always happen. Neither are the theological idiocies crucial; they will never endure. What is decisive is not even sin, as fearful as it is, because it can be forgiven. Rather, what is essential, what determines everything, is that the community knows itself called by God to make God's plan for the world visible and to be a place of constant reconciliation and constantly recovered peace within the world—the Body of Christ.

As Paul says again and again, God has particularly chosen the weak, the poor, the ignorant, the totally incapable in order to work in the world through them (1 Cor 1:18-31), because the clever and wise people of this world are busy cultivating their own wisdom.

In all this I have been trying to remove some of the varnish from the picture of Paul so that the colors of his life may emerge more clearly. This was, in the first place, about the synagogue as catechumenate for the Gentiles, and second, about the role of the Christian house. In the third place I told about a leatherworking shop that was the base for the Pauline mission, and fourth, I have tried to say something about the way Paul gathered coworkers around him and how lovingly he was united with them. You have, of course, noticed that the scarlet thread through all that I have said is the Christian community. If we do not see what Paul invested in building up living communities he will always remain the great unknown for us. But in this connection I must necessarily approach a fifth (and final) point that is absolutely essential. I call it "a theology of history suppressed."

A Theology of History Suppressed

The letter to the Romans not only contains a list of greetings that lets us see deep into Paul's heart. It also includes, in chapters 9–11, a piece of theology of history that was not acknowledged in the church for many centuries—that, in fact, has remained foreign to Christianity to a large extent until today. Had this theology of history remained present to the minds of Christian theologians and the Christian people there could never have existed that Christian anti-Judaism that ultimately made Auschwitz possible.

Paul begins this theology of history with a list of all that God's adopting love had given to God's people Israel in the course of time:

> I have great sorrow and unceasing anguish in my heart. For I could wish that I myself were accursed and cut off from Christ for the sake of my own people, my kindred according to the flesh. They are Israelites, and to them belong the adoption, the glory, the covenants, the giving of the law, the worship, and the promises; to them belong the patriarchs, and from them, according to the flesh, comes the Messiah. (Rom 9:2-5)

The greatest sadness, the deepest sorrow in Paul's life was thus the fact that a large part of Israel had taken offense at Jesus. Paul cannot be content with the fact that only a remnant of Israel, namely, the Jewish-Christian church, has come to believe in the Messiah. What part, he must have asked himself over and over, did the unbelief of by far the larger part of Israel have in God's plan? Paul seeks an answer.

First he says: through the unbelief of the greater part of Israel came the salvation of the Gentiles (cf. Rom 11:11). Paul is thinking quite concretely here. He had always preached first in the synagogues, and only if his own fellow Jews refused to hear him there did he turn to the "uncircumcised"; as we have seen, these were the Gentiles sympathetic to the synagogue. The unbelief of the one thus brought salvation to the other. The rejection by the unbelieving part of Israel led to Gentile Christian communities being formed everywhere. But Paul cannot be content with this thought. That the unbelief of Israel brought salvation to the Gentiles is not an adequate answer for him. He goes a step further.

Paul is convinced that it is precisely the phenomenon of messianic salvation making itself visible in the Gentile Christian communities that will bring Israel, now standing aside, to see what is happening. He formulates his insight this way: "So I ask, have they stumbled so as to fall? By no means! But through their stumbling salvation has come to the Gentiles, so as to make Israel jealous" (Rom 11:11). He means to say that the fascination of the messianic reality that is now taking a social form in the Gentile church will shake Israel and stimulate them to imitation. Israel will see in the Gentile Christian communities that the messianic transformation of the world has already begun, and that very thing will bring it to believe in Jesus as the Messiah. The crucial text toward which the whole argument of the chapter is heading is this: "a hardening has come upon part of Israel, until the full number of the Gentiles has come in. And so all Israel will be saved" (Rom 11:25-26).

This talk of the "coming in" of the Gentiles shows that Paul is thinking of the pilgrimage of the nations that is repeatedly spoken of in the Old Testament. The Gentile nations learn from Israel or even, by coming to faith, perform pilgrimage to the eschatological community of salvation that is Israel. By "the full number of the Gentiles" Paul refers not only to a numerical entity but also to the moment when, through the crowding of the Gentiles toward the eschatological Israel, the fullness of the messianic reality will shine forth, so that it will be evident that the Messiah must already have come.

Then, Paul says, the whole of Israel that until then has remained unbelieving will come to faith. The "fullness" or "full number" of the Gentiles then corresponds to the "fullness" or "full number" of the Jews—and that will appear miraculous in the eyes of the rest of the world, a miracle that will lead to the final turning toward life:

> Now if their stumbling means riches for the world, and if their defeat means riches for Gentiles, how much more will their full inclusion mean! . . . For if their rejection is the reconciliation of the world, what will their acceptance [by God] be but life from the dead! (Rom 11:12, 15)

What is so remarkable about this passage, so remote and strange to us? For Paul, Israel is the basis for the church. The church has not taken Israel's place, nor does it stand at Israel's side; it is the eschatological perfection of Israel. But as long as part of Israel cannot believe, the church as the eschatological Israel is still unfinished, still unperfected, still has not reached its goal.

But how is Israel to come to believe? The still-unbelieving Israel will come to believe by being made "jealous." How shall that be? It will happen if Israel is fascinated by what it sees in the Gentile Christian communities: the messianic power of those communities. So mission occurs here not by a fanaticism for conversion, most certainly not through indoctrination, but through fascination! Paul expects the repentance of the still-unbelieving part of Israel to be brought about because of the messianic radiance of the Gentile Christian communities.

How horribly Paul's expectation has been smashed in the history of the church! Ghettoization instead of brotherly and sisterly neighborliness, forced baptisms instead of conviction brought about by the fascination of messianic communities, persecution instead of fraternal and sororal love! Throughout many centuries, in this way, Paul became the great unknown.

I hope there will never again be persecutions of Jews by Christians. But that is not enough. It would in any case have been absolutely anathema to Paul. The direction of Romans 9–11 is quite different: Christian communities are empowered to live in such a way that a radiance goes forth from them that will let Israel see that the Messiah must already have come. The messianic abundance is already breaking forth.

What trust Paul shows in the power of God! How much he relies on God's mighty acts in the Christian communities! And what an idea of the church he has! Do we believe in the picture of the church Paul teaches when he says, "we, who are many, are one body in Christ, and individually we are members one of another" (Rom 12:5)? I believe that here, precisely at this point, Paul remains profoundly unknown to us. Are we really aware that every community is the Body of Christ? That is not something purely internal, purely spiritual, purely mystical! The image of the body refers to a visible social unit where people have joined their lives together. Here Paul is still a stranger to us.

But we have to overcome that gap, for here, at this point, the future of faith in Europe and elsewhere will be decided. Will our parishes become living communities that witness to Christ through their lives, through their way of being together; communities that show through their unanimity that redemption is real; congregations that show by their constant reconciliation that there can be peace for this world?

You may be thinking, "Oh, community; he talks all the time about community!" Is that really so important for faith? Yes, absolutely! Without the theme of "community" we will never understand Paul. It is no contradiction, none at all, to his great theme of justification and salvation through Christ alone, for the church and its congregations are for Paul the Body of Christ, the real space in which salvation through Jesus Christ takes place and becomes visible.

I am certainly aware that we cannot translate the form of early Christian communities in all its individual elements into our present church. That would be sentimental romanticizing of the primitive church. But if the church is not to become paralyzed it must, like any living thing, grow continually into new forms and shapes. And yet at the same time the spirit and the fundamental structures of the apostolic period must be retained; otherwise the cells in the church body will sicken and become incapable of living. The question of the right shape for our communities remains one of the fundamental issues in the present church, and in this regard we can learn infinitely much from Paul.

Chapter 16

How a Sacrament Works

The church's sacraments are something precious, but anything precious is always in danger of becoming routine. I am thinking especially of the Eucharist. Approaching the communion rail has become a simple matter of course for many people. Communion is part of the Mass (something that was not true for many even through the nineteenth century). We get used to everything, even the most beautiful and priceless; it becomes a habit.

This is true in all areas of human life. What brilliance there can be in the first encounter with someone—and how bleak and gruesome do many marriages, and most certainly many "partnerships," seem after only a few years! Erich Kästner depicted this situation in his poem, "Sachliche Romanze," as follows:

> When they had known each other for eight years
> (and it is true to say they knew each other well),
> their love suddenly got lost,
> as other people lose a cane or a hat.
>
> They were sad, they tried to be nice,
> they exchanged kisses, as if nothing were wrong,
> and looked at each other and knew not how to go on.
> Finally, she wept. And he just stood there.

From their window you could wave at the ships.
He said it was already a quarter past four
and time to go somewhere and drink coffee—
next door someone was practicing the piano.

They went to the tiniest café in the place
and stirred and stirred their cups.
By nightfall they were still sitting there.
They sat alone and spoke not a word
and simply couldn't grasp it.[1]

Thus Kästner's masterful poem about how love can get lost. The couple's love did not vanish "suddenly," of course. Kästner's use of "suddenly" simply describes the abrupt awareness. In such cases it is usually preceded by a long erosion in which the foundation of union gradually crumbles. In the end the loveliest symbols and gestures ("they exchanged kisses, as if nothing were wrong") become utterly empty and meaningless actions.

Isn't it much the same with us and the sacraments? They have become the normal thing for us; they no longer shake us and turn our lives around. Above all, the Eucharist, the center of Christian life and the sacrament of Christ's most profound presence, is threatened by this reduction to routine and gradually becomes more and more fragile.

A Classic Definition

But I don't want to begin with the Eucharist in my attempt to bring myself and you closer to the sacraments again; instead, I will start with a sacrament that is celebrated much less often and therefore more strongly radiates the original brilliance that is proper to all the sacraments. I mean holy orders.

The sacramental action that gives priests their authority to act *in persona Christi capitis*, in the place of Christ, the head of the church, has a clearly visible and unmistakable high point: when, after the reading of the gospel, the address of the bishop, and the solemn litany of all the saints, the candidates for ordination kneel before the bishop and, while the assembly keeps silence, the bishop lays hands on each one's head. Other priests who are present join in this gesture, laying their hands on the candidates for ordination. Then the bishop, surrounded by the presbytery, sings the ordination preface, which summons the Holy Spirit on the candidates for ordination. It is precisely at this climactic point in the ordination of priests that we can see most vividly illustrated what a sacrament is. Let me first give a definition of what Catholic theology understands a sacrament to be.

I must preface this by saying that this definition can in no way encompass the wealth of the whole church's sacramental theology, above all, that of the patristic and medieval periods. I choose it primarily because it plays a major role in the catechisms of the Roman Catholic Church. So I will refer to it first. In the course of this chapter I will certainly go beyond it. But for now, the simple definition:

> A sacrament is a visible sign [the whole of the sign includes the interpretive word], instituted by Christ, that points to an invisible reality and, through the church and within its life, gives a share in that reality.

Now let us simply test whether this classic definition of sacramental theology applies to the ordination of priests.

Holy Orders as an Example

The ordination of a priest involves a number of visible signs: the candidates' prostration during the Litany of the Saints, the anointing of their hands with chrism, the presentation of chalice and paten, and the exchange of peace with the bishop. But the central sign that is indispensable for the ordination of a priest is the imposition of hands by the bishop. This laying on of hands, while all those present are silent, is so eloquent that probably most believers assume that the sacrament is thus conveyed. But that is a mistake, because the sign of the laying on of hands must be joined with another, namely, the word, in this case the preface for ordinations, which calls down the Holy Spirit.

The preface is here as essential as the imposition of hands. We can illustrate the necessity of the addition of words by considering the sacrament of baptism. In that sacrament, nowadays, water is poured on the head of the baptizand. In the early days of the church the person being baptized was immersed entirely in water (and then anointed with blessed oil). But if the word, namely, the baptismal formula, "I baptize you in the Name of the Father, and of the Son, and of the Holy Spirit" (the trinitarian baptismal confession in the early church), were not spoken, baptism would be theologically indistinguishable from a bedtime bath or a quick wash in the morning.

So the sign dimension of the sacraments includes not only visible signs such as pouring water, anointing with oil, eating bread, the laying on of hands but also the word that always accompanies these; originally it was most often a solemn appeal for the Holy Spirit. This accompanying and clarifying word that makes a sacrament truly a sacrament is not visible, but it is audible, so it is just as much a sign as the imposition of hands. It is a sign that interprets the visible action and makes its meaning clear. After all, language is also part of the world of signs. For modern semiotics that is obvious: language is nothing but a system of signs.

But now to address another part of our definition: "The visible sign points to an invisible reality and gives a share in that invisible reality." What, in priestly ordination, is the invisible reality to which the complex of signs points? That is quite clear: it is Christ's sending the apostles to proclaim the reign of God and to gather the people of God, for laying on of hands was already a visible sign of mission in the New Testament (cf., for example, Acts 13:1-3).

Within the complex of signs at priestly ordination the bishop represents Jesus Christ himself, who sends his disciples to all the people in Israel and then to the ends of the earth. So within the framework of the sacramental event the bishop represents Jesus Christ. The bishop's imposition of hands is a sign of the authority that Jesus once gave his apostles and that he gives in the same way today, as the Risen and Exalted One—an authority priests cannot take for themselves but can only receive.

So we must say that something that happened two thousand years ago, namely, the sending of the apostles, enters our present in the ordination of priests; it becomes tangible, visible, audible reality. At that time Jesus Christ empowered his apostles and sent them forth. In the sacrament, that past reality becomes present. When in some cathedral in Germany, on the feast of Saints Peter and Paul, men are ordained priests, exactly the same thing takes place as what once happened in the year 30: in the person of the bishop, Jesus Christ himself empowers the candidates for ordination and sends them to proclaim the Gospel and gather the people of God. The external sign thus points to something invisible; indeed, the external sign, including the preface for ordinations, gives the candidates a share in that invisible, apparently long-ago event.

Anointing of the Sick as an Example

Something similar is true of the anointing of the sick. When the priest, in place of the bishop, anoints the forehead and hands of the recipient with oil and speaks the interpreting word, the celebrant is doing nothing other than what Jesus did for the sick and suffering in Israel. Jesus repeatedly healed sick people and spoke God's forgiveness to those who had fallen into sin. Jesus wanted to bring Israel to the condition that was intended for it from the beginning: Israel is to be "the world" under the rule of God. And life under God's rule can only be conceived as *healed* living.

It is true that the "healing" of humans has many dimensions. It can mean being freed from an illness, but it can also mean becoming whole within, achieving inner peace, placing one's whole life in God's hand, being reconciled to God and other human beings, and in this way becoming whole and healthy. The path to that state passes by way of repentance, away from one's own ideas and patterns of behavior and toward God's saving thoughts. We should note these several dimensions of "healing." It is not only a question of healing the body; it is just as much about the healing of life, of one's own history. There are so many things we drag around with us: wounds, irritations, things unspoken, unredeemed, confused, unclarified—and above all the guilt that burdens us. All those things are among our illnesses; all stand contrary to the brilliance of the reign of God. The whole requires healing.

The New Testament shows how Jesus' healing activity continued among the disciples and apostles after Jesus' death and resurrection. They not only visited the sick and comforted them; no, their task was to *heal* the sick. They were meant to cure them, that is, to overcome evil at its roots: "As you go, proclaim the good news, 'The kingdom of heaven has come near.' Cure the sick, raise the dead, cleanse the lepers, cast out demons!" (Matt 10:7-8). Over the centuries the church has always known that it has this commission to heal. And so the anointing of the sick also joins us directly to Jesus, healing and blessing, opening for us all the reality of the saving reign of God.

But how is such a thing possible? How do the sacraments do that? How are they able to join us directly to Jesus and his praxis of the reign of God? How do they manage to leap over time and unite us to the actions of the earthly Jesus and the apostles?

This brings me to the real question of this chapter: how does a sacrament work? In order not to go astray in attempting an answer, I would like first to describe two positions that are not at all uncommon but are certainly false. The first imagines that the working of the sacraments is "magical," while the second says the sacraments are "only" signs, "only" symbols, "only" aids to thought, "only" visualizations—that they are to be thought of as a kind of pious didactic tool but accomplish nothing by themselves.

The Temptation to Magic

First let me speak about the first notion, that the sacraments are acts of magic: the best example of such an idea is found in the eighth chapter of Acts. There we read of a man in Samaria named Simon, who earns his living as a magician and miraculous healer. As usually happens with healers and people who pray for healing, he had a huge following. When he saw how the apostles laid hands on those who came to believe and so gave them the Holy Spirit—the fact that they had received the Holy Spirit was obvious from their joy and enthusiasm—that is, as Simon saw the effects of reception of the Spirit, he wanted to have that same "power." He went to the apostles and offered them hard money, hoping they would sell him the ability to convey the Spirit and to heal.

How, according to Acts 8, did this Simon imagine the Holy Spirit? Evidently he thought of it as a kind of *mana*. The word originally comes from Polynesian culture, where it means "effective" or "powerful." *Mana* has become a specialized term in religious studies to refer to a potential for power concentrated in persons and objects, weapons and utensils, but also in relics and graves. It can be beneficial, but it can also be highly dangerous. It is possible to cause *mana* to flow, to transfer it to others, to accumulate it, but also to lose it again. Simply think of the power potential of an electrical charge. People thought of *mana* as a cosmic power, a flowing energy, a life force that heals and gives a higher quality of life but that can also vanish, leaving illness and evil behind it. This notion of *mana* was widespread among ancient peoples.

But many of our contemporaries think the same way. You only need to leaf through ads for wellness cures to find the old idea of *mana* gussied up in modern dress. To quote from the wellness pamphlet advertising a German spa: "As your skin is stroked and gently massaged with silk gloves, your body will nestle itself into the positive vibrations of our spa bath, in which countless people have for centuries found their way back to themselves. After the massage you will walk sensitively and with feeling over our barefoot path of fine sand and stimulating pebbles and feel the powers of the earth streaming into you . . . ," etc. The composers of advertising texts spread this dishonest language on us nowadays like butter on bread. If only it really *were* butter! It is more like cheap margarine manufactured by the word industry.

In the popular notion of *mana*, then, human salvation is something like a cosmic power potential that can pour into human persons or be transferred to them. I suspect, unfortunately, that in our worship services some people still think in fundamentally magical terms when receiving a blessing (for example, on St. Blaise's day) or taking the host at Communion, namely, that at such a time a kind of divine power potential flows over one and makes one whole and healthy.

We must say a determined farewell to such ideas. The Christian sacraments have nothing to do with magic; they are something altogether different. Communion is not medicine and most certainly not a drug. It is encounter, direct and immediate encounter with Jesus Christ.

It is quite another matter that when God acts in us that action can take place through the natural forces in the world, nature, the soul, the wisdom collected through the course of history. Above all, God acts on us through other people; it is in them that God encounters us, as well as through events and even objects. To put it another way: God always acts on us through creation and history, never outside of or contrary to creation and history. But what is crucial is that it is God who acts. The sacraments are about the coming of the reign of God, and consequently God's actions have nothing to do with magic, nor do the sacraments. It is not human beings who set divine powers in motion through the sacraments; instead, in the sacraments it is God who acts.

Only a Sign?

But now to the second position I mentioned, which is equally false: this says that the sacraments are "only" signs or "only" symbols; they simply offer us a kind of illustration or assurance but accomplish nothing in themselves. What gives us grace is faith only. The sacraments, it is said, are only *posterior* concretizations and illustrations, memorial signs for what has already occurred in the act of faith.

The Catholic churches have rightly objected to this, the Roman Catholic Church above all at the Council of Trent, which said that the sacraments are not mere secondary means of making visible a grace that is given independently of them; rather, they *effect* grace, they themselves mediate it. But how do they do that? How is it possible without magic and sacramental flim-flam? This brings us finally to the real question that is of interest here, namely, how does a sacrament work?

I will attempt an answer in three steps. The first speaks of the presence of the risen Christ. The second considers how we can enter into that presence. The third expands on the second and speaks of the church as the fundamental sacrament. At the end I will then show how all creation reveals certain similarities to what happens in the sacraments.

The Presence of the Risen One

I fear we are not often clear about how radically resurrection must be thought. Resurrection does *not* mean that our life continues with God in the same form as we have lived it here—in a rhythm of hours, days, and years, located within a space that encompasses us and that we cannot escape. In the resurrection, earthly time ceases to move forward; rather, the resurrection is the sum of all the time we have lived in the world, transformed and glorified. Resurrection is the harvest of our history.

What we have lived in the many years of our lives will be transfigured into a new form of existence with God that we cannot even imagine. Resurrection is history gathered together. In it everything we have lived and everything belonging to the history of our life will become a concentrated present, beyond all passing time. In the resurrection all earthly time will be abolished, and the past of our life will be transformed into pure presence.

But we must think of the reality of resurrection just as radically as far as space is concerned. In our earthly existence we are always tied to the space that surrounds and encloses us. When I am in Munich, I cannot be simultaneously in Paris. I am harnessed to the coordinates not only of time but also of space. But resurrection is the removal of limits not only of time but also of space. The resurrection body is no longer bound to earthly space. It is beyond all space. Here it is also true that it is pure presence.

I have said all this in general about the reality of resurrection, but properly I should have formulated it in light of the risen Christ and even in view of the thought on resurrection that was already being developed in Old Testament Israel. In any case, the truth is that without Jesus Christ there would be no resurrection for us. Christ is the "firstborn from the dead" (1 Cor 15:20) and thus the ground and the first, the beginning of all resurrection from the dead. Ultimately it is only possible to grasp what resurrection is in light of Jesus Christ.

But it is true to say of Christ, the Risen and Exalted One, that in him his whole life, everything he said, everything he did and suffered, up to his death on the cross, is forever present. The Fourth Gospel expresses this by saying that the wounds were still visible on the body of Christ risen and glorified (John 20:19-29). And Revelation describes the already exalted Christ as the lamb that is slain (Rev 5:6). Such statements presuppose real experience. The disciples who "saw" Jesus after Easter experienced him as the Risen One, but as the One in whom his whole history, his whole earthly activity, and above all his suffering, as glorified suffering, are risen as well.

Thus the Risen One is present to us with his whole life, everything that was in him and made him, his Good News, his sending of the apostles, and his passion. He is present as the whole Christ, but not as someone who carries his past around with him as mere past; instead, he is the one who *is* his past, the one who preaches, heals, sends, hangs on the cross, rises from the dead. The existence of the Risen One is living presence and thus no longer subject to our space and time.

This all means that the Risen One is pure, unimaginable presence. He is so close to us that we cannot conceive it. In terms of space, he is not somewhere distant. In terms of time, he is not somewhere in the past. He is closer to us than we are to ourselves. That is the first, the basic precondition for understanding how a sacrament works: the Risen One—and he is, in fact, the epitome of all grace and salvation—is indescribably close to us, together with his whole life.

But how can this ungraspable closeness come to us? Here I must take the second step in my reflections, asking how we can enter into this immediacy of the Risen One. And at this very point we must think more precisely about the concept of sign.

Sign as Communication

There are many kinds of signs in our world. You might say that we are surrounded by signs, everywhere and unremittingly. For example, when I drive my car I constantly encounter all sorts of signs. It begins as soon as I start off: uh oh, I haven't fastened my seat belt! My VW Golf immediately produces an acoustic sign to encourage me to put on my seat belt right away. A few minutes later comes another sound: the external temperature has fallen below thirty degrees Fahrenheit. That means I may have to watch out for ice on the road. And so on.

If, before I start on a trip to an unfamiliar destination, I set my GPS, the display lights up with a whole series of optical signs: a stylized Autobahn sign as an icon for the navigation menu, a stylized strip of film as an icon for the choice of video displays, a stylized loudspeaker as an icon for music, a stylized traffic sign, which directs me to the menu listing road repairs and traffic jams along the route I have chosen—and so on. I won't even begin to talk about the hordes of traffic signs that line the roads and most certainly not about the millions of abbreviations and acronyms that make life easier, such as Matt, Rom, Heb, Inc., US, SJ,

WCC, UAW, POTUS, BBC, PBS, and on and on. In short: modern life is alive with signals, symbols, icons, and abbreviations.

But there are other signs in our lives that are much more important and also much more human than all the mechanical signs that clever people have invented at one time or another. Suppose I am standing somewhere in the Munich airport. Passengers are arriving from a long flight from America. A lot of people have been waiting an hour already for those who are coming; the flight is late. To my right and left there are wild scenes of greeting. Right in front of me a man and a woman embrace, hugging each other as if they would never let go. I see tears. Between hugs they draw back and look at each other as if to make sure that the other is really there. I don't need to go on describing the scene.

Such greetings and embraces also fall within the category of signs, but different kinds of signs from traffic shields and graphic symbols. These are familiar, intimate signs exchanged between persons. And here we are very close to what we already proposed as a definition for the sacraments: a visible sign that expresses something invisible. The visible sign is the embrace, the kissing, the whispering in the ear. And the invisible? It is the love between the two, the bond between two persons, the communion of two people. And yet this invisible reality needs to be made visible. But at the same time, the visible needs the invisible; otherwise the embrace would be empty, soulless, and a dreadful externality. Remember:

> They were sad, they tried to be nice,
> they exchanged kisses, as if nothing were wrong,
> and looked at each other and knew not how to go on.
> Finally, she wept. And he just stood there.

This is important: when the two people met in the airport the mutual love, the invisible bond between the two, was apparently there already. What had already been present for a long time wanted to express itself anew and physically. But it also happens that mutual love comes to expression for the first time: the first tender touch, the first kiss, the first embrace. Then it is a matter not of deepening and renewing something already there but of beginning something.

Everything I have just described falls within what sociologists call communication events. They too would distinguish between the external and internal sides of each communication, and they would also say that every communication, without exception, takes place through signs; of course, language is also a type of sign. Finally, they would say that signs strengthen and deepen communication but can also initiate it.

Jesus and the World of Signs

At this point I have to point out once again that the sign dimension also played a decisive role in the life of Jesus. He healed sick people again and again—but how? He touched them; he laid hands on them. He put his fingers into the ears of the deaf. He made mud out of dirt and saliva and spread it on the eyes of the blind. But he not only healed the sick; he embraced and blessed children, ate and drank with toll collectors and sinners. He washed his disciples' feet and celebrated the Last Supper with them.

All these signs reach deep into the bodiliness of human beings and take it seriously. Of course, these physical gestures were always accompanied by Jesus' words. The word, itself a sign, a linguistic sign, takes away the undefined and ambiguous character of actions. Jesus joined signs with words as a single whole. To that extent everything he did already had a basic sacramental structure. The post-Easter sacraments are all grounded in the actions of the earthly Jesus. In fact, we must go much further back: sacramental reality extends deep into Old Testament Israel. Consider the circumcision of males: the theologians of the early church had no problem at all in calling it a "sacrament of the Old Testament."[2] I think also of the sign-actions of the prophets, combining visible signs and audible, interpreting words. I cannot go into all the details here; that would take us too far afield.

So let me return to Jesus. After Easter, what the earthly Jesus had begun was further developed as the sacraments became a communication between the risen Christ and Christians. This encounter, this communication, takes place in signs: in the sign-action and the word that accompanies it. Everyone who receives a sacrament encounters Christ and is received into the life, death, and resurrection of Jesus. This encounter is mediated by the sacramental signs.

All this has probably made it clear that to talk of a sacrament as "only" a sign or "only" a symbol is not only naïve but positively stupid. Real encounter, real becoming-one can take place for us in this world only through signs. (And let me here emphasize again that language is always part of this web of signs.) Imagine a marriage in which the partners no longer speak to one another, in which the whole day long not a word is exchanged, in which there are no more tender glances, no tendernesses, no touches, no kisses, no embraces. That marriage will end very soon, or rather, it is already at an end. Signs are essential to human beings; without them we cannot exist. They open communication and create encounter ever anew.

To this world of signs that saturates everything belong the sacraments as well. They are thus something profoundly human, something indispensable. They make possible the encounter between the risen Christ, always present to us, and those who believe. They build the bridge between the visible and the invisible, between time and eternity—or we might better say between earthly time and the glorified time present with God.

Signs That Are Given

Now let me present an objection of my own. A sacrament has nothing to do with magic; no drugs are shared; no *mana* is conveyed. But it is not a mere memorial sign. It is genuine encounter, uniting—put simply, it is communion. And now the objection: how can a human being presume such an encounter, such a union with the Risen One? In the airport scene two people approached one another, two human beings who are, so to speak, on the same level and see eye to eye. Each brought her or his own love to the encounter; each was equally giver and receiver. But can we say the same thing of our encounter with Christ in the sacraments? Are we *partners* in it? Are we not solely and exclusively recipients? Can we and may we in any way think of this encounter in terms of the encounters we are used to? Have we not overlooked something fundamental?

I consider this objection justified and even necessary. It can help us to make more precise what we have already said. In a human encounter like the one I have described, one party can begin, for example, by fondly embracing the other, taking the other in her or his arms. It is different with a sacrament; there we cannot take the initiative. We cannot say: now I am going to meet Christ. The encounter with Christ is not something the human being can bring about, arrange, precipitate, certainly not compel. It is always something imparted and given. How could we possibly, of ourselves, approach the reality of the Risen One, even though he is so near to us?

So Christ himself must take the initiative, must give the sacraments, must institute the encounter. The sacraments are gifts, presents from the Risen One to us. You will notice that I am repeating the statement that was part of our definition from the beginning: "A sacrament is a visible sign instituted by Christ . . ." The institution of the sacraments by Christ is in fact something essential and indispensable, because it says: it is not *we* who can open the event of communication. The encounter with the Risen One in the sacrament is instead pure gift arising solely out of his love. We ourselves cannot open the door to the world of the Risen One; every time we receive a sacrament, it is opened to us by him.

We should not, however, think of the gift of the sacraments by Christ as if he had instituted each individual sacrament in a separate juridical act. Jesus most certainly did not do that, nor was it necessary. What he instituted was the church as the new, eschatological Israel that was to be gathered, and the church is itself a sacramental reality. The church is sacrament, and all the sacraments are nothing other than the fulfillment of the church's essential reality. I want to speak of this now in a third step, the most important of the three we are taking together.

Church as Basic Sacrament

In one of his books the great theologian Romano Guardini asked himself the question: how can we ever know that God is real? His answer was: we can only know it by looking at Jesus Christ. He is the image of the invisible God, the icon of God. From Jesus' words and actions we experience who God really and ultimately is.

But then Guardini asks, more penetratingly: and how do we know who Jesus was? Are there not many images of Jesus, assertions about Jesus, different interpretations, conflicting opinions about him? His answer: ultimately it is only through the faith of the church that we know who Jesus was. Only in the faith of the church, only in the company of the faithful, only on the basis of believing communities do we find access to the real Jesus.[3]

This insight is crucial also for our understanding of the sacraments. The encounter with Christ in the sacraments that I have been speaking about is not a private encounter between Christ and the believer. Every sacramental encounter takes place on the soil of the church or it does not happen at all. I would like to illustrate this with what seems at first an external phenomenon. If someone asks you how many sacraments there are, you will immediately say "seven." And that is quite correct. But we have to be clear about the fact that these seven individual sacraments are only developments and expressions of the fundamental sacrament that is the church. How is it that we can call the church a sacrament? Very simply because it is something visible and yet is grounded on something invisible: Jesus Christ, the Risen and Exalted One. He is preached in the church, and he acts on those who believe in him. Where two or three are gathered in his name, he is in their midst (cf. Matt 18:20). Our definition of sacrament thus applies not only to the seven individual sacraments but also to the church as a whole. That is why recent theology calls the church the "basic sacrament."

This insight is of extraordinary importance for our question about how a sacrament works, because it makes it clear that the encounter between the risen Christ and the believing Christian is not a meeting of two individual, discrete persons. The Risen One is not alone; he is surrounded by the saints, those who have reached the completion of their lives. And I as a believer am not alone. I could not believe at all without the others. I could not follow Jesus without many other people. *A* Christian (alone) is *no* Christian.

That is why the sacramental encounter with Christ always takes place on the soil of a community. And when someone seeks the external ritual of a sacrament but not life in the church, in the congregation, the sacrament threatens to become a perversion. In such a case the sacrament is ripped from the soil in which it is rooted, and it can only wither. It cannot bear fruit.

The church is the basic sacrament, and all the individual sacraments are expressions of the church's essence. This is a theological insight we must relearn. At First Communion, at confirmation, and at the ordination of priests we have somehow always known that: these were occasions for the whole congregation to celebrate. It was certainly obvious in the celebration of the Eucharist. We know—at least since the twentieth-century renewal of the liturgy—that the Eucharist is a shared meal that draws us into Jesus' sacrifice of his life and also into his resurrection.

This has been more difficult with regard to baptism. I myself was baptized in a hospital chapel. There was no congregation present, only my family and the sponsor. The same was true for many of us. Only gradually, in the last decades, have our parishes come to understand that baptism is a celebration for the whole community and not only for the family involved. It is still more blatant with regard to the sacrament of marriage, in which the couple say an eternal yes to one another and affirm that their union reflects the love between Christ and the church. Such a thing cannot be a private matter for the families concerned. A marriage is something for the whole congregation. The community, after all, must help the marriage to succeed, and it must be there to assist when a marriage is in crisis. How far removed we are from all that!

And what can we say about the sacrament of reconciliation? Do we still remember that constant reconciliation is something the whole parish must do? Obviously this is not to detract from the absolute intimacy of the confessional; obviously the secret of the confessional remains sacred. And yet mutual reconciliation in anticipation of the sacrament of reconciliation and beyond the confessional is a matter for the whole parish. This sacrament, like all the others, must have a space and frame of its own, namely, the common life of the community, which offers mutual aid and strengthens faith. Only in such a space can the sacraments bear fruit; only there do they develop their full power.

You will have noticed that we have moved into a broader field. The sacraments are genuine encounters of each individual with Christ, but they presuppose the foundational sacrament "church" or "community." The present crisis of the church in Europe and elsewhere consists precisely in this, that the sacraments have become detached from the basic sacrament "church" and for many have become mere rituals. That would require a long discussion.

But my primary interest here is to show how the sacraments are rooted in the human, to make it clear how deeply they match our bodiliness, though that is always saturated and formed by spirit. The church's sacraments are not something abstruse; they are not magic, not hocus-pocus. They are the absolute culmination of what happens constantly in our lives, namely, that we communicate uninterruptedly with one another through signs. The sacraments are the highest and loveliest form of all human signs. They are signs given us by Jesus Christ, in which he joins himself with us on the soil of the church and in which our eternal encounter with God is already anticipated.

The Cosmic Dimension

Before I close, let me point to a very special aspect of the sacraments. As we have seen, there are many elements belonging to the nature of sacraments, among others that in them the invisible reveals itself in the visible. Nonetheless, this important structure, which is proper to all the sacraments, is true of creation as a whole. We are surrounded by visible and audible realities: flowers, trees, meadows, forests, rivers, lakes, mountains, stars, animals, human beings. We see around us a wealth of human faces and hear countless voices, from the sound of the sea to the harmonies of language. All about us we find an infinitely rich creation that addresses us in various colors, forms, and voices.

But what does it speak of? The great theologians of the early church as well as those of the Middle Ages were convinced that the whole creation is structured so as to speak to us about God. The wisdom teachers of the Old Testament had the same conviction. They were certain that all things were originally made to speak to us about God, that is, to be transparent to God in order that God can be known in them. This is expressed with particular beauty in Psalm 104, which sings of God's glory in the works of creation:

> Bless the LORD, O my soul.
>> O LORD my God, you are very great.
> . . .
> You make springs gush forth in the valleys;
>> they flow between the hills,
>> giving drink to every wild animal;
>> the wild asses quench their thirst.
> By the streams the birds of the air
>> have their habitation;
>> they sing among the branches.
> From your lofty abode you water the mountains;
>> the earth is satisfied with the fruit of your work.
> You cause the grass to grow for the cattle,
>> and plants for people to use,
>> to bring forth food from the earth,
>> and wine to gladden the human heart,
>> oil to make the face shine,
>> and bread to strengthen the human heart.
> The trees of the LORD are watered abundantly,
>> the cedars of Lebanon that he planted.
> In them the birds build their nests;
>> the stork has its home in the fir trees.
> The high mountains are for the wild goats;
>> the rocks are a refuge for the coneys.
> You have made the moon to mark the seasons;
>> the sun knows its time for setting.
> You make darkness, and it is night,
>> when all the animals of the forest
>> come creeping out.
> The young lions roar for their prey,
>> seeking their food from God.
> When the sun rises, they withdraw
>> and lie down in their dens.

People go out to their work
> and to their labor until the evening.
O LORD, how manifold are your works!
> In wisdom you have made them all;
>> the earth is full of your creatures. (Ps 104:1, 10-24)

What an intriguing and blissful perception of reality! Wild asses, storks, wild goats, young lions—this sweeping view encompasses them all. "The earth is full of God's creatures." And this very regarding of the whole creation in its abundance and concreteness must lead to praise of God, as Psalm 104 formulates it at the very beginning, setting the program for the whole:

> Bless the LORD, O my soul.
>> O LORD my God, you are very great.

The psalm says in its own way what is found in Isaiah's call vision:

> Holy, holy, holy is the LORD of hosts;
>> The whole earth is full of his glory. (Isa 6:3)

You notice, of course, that if one can regard the whole creation in such a way that it is transparent toward God and leads to praise of the Creator, this is already a manifestation of something we have recognized as one of the basic structures of the sacraments: the visible becomes a sign of the invisible. The visible creation becomes a sign of the invisible God. This does not mean, of course, that creation is itself a sacrament in the proper sense, but it reveals a basic structure that it has in common with the sacraments.

Evidently God intended creation to reflect the glory of the Creator through a thousand facets. But this means that creation has a kind of sacramental structure. The visible is a medium for the invisible. Visible creation is transparent to the invisible glory of God. Thus fundamentally the whole universe is a basis for the sacraments themselves. And yet— then comes the "but." This is how we really should perceive things, but we all know that is not so. For the most part we see the world differently. Our eyes behold the infinite suffering in the world, its misery, its dark places, the unending conflicts and catastrophes of history. We see the hunger, sickness, death. And even nature can present itself in ways that make us shudder: in the coldness of space, in natural catastrophes, in the apparently absurd cycle of eating and being eaten.

Reinhold Schneider, in his book, *Winter in Wien*, writes of a visit to the Vienna Museum of Natural History, where he saw Japanese crabs that seemed to him like something out of the Inferno. Then he describes a frog "that, standing erect like a human being, was sucked dry by a leech that wrapped itself around it." In the same context he speaks of the "absurd architecture" of the dinosaurs, which he calls "cathedrals of absurdity" as "a will to live that cannot live." Then he writes:

> The horror is that human forms wind through the monsters: the dinosaur's knee recalls a human knee, and the fivefoldness of fingers and toes appears again in the elephant seal's flippers. The loveliest bird snatches the most beautiful butterfly in its flight, plucks off its wings and lets them float away while it devours the tender body that, during its short life, was content with a little nectar and, defenseless, gave to the world its play of colors, a bolt from the hands of the Father. It seems also as if a green-gold shimmering beetle had been created solely for the destruction of roses. I saw it at work in Muzot. Unclean disaccord, it spared not a rose. And the face of the Father? That is wholly incomprehensible to us.[4]

How is it that creation, which as a whole truly should be something similar to a sacrament—that is, revealing the brilliance of the visible God's invisible glory—so often appears not as a sacrament but rather as a disgusting contrariety, a bizarre absurdity, a dark mask that conceals God instead of revealing?

To give a sensible answer we need first to consider some very simple things that Reinhold Schneider passes over far too quickly: the fact that we are repelled by things that sting, stick, or stink, that are slimy and hairy, crawling and crunching (as when, for example, a lion gnaws the bones of a young gazelle), that they evoke alienation and disgust in us, is not simply objective. It presupposes the development of some very particular cultural points of view.

There are tribes that devour earthworms with pleasure and enjoyment, while the very idea is nauseating to many Europeans or Americans. There are countries in which roast dog is a banquet. The world can, after all, be experienced in very different ways. I get annoyed when a mosquito attacks and bites me, but on the wall of my office is a photograph of a mosquito, very much enlarged and backlit; with its beating wings it is almost the image of an angel. Biologists in particular often see and experience slimy or hairy, long-legged or spiky little beings quite differently from the average observer. I once knew an arachnologist who was spellbound by the beauty of spiders; his wife was not allowed to kill a spider in their house. Their marriage nearly broke up over it.

To make a long story short: we are simply unable to take an objective view of creation. Our point of view is not only formed by evolution but even has theological backgrounds. It is also connected to the disastrous history that shapes us much more deeply than we suspect. Our ability to fully appreciate the glory and the dimensions of meaning in creation is restricted. We got here through a long history of sin, a constantly renewed story of human refusal, a history in which the ancient burdens of human guilt have steadily piled up—in short, a universal history of sin and guilt that disrupts and distorts our view of creation. It is not that nature itself is evil or disgusting, but it quite often appears so to us because our vision is dulled. In truth, creation and history should be absolutely transparent to God, but they are so no longer, because the latent guilt in history has shrouded our eyes. We can no longer appreciate what creation really is.

For that reason, and only because of that, God began a counter-history within the darkness of this history of sin and guilt. God created one people for God's self, in the midst of all the nations, in order to make visible in that people how the world really ought to be. Therefore Israel exists, and the church as the eschatological Israel; therefore the sacraments exist as the expression of the church's nature, in order that here, at least, the beauty of creation and with it the meaning of the world may appear.

The sacraments are thus a restoration of creation, intended to make God's world appear. They are to make the brilliance of creation visible once again. They give us a share in God's new creation.

The Sacraments and the Cross

Now yet another "but": if our eyes are clouded by sin because the ancient burdens of the human history of sin and guilt are so heavy, if human sin really spoils and defaces the earth, then the sacraments cannot simply draw back a curtain and make the world stage appear illuminated by shining beams of light. No, the world's misery, which we have caused, has its cost and cannot simply be eliminated at the wave of a magic wand. When people have taken action against the multitude of human sins it has quite often cost them their lives. It has taken the lives of many, many prophets. When John the Baptizer opened his mouth, it cost him his life. When Jesus preached and lived the reign of God, it was at the price of his life. But with his death he also showed us, at last, the way out of our misery, so that in following him we ourselves can journey on that same path.

Therefore all the sacraments, which in themselves ought to show us the glory of creation, are also indispensably connected to Jesus' passion and death. Baptism means dying with Christ, and it is only in that dying with him that our rising with him can occur. The sacrament of reconciliation means placing oneself now already under the final judgment and in that judgment, through the mercy of God, being acquitted and set free. Eucharist means participation in Jesus' last meal, and the bread that is broken there is participation in his death, the crushing of his body, his self-surrender. Likewise the wine he gave to his disciples: it is a participation in his blood. The ordination of priests is certainly their authorization and empowerment to speak and act *in persona Christi.* But those who do that share also in the fate that fell upon Jesus: rejection and often disappointment after disappointment.

So, because of the distortion of creation by sin, every sacrament is at the same time a participation in Jesus' suffering and death. That is an aspect of the sacraments that must not be suppressed, any more than the other aspect, that all sacraments give a share in Jesus' glory and the brilliance of his resurrection. All sacraments lead to the cross. Nevertheless, they give us a share in resurrection to new life. And because the resurrection is beginning already through the seven sacraments, they all have something festal about them.

Every baptism is a festival of the people of God, a crossing over into God's new world. Every celebration of the Eucharist is a feast, the beginning of the eternal banquet with God. Even the sacrament of reconciliation is a festival: liberation from the burden of guilt and the realization of what Jesus described in the parable of the lost son. Every sacrament, despite its link to Jesus' passion, is already the beginning of what eventually will be the final reality: resurrection. But it is so with an important difference: in life with God, when we have crossed over the boundary of death, we will no longer see God through the medium of signs. Then we will experience God's glory face-to-face.

Chapter 17

A Catastrophe in the Life of David

Not long ago, somewhere in Upper Bavaria, I went into a church, rejoiced in its silence, prayed, looked around, and saw that the door to the confessional was leaning against the wall. Anyone could look inside, and there stood the broom, mop, bucket, and a snow shovel. The cleaning cloth was hanging, still damp, on the edge of the bucket. It seems, therefore, that the cleaning materials were diligently used. Apparently no one had confessed there for a long time, and the confessional had become a broom closet. I started thinking about the phenomenon of the empty confessional. The one I saw there was not the only confessional box put to other uses in the twenty-first-century church.

As a young assistant in the early 1960s I used to hear confessions every Saturday for hour after hour. During Holy Week the two assistants and the pastor sat in the confessional for many hours over the weekdays as well. What explains the enormous decline in confessional practice in Germany and elsewhere?

There are probably a number of reasons: for example, experiences with bad confessors who harped on a single sin or contrariwise declared things one had confessed as sin to be something normal and tried to deny any guilt at all. The latter became more and more frequent. It was also hard for Christians who had carefully prepared themselves for confession to run into priests who treated it as routine or a mere formality. Another and very different reason is shyness and even fright at the prospect of confessing. But that cannot be the whole reason because that shyness always existed, and an honest confession is always, in the end, an extraordinary liberation.

Another reason for the decline in confessional practice is probably the isolation of the sacrament of reconciliation. It no longer has sufficient soil under it, because there is no living community surrounding the sacrament—living community in which many live in the awareness that we are placed within a history with God to which belongs a constant repentance and constant forgiveness. We could also say it in theological terms: the basic sacrament "church" is lacking. More baldly: there is no "biotope" of a believing community in which it is simply a matter of course that one goes to confession.

And yet there is still another reason, and probably the decisive one: in our society the awareness of personal sin is vanishing. There are many causes for this, and I want to present a series of them. They are responsible for our increasing inability to perceive sin and guilt at all.

Pseudo-knowledge of Other Peoples

First, we have to be clear that as late as the Middle Ages practically nothing was known about foreign lands. Knowledge of Asia, Africa, and America, of Indian, African, and East Asian cultures began only with the great voyages of discovery. Everything previously known (in Europe) was fragmentary. But with the voyages of discovery in the modern era came a sudden deluge of knowledge (and pseudo-knowledge) of other cultures. As people began to know more about other cultures, they told themselves, in Europe for example, that in other lands there were native peoples who simply exposed those who had grown old or become sick and helpless; they were thus killed and everyone in the tribe (including those directly involved) found this completely normal and right.

But what was perceived in the modern era more as a curiosity or regarded with revulsion as the squalid behavior of so-called savages gradually led, in the minds of Europeans, to the notion that manners and morals are different everywhere and therefore entirely relative. "Apparently each one does it differently" slowly became "Everyone can do as she or he wants."

We are not so fond of acknowledging that in all peoples without exception we find the phenomenon of conscience, as a deep awareness of things that one must do or may not do, and that in all peoples the phenomenon of guilt is to be detected in a wide variety of expressions.

Indeed, it is far less interesting to observe that all cultures have an experience of guilt than for ethnologists to demonstrate, supposedly, that in earlier times certain tribes in the Pacific practiced complete sexual license, and for that very reason the people there lived in profound happiness and social peace. Incidentally, the supposed examples of happy societies without sexual taboos have been repeatedly refuted by later researchers. The "noble savage" who lives promiscuously and therefore in peace and free from violence is a dream-wish in the minds of human males.

Pseudo-knowledge from Psychology

A much more important reason why sin is no longer perceived as such, however, is psychology. I will simply quote a sentence at random from a newspaper. There, for example, I read a few days ago: "The bus driver who caused the serious accident is still in shock. As soon as he is able to engage, a psychologist will be made available to him."

Similar notices appear more and more frequently. The psychologist has replaced the pastor. To avoid misunderstanding, let me say that obviously psychological or psychiatric help can be a good thing, and often it is urgently necessary. It only becomes dubious when it is regarded as the sole and ultimate need and it is no longer acknowledged that there is a dimension to human beings that cannot be reached by psychology. The case is simply this: no psychiatrist or psychotherapist can forgive sin, but ultimately it seems that many pop psychologists and psycho-technicians are moving precisely in that direction. Of course, they are doing so not by way of repentance and forgiveness but instead by bringing all guilt feelings into the light and discussing, arguing, and picking them apart until they vanish into thin air—something that is entirely different from sacramental absolution.

Psychotherapists speak of guilt feelings, "shadows," the superego, the aggressive drive, neutral forces, complexes (including guilt complexes), reprocessing, grief work—but not of guilt or sin in the theological sense. Of themselves they cannot speak of such a thing, because that would take them beyond the limits of their professional field. They are simply not competent to do that, nor are they responsible for doing so. If they really are good psychotherapists and recognize that those sitting or lying before them, seeking help, are believers, they point out to them the possibility that their faith may lead them to seek forgiveness, and they build that possibility into their therapy. But that seems to happen rather seldom.

In the media the dominant strain is a pop psychology that operates on this principle: "Throw those stupid feelings of guilt out the window once and for all!" Or still more simply: "Go ahead and do what you have always wanted!" More and more self-designated life counselors on television, in magazines, and in the rising tide of self-help literature recommend much the same things. But even more effective than these direct instructions are the models of behavior that are spooned out for us in small doses in television films. Those series love adultery, for example. An "affair" is always titillating. And when afterward the husband confronts his wife, or the wife her husband, television loves fixed formulae. The tele-husband commonly says to his wife, "I can explain everything. It has nothing to do with *the two of us*." And the tele-wife in such a scene will say to her husband, "It just happened. It doesn't mean *anything*." The whole thing is almost a ritual. Both husband and wife absolve themselves of any guilt. And that is precisely what the television series want to communicate: "It doesn't mean anything." Absolving oneself of all guilt is one of the favorite occupations of people today.

Pseudo-knowledge from Natural Science

Still another reason for the suppression of guilt in our society is pseudo-science derived from the natural sciences or, more often, from bad popularizations of the results obtained by the sciences. For example, we have been flooded for years now with news about the decoding of the human genome. Genetic technology celebrates triumph after triumph. We are promised that in the future (almost) all illnesses will be curable, and still more, that very soon all parents will have the ability to bring only genetically perfect children into the world. Once human beings are genetically impeccable, the genetic technologists gleefully insinuate, they will also be "good."

Obviously not all biologists are so daft, but it is amazing to what extent a purely materialistic and mechanistic view of the world has been bubbling up in recent years, a view we had thought belonged to the nineteenth century and had long since been overcome. Human beings are presented as purely the product of their genes. Some even project that in the near future parents will be able to check off the desired characteristics of their hoped-for heir or designer baby: boy or girl, dark hair or blond, blue or brown eyes, tall or medium tall, obviously healthy—and also vital, intelligent, charming, and outgoing. A good character will accompany all this—many people really imagine that! Who can talk about sin anymore?

Popularization runs in much the same direction among a particular group of brain researchers. They see it as almost a matter of course that every human action is determined by a corresponding stimulus in the brain. Free will is said to be a figment of our imagination, a juggling of neurons in the brain. That, of course, represents a fundamental affirmation, namely, that there is no such thing as the human spirit and that the world exists only as spiritless matter. This basic or preliminary affirmation is not even discussed any longer. Why should these researchers be hampered by the contradictory evidence that each person lives as if she or he were free—when, for example, individuals assign guilt to themselves or to others—in asserting that we are only cue balls for the currents in our brains? The schizophrenic researchers who have just declared themselves nothing but marionettes insist, in the next instant, that their freedom and human dignity ought to be respected.

On the whole we have to say that we live today, willy nilly, in the midst of pseudo-scientific models of explanation that no longer allow any space for human freedom and therefore the ability to sin and incur guilt. Unsound natural scientists assert, "What you do comes entirely from your genes or electric impulses in your brain." Unsound psychologists say, "What you do has already been determined by your childhood experiences." And unsound sociologists tell us, "What you do is determined by the environment that has shaped you." There is no place left for freedom of the human will—and, of course, none for anything like sin and guilt.

The Push for Absolute Self-Determination

The inability of people today to accept their own guilt in any way derives, however, not only from anthropology, psychology, biology, and sociology. We are faced with a very strange paradox: while the trend of today's science is toward denying human freedom, at the same time people are claiming, beyond all measure, the right to be independent, masters of their own lives, autonomous, self-determining, and entitled to every imaginable freedom. This goes so far that people deny their own guilt. In Jean-Paul Sartre's play *The Devil & the Good Lord*, General Goetz says: "There was no one but myself . . . I who accused myself today, I alone who can absolve myself . . . I alone."[1]

In addition, there is a growing chorus of voices asserting that most of the misery in the world comes from Christianity, because it is Christianity that has hammered into us this horrible consciousness of sin we are having such a hard time getting rid of. The church's constant talk of sin and guilt flows in our blood like poison and makes us unfree. We constantly hear about commandments we must obey; we must accommodate our-selves to them, behave, submit. There is unremitting talk about the jeal-ous God who is watching to see that we obey. That is what makes us so evil: that we want to be different from what we are allowed to be.

What I have just described is not a figment of my imagination. These were the ideas presented by the celebrated author Martin Walser in an essay that appeared some years ago in the *Neue Zürcher Zeitung* under the title "Ich vertraue. Querfeldein."[2] What he says there is the credo of neopaganism. Often guilt feelings are regarded as positively pathologi-cal, something that should not exist and therefore must be cured.

Certainly there can be guilt feelings that should be classified as pa-thologies, but that is not the norm. What is normal is that one has guilt feelings because one is guilty—because one has disdained another, lied, been unfaithful, egoistically sought only one's own advantage, caused serious damage to someone else.

It must be admitted that we Christians are not without complicity in the present resistance to guilt feelings. Have we not all too often repre-sented God as a policeman, a watchdog, and the church as the purveyor of institutional morality? Still, we have to be aware of what would hap-pen if there was no longer any awareness of guilt and sin, if there were no commandments valid for everyone, if each individual lived only her or his private reality, or if only the law of the strongest prevailed. We need not tax our imaginations to know what would happen. The experi-ment has already been made. Adolf Hitler deliberately separated himself from Christianity, from Jewish morality and "Jewish conscience," as he called it, following Friedrich Nietzsche. Accordingly, as the foundational action of his thousand-year empire he organized within a few years the greatest mass murder of all time, with millions of people driven into refuge, starved, gassed, shot, and hanged.

An Exemplary Story

It is therefore useful—no, it is bitterly necessary—to reflect on what the Jewish and Christian tradition says about sin and guilt. But I do not want to do that in purely theoretical terms. The Bible is not theoretical about it either; it tells stories. The people of God tells itself stories and in them expresses its gathered memory, its ability to distinguish between God and the world, its knowledge of sin and forgiveness. Let us now listen to one of these great narratives, which is part of world literature. It is the biblical story of the sin of the great King David.

[Once upon a time] in the spring of the year, the time when kings go out to battle, David sent Joab with his officers and all Israel with him: they ravaged the Ammonites, and besieged Rabbah. But David remained at Jerusalem.

It happened, late one afternoon, when David rose from his couch and was walking about on the roof of the king's house, that he saw from the roof a woman bathing; the woman was very beautiful. David sent someone to inquire about the woman. It was reported, "This is Bathsheba daughter of Eliam, the wife of Uriah the Hittite." So David sent messengers to get her, and she came to him, and he lay with her. (Now she was purifying herself after her period.) Then she returned to her house. The woman conceived; and she sent and told David, "I am pregnant."

So David sent word to Joab, "Send me Uriah the Hittite." And Joab sent Uriah to David. When Uriah came to him, David asked how Joab and the people fared, and how the war was going. Then David said to Uriah, "Go down to your house, and wash your feet." Uriah went out of the king's house, and there followed him a present from the king. But Uriah slept at the entrance of the king's house with all the servants of his lord, and did not go down to his house. When they told David, "Uriah did not go down to his house," David said to Uriah, "You have just come from a journey. Why did you not go down to your house?" Uriah said to David, "The ark and Israel and Judah remain in booths; and my lord Joab and the servants of my lord are camping in the open field; shall I then go to my house, to eat and to drink, and to lie with my wife? As you live, and as your soul lives, I will not do such a thing." Then David said to Uriah, "Remain here today also, and tomorrow I will send you back." So Uriah remained in Jerusalem that day. On the next day, David invited him to eat and drink in his presence and made him drunk; and in the evening he went out to lie on his couch with the servants of his lord, but he did not go down to his house.

In the morning David wrote a letter to Joab, and sent it by the hand of Uriah. In the letter he wrote, "Set Uriah in the forefront of the hardest fighting, and then draw back from him, so that he may be struck down and die." As Joab was besieging the city, he assigned Uriah to the place where he knew there were valiant warriors. The men of the city came out and fought with Joab; and some of the servants of David among the people fell. Uriah the Hittite was killed as well. Then Joab sent and told David all the news about the fighting; and he instructed the messenger, "When you have finished telling the king all the news about the fighting, then, if the king's anger rises, and if he says to you, 'Why did you go so near the city to fight? Did you not know that they would shoot from the wall . . .?' then you shall say, 'Your servant Uriah the Hittite is dead too.' "

So the messenger went, and came and told David all that Joab had sent him to tell. The messenger said to David, "The men gained an advantage over us, and came out against us in the field; but we drove them back to the entrance of the gate. Then the archers shot at your servants from the wall; some of the king's servants are dead; and your servant Uriah the Hittite is dead also." David said to the messenger, "Thus you shall say to Joab, 'Do not let this matter trouble you, for the sword devours now one and now another; press your attack on the city, and overthrow it.' And encourage him."

When the wife of Uriah heard that her husband was dead, she made lamentation for him. When the mourning was over, David sent and brought her to his house, and she became his wife, and bore him a son.

But the thing that David had done displeased the LORD, and the LORD sent Nathan to David. He came to him, and said to him, "There were two men in a certain city, the one rich and the other poor. The rich man had very many flocks and herds; but the poor man had nothing but one little ewe lamb, which he had bought. He brought it up, and it grew up with him and with his children; it used to eat of his meager fare, and drink from his cup, and lie in his bosom, and it was like a daughter to him. Now there came a traveler to the rich man, and he was loath to take one of his own flock or herd to prepare for the wayfarer who had come to him, but he took the poor man's lamb, and prepared that for the guest who had come to him." Then David's anger was greatly kindled against the man. He said to Nathan, "As the LORD lives, the man who has done this deserves to die; he shall restore the lamb fourfold, because he did this thing, and because he had no pity."

Nathan said to David, "You are the man! Thus says the LORD, the God of Israel: I anointed you king over Israel, and I rescued you from the hand of Saul; I gave you your master's house, and your master's wives into your bosom, and gave you the house of Israel and of Judah; and if that had been too little, I would have added as much more. Why have you despised the word of the LORD, to do what is evil in his sight? You have struck down Uriah the Hittite with the sword, and have taken his wife to be your wife, and have killed him with the sword of the Ammonites. Now therefore the sword shall never depart from your house, for you have despised me, and have taken the wife of Uriah the Hittite to be your wife. Thus says the LORD: I will raise up trouble against you from within your own house; and I will take your wives before your eyes, and give them to your neighbor, and he shall lie with your wives in the sight of this very sun. For you did it secretly; but I will do this thing before all Israel, and before the sun." David said to Nathan, "I have sinned against the LORD." Nathan said to David, "Now the LORD has put away your sin; you shall not die. Nevertheless, because by this deed you have utterly scorned the LORD, the child that is born to you shall die." Then Nathan went to his house.

The LORD struck the child that Uriah's wife bore to David, and it became very ill. David therefore pleaded with God for the child; David fasted, and went in and lay all night on the ground. The elders of his house stood beside him, urging him to rise from the ground; but he would not, nor did he eat food with them. On the seventh day the child died. And the servants of David were afraid to tell him that the child was dead; for they said, "While the child was still alive, we spoke to him, and he did not listen to us; how then can we tell him the child is dead? He may do himself some harm." But when David saw that his servants were whispering together, he perceived that the child was dead; and David said to his servants, "Is the child dead?" They said, "He is dead."

Then David rose from the ground, washed, anointed himself, and changed his clothes. He went into the house of the LORD, and worshiped; he then went to his own house; and when he asked, they set food before him and he ate. Then his servants said to him, "What is this thing that you have done? You fasted and wept for the child while it was alive; but when the child died, you rose and ate food." He said, "While the child was still alive, I fasted and wept; for I said, 'Who knows? The LORD may be gracious to me, and the child may live.' But now he is dead; why should I fast? Can I bring him back again? I shall go to him, but he will not return to me."

Then David consoled his wife Bathsheba, and went to her, and lay with her; and she bore a son, and he named him Solomon. The LORD loved him, and sent a message by the prophet Nathan; so he named him Jedidiah [the LORD's beloved], because of the LORD. (2 Sam 11:1–12:25)

What we have read here is the description of a crime, committed not by just anyone but by the celebrated King David, the great king of Israel. David was not just another scoundrel; he was a believer. Later, the psalms were attributed to him, and it was in the figure of King David that Israel's hope for the messianic king of the end time was kindled. This David committed the crime that is told to us in such unadorned fashion.

We can only be amazed at the people Israel, which did not stylize its greatest king—as was common for other nations—into an untouchable hero-figure but said with the utmost sobriety and unsparing candor: so it was with David, and so it has been with many others in Israel. God's project is furthered not only by perfect people (who are very rare!) but also and above all by sinners. What is decisive for the history of God in the world is that there are people who listen, who allow themselves to be instructed, who repent and in doing so serve God's plan.

David's Sin

What kind of sin was it that David fell into? If we look closely, we see that the narrative does not develop the account of the sexual transgression as the sin itself, even though the whole thing starts there. David's real sin is his misuse of power; it is brutal violence. The fictional case of the poor man's lamb that the prophet Nathan tells the king in order to make clear to him what he has done shows it with the utmost clarity: David unhesitatingly takes whatever he wants. In doing so he meddles recklessly with Uriah's rights, showing his contempt for other human beings. That is described in the inner world of the narrative as the sin itself.

Then, with a high degree of narrative skill, the story shows that David slips deeper and deeper into sin, involves himself in worse and worse guilt. First, it is only a matter of lust—the Bible calls it "the lust of the eyes" (1 John 2:16). Then the desire becomes deed. David has to have this woman in his bed. So Bathsheba becomes pregnant, and her pregnancy has to be hushed up—hence the attempt to bring Uriah by any means to sleep with his own wife. Because Uriah, the clever officer, immediately sees through this wicked game he has to be gotten rid of, and in order that it should not attract attention any number of soldiers, even especially seasoned ones, have to die with him.

This is a narrative skill that grabs us by the throat. It shows how one thing leads to another, once the sequence has begun. Mere desire leads in the end to murder of David's own subordinates. Every sin leads further downward, the story says; every sin widens the circle around it. Once David has summoned Bathsheba to his house, he gets into a pickle. Despite the energy with which he does everything, he seems like someone blinded, deafened, crippled.

Who can draw him out of his blindness? He cannot do it himself. His conscience tells him—nothing at all! David has no self-perception. He has achieved everything he wanted. The story seems to have come to an end: when Uriah's wife hears that her husband is dead, she laments for him, but as soon as the mourning period is over, David has her brought into his palace. She becomes his wife and bears him a son. David is altogether satisfied with himself.

But God is not at all satisfied with the whole business. At the exact moment when the story could be at an end, there stands like handwriting on the wall, like a hideous sign, the statement: "But the thing that David had done displeased the LORD." God has not appeared anywhere in the story before this; it was told in entirely secular terms. Only now, at this point, the narrative makes clear with the utmost brevity that the world is not exhausted in its superficial appearance. It has another horizon, namely, God!

That is precisely the point. That sin is sin and guilt is guilt cannot be explained by either psychology or sociology, and not even by the Golden Rule—"do not do to another what you do not wish to have someone do to you"—because one can still say: if I have the power, why should I not do what pleases me and what *I* want? I will decide for myself what is good, and that is always what is good for *me*. This devilish logic cannot be stopped, except by these words: "but the thing that David had done displeased the LORD."

The Role of the People of God

If it is not God and God's plan for society that is the ultimate standard by which our behavior can be measured, then at some point every ethic shatters and all human rules break down. Conscience alone is no help at all, because conscience has to be educated—and what would be the ultimate measure by which it can be educated if there were no God?

Still, who hands on this ultimate measure? Who conveys God's will to us? Who teaches us to determine what is true and what is false, what is good and what is evil? It can only be the people of God, which through its long history with God has learned to know God's will and has struggled to attain the gift of discernment. That is precisely what I meant at the outset when I said that the sacrament of reconciliation today lacks a living community that surrounds it and in which it is embedded. The sacrament of reconciliation is a church thing. It needs communities that have a history with God; it needs congregations in which guilt is understood as guilt and forgiveness and reconciliation are really lived.

In our story the prophet Nathan represents this experience of God's people, the experience of the community of Israel. Only through that is he in a position to snatch David out of his blindness and self-satisfaction.

But he does not hit him on the head with a moral hammer. Instead, he presents him with a legal case for the king to decide. David, who despite all his sins is a great king and an incorruptible judge, delivers his judgment immediately: "The man who has done this deserves to die." And in saying this he has imposed a death sentence on himself. That is the linchpin of the whole narrative, and it must not be overlooked: David utters his own death sentence. The fact that God does not carry out that death sentence is pure grace and concessive mercy. That mercy is possible because David repents. Listen again to the crucial sentences: "David said to Nathan, 'I have sinned against the Lord.' Nathan said to David, 'Now the Lord has put away your sin; you shall not die.'"

The Incident Is Not Over

Thus the sentence against David is abrogated immediately after his repentance and confession of guilt. The prophet absolves David in the name of God. Now we are again at a point at which the story could end, because it appears that everything has been put right, just as everything is apparently settled after an honest confession. The penitent leaves the confessional, prays an Our Father and a Hail Mary, and goes home happy.

But the story continues, and something bad happens. The child David had begotten with Bathsheba dies. Moreover, there are indications of terrible things that have yet to happen in the royal family. What is that all about? Didn't God forgive? Can it be that we get a glimpse here of that God of the Old Testament whom many Christians still think was a violent and vicious God, a God of vengeance, perhaps even a demon whose horrid image has only been erased by the New Testament?

No, that is not the case; all that is theological nonsense. What is revealed here is rather a reality connected with sin, something we have to speak about in conclusion. The guilt of sin can be forgiven, and the guilt itself is erased; it is no longer present. That is profoundly liberating. But every sin changes something in the world for the worse. Every sin leaves its traces. Every sin has consequences, often horrible ones. To give one simple example: if someone has set fire to his or her neighbor's house, that person can regret the deed afterward and be forgiven. But the house is still in ruins.

The consequences of sin are not always external and material. Something can also be destroyed within someone's heart. Other people's trust can be smashed. Faith can be extinguished. Do we really have any idea of what we can destroy in others through our idleness, our minimal faith, our cynicism? Sin always makes itself incarnate, and precisely in those around us, those who depend on us, those who look up to us.

So David's sin will also have its consequences, and they will show themselves in his own family. David's son Absalom will later revolt against his father, stir up a rebellion in order to make himself king. He will break into David's harem and rape his father's wives. All Israel will speak of this shameful deed. So in his own way the son will repeat exactly what his father David had done.

If we understand all that within the concept of punishment, if we say that God forgave David but still punished him, according to the formula "I forgive you, but you have to take your punishment!" we are not doing justice, theologically, to the story. It is not God who ambushes the human being after the fact; it is human beings themselves who create their own misfortune with every sin, and the evil is not simply eliminated by pardon. The consequences are often felt in the world, in society, in the family for many generations. In our story it even happens that God limits the fatal consequences and offers David's family another chance through the birth of Solomon. God creates a new beginning.

Sin and Salvation

So the story of David and Bathsheba contains a highly refined theology of sin. It shows us the whole misery of the human being but also humanity's greatness—provided we repent. But above all it shows that sin is not only committed against our fellow humans. Every sin is directed against God—not because we can insult God, but because God is personally affected when the happiness and grace God wants for the world is dimmed or destroyed by sin. Therefore David confesses: "I have sinned against the Lord."

That is Israel's true insight: when we sin we not only destroy a piece of the world but also delay God's plan to bring grace and salvation to the world. To that extent we sin against God and God's project. But the reverse is also true: when we join in helping to build up the people of God, when we never tire but rather cooperate in the power of our common effort to create living communities, then we help to bring the world to salvation and cover a multitude of our sins.

Chapter 18

On the Sense and Nonsense of Good Intentions

Recently there appeared alongside the German superhighways a sign designed to educate drivers. It read, in large letters: "Fester Wille: Null Promille" ["Firm your will: alcohol nil."]. It was a clever composition, if only because the rhyme unavoidably fixed itself in people's minds. But the author not only made a good rhyme; he or she took the small liberty of playing with our unconscious, since when we think "your will," we almost inevitably shift to the idea of "last will (and testament)." Thus the thought of one's own last will lurks in the background and with it the idea of death or a fatal accident.

The writer, in fact, struck even deeper into the unconscious, doing what has been fashionable in the advertising industry for a long time now: exploiting the Christian tradition and its important words. If only in the form of a long-lost cultural inheritance, the thought of firmly fixing "my will" still recalls to many what they learned a long time ago in preparing for First Confession. A necessary element of confession, they learned (one hopes!), was a "good intention." The Catechism says that receiving forgiveness in the sacrament of reconciliation demands a "firm resolve" to avoid sin and the near occasions of sin. Otherwise repentance is not genuine.

That, like the whole Catechism, is altogether reasonable. The "firm resolve" that is one of the five elements of the sacrament of reconciliation too often becomes, however, in catechesis and in practical living, nothing but a bunch of toothless "good intentions."

Intentions on a Sour Stomach

Such "good intentions" still exist in secularized form; they are amazingly tenacious on the social level. They surface especially on special birthdays (forty, fifty, etc.), New Year's Day, and Ash Wednesday: "From today on I will smoke less, drink more moderately, give up chocolate entirely, go to bed earlier, watch less television, be more patient with my wife/husband," or in radical form, "From today on everything will be different."

In reality, nothing changes at all. Intentions on this level, declared to be fixed and unchangeable, are quickly altered, often within a few hours. First we make an exception and allow ourselves just one little pleasure, then we delay the beginning of the new life to the following week. But by then everything is gone with the wind, and life goes on as it always has.

I recall a cartoon that fits this context. An elegantly clad man is seated in a kind of executive chair behind a wide desk, facing front. His eyes are half closed. Evidently he is weary. It must be early on New Year's Day, because he is listlessly drinking a glass of champagne and philosophizing. The balloon over his head reads, "If I could start all over from the beginning, I would probably do everything differently." Then comes the second panel, with exactly the same person in exactly the same chair. But the balloon reads, "Thank God that is impossible."

Why is this? Why is it that good intentions of this kind, and certainly the misery depicted in the cartoon, don't get us anywhere? Why are our intentions such a dubious proposition? What does the Bible say about it?

To begin with, the concept of "good intentions" does not exist in the Bible. It comes from ancient philosophy, which reflected on the fact that one can only do good when one has determined to do so through an inner choice (*propositum*). This valid insight became, from the Middle Ages on, an aspect of the theology of the sacrament of reconciliation: repentance is not sufficient in itself; it must be combined with the solid intention not to sin in the future. This solid will to avoid sin is part of the seriousness and joy of the sacrament. It is poles apart from the attempts at self-reform that begin with a sour stomach on New Year's Day or Ash Wednesday.

Reversal, Not Touch Up

As I have said, the concept of "good intentions" does not appear in the Bible. But the prophets and teachers of God's people did indeed speak, and in radical fashion, about the subject covered by the phrase. They did so when they called for repentance, reversal of one's whole life.

Repentance/reversal presumes that one is running in the wrong direction and getting farther and farther from the goal. In contrast, the usual "good intentions" suggest that, all in all, everything is fine. They presume that there are, in fact, some aspects of myself that can be improved. Some touching up is needed here and there; a few things need polishing. But fundamentally, the direction of my life is correct, and the improvements remain on the level of repair work. Precisely at this point the Jewish and Christian tradition thinks much more radically. On Ash Wednesday, as we receive the ashes on our heads, it tells us, "Remember that you are dust, and to dust you shall return."

That is the real human situation. In line with its seriousness, the Ash Wednesday liturgy quotes the prophet Joel: "rend your hearts and not your clothing. Return to the LORD, your God!" (2:13). As long as we have not recognized our true situation, as long as it does not rend our hearts, we cannot reverse course and form the one intention that deserves to stand before all others: to serve God with our whole existence and give honor to God alone. "Good intentions" in the ordinary, watered-down sense conceal the real situation. Their intent is superficial cosmetic change, when in reality we need a new heart and a new spirit.

The usual kinds of "good intentions" are also questionable, however, because they presuppose that we can change ourselves if we try hard enough. This degrades the Christian faith to a kind of moral armament, indeed to self-redemption. Those who say, "Starting today I will change my life," know very little about the human being and not at all what faith is. I cannot change myself by my own efforts. If I repent, if something new comes into my life, it is always given to me, is always grace, even though the repentance is my own and depends altogether on what I myself do. The Lamentations that are attached to the book of Jeremiah in the Greek and Latin Bible conclude with the plea, "Restore us to yourself, O LORD, that we may be restored; renew our days as of old" (Lam 5:21). The best theology could not state it better. Every repentance, every return, comes from God. It is God's work when people freely turn back. Repentance solely through one's own strength is impossible.

In the Force Field of God's History

When Lamentations speaks of human restoration as coming from God's initiative, that is not merely pious mouthing. These poems look back to the fall of the Southern Kingdom and the destruction of the temple in the year 586 BCE. They contemplate one of the most dreadful and shattering occurrences in the history of Israel. The "we" of the text is the "we" of the battered and scattered people of God.

Apparently Israel could not really repent so long as its faith was tied to its existence as a political state. It was only the catastrophe of 586 that opened the people's eyes. Now they beg for restoration to a new form of life. This defines the place of all repentance and restoration. God gives it not magically but by opening our eyes to the history within which we stand—our own history, that of the people of God, and that of the nations. The Bible would say: to the history in which God destroys and overthrows but also builds up and plants (Jer 1:10). It is only shock in the face of a history of horrid destruction and miraculous grace that leads to true repentance. Human beings have to confront the misery they themselves have caused as well as the new thing that God creates out of the catastrophes of the nations.

The "room" in the gospel for Ash Wednesday, behind whose closed doors we are to pray (Matt 6:6), does *not* mean that the coming of grace is a private matter and grace itself a mysterious fluid that descends on us vertically from above. The closed room is only an illustration of the fact that we are not to make a show of our faith; it is not an image of our encounter with God's grace.

Grace always comes to us from without, never from our own selves. Even if it sometimes seems to us that it grew from "within us," that "within" has long been in a process of formation "from without" that we cannot comprehend. Our inwardness is unthinkable without the word of Scripture, the tradition of the church, a living transmission of the faith, sharing in divine worship, the rousing history of the people of God.

Repentance in the biblical sense always takes place within the force field of church and community. It presupposes an encounter with people who authoritatively show me the way, in the name of Jesus. "We are ambassadors for Christ, since God is making his appeal through us," Paul writes in the New Testament reading for Ash Wednesday. He continues: "we entreat you on behalf of Christ, be reconciled to God" (2 Cor 5:20). That too is part of the basic structure of all repentance: others who

speak for Christ open my eyes to my true situation and offer me reconciliation with God.

Thus repentance is more than a drawer filled with good intentions. It
is a profound event that incorporates me in the history of God with God's
people and that normally is made possible only in an encounter with
that history. Repentance presupposes that we have tasted something of
the new thing God is creating in the world. How can anyone change the
direction of an entire life without having seen and tasted, experienced
a joy never known before?

Repentance in Joy

Obviously repentance is often a reaction to elemental crisis, as is shown
not only by the Old Testament lamentations; the lost son in Luke 15 had
to waste his money on prostitutes, become a swineherd, and literally lie
in filth in order to repent. But even that repentance out of misery would
not have been possible for him if he had not had the picture of his father's
house before his eyes. There everyone rose from the table satisfied. What
causes the lost son to get underway is the catastrophe of his life, but what
draws him home is the love of his father and the joy that awaits him
there. A feast will be prepared for him.

Repentance is a radical event with many components. One of them is
a good intention. In the case of the lost son it is: "I will get up and go to
my father" (Luke 15:18). The Greeks were right in thinking that one can
only do what is good and right if one has first made an inner choice. The
lost son's choice, his statement, "I will get up . . ." changes his whole
life. That choice, that intention, causes him to set his feet in motion.

So the Bible describes the location of what we call "good intentions."
Its place is in real history. That history, which the parable of the prodigal
son also tells about, is the coming of the reign of God. God acts today,
in our days, and God's action changes everything. God's action creates
a new situation in the world in which people and things can change at
depth. Nothing need any longer remain as it is. Paul describes this new
"moment" in history in the Ash Wednesday reading by saying, "See,
now is the acceptable time; see, now is the day of salvation!" (2 Cor 6:2).

Placed within this history of God with the world, even "good intentions" have their justification in the end. They are then no longer something we ourselves create but come to us from without—from the
encounter with those who show us the way in the name of Jesus. And
then they no longer serve to build up one's own self but enable us to

cooperate in God's work in the world. They are relevant, issue-related— namely, related to God's project. Therefore they also lead us further, into the new creation God is building up from the dust of our mortality and our self-created catastrophes.

Chapter 19

Has the Church Been Deprived of Fasting?

Rhesus monkeys, mice, and even worms whose daily caloric ration is reduced by a third live longer than others of their species. They less frequently suffer from cancers, and they are healthier on the whole. Broad-based experiments undertaken in recent years have shown this. Thus far the scientists have not been able to determine the exact working of this reduction in calories, but they suspect that metabolism is purified of damaging byproducts by a regulated diet, and therefore the immune system functions better.

Thus modern medicine is reacquiring the knowledge that physicians in antiquity had gained by practical experience. Of course, the religions have possessed that knowledge even longer. When they imposed periods of fasting on their adherents it was not merely about renunciation but also about well-being. Human life is meant to succeed; it must be ordered and protected. There is practically no religion in which fasting plays no role. In Judaism and Christianity it also occupies a significant place. The church permits itself a forty-day period of penance beginning with Ash Wednesday, a day of strict fasting and abstinence, and culminating with Good Friday, another day on which Christianity has fasted from the very beginning.

Secularized Fasting

At present, however, fasting is being abolished in the religions and in Christianity as well. To the same extent that people are eating unthinkingly and greedily in the wealthy industrialized countries, and the diseases of civilization, such as gout, diabetes, and hypertension are increasing, we find in the same countries an effort to lead a way of life that is tied to a correct diet. An infinite number of sanatoria can be found in which one can fast at great expense, a vast array of beauty farms where one is placed on the strictest diet, a powerful wave of wellness programs whose utmost article of faith is the ability to shape one's own body. These involve larger and larger numbers of people and have produced one of the fastest-growing branches of the economy: the well-being and healthful living industry.

Apparently a deep satisfaction comes from modeling one's own body. Cindy Jackson, who has had (thus far) thirty-eight beauty operations because she does not want to go on being a rather plump American girl from Ohio but instead would like to be a live Barbie doll, is an extreme case, but she is not unique. The great vision of many young women and men is absolute thinness, a delicate figure. Starving and fasting are the means. The perfect human being of the future drinks vegetable juice in the morning, eats nothing at noon but a salad with soy dressing followed by daily nourishment-enhancing capsules, then spends an hour in a fitness studio; this individual has a body-mass index of twenty-one and a washboard belly. She or he works on her or his own body as an earlier artist sculpted a statue and does not neglect to rub in algae extract every day. Sunday mornings these folks go for a walk with their blow-dried dogs and display their bleached teeth when they greet other walkers.

Is there any place left for Christian fasting? Everything depends on how, in the future, it will be understood and interpreted. We have to recover a clear idea of the specific point of Jewish and Christian fasting: it was an aspect of repentance and renewal, not only of the soul, but also of the body, but that meant the ordering of every part of life to God's project.

When Jews fast on the Day of Atonement, it is for the sake of Israel, that it may turn from its own will to that of God, and the church's proper fast day was always Good Friday. But fasting on Good Friday means a lacerating memory of Jesus' death, making it present; it means dying and rising with Christ—dying to one's own gods and rising to a new life in the common life of the community. Therefore Jews and Christians have always been far in advance of every kind of fasting merely for the sake of health—though the latter, of course, can make good sense. For them wellness was more than health. If fasting (and restriction of the urge to consume) became part of a movement of repentance and renewal in the church, Christians would not have to let themselves be fascinated by the weight-loss acrobatics of their overfed environment.

Fasting and Feast

The problems with church fasting, however, are not confined to its secularization. Every Christian practice of fasting lives in a peculiar dialectic: Jesus himself fasted, and he spoke about fasting—and yet he and his disciples did not observe the customs of their pious contemporaries in that regard. For that they were despised and slandered. It must have been in reaction to such attacks that Jesus said, "the wedding guests cannot fast while the bridegroom is with them, can they?" (Mark 2:19). He thus declared the era that has dawned with his coming to be a time of salvation, a time of rejoicing and feasting. That was so aggravating that his opponents called him "a glutton and a drunkard" (Matt 11:19). The post-Easter community took up that annoying saying about the never-ending wedding at which one cannot fast and added: "The days will come when the bridegroom is taken away from them, and then they will fast on that day" (Mark 2:20). The addition was theologically legitimate; it emphasizes the dialectic between the messianic time whose jubilation must never be silenced in the church and the still ongoing time of tribulation and hardship.

The church has always been aware of this fruitful tension between feast and fasting. Even Jesus' great precursor, John the Baptizer, did not have the contempt for food we ordinarily think of in connection with him. He ate "locusts and wild honey" (Mark 1:6). But roasted and salted locusts are regarded in the Near East even today as particular delicacies, and most certainly the same is true of honey from wild bees. It is only that one does not find such delicacies in the wilderness every day. The information about the eating habits of the Baptizer is therefore intended to depict not a grim ascetic but a person who left food and life entirely in the hands of God. Life in the wilderness brought with it fast days and feast days.

The same dialectic structures the church's year. While the church has preceded its great feasts with days of fasting and repentance, there always follows the brilliance of the feast as a celebration of the messianic time of fulfillment that has already begun. Can we maintain that dialectic today?

Sometimes one gets the impression that we are no longer in control of either: fasting as a sign of radical renewal or the celebration of real festivals. Fasting has been emptied of its meaning, but eating is reduced to the consumption of factory-made products. It is not *that* we don't eat—but *how*?

The Triumph of Fast Food

In the supermarkets, the cases of frozen food and shelves of precooked meals take up more and more space. Teachers report a growing number of children who are sent to school without breakfast; after all, there are breakfast candy bars with crunchy oatmeal available at school. Any passionate reader of mystery novels can observe a strange phenomenon: increasingly, there is a pleasurable and detailed description of what the detective eats and drinks. His or her culinary expeditions are nearly as important as the search for clues to the murderer. Apparently these authors of popular literature are well aware of what their readers want today.

Cardinal Jean-Marie Lustiger of Paris is supposed to have answered a question put to him by a woman at a Catholic academy about what the church's deepest crisis is today by saying: "That women can't cook anymore." His answer hits the bull's-eye. The deficiency his *bon mot* addresses is not solely about mere culinary matters. The most precious sacrament Jesus endowed was enacted at a table, and its place ever since is within a meal. The table of the Eucharist must continue its life at the tables where Christians eat together as a "new family," recollect in unanimity, speak with one another, join their lives with those of others. This presumes a culture of the table, of conversation, of community. This common life around the common table is being lost, however, even in many religious houses and monasteries. It may be that the elimination of fasting and the formlessness of many Christians' meals have more to do with each other than we suspect.

Babette's Feast

One of the best things Karen Blixen (Isak Dinesen) wrote was her novella, *Babette's Feast*. A French cook, driven to Norway by the revolution, is servant to a pair of elderly siblings who belong to a Pietist sect.

> Its members renounced the pleasures of this world, for the earth and
> all that it held to them was but a kind of illusion, and the true reality
> was the New Jerusalem toward which they were longing. They
> swore not at all, but their communication was yea yea and nay nay,
> and they called one another Brother and Sister.[1]

One day Babette wins a lot of money in the lottery, and because cooking is her whole passion—she had been one of the best cooks in France—she wants, one last time in her life, to prepare a great feast. She manages to give the pious congregation a banquet with expensive delicacies she has to order from France. Those invited have no use for such goings-on and they are resolved to get this meal over with, keeping their taste buds under control. They have only attended out of politeness and tact.

But Babette has not only prepared a marvelous meal but also decked the table with the finest linen and the most beautiful dishes she can find. She invests her whole lottery prize in this meal. And then something happens that no one could have anticipated. At the end of the evening her guests are like people transformed. They are playful as children with one another, bury all their old enmities, and sense that the New Jerusalem can sometimes appear on earth:

> Taciturn old people received the gift of tongues; ears that for years
> had been almost deaf were opened to it. Time itself had merged into
> eternity.[2]

What Isak Dinesen narrates in this novella is the spirit of the Gospel. Jesus wanted to save not merely souls but also bodies and clothing, food, drink, sleep, our houses and our life together, our time and our wealth. Everything in this world, including fasting and feasting, is to reveal the brilliance of the reign of God—and the one cannot exist without the other.

Chapter 20

Prayer as Access to Reality

I am doing something I really should not do: I am listening to two young people in love—and not just a little bit in love, but powerfully, lastingly, and passionately. I hear the two of them talking—they talk with each other constantly. They tell each other everything, even the tiniest details: what each one has done that day, what they did yesterday, what they did in the past, what they will do tomorrow. They want to know everything about each other, nothing left out.

They thank each other often, even for the least little thing. They find it wonderful to be able constantly to thank each other. They sense this mutual gratitude as a sign of their familiarity with one another. They giggle, whisper in each other's ears the names they have invented for each other, names that are by no means to be made public, since they would be thought silly. But they are not silly to the couple; they are little tendernesses. They praise each other again and again; sometimes they almost congratulate themselves.

I break off at this point, leap over many years, and listen in to the conversation between the two at this point. They have been married a long time, and they have held fast to one another. But their language has changed. The first thing I notice is that they no longer have much to tell each other. Instead, there are new forms of speech between them that scarcely existed at the beginning: for example, long discussions of money matters, crises in their children's upbringing, problems with their house, and above all the annoyances of the workplace.

One form of speech is completely new; it did not exist between them at the beginning: grumbling. And there is another form never used by the couple before: complaint. One complains constantly to the other; more and more often one complains about the other. Often they are silent—a long, persistent silence. They ignore each other, and then in the evening they insult each other. It is a horrible scene, but it ends positively: both of them apologize, at first only formally. But on the following day, when they see what they have done, they plead for forgiveness. And then the young woman begs the man to make things between them the way they were at the beginning. She pleads with tears in her eyes.

From that point something changes. Their language shifts again. I hear tender tones return, but now tinged with patience and a new awareness of the fragility of life.

What Speech Can Do

Why have I developed this scenario? In the first place for a very simple reason: I wanted to show something about the nature of speech. Human language can do an enormous amount. It is not only that it creates communication or destroys it. It is also capable of an endless number of nuances and it has infinite facets. It moves constantly between one attitude and another. It can convey something; it can narrate. It can list, and it can recall. It can bring close what is distant and remember things that are past. It can ask and plead, lament and accuse, appeal and demand. It can express outrage, but it can also acknowledge and appreciate. It can praise, exalt, and glorify. It can rejoice and celebrate and give heartfelt thanks.

Language can do all those things; human beings can do all those things. And all of it happens in prayer as well. The whole spectrum of the numerous attitudes in speaking I have indicated in my scenario exists in prayer also. As regards the multiple ways of speaking, we can learn an unbelievable lot from the biblical psalms. They tell about what God has done for the people of God. God's deeds in history are remembered. The beauties of God's creation are regularly listed. God's glory is sung.

But there is also imploring prayer to God, who is not only asked but also begged for help. The psalmist's own need and that of the people of God are described—*and how!* The whole misery, all the secret contingencies of life: all these are held before God's eyes with terrible realism. Often in the psalms lament precedes petition, and that lament pulls no punches. It not only mourns; at times it positively accuses God. It says to God's face what promises God has made to Israel in the past and apparently not kept. The psalmist demands of God: "Come to our aid at last!" "Don't leave us in the lurch this way!" "Remember your promises of fidelity in the past!" The whole Psalter, with its 150 psalms, is a dramatic dialogue between Israel and its God. And how does the dialogue end?

After all the laments, petitions, challenges to God, the Psalter ends, in Psalms 146–150, with a chorus of praise. All creation is called upon, all the beasts, all the people, all the nations, all the voices of the universe, even all musical instruments, to join in eschatological praise of God. At the end of the Psalter, all creation has become pure praise!

It is really thus: in a *biblically* shaped prayer nearly all speech attitudes of which human beings are capable are brought to bear, from outrage to praise, from deepest lament to shocked thanksgiving, from brief outcry to long narration. And I will say that in this way, with this kind of multifaceted prayer, the human being suffers no divorce from reality but instead gains new reality. An infinitely broad horizon opens to us that otherwise would remain closed. Still more, we become, for the first time, human—and God becomes for us, for the first time, God.

In what follows, of course, I cannot give an overview of the whole spectrum of forms of speech in prayer. Therefore I will choose four attitudes that play a fundamental role in biblical prayer: lament, petition, praise, and thanksgiving.

Lament

The deepest and most dreadful lament in the Bible is familiar to everyone; it is the beginning of Psalm 22: "My God, my God, why have you forsaken me?" In these words, Jesus cried out to God in the agony of death. It is often said that this cry expresses ultimate and profound despair, but that is not true. Jesus died not with a scream of despair on his lips but—as was a matter of course for a faithful Jew—with a dying prayer.

Jesus' prayer was Psalm 22. It begins with a cry of utter abandonment, but gradually the psalm's attitude and language change. Lament becomes petition, and petition suddenly, in verse 22, becomes assurance of rescue. The perspective broadens from the psalmist's own crisis to the salvation God will inevitably give not only to the people of God but to all nations. It is only when one sees this connection that Jesus' death appears in its true light. Jesus died not in despair but in utter trust. Still more, Psalm 22 is an *exemplary* demonstration of how, in prayer, profound lament can be transformed into confidence. That happens again and again.

Someone begins telling God about her distress. It erupts from her; she tells God in detail how things are, and that listing of her needs condenses into an accusation against God: "Why are you doing this to me? Do you want to go on piling things up? Have you no mercy? Where is your help?" And then, in the midst of these complaints, something in the person changes; the complaint becomes a plea and the plea a silent confidence. Countless believers have experienced that. One's perspective changes in the course of prayer—no, not only the perspective. Reality changes, because it reveals itself suddenly from the other side and thus as something new. At first the complaint can be so radical that it becomes cursing. I do not mean cursing God but cursing life and its circumstances, or cursing other people.

One example of this is Psalm 137, in which the deportees in Babylon complain to God of their distress. They have been transported out of Israel and now have to do slave labor in the land between the rivers, for example, cleaning out irrigation canals that have filled with sand or marsh growth. The psalm begins:

> By the rivers of Babylon—
>> there we sat down and there we wept
>> when we remembered Zion.
> On the willows there
>> we hung up our harps.
> For there our captors
>> asked us for songs,
>> and our tormentors asked for mirth, saying,
>> "Sing us one of the songs of Zion!"
> How could we sing the LORD's song
>> in a foreign land? (Ps 137:1-4)

The psalm ends with hope for a divine judgment on Babylon. Its conclusion is so dreadful that many Christians have thought they cannot pray anything of the sort. After Vatican II the conclusion was therefore deleted from the Liturgy of the Hours. It reads:

> O daughter Babylon, you devastator!
>> Happy shall they be who pay you back
>> what you have done to us!

> Happy shall they be who take your little ones
>   and dash them against the rock! (Ps 137:8-9)

That describes the brutal customs of war at the time, but it is, in fact, horrible. How can anyone pray such a text? Isn't it absolutely unchristian? Careful, though! The Psalter is neither a handbook of moral theology nor advice literature with rules for behavior and decency. The Psalter lets out everything that lies within the human heart: rage and fury, fear and terror, sighing and longing, trust, rejoicing, and delight.

The Psalter is a book of powerful emotions. It suppresses nothing of what riots within: unremitting rage at injustice received, unbridled pining for justice, longing for an evil past to be repaired. All that and much more lies deep within us and wants to be let out, and it is good for that to happen. The question is only what we will do with the rage and bitterness that rise up in us. And here Psalm 138, following immediately after Psalm 137, gives an amazing answer. As its superscription says, it is a psalm "of David," meaning that, in the mind of the redactor of the Psalter, it is to be read as a psalm by David, that is, ultimately, a psalm from the lips of the Messiah.

This psalm of David is firmly linked to Psalm 137: the deportees do not want to sing the Lord's songs "in a foreign land," that is, in a place where other gods have their home. But now the coming Messiah says to God:

> I give you thanks, O Lord, with my whole heart;
>   before the gods [of Babylon] I sing your praise.

Those complaining in Psalm 137 do *not* want to do that. The Messiah continues:

> I bow down toward your holy temple
>   and give thanks to your name
>   for your steadfast love and your faithfulness. (Ps 138:1-2)

The speakers in Psalm 137 do not want that either. This means that Psalm 138 is an antithesis to Psalm 137. The Messiah has no problem singing "with the whole heart" the ancient songs of Zion even in a hostile land, in the face of the foreign gods—and with him, now the deportees have no more hesitation either. They simply sing their songs in the direction of Jerusalem.

And how is that all possible? When the Messiah lifts up his voice, history will continue. The circumstances will change; the nations and their rulers will turn to the God of Israel. Psalm 138 formulates it thus, as it continues:

> All the kings of the earth shall praise you, O Lord,
>> for they have heard the words of your mouth.
> They shall sing of the ways of the Lord,
>> for great is the glory of the Lord. (Ps 138:4-5)

That is not yet the present. It is still a vision. But the vision expresses an enormous hope, and that hope, in itself, changes everything. That hope gives the inner freedom to praise the God of Israel, even in a foreign land. The burning desire for revenge on Babylon and its children is silenced; it plays no part any more. Suddenly the oppressors are regarded with new eyes. There is to be hope even for them. How stupid to destroy such a dialogue of the psalms with one another by simply rubbing out an essential part of the conversation!

So Psalm 138 is in dialogue with Psalm 137. It does not erase its distress; that has to be expressed first of all. But Psalm 138 offers a completely different solution in which violence and vengeance have no more place, and that new solution holds within it an insurmountable confidence about the world's history of violence.

What thus plays itself out between Psalms 137 and 138 happens again and again in the hearts of those who pray in faith. First there is wrath, outrage, anger, perhaps even hatred. All that needs to come out; it must come out. Beware when it remains seated deep in the soul and poisons one's whole body. But when this outrage takes place *during* my *prayer* and not just anywhere and at any time, I suddenly realize: no, I must not think that way. I must not pray that way. And then, perhaps very softly and unnoticeably, my view of things and people changes—and thereby reality itself is changed. My prayer that began so wrathfully has opened a new reality to me.

Petition

More and more Christians—including those who believe deeply—are asking themselves: is there any point to petitionary prayer? Is it even right to ask God for things? Would God's hearing my prayer not presuppose that God would intervene in the way of the world *for the sake of my little prayer*? Isn't someone who asks God for something wanting God to change the course of history? Does God even do such a thing? Dare one make such a prayer at all?

Suspicion that God will probably not intervene in the world's history for the sake of our prayers is deep-seated and goes back a long time, to the beginning of the European Enlightenment. Later, Jean-Jacques Rousseau and Immanuel Kant developed their own objections of precisely this sort. Today this skepticism is widespread, and many Christians are not at all aware of its origins. Does God really intervene? Does God meddle with history?

Many Christians *and* many theologians take a position that tries to eliminate the whole problem of God's intervention from the outset. It simply assigns a different role to petitionary prayer, saying that its purpose is not at all to move God to help. Its only task is to change the person praying. When we pray to God for others or for ourselves we discover that we have to change ourselves. Our petition, so this position holds, confronts us with the will of God, and by that very means makes us aware that it is our task to act in the world ourselves.

For example: there is little point in praying for starving people if we do not afterward do something ourselves to alleviate hunger in the world. For those who do nothing for the starving except pray for them, prayer is purely a substitutionary act, that is, a substitute for not acting. Prayer for the hungry only makes sense, it is said, if it awakens our social conscience. Our *prayer* for the hungry must lead to *action* on their behalf. Only then is it legitimate, and that is its whole meaning and purpose.

A good deal about this position is correct; I have no doubt of it. Those who pray honestly change themselves in the process, or, to put it better, they allow themselves to be changed by prayer. And insofar as they allow themselves to be changed, God can act in the world through them. That is an altogether important and often undervalued side of petitionary prayer. Here again we clearly see something that appeared in our discussion of "lament": imploring prayer changes the one praying, broadens her or his perspective, and shows her or him the true reality of the world.

I am not simply rejecting the position I have described, but I would *radicalize* it: anyone who earnestly prays to God says: I cannot do it myself. I am helpless. I cannot change myself or my fellow human beings, much less the world. You alone can do it. Only your Holy Spirit can renew the face of the earth. That is: every honest and unrestrained petitionary prayer liberates us from the arrogant assumption that we ourselves can bring truth and love into the world. Only God can do that.

We can only open ourselves wide, so that God can act through us. In that process we recognize God as who God is: the holy, almighty One who is infinitely close to us. Petition is ultimately the acknowledgment of what *we* are and who *God* is. For that reason alone it has a profound meaning.

But despite what I have just said, the question remains: does God intervene in the world? Does my prayer cause God to act? Or does God act *only* in the sense that my own prayer changes me? There is probably no one who painted the supposed futility of petitionary prayer more vividly and drastically than Bertolt Brecht. In the eleventh scene of his *Mother Courage and Her Children*, he tries to show Christians that their praying is utterly in vain. More than that, it is dangerous, because those who pray are prevented from acting in the very moment when they should act. Prayer produces no *gain* in reality but a *loss* of it. How does Brecht try to show that?

We find ourselves in the time of the Thirty Years War. In the eleventh scene of *Mother Courage* the imperial troops are closing in on the city of Halle in the middle of the night. In a farmstead near the city, soldiers are trying to force a group of peasants to show the imperial forces a secret way into the city. The farmers are unable to do anything but wail and pray:

> Our Father, which art in heaven, hear our prayer, let not the town perish with all that be therein asleep and fearing nothing. Wake them, that they rise and go to the walls and see the foe that comes with fire and sword in the night down the hill. . . .
>
> God protect our mother and make the watchman not sleep but wake ere it's too late. And save our son-in-law, too, O God, he's there with his four children, let them not perish, they're innocent, they know nothing. . . .
>
> Heavenly Father, hear us, only Thou canst help us, or we die, for we are weak and have no sword nor nothing; we cannot trust our own strength but only Thine, O Lord; we are in Thy hands, our cattle, our farm, and the town too, we're all in Thy hands, and the foe is nigh unto the walls with all his power.[1]

So much for the peasants' prayer. It is, of course, a clever satirical compilation of many Christian prayers: "make the watchman not sleep"; "don't let anything happen to my child." Who among us has not prayed in much the same way? But why shouldn't one do so? This is a prayer full of trust in God's omnipotence. And what happens in Brecht's version?

While the peasants are praying this way, Kattrin, Mother Courage's dumb and crippled daughter, seizes a drum, climbs to the roof of the barn, pulls up the ladder after her, and starts drumming. The soldiers can't reach the roof, so they shoot the girl down. Her drum has been heard in the town, however, and raised the alarm. Kattrin is dead, but the town is saved.

Don't pray; act! That is the inflammatory conclusion of this eleventh scene. Prayer is flight from reality and from personal responsibility. Brecht has dramatized this maxim in the most impressive way. But it does not seem to occur to him that God might have acted *through Kattrin*. If, that is, we take Brecht at his word, Kattrin must have been driven to action precisely through the prayers of her mother and the peasants.

I am convinced that one could develop an entire theology of God's action in the world on the basis of this scene from Brecht. God does not act in a way that we can calculate in advance. God is not a vending machine into which we drop our petition, press the knob, and down comes the help, precisely as a vending machine is programmed to do. God hears all our prayers, sometimes with an almost frightening directness, but often diametrically differently from what we have imagined. The peasants' prayer was heard, after all—but in a way different from what they had imagined. That way even led through a terrible sacrifice, the death of an innocent girl. And that too brings us to the center of Christian faith. For coming to the aid of the world, changing the world, does not happen in most cases without sacrifice, because the world is profoundly resistant. Genuine rescue and true aid usually demand sacrifice. Redemption is not accomplished by magic.

I think that, without meaning to do so, Brecht in this moving scene from *Mother Courage* has revealed something about the mystery of God's intervention in the world. God does intervene, but mainly in very different ways from those we ourselves expect. Many Christians have the overwhelming and even terrifying experience of the precision and lavishness with which God listens to prayers. The experience is *sui generis*. One cannot argue with it; it cannot be tested experimentally; it most certainly cannot be marketed. It can only be received, ever anew, by individuals, Christian communities, or the whole church. But there is also—just as terrifying—the experience of God's silence, apparent nonintervention, even apparent doing of just the opposite of what is implored.

These two experiences cannot be set in opposition to one another, and those who have knowledge of both would never think of doing so, because they have often found that God is present in the midst of and despite silence, that God does *not* listen to prayers and yet hears them in a different way, that the process of petition itself can become a liberating, meaningful transformation of reality.

At this point I want to refer to a particular experience many believers have had: living or working in such close companionship with others that there are frequently points of friction that demand a lot of effort and cannot simply be alleviated by open discussion, not even with all the techniques of communication so highly praised by social engineers nowadays. In such cases the only possibility may be to pray for the one who irritates us so dreadfully, to beg God for help, and to complain to God that one is unable by oneself to change the situation. Then suddenly one finds *that* the situation changes. I see the other person with new eyes, and the other sees me with new eyes as well.

You may explain that however you will and make use of processes that work through the unconscious and by no means exclude a lot of subtle psychology. In any case, my experience of such cases is that petition on behalf of the other and a prayerful admission of one's own helplessness is the best way to go forward. Often it is a kind of miracle how relationships can then change.

Praise

Not long ago it happened that a butterfly with brilliant, black-rimmed red wings fluttered through a clearing in the forest. Those walking by thought it was so beautiful. A boy wanted to run after it and catch it but got tangled up in nettles and gave up. His father took the boy by the hand and lectured him. (The father was a biology teacher.) He asked his son, "Do you know why that butterfly is so red?" "No," said the boy, "there are red ones and blue ones and yellow ones and white ones. But I never saw one *so* red."

"Now listen," said his father. "I will explain to you why this kind of butterfly is red. It has to do with evolution. The process of evolution caused the butterfly to develop this way. The blood-red color of its wings is a signal; it tells the hungry birds, 'I taste poisonous. My flavor is nasty. You would be nauseated.' So that the birds will know that and don't even try to find out whether the butterfly really tastes bad, they get the signal 'red.' It tells them: 'It's no use testing it.' And the birds react to the red color; they leave the butterfly alone."

The father, proud of this naturalist lecture for his son, was a little irritated when the son only made a face and said, "But I don't think it's nasty. It was pretty."

So who is right? The father or the son? Both of them, of course. You can look at a butterfly in purely biological terms, making it an object. You can dissect it. You can analyze its genetic code. You can look for the evolutionary factors that have led to its phenotype. But you can also look at the beauty of a butterfly and be amazed and start to feel happy. You can even regard it as a piece of the endlessly variegated creation of *God*, which—together with many other things—also serves to enchant human beings. It is something like what Lothar Zenetti once wrote in a short poem entitled "The Bill Comes at the End":

> One day, most certainly
> we will get the bill
> for the sunshine
> and the whispering of the leaves,
> the tender lilies of the valley,
> and the dark evergreens,
> the snow and the wind,
> the flight of birds and the grass
> and the butterflies,
> for the air
> we have breathed,
> and our view of the stars,
> and for all the days,
> the evenings and the nights.
>
> One day it will be time
> for us to get up and pay;
> let me have the bill, please.
> But we were forgetting
> about the innkeeper:
> I have been your host,
> he says and laughs,
> as broad as the earth:
> It was my pleasure![2]

With that we are already landed in the midst of "praise." The psalms know not only profound lament, not only desperate pleading. They also know the praise of creation. It can all be detailed in long lists: day and night, sun and moon, wind and stars, mountain goats and young lions, mountains and clouds. All creatures reflect the glory of God, God's open hand (Ps 104:28) and life-giving breath (Ps 104:30).

As we view this infinitely broad, colorful, and manifold creation, praise arises. It is not something a person must force and wrestle for. We only have to open our eyes and see God's care for us in all things. What does God say in Zenetti's poem? "I have been your host. . . . [I]t was my pleasure."

Looking at the world this way, however, is not just a matter of course. We can see it very differently: the animal world as an eternal and monstrous devouring and being devoured; human society as an unending process of tapping in the dark with our eyes blindfolded, always on the brink of the abyss; the starry heavens as an endless, cold space that would destroy us instantly if we were not wearing spacesuits.

The psalms are aware of all that. They know the threats to which we are exposed. They know the chaos from which God continually rescues creation. They know the crises of the nations, the arrogance of the powerful, the deadly rivalries in the midst of the people of God. Praise of creation in the psalms is such *despite* these chasms. And that is the only way in which it can make biblical praise possible, the recognition of God's glory beyond all distress and beyond the apparent void of meaning.

Praise opens for us the meaning of the world. It expands our horizon. It draws us out of our depressions, out of the despair that sometimes sneaks up on us. It does not narrow our gaze but opens our eyes to the whole breadth of reality.

Obviously I can consider the colors of a butterfly that flutters across a clearing as the complicated result of a long chain of mutations and selections. I must, in fact, do so. And obviously I may regard the song of the rising lark as an effective marking of his own territory. I have to do so. And obviously I can define a mighty, marvelously spreading beech tree with broad, welcoming branches as a "a plant with an elongated stem, or trunk, supporting leaves or branches." Thus the definition of "tree" in Wikipedia.

And yet I can say, with Günter Eich, "who would wish to live without the comfort of trees!"[3] and I can see the colors of the butterflies and the song of the birds as the gift of a Creator who cares for the world, there for no other purpose than to make me happy.

All this means that the world has dimensions that cannot be comprehended purely through the natural sciences. They evoke in us happiness, joy, enchantment, security, or comfort. But these other dimensions of the world open themselves in their full profundity only in praise of God.

Thanksgiving

I have spoken at some length about nature and creation. But in the psalms, and throughout the Bible, something else plays a much more important role, namely, history. God is not only praised as the one who made heaven and earth but still more often as the one who led Israel out of the slave state of Egypt and raised Jesus from the dead.

The Bible looks not only at creation but much more intensely at God's deeds in history. And from that arises another attitude of prayer: thanksgiving. It is closely akin to praise. Giving thanks for God's deeds presupposes, of course, that one believes in God's actions in history, and that one tells of God's deeds. But that in turn presupposes that there is a place where one can tell of those deeds, that there are believers who listen trustingly and in turn, filled with gratitude, relate their own experiences with God.

The Acts of the Apostles says that the assembled community is the place where the deeds of God—including especially God's current acts— are reported (cf., e.g., Acts 14:27). In this the young church followed a basic structure already given it by Israel. We can describe that basic structure: crisis—plea to God for rescue—rescue by God—Israel's public thanksgiving. For example, when someone in Israel was in deep crisis, he made a vow, and when God had then delivered the individual from the crisis, he brought a thanksgiving sacrifice to be offered in the temple. The summit of this thanksgiving sacrifice was the *todah* meal.

For the *todah* sacrifice and the banquet that followed, the individual in question gathered her family and friends. During the meal she told what God had done for her and her family, how God had helped her and brought her out of her distress. The assembled company made the thanksgiving of the rescued individual its own, and in doing so knew itself joined to the whole of God's people, because help for every individual was help for all Israel.

Another opportunity to thank God for God's deeds came at the great temple feasts: Passover (Easter), Shavuot (the feast of Weeks), Sukkoth (the feast of Booths), Rosh Hashanah (New Year), and Yom Kippur (the Day of Atonement). All those feasts were, from a very early date, historical festivals at which all Israel came together to thank God for God's deeds in history, above all, for leading the people out of Egypt. That is especially obvious at the Seder, the beginning of the Passover feast. Passover is remembering and giving thanks for the leading of Israel out of Egypt, out of a totalitarian state into freedom.

But it was not only at the major feasts that Israel remembered God's great deeds in history and gave thanks. At every Sabbath worship the Torah is read, and so the history of the people of God is made present. Christian worship joins the two: the liturgy of the word from synagogue worship and the great thanksgiving of the Jewish festivals, above all, of course, the Seder. That is why the highest form of all Christian assemblies is called *eucharistia*, thanksgiving. And within this great feast of *eucharistia* a central part stands out as the high point of all Christian thanksgiving: the eucharistic prayer. It reaches from the solemn opening ("Let us give thanks to the Lord, our God") to the great doxology at the end and the affirming "Amen" of the whole assembly—the most important of the many "amens" in Christian worship.

This powerful eucharistic prayer is the church's basic act, which is to say, the basic action of the church is thanksgiving. We see this from the fact that this eucharistic prayer gathers everyone around it: those near and far, the living and the dead, the ordained ministers and the people of God. The eucharistic prayer gathers them all by remembering them or even calling them by name.

But every eucharistic celebration gathers not only the earthly church; it calls together the church already perfected as well. All the angels and saints are assembled, and in that gigantic assembly God, the Father, is thanked for the divine saving action. The Father has rescued Jesus and, with Jesus, his people as well from death and led them into the light of resurrection—and is still doing it.

Forgive me for reciting things you have long known. In doing so, I am aiming at this: if God is the Creator of the world and the Lord of history who created us, sustains us, holds us in life every second of every day, constantly rescues God's people from their self-created chaos, and desires nothing but the salvation of the world—then giving thanks to God is the most elementary thing in our lives. Then this thanksgiving is not something that exists alongside a lot of other things; it is something like the steady breathing without which we would suffocate. God's saving grace that surrounds us and our thanksgiving that responds to it are the foundation on which we exist. Whoever stands on that foundation stands within reality. Whoever denies or suppresses it moves out of reality into the abyss, into pure unreality. Therefore prayer in all its forms is infinitely more than a mere psycho-pharmaceutical, infinitely more than a kind of life support, infinitely more than mere hygiene for the soul. Prayer tears away the curtain to reveal true reality, what we are and what keeps us alive.

Stories of Prayer

At the beginning of this chapter I presented a fictional scenario: the shifting ways of speaking during the lives of two people who love each other—how they are constantly telling each other new things, thanking each other, giving each other nicknames, but also how they complain and quarrel—and finally forgive each other and remember the beginnings of their love. I described this scenario to show how many ways of speaking there are and how important they are for prayer. But obviously I wanted to do a lot more, and you will have noticed that right away.

Every love has its history: its springtime, its summer, its cold and frosty nights. And it has its autumn, which is often much more beautiful than spring and summer because one has gone through good and bad days and allowed mutual love to ripen.

But just as there are infinitely many love stories, each of us has her or his own very personal history of prayer. In those stories there are hours of overflowing gratitude but also those of dryness and desolation. In those stories of prayer there are times in which modern prayers with new, bold formulae appeal to us, but there are also phases in which we learn again how much power is concealed within the ancient prayers of the people of God, especially the psalms. In the history of our prayers there are times when all the words we say to God seem to us inadequate, and we can do nothing but hold out our lives to God in silence. But there are also times when we are driven to speak out loud and in public, with the congregation assembled before God.

In the history of our prayer there are hours when prayer seems to arise of itself and fulfill us, but there are also phases when we perhaps cannot pray at all for a time. I myself have always noticed very quickly how disordered and unreal my life becomes in such times, but not primarily because I was lacking the correct hygiene for the soul. Praying or not praying goes deeper. To repeat: it is about the foundation, the roots of our existence. We pull up those roots when we no longer speak with God, when we do not complain to God, plead in earnest, praise and thank God. It is when we address God in complaint and petition and praise that God really becomes our conversation partner, that is, a person, the living God.

A fifteen-year-old once complained to me about his suffering. He lived with his brother, two years older, in the same family, in the same house. But because he supposedly had insulted his brother at some time or other, the brother had not spoken a word to him for years. The older brother completely ignored the younger one, did not take note of him, deliberately looked past him. The parents were helpless. I could not even imagine the situation, but that is how it was. And I would say: it was a crime, because in this way the younger brother was degraded to a non-person. He was not even an object. His existence was denied.

People between whom community exists *must* express that community. They look at each other. They talk with each other. They say "good morning." They say "good night." They say "enjoy!" at table. There are thanks and requests that pass between them. If none of that exists, their life together becomes an act of mutual destruction.

The same is true of our relationship to God: if there is no living conversation between us and God, neither lament nor petition nor thanksgiving, God will never be a person and therefore, in the long run, will be nonexistent. But for those who pray, God becomes the living God, a person, a partner. People who pray find that God looks at them, gives them a thousand signs that God is constantly putting new joy into their hearts, and that for them nothing is "in vain." They have grounded themselves in God.

In the third part of this chapter I quoted a poem by Günter Eich that begins with the cry: "who would wish to live without the comfort of trees!" In conclusion I will adapt that statement a little and say: "who would wish to live without the comfort of prayer!"

Chapter 21

What Distinguishes Christianity from the Religions?

For quite a while now, many neopagans and quite a few of the baptized have been making up their own religions: they cobble together a private faith out of mismatched bits of the widest variety of religions and worldviews, because the church has scarcely anything to say to them or is simply irritating. Even among some "confessing" Christians, faith in central parts of the creed is gradually fading—the resurrection of the dead, for example. A good many orient themselves to foreign beliefs such as Buddhism or nature religions, or they make up their own mixture altogether. A statement from this thirty-five-year-old is typical:

> I don't really know what my religion is. I was baptized, but I haven't gone to church for a long time. Jesus was certainly an important person, and I believe in the divine element in the world. But I can't deal with the church. The Dalai Lama appeals to me more: his humanity, his humor, his sanity. Reincarnation would be nice; it makes some sense to me. But the most important issues for me are protection of the environment and the problem of climate change. For that we have to learn from the Indians.

Fifty years ago scholars predicted that through the sciences, especially the natural sciences, the Enlightenment would gradually bring an end to religion. Today a good many religious sociologists are surprised to find that exactly the opposite has occurred: religion is enjoying a renaissance—not, however, the church religions, but private religion, with all the arbitrary characteristics that are associated with what is private.

The prognosis of the religious sociologists is, however, also being shattered by the fact that Islam has awakened to new vitality, not only in its core regions, but far beyond them. In that case, of course, it is by no means a matter of arbitrary religious choice but rather the contrary.

Add the following: many Christians who once could "believe along with" the "established church" without having to give much thought to the foundations of their faith are suddenly faced with decisions they are in no way capable of resolving on their own. That is our situation: much insecurity, a degree of helplessness, and the erosion of faith.

What Is the Difference?

For all these reasons it is the church's urgent and even essential duty to make clear what is specifically Christian. This distinctive Christian reality is not easily delineated, because at first glance the religions and Christian faith seem to have an extraordinary amount in common. Hindus go to their temples, and Christians to church. What is the difference? There are glittering festivals in all the nature religions, and Christians also celebrate their great feasts. What is the difference? Many Muslims pray a rosary of ninety-nine beads; many Catholics pray a rosary of fifty-nine beads. What difference can we find there?

Buddhist monks meditate, and so do Christian monks. Hindus have their ancient Vedas, seen by them as revelation, and Christians have the Bible, which they regard as revelation. There are sacred songs in all religions, and Christians sing hymns as well. Visitors to the temples of all religions bring sacrificial gifts to worship, and the offering basket circulates in Christian churches. In all religions, including Christianity, there is a demonstrable conviction that one must do what is good and not do what is evil, and that doing good is not in vain but brings promises with it.

What Is Religion?

I could go on like this for a long time and list one common feature after another. At first sight there are an extraordinary number of correspondences between Christianity and the religions. Often their external forms differ, but many scholars of religion assert that the same basic movement, the same basic attitude, underlies all the variety of external forms. Religion, they say, is the transcendence of the self, surrender to a cause that is greater, holier, and more global than the self—indeed, religion is not only surrender to this greater and holier thing but absolutizing it. And that is true of all religions. They all, so it is said, reach out toward the One, the Unnameable, the Incomprehensible. Nothing differs except the external forms and rituals, and those are simply a matter of the multiplicity of human cultures.

In the year 384 CE, when Christianity was already on its way to becoming the state religion of the Roman Empire, the Roman senator and city prefect Symmachus handed a petition to the Roman emperor Valentinian II, requesting the restoration of the goddess Victoria in the senate house; at the same time he presented a defense of the ancient Roman religion. Essentially he was defending not only Roman religion but also the pluralism proper to it: the gods were interchangeable. No one saw any difference between Roman Jupiter and Greek Zeus. A short passage from Symmachus's petition has become famous because it corresponds precisely to our contemporary mind-set:

> It is just that all worship should be considered as one. We look on the same stars, the sky is common, the same world surrounds us. What difference does it make by what pains each seeks the truth? We cannot attain to so great a secret by one road. (Symmachus, *Relatio* 3.10)

This is neoplatonic, pious, tolerant, and appealing: every religion reflects something of the one great truth, but none of them has the whole. It is only against the sunset horizon of this late ancient piety that the enormity of what Jesus says in the Fourth Gospel is apparent: "I [alone] am the way, the truth, and the life" (John 14:6). For the Roman city prefect Symmachus and for by no means few Christian theologians (theological representatives of so-called religious pluralism) it is all about the one, hidden mystery of the divine. Rituals, customs, external paths leading to this mystery of the world are culturally different, but all lead to it in the end. Each should follow her or his own path.

To this I want to say in advance: if you look more closely and with a sharper eye you will see even in the external rituals the fundamental differences between the religions and Christianity.

Christian Prayer

For example, the Christian prayer of petition is fundamentally different from that in the religions. I will use a pointed expression, at the risk of oversimplification: petitionary prayer in the religions wants something from God. It tries to move God, to interest the deity in one's own cause, to bring the god to one's own side; in fact, it tries to change God's mind. In Christian prayer, by contrast, it is not a question of what *I* want but what *God* wants. Christians pray to know the will of God and to turn themselves to that will.

Of course, Christians are in constant danger of descending to the level of the purely religious, that is, seeing everything as revolving around them and regarding God merely as the legitimation of and aid for one's own interests. Christian prayer too quite often has the basic structure: "Dear God, please make my wishes your own! See to it that you want what I want!" There is the constant threat, within Christianity, of slipping into religion. Christian faith is, consequently, a constant return, a steady reflection on what is distinctively Christian, as the Bible and—building on the Bible—the church's tradition teaches.

I could view all the phenomena that Christianity, at first glance, seems to have in common with the religions in the same way. Sharp differences would appear everywhere. Christian baptism is something fundamentally different from Hindus' bathing in the waters of the Ganges. Jesus Christ's sacrifice on the cross is something completely different from the countless sacrifices throughout the history of religions. And when Christians assemble for Eucharist, that is also something different from the visit of a group of Japanese to a Shinto temple.

But I do not want to make that sort of comparison here. Instead, I want to move directly to the center, the place where all merely external phenomena have their basis, and I will do this in three steps. If one wants to know the nature of a terrain, what is hidden in its depths, it is unnecessary to dig up the whole plot. One uses test wells. Likewise, I will sink three test wells into the soil of Jewish and Christian faith.

First, though, I have to offer a brief aside. As you have certainly noticed long ago, I do not count Judaism, from which the church emerged in closest contact, among the religions any more than I do Christianity. In biblical Israel and the church all religions were redeemed. Therefore a Christian theologian may never and in no case place Israel alongside the religions. Certainly one must also speak of the differences between Judaism and Christianity, but that is a separate subject, one I will not address at this point. What I will discuss here, in my three test probes, is based on the commonalities between biblical Israel and the church.

The first of these three test probes could be entitled:

God Is God and Not World

You may be surprised that my first point is not that for Jews and Christians there is only one God and not a plurality of gods. I could have said that, of course, and it would have been quite correct. But the real difference between Israel's faith and that of the majority of the religions was not only the number of gods, whether one or ten or thirty or seventy. The difference lay at a deeper level: for the most part the gods of the Gentiles were powers of this world that were absolutized; people subjected themselves to those powers and elevated them to the level of deities.

For example, people continually find it an enormous temptation to dominate others, and they therefore act as if the possibility of ruling over others were something divine, that is, something ultimate, unconditional, and absolutely fascinating. So they serve power and give it names such as Zeus, Jupiter, Baal, or Donar, and in worshiping Zeus they worship the power to dominate and derive from that their own right to dominate others. Or they experience again and again the seductive temptation of sexuality, rip it from its context in creation, and say: sexuality and Eros are something divine, an ultimate meaning, a final goal. Sexuality is the highest thing there is; I will submit to it. And then they give that temptation names like Aphrodite or Venus, and in worshiping the goddesses of love they isolate sexuality from its context and claim the right to serve it without restraint.

Thus human beings make every great and fascinating reality in the world into a god and surrender themselves to those gods: nature and the homeland, intoxication and war, money and knowledge, love and hate, life and death, and many other powers as well. All of them become gods for humans, to which—according to the situation—they subject themselves and by which they allow themselves to be governed.

I think it is clear enough that Israel's faith in a single God did *not* mean that it had made a single god of all those many gods, concentrating the multiple powers of the world in a single Power. If that had been so, then Israel's faith would not be really different from the Gentile religions. What happened in the people of God of the Old Testament was utterly different. In a thrilling process of enlightenment, Israel was made to know that God is not world; God stands over against the world as the Wholly Other who created the world and for that reason is not world. With that insight, the world was de-divinized. It was emptied of the gods imagined by human beings. It was freed from the self-created demons that had again and again driven people about in fear and unfreedom.

This de-divinization of the world was not a loss; it was not a banalization of the world. On the contrary: only at that point did the true brilliance, the true beauty that the world possesses because it is God's creation, become evident. The de-divinization of the world created for the first time the possibility of giving a redeemed form to the world's great realities such as love, power, and society, of forming them into what God intends them to be.

Israel's breathtaking step from the many gods to the one God was thus not simply a subtraction from the number of gods; it implied a completely new knowledge of who God is: not a power of nature, not a piece of the world, not the foundation of the world, not the pinnacle of the world, but the Wholly Other, the one who is altogether *not* world but Creator, Fashioner, Sustainer, and Perfecter of the world.

I am not sure that we have really grasped this revolutionary recognition by Israel in its full depth. The history of European thought, the development of the natural sciences, indeed, our whole culture, would have been unimaginable without this de-divinization of the world. And contrariwise: when belief in the Jewish-Christian God, the Creator of heaven and earth, is snuffed out, then inevitably the old gods return. Then people fall back into nature mysticism, belief in fate, new forms of magic, fear of a variety of powers. They are again afraid of drawing the gods' attention to themselves, lest they be robbed of their happiness. They again have demons on their backs or descend into pure irrationality. They embrace trees, plumb their horoscopes every week or every day, call falling stars a good omen, join Franz Beckenbauer in believing in metempsychosis, are afraid of secret rays, and hang semiprecious stones on their bodies to heal their livers. It is not a matter of irrelevance to fall back behind the biblical belief about creation. In the long run it has enormous consequences. We can already sense them quite clearly. Pagan anxiety is growing.

Redemption by God or Self-Redemption?

I am now at my second point—if you will, my second test well. I do not know if you have ever noticed, when visiting a bookstore, what a horde of self-help literature is to be found there. The shelves are brimming over with titles such as "Eating Right" and "Living a Healthy and Happy Life" and "Avoiding Electromagnetic Pollution" and "Writing a Letter of Application" and "Everything You Need to Know about Body Language" and "Now at Last: A Healthy Figure" and "Baby Care Is Child's Play" and "My Child Is at the Awkward Age" and "The Husband Every Woman Wants" and "The Wife Every Husband Wants," and so on and so on.

Books like these can be very practical. They often make you laugh, and sometimes they are simply laughable. But on closer inspection they reveal a particular tendency. They are not only written because the circle of experience once provided by the extended family, in which a great many life experiences were handed on from generation to generation, is now absent. No, there is another reason for a broad sector of self-help literature: it betrays a deep longing, a desire not to have to depend on others, the urge to be self-sufficient in everything. Behind this, still deeper, lies the will: I want to be my own master. I won't let anybody tell me how to live. A book is something I can keep at a distance; basically I don't need anyone else. What I am, I am on my own initiative. And behind that, still a level deeper, lies the desire to save oneself.

Not long ago a magazine on the subject of modern pastoral care arrived at my house. The cover advertised a lead article entitled "Becoming Human." If you are thinking, "Ah, that was the Christmas issue," you are right. But if you think the article was about Jesus' incarnation, you are mistaken. It was, rather, about becoming human oneself. The subtitle was "Being Holy Means Being 'Myself.'" Instead of "Becoming Human," the title could have been "Self-Redemption," because that is what it was about.

The article invited the readers to find themselves, experience themselves, discover themselves, develop what is within them, bring their humanity to fulfillment, become a blessing to themselves. Its recommended subject for meditation had nothing at all to do with Christian meditation. It was about one thing only: finding one's true self through self-redemption.

What is now being propagated by quite a few pastors and theologians in the church, quietly or even loudly and unconcealed, is exactly what has always existed in the history of many religions: self-redemption! It invites people to save themselves through outward and inward cleansing, physical exercises, meditation techniques, renunciation, correct nutrition, ascesis, concentration, discovery of the true self.

Some time ago our letterboxes in Munich contained an ad for the local esoterica fair. The major part of the leaflet was devoted to self-recommendation by Thea, the wise witch:

> Primal knowledge and primal strengths slumber within all of us;
> they must simply be awakened. My experience and knowledge can
> help you to discover this primal knowledge in the depths of your
> own soul, so that it can heal you.

What is healing, what is divine, lies in all of us, then. It only has to be awakened. This kind of yearning for self-redemption is very ancient. Indian Kundalini yoga offers the following idea: at the lower end of the spine there slumbers a divine energy, coiled like a snake. It is called Shakti, the name of the god Shiva's consort. Correct meditation can awaken it, and it will traverse the spine upward, travel through the various ethereal centers of the channels of energy in the body, and ultimately unite with Shiva. Then the one meditating enters a condition of limitless knowledge and bliss.

"Gnosis" in the early church offered a very comparable model of salvation. The church engaged in an unexpectedly difficult defensive battle against Gnosis in the second and third centuries CE. Gnosis means "knowledge" or "awareness." The true Gnostic, according to this heretical form of Christianity, recognizes the divine in herself or himself, thus grasping one's individual heavenly origin. In this way the Gnostic saves himself or herself from the misery of the world. Educated people in particular were fascinated by such a doctrine of salvation at that time, not only because Gnosis cleverly adapted every text from Homer to the Bible to its own ends. What was so seductive was the message that human beings conceal the divine within themselves; it is their hidden, true self that must only be recognized and liberated.

There are many indications that for some decades now, almost unnoticed, a new Gnosis has spread through the church. All too often there appear in sermons and teaching models words such as "encounter with the self," "being in accord with oneself," "living in harmony with oneself," "accepting oneself," "self-realization." Such language aims, consciously or unconsciously, at self-redemption. One's ego is made the highest and the ultimate and becomes sufficient in itself.

There is a terrible temptation in the religion of self-redemption, because it comes to meet people where they are. They want to be divine, that is, they want to be masters of their own lives. And at this very point the Bible says, with immense energy: you cannot save yourself. You are not God. You are a creature, and therefore you are dependent on God and your fellow human beings with your whole existence. That you live at all is pure gift. You need constant help. You are unceasingly directed toward others.

Some time ago a teacher told me the story of a boy whose parents had enrolled him, three years earlier, in an elementary school in Munich where she herself taught. No private school would accept this boy. From the beginning, he acted like a little beast. He began to fume and break out in rage the moment he felt he was not the center of attention. He cried and shouted if something he was doing did not succeed—and that was often the case. He repeatedly struck other children or ran around the classroom like a wild thing. Then he would sink into a depressive phase. His mother feared that her child could not stay in the school. Later she said that during the first weeks she sat near the phone, shaking, and expecting that any minute she would get a call from the school to say, "Sadly, we cannot keep your child here." After all, that had happened many times before. The mother's panic was as severe and devastating as her child's disorder.

It was due to understanding teachers that slowly, through unspeakable effort, things got better; the child even skipped a grade. But it was not the teachers alone. The boy was indebted also to the help of his fellow pupils and the understanding and cooperation of the other parents. He owed it all to the community spirit and common care of many who worked together in that school in admirable fashion. The whole was also supported by a physician who brought his experience and advice to the project.

The child would never have escaped the vicious circle of disturbed behavior and woundings by his own strength. He needed help. He could not free himself. But above all, his parents needed help, and so did the teachers—namely, the help of a genuine cooperation in which people worked together and not against each other.

What the teacher told me seemed to me a veritable paradigm for all our lives. We cannot save ourselves. We can only open ourselves to the help that comes to us from without, from others, ultimately from *one* Other. We can see from this example how rescue, liberation, redemption happens, the kind of thing the Bible talks about: that we enter into a space where help, liberation, and rescue are already given. Christians call that space the people of God, or the church.

How Redemption Enters the World

This brings me to my third point, the third test well. The question now is how, in what way, redemption can be brought to the world. Many have tried to redeem the world, to change it. Every revolution is aimed at freeing the masses, releasing people from their misery, altering every condition of life. Every revolution desires a new consciousness, a new society, a new economy, a new art, a new humanity.

But revolutionaries have a fundamental problem: they have no time. Individual lifetimes are limited, and the masses are inert. If revolutionaries are to see the new society they long for in their own lifetimes, they have to change the old society in a relatively short time, and they can only do that by force. Why force? Quite simply because, in the first place, it is quick, and in the second place because they do not believe in a freely chosen reversal of things. They prefer to rely on force.

Current scholarly definitions of revolution, in fact, contain at least three elements: first, that the masses are involved; second, that the social upheaval takes place rapidly; and third, that the overthrow is to be accomplished through open and direct violence. The last paragraph of the *Communist Manifesto* reads:

> The Communists disdain to conceal their views and aims. They openly declare that their ends can be attained only by the forcible overthrow of all existing social conditions. Let the ruling classes tremble at a Communist revolution. The proletarians have nothing to lose but their chains. They have a world to win. Working men of all countries, unite!

At the center of this decisive closing section of the *Manifesto*, violence is explicitly proclaimed as a necessary principle of the world revolution. There is no other possibility if one has little time and the whole world must be saved at one blow. Human freedom is, however, left behind in the process. Countless people are defiled and left in the mud.

God's principle is different. To put it somewhat crudely: God is a better strategist. Like all revolutionaries, the God of the Bible desires a total overthrow, a radical alteration of world society, because revolutionaries are right about one thing: this is about the whole world, and the change must be radical, simply because the misery of the world cries out to heaven and because it begins deep within human hearts. But how can anyone change the world and society at the root without taking away freedom?

It can only happen if God begins "small," starts at one place in the world. There must be a place—visible, comprehensible, subject to testing— where the redemption of the world begins, that is, where the world becomes what, in God's sense, it should be. The new thing in the world can then spread from that place outward, but certainly not by propaganda, not by indoctrination, not by force. People must have the opportunity to come and see, to view the new thing and test it. If they want to, then, they can allow themselves to be drawn into the history of blessing and peace that God is bringing about. Only in that way is the freedom of the individual preserved. What drives them to the new thing must not be compulsion or moral pressure but only the fascination of an altered world.

So God, in contrast to the revolutionaries, must begin in a small way, with a little nation. More precisely, God cannot begin with a nation or a people. God must start with an individual, because only the individual is the point where God can count on *repentance in freedom*. That is precisely what the ancestral narratives in Genesis are about. The first pages of the Bible had told of the creation of the world, the development of human history, and—with only a few hints—the evolution of human civilization and culture. But in all that, the Bible also told right away about disobedience to God and so about the growth of destructive rivalries and brutal violence.

But then, in chapter 12, Genesis begins something new. Suddenly it is no longer focused on humanity as a whole but starts again with an individual: Abraham. God begins to transform the world by starting anew in a particular place in the world with a single person:

> Now the LORD said to Abram, "Go from your country and your kindred and your father's house to the land that I will show you. I will make you a great nation, and I will bless you, and make your name great, so that you will be a blessing. I will bless those who bless you, and the one who curses you I will curse; and in you all the families of the earth shall be blessed." (Gen 12:1-3)

So God begins anew, with an individual. But the story will not be simply about this individual; he is to become a great nation. That is unavoidable, because a single individual could not show what God wants to establish: *a new society*. The individual must therefore be at the beginning, but the end result must be a new society, for redemption, salvation, and peace always have also—and primarily—a social dimension.

Still, this nation God will create remains aware of the irreplaceability of the *individual*. The people of God may never become a pure collective reality, a mass; it must always also be "Abraham," that is, a people in which every individual is constantly called by God to her or his particular duty.

Something else is also true of this people: it does not remain in and for itself. Its goal is not its own existence; it is not there for itself but is called out of the mass of the peoples *for the sake of the nations*. In it must become clear, visible, and tangible what God desires of the whole world: freedom, peace, nonviolence, salvation. Because God desires the salvation of the whole world, that salvation, that well-being, must be prepared for and made tangible in the experimental field of a tiny nation, just so that the other nations can see that there really can be justice and peace in the world. It is there so that the nations can see that justice and peace are not a utopia, a "nowhere," and so these other nations can accept the new social order in freedom, simply because they are fascinated by it.

That, of course, places a frightful burden on this tiny people of God, the burden of election. For if God's people do not do justice to their task, if it becomes riddled with strife instead of peace, violence instead of nonviolence, ill-being instead of well-being, it cannot be a blessing for the nations. Then it falls short of the meaning of its existence, and then it will be not only an object of derision to the nations but a force for evil.

God's way is the strategy of a silent revolution, the knowing that everything done for the sake of humanity must begin small, with a tiny nation. That is the only way the freedom and dignity of human beings can be preserved. It is only in this way that the nations can know, not by compulsion, but through immense fascination, what God desires in the world. Therefore God needs a people *of God's own* in the world, and that is why the whole Bible is so pushy about it, speaking again and again about this one nation among the nations, its failure, and the evil that repeatedly spreads out from this people, but also about the new and revolutionary thing that has come into the world through that nation.

In speaking, in this third point, about Abraham and the history that begins with him, I have zeroed in on the issue I want to focus on. I could just as well have chosen any one of a number of biblical texts, especially the gospels and the story of Jesus. With Jesus, this action of God within world history reaches its culmination. Everywhere, as with Abraham and his calling, it is clear that, for Christians as for Jews, salvation happens in history, in the midst of our story, in the midst of our world, on this earth, here and nowhere else.

In this the biblical tradition is already keenly distinguished from many religions—for example, the numerous forms of Gnosis, and from Buddhism, which today exercises a strange fascination for so many. For

Buddhism, salvation is escape from the world. All will, all desire is evil, that is, it causes suffering. And because in this world the human always wants something, always desires something, one must overcome the world. Nirvana is the end of all willing, the end of all desiring.

The Jewish and Christian tradition says precisely the opposite: creation is good. Human will and desire are good. You may enjoy a good meal. You may savor a good wine. You may be happy in embracing your wife or husband. You may rejoice when you succeed in doing something good. You only may not desire what is evil, not wish for something that is against God's order of creation and your own calling. Salvation lies not in exile from the world; the world itself is endowed with salvation to its depths through the history of redemption that began with Abraham and reached its goal in Jesus Christ.

Jesus Christ, his coming, his incarnation show that salvation consists in a deeper and deeper incarnation of God in our world. That is the perfection of the uniquely Jewish-Christian faith: that God, the Wholly Other, who is not world, enters radically into our world, takes up residence in it, and, not only that, becomes flesh, as the prologue to the Fourth Gospel formulates it: "And the word became flesh and lived among us, and we have seen his glory, the glory as of a father's only son, full of grace and truth" (John 1:14).

So the salvation of which the Bible speaks does not happen only in a world beyond. It is present among us already. And it touches not only the soul but the whole person—spirit, soul, innermost as well as outermost being: all one's senses, body, food, work, sleeping, dwelling, environment—everything in us and around us without exception. Christianity is about the redemption, the transformation, the overturning of the whole earth. And as we have seen, the redemption of the world does not happen with a trumpet blast; it does not just fall from heaven. Redemption is no hocus pocus and has nothing to do with magic. The redemption of the world began when a man of the East called Abraham packed up his goods and took to the road.

It is true that redemption is pure grace, something we ourselves cannot effect, but that grace has to be accepted by us, and so it develops as history, a long process of the here and now of our repentance and renewal. Therefore this grace, this redemption needs a people, one that has a memory, is itself a people of memory, a people in which individuals tell each other again and again what God has already done, a people that in every sphere of its life, from the economy to culture, lives this new, saving reality in the world. Therefore this grace needs living communities that do not dwell apart from the world but in which the world is transformed every day.

Such communities are more than clubs, more than a gathering of individuals who are connected simply by the parish office, the bishop's chancery, and the Roman curia. They are more than a service organization for religious needs, more than a group that comes together to organize church picnics and trips. These communities are a space for the rule of God, the Body of Christ, the beginning of the new city of God, the eschatological Jerusalem.

Redemption comes to the world in this way: through a real history that takes place within the world, plays itself out in a people, and then culminates in the life and death of a single individual who draws together in himself all that this people was created to be—such a redemption *within history* exists in none of the religions. It exists only in Israel and the church.

Summary

I have now made test probes at three points in a broad field, so broad that sight can scarcely encompass it. With all of them I wanted to discover what the nature of Christianity is, what distinguishes it, beyond all external features and similarities, from all the religions. Of course, we could have sunk our wells in many other places, but we have to be content with three.

It thus appeared that in the Jewish and Christian tradition God and world are absolutely different. God is not world, and the world is not God. That eliminates many religions already—all the nature religions, almost all the ancient religions, all modern nature mysticism—because they all mix God and world together.

It then was evident that, according to the highly realistic perspective of the Bible, human beings cannot redeem themselves, cannot save themselves. That cuts out all the religions that propose self-redemption, especially Buddhism, all the modern esoteric private religions, but also all recent pseudo-religions such as Stalinism.

The third reality that came to light was that at the center of Jewish and accordingly of Christian faith is the insight that God wants to have a people in the world. Salvation and redemption are for the whole world but must come to them in freedom, without compulsion, and therefore God needs a people, needs communities, that are visible in the world as places of transformation, loci of the silent revolution. That eliminates practically all the world's religions, which is to say, here Israel and the church are distinct from all religions. Judaism and Christianity are not "religions." They are something entirely different. Israel and the church are the redemption of all religions, because here the world and its history are taken with absolute seriousness. Salvation happens in history and through history and beyond.

Finally, it should also have become apparent how deeply the three points I have described are connected with one another: because God is not world, because God is not identical with nature and the powers of the world but has created the world out of love, God is altogether devoted to the world. This is no God of silence but one who hears, speaks, and acts. God has personally entered history because God cannot leave human beings, who turn away from God and therefore suffer and struggle, to remain alone. Only because God is not world can God enter history; only so can there be a history with God. And only because human beings are needy, not divine and not holy, not omnipotent and constantly in need of help, is there a history of redemption.

What about Islam?

It would seem that Islam falls outside our framework, because it makes a sharp distinction between God and the world, and it is also about *umma*, the community of all Muslims. But precisely here the above results are validated again, because at many points Islam is dependent on Judaism and Christianity. This should not be understood to mean that Muhammad stitched together parts of the Jewish and Christian traditions that appealed to him, in a kind of patchwork. He had many opportunities to encounter Israel and the church; for example, it is not impossible that even before him there had been an Arab group of worshipers of an overarching High God, tracing itself to Abraham. It is certainly not beyond the realm of possibility that, on the basis of many influences from Judaism and Christianity, the worship of one single God impressed itself on him so much as to take visionary form. In that case also, a dependence on Israel and the church will have existed. At any rate, it is evident in countless passages of the Qur²an.

But, despite all that it derived from Judaism and Christianity, Islam lacks what appeared in our third point. The God of Islam is far from having the same relationship to history as does the God of the Bible. Certainly, the God of Islam speaks, promises, demands, utters threats. He has sent a long series of prophets (I will list the "biblical" prophets among them, to illustrate how close the Qur'an is to the Bible): Adam, Enoch, Noah, Abraham (= Ibrahim), Lot, Isaac, Ishmael, Jacob, Joseph, Jethro, Moses (= Musa), Aaron, David, Solomon, Elijah, Elisha, Isaiah, Jonah, Job, Zechariah, John the Baptizer, Mary (= Marjam), and Jesus (= Isa). And yet Allah does not act in history as does the biblical God. His actions are confined primarily to giving instructions, the last, greatest, and concluding of which is the Qur'an. This is the central saving event of Islam, and it takes the form of definitive teaching: Allah sends his word for the guidance of humanity into the heart of Muhammad and by that channel into a book. God does not become human; God's word becomes "book."

In this way revelation becomes ultimately only instruction or information. But in the Old Testament it was already more than that. The whole Old Testament is a dramatic dialogue between Israel and its God—and still more, it is a dramatic *event* between Israel and God. God leads the people of God out of Egypt and rescues them from the hand of Pharaoh. God fights for this people in the wilderness. After they worship the golden calf, God threatens to create a new people and retracts the idea in response to Moses' intervention. God casts the people into exile and brings them back to Zion in a new exodus. God struggles for this nation, loves it like a bride, listens to its complaints, suffers with it, renews the covenant with it, leads it again and again to new life. It is a dramatic story.

The story then finds its end, its goal, in Jesus. Whoever hears him, hears God. Whoever sees him, sees the Father. In him the Word of God has become flesh. What the Bible thus depicts is a different, an infinitely more profound relationship of God to the world and history. Therefore, in addition, the Muslim *umma* is something different from the biblical people of God; the two are scarcely comparable.

When one reads the Qur'an all that leaps into view, not only in the content, but formally as well, for the Qur'an has no narratives like those of the Bible. There are many passages that refer to actual events, but they are not narrated in the proper sense of the term. There are many narrative texts, but characteristically those texts take their material from the Bible. Thus, for example, in *Sura* 12 there is a recitation of the Joseph story from the Old Testament, though in time-lapse style and without the colorful details of the biblical text. The story of Moses in *Sura* 20 and the annunciations to Zechariah and Mary in *Sura*s 3 and 19 are told in similar fashion. Whenever there is narrative, then, it is through reference to the Bible, and in the process the biblical narratives are transformed into moral examples. It is really not possible to tell of Allah and his actions in history independently of the Bible. From Allah we have only words, endless series of words.

And now we come to the crucial point: all biblical narrative reaches its culmination in the story of the death and resurrection of Jesus. The one in whom God is altogether present is put to death on a cross, and yet this is how the history of liberation God has been pursuing since Abraham reaches its climax. For the Qur'an this is an impossible story. The real Jesus, says *Sura* 4.157–58, was neither crucified nor killed.[1] This emptying of the crucifixion, making it only a phantom event, is something Muhammad adopted from Christian heretics. Ultimately it is connected to Muhammad's passionate rejection of the trinitarian God. How so? In Christian trinitarian doctrine the "procession" of the "Son" from the "Father" is revealed as a "sending" of the Son into the world. That is how the doctrine of the Trinity substantiates the radical self-communication and self-surrender of God to the world.

Islam is dependent on Judaism and the church in many respects, directly or (which makes no difference) indirectly. That dependency gives it its strength. To put it another way: where it proclaims truth and lives it, it draws on strengths that are constitutive for Jewish and Christian revelation. That is the only explanation for the historical momentum of Islam. But at the same time it has missed the innermost truth of Israel and the church.

Every Truth Comes from the Holy Spirit

But I do not want to finish with this opinion, however accurate I consider it to be. I want to conclude with something different, something that has received far too little attention in this chapter thus far. It is true that we must learn to see what is distinctively Christian—and above all to live it. This is, in fact, urgently necessary in our society, which tries to level everything and obliterate whatever is distinctive. But we must, of course, also see that all religions have always been on pilgrimage in search of the true God, and obviously they have not simply gone astray in their search. From the beginning, they have recognized partial truths, and those partial truths can be so significant that both Jews and Christians need to learn from them.

The Kabbala, a form of Jewish mysticism, considers the long residence of Israel's children in Egypt as a kind of stratagem of providence: all the sparks of truth scattered through the Egyptian temples are said to have entered into the flame of Israel's knowledge. Justin, Irenaeus of Lyons, and Clement of Alexandria, all great theologians of the early church, speak of the multiform "seeds of the *Logos*" among the Gentiles. They are referring not to the Gentile religions, of course, but to the pagan philosophers whose critique of religion paved the way for the truth of Christianity.

The Apostle's Creed points in a similar direction: the breathtaking image of Christ's descent into Hades is interpreted to mean that, in his death, Christ has reached out to, liberated, and brought into the light all the truths the people of the world have ever discovered. Thomas Aquinas even dares to say, "*Omne verum, a quocumque dicatur, a Spiritu sancto est.* [All truth, no matter who has spoken it, comes from the Holy Spirit.]"[2] What is so magnificent and for me so continually fascinating is that so much is gathered and brought together in the church: the truths of the pagans, all the knowledge of true philosophy, the wealth of the arts—but it is not simply tossed together. It is purified, clarified, redeemed.

All that is true not only of the past. The process of gathering and bringing together is ongoing. God can also allow truths to appear outside the church, truths that had been buried in Christian consciousness or had never really come to the fore. For example: the church of the first three centuries was clearly distanced from the Roman state, not only because the state was profoundly shaped by paganism or because it persecuted Christians from time to time. No, the early church was aware that it was a unique society that must under no circumstances get mixed up with the state. After Constantine, that awareness was gradually lost, in the East more thoroughly than in the West. But then, centuries later, the secular state arose. It dissolved the marriage of church and state in a sometimes violent process of secularization—and that was indeed a blessing for the church. Thoroughly secular forces in this way brought the church back to an awareness of its uniqueness, and in doing so they exercised a prophetic function. They brought about reform in the church, at first contrary to its own ideas of itself—or they did so at least in part, for there are still Christians who think they have to make use of the state in order to preach their message.

We must expect similar processes, in which God intervenes from without, so to speak, at any time. What is God saying to the church through the present worldwide revitalization of Islam? Most certainly not that it should retreat to the mixing of state and religion, or even to the medieval exercise of violence, things that were a matter of course in Islam from the beginning. But can it be that, through the confrontation with Islam,

God wants to say, to a weary and deeply divided Christianity that practices its Christlikeness at most on Sundays, that faith demands one's whole life, that it demands public acknowledgment from every individual, and that if Christians do not come to understand that, it will be extinguished in Europe?

Chapter 22

Where Do We Get Our "Values"?

We hear more and more talk in our society about "values." "The schools have to get back to teaching values," the secretaries of education say. A German president demands "a stronger determination to educate people in values." A variety of public figures of very different political stripes sign a "values initiative." Even NATO was recently called a "society of values."

Serious Competition over a Word

In pedagogical literature especially, but not only there, for some time there has been a plethora of expressions such as these: experiencing values, reliving values, ideas of values, awareness of values, ordering of values, conveying values, educating values, values didactic, determining values, consensus on values, canon of values, index of values, advance in values, conflict over values, changing values, loss of values, decline of values, betrayal of values. Even such an orotund expression as "values arena" has survived for some years now in the equally pompous form "language arena."

None of these words[1] appeared in the hefty Duden Universal Dictionary of 1983. Where does this sudden inflation of "values" words come from? The reason is simply that our society is anxious about apparent signs of disintegration and still more fearful of social chaos. The media present us continually with expressions such as these: national debt crisis, debt trap, educational emergency, youth criminality, shoplifting, media seduction, vandalism, armed autonomy, drug crime, forced prostitution, child pornography, corruption, running amok, lack of childcare, trafficking in organs, human trafficking. We could let the list run on endlessly. And since in a pluralistic society no one dares to speak of the Ten Commandments anymore, we prefer to talk about values and corresponding "rules."

The latest call for communicating values was apparently evoked by economic fears. The financial crisis showed palpably—so we read—that an economy lacking values and conscience cannot function but will throw whole countries into nearly insoluble crisis.

So society is afraid of chaos, and it is fearful that the moral education of youth is collapsing. A word like "moral," however, sounds disgustingly old-fashioned to most people; hence the call for "values." Just as "garbage" is no longer "garbage" but instead has become "scrap" or "recyclable resources," morals are no longer morals but "adherence to values." But it seems that "values" is also a word that can be used to dissolve the connection to the indispensable nature of the human. Values are something passing, changeable, arrived at through discussion and consensus building; they are not, in their nature, binding.

Robert Spaemann points out that when Western visitors remind them of "our values" at the completion of their required program, Chinese politicians are accustomed to answer, with a certain justification, "You yourself say that these are *your* values you are upholding. We have our own values, different from yours. So what do you expect of us?"[2]

What the State Cannot Guarantee

There is yet another and more profound reason for the popularity of the word "values," namely, current discussions about democracy. A phrase of the jurist Ernst-Wolfgang Böckenförde (the so-called Böckenförde Paradox) is repeatedly quoted. He wrote that the modern liberal state is founded and maintained by powers and forces outside itself: *"the liberal, secularised state is nourished by presuppositions that it cannot itself guarantee."*[3] Concretely, that means that pluralist, democratic societies depend for their survival on political virtues such as public spirit and a willingness to compromise and cannot exist without them. But above all, they are grounded in basic values such as freedom, equality, tolerance, and solidarity. Without a social consensus that these and other basic values must be respected, a society would rapidly dissolve. The liberal democratic state cannot, however, guarantee that consensus, and it most certainly cannot impose it. It cannot by its own means even demonstrate the truth of its foundational values and the basic rights that flow from them.

To put it another way: in a democracy, the majority rules. Should it happen that the majority chooses negative values, for example, inequality or the destruction of supposedly "worthless" lives, the formal rules of democracy can ultimately not prevent it from happening. Not even the "basic rights" guaranteed, since May 23, 1949, by the first nineteen articles of the German Constitution (e.g., human dignity, personal freedom, the right to life, freedom of belief and conscience, freedom of opinion, the right to assemble, the inviolability of one's dwelling, etc.) can be sustained without social consensus. It is true that in article 79, paragraph 3 of the Constitution there is a so-called eternity clause, according to which the human rights anchored in article 1, paragraph 2 cannot be removed by a majority vote to amend the Constitution, nor can the principle of democracy. In a nutshell: there are rights that are not subject to a vote.

But that eternal guarantee rests on shaky ground. After all, laws do not need to be repealed. If the consensus wanes they can be restricted or reinterpreted. Consider how our society deals with the not-yet-born—in real life and also in law. Here one can see that it is already in the process of severely restricting one of the basic human rights, namely, the "right to life" from article 2, paragraph 2 of the Constitution. There are evidently any number of possibilities for avoiding even the basic rights in the Constitution or, still worse, applying them "intelligently."

So democratic society is like a tightrope walker. The rope is thin and the abyss is deep. The rope that crosses the abyss is made up of the basic rights or basic values, which ultimately depend on the consensus of society. Will the anchors holding the rope hold? Can the consensus be maintained? Or is it already unraveling? Has the process of erosion already begun? That is the reason for the deep-seated anxiety of many people and ultimately for the inflation of the word "values."

The Source of Values

This makes all the more important the question: where do the basic values enunciated in the German Constitution or in comparable constitutions of other countries come from in the first place? An initial answer can only be that our knowledge of the fundamental values that sustain our basic rights, such as freedom, equality, human dignity, equality of rights, and many more, has come to us from without, by way of history. Basic values are found in history, where they have been formulated and fought over. They were by no means universal and obvious from the beginning.

It is not my intention at this point to trace the multiple branches of our basic values and rights to their roots. That would be a complex and nearly impossible task. We would have to discuss the law collections of the Sumerian king Ur-nammu, the Babylonian Codex Hammurabi from the eighteenth century BCE, the wisdom of ancient Egypt, Plato, Aristotle, and the Stoics, then Roman legal thought, and much, much more. I have to leave all that aside.

I am concerned with something else. I want to point emphatically to a particular root that is often overlooked and is even suppressed and not infrequently muzzled: that is to say, *the* place in the world in which modern basic rights are most strongly rooted, and from which they derive their momentum, is Israel and, later, the church. The people of God, through a long history and with many sacrifices, traveling by way of "trial and error," made an essential contribution to the fundamental rights on the basis of which Western society lives today.

All those who live through faith will say still more: these basic rights were given to Israel by God; they were "revealed" to the people of God. That does not exclude describing the whole process initially "from below," since Israel discovered essential parts of the fundamental rights on the basis of which we live today, and not only discovered them but put them into words—in the law of Sinai, the Torah.

The Torah, the "five books of Moses," was composed and written down, essentially, in the royal period and the subsequent time of exile, as well as in the early postexilic period, encompassing approximately the years 900 to 400 BCE. Oral layers of the Torah are still older. In his message of the reign of God, Jesus fulfilled and at the same time sharpened the Torah. Both of these, the Torah and Jesus' message, are an essential foundation for our basic rights. The great concepts of modern democratic history—liberty, fraternity/sorority, human dignity—reveal as much.

The Role of Israel's Exodus

Looking back, Israel focused the reception of the Torah at a single point: the event at Sinai. There, according to the book of Exodus, Israel received the Torah, a social order such as had never existed before in the world, from the hand of God.

The event at Sinai is preceded by the exodus from Egypt. For the Bible, the two form an inseparable unit. The liberation from Egypt is completed only with the gift of the Torah, which is thus characterized as an order for society that leads to freedom. It does not create a new state like Egypt, where Israel had to perform slave labor; rather, it gives a new order born of freedom.

This connection between the exodus from Egypt and the new social order of Sinai has been like priming powder for the history of freedom in the West. At least in the two great representative freedom movements the Exodus texts were repeatedly cited as criteria: in the English Revolution of the seventeenth century, the mother of all later revolutions, and then in the eighteenth century in the American Revolution. The social philosopher and political scientist Michael Walzer offers a wealth of citations in his book *Exodus and Revolution*.[4]

Oliver Cromwell (1599–1658) opened the first session of the first elected Parliament under his Protectorate with a long speech in which he compared the new situation in England to the exodus of Israel and warned against a return to Egypt, to "bondage under the regal power." Obviously, Cromwell's politics had its dark side: his rule was at times nothing but a military dictatorship. Still, his importance for the history of freedom in Europe should not be underestimated, and for the establishment of his new republic he appealed to Israel's exodus.

In 1776, Benjamin Franklin suggested that the Great Seal of the United States should show Moses with rod uplifted and the Egyptian army drowning in the sea. His suggestion was not accepted, but that he made it at all shows how deeply aware people were, even then, of the biblical roots of their own revolutionary actions.

So in the development of modern democracy the memory of the connection between Israel's exodus and the beginning of a new order of society played an extraordinary role. The Puritans, the Quakers, the Baptists, all of whom received a good deal of impetus from the English and American revolutions, were continually moved and shaped by the Bible. Their preachers referred with unusual frequency to the biblical account of the exodus. Moreover, the Sinai covenant that followed the exodus gave a crucial impetus to contractual theory in the early modern period, because there the whole people accepted God's offer of a covenant (Exod 19:8). Correspondingly, in the (hypothetical) social contract the state depends on the assent of the people.

In the French Revolution the idea of *fraternité*, of brotherhood and sisterhood, that is, solidarity, played a significant role. It too comes from the Bible. In the book of Deuteronomy all who belong to the people of

God are called and addressed as "brothers [and sisters]." But it is not just a matter of terminology. The Torah demands that all the people in Israel are to be treated as brothers (and sisters), even the foreigners. Leviticus 19:33-34 reads:

> When an alien resides with you in your land, you shall not oppress the alien. The alien who resides with you shall be to you as the citizen among you; you shall love the alien as yourself, for you were aliens in the land of Egypt; I am the LORD your God.

Even today our society is far from making such texts a reality. "Love him or her as yourself" means giving the person your attention, feeling concern and caring for her or him as for one's own family. "Yourself" is by no means a single person, an individual, but one's own family and clan, within which as a matter of course there are solidarity and mutual aid.

Human Dignity

The German federal constitution begins with this statement: "Human rights are inviolable" (art. 1.1). The fundamental right to human dignity is also deeply rooted in Israel's Torah, for it says that all people are created by God, even "in [God's] image, according to [God's] likeness" (Gen 1:26). Therefore every human being is infinitely precious and is unique. Since the time of Pope Leo the Great (440–61) the church has prayed in its liturgy: "O God, you have wonderfully created and still more wonderfully renewed human beings in their dignity [*dignitas*]." This fundamental conviction on the part of Israel and the church was essential for the concept of human dignity. The well-known educator Hartmut von Hentig wrote in his book, *Ach, die Werte: über eine Erziehung für das 21. Jahrhundert*:

> Human dignity is a Christian element in our secular constitution. The ancient Greeks found it difficult to construct such an idea and to apply it consistently because some of them had come into the world already slaves, and in their view anyone who was not free was only half human.[5]

We are thus indebted to Israel's Torah for essential impulses toward the concepts of freedom, human dignity, and a fraternity/sorority that extends to everyone. Other basic concepts of democracy come also from that little nation: the right to inviolability of one's dwelling (Deut 24:10-11), the idea of division of powers within the state. In chapters 17–18 of Deuteronomy there is a clear division between the office of the king, that of the priest, and that of prophets. These three offices are there seen as independent of one another and each has its own function within the whole society. And the king is subject to the Torah, just as are the priests and prophets. It is constitutive. Accordingly, Deuteronomy 17:18-20 says of the king:

> When he has taken the throne of his kingdom, he shall have a copy
> of this law written for him in the presence of the levitical priests. It
> shall remain with him and he shall read in it all the days of his life,
> so that he may learn to fear the Lord his God, diligently observing
> all the words of this law and these statutes, neither exalting himself
> above other members of the community nor turning aside from the
> commandment, either to the right or to the left.

Israel's Ability to Discern

Obviously it was not only Israel and the church that made possible our present constitutional state. Other peoples and cultures developed progressive systems of law, created the preconditions for human rights, and advanced the humanization of society. We must even say that Israel adopted a good deal from the peoples around it. After all, it was surrounded by great empires: Egypt, Assyria, Babylon, and, after Alexander the Great, the Hellenistic empires. It was constantly forced to engage with the religion, cultures, and social forms of the neighboring peoples.

Israel not only sat "in the center of the nations" (Ezek 5:5) but had them in its own midst. Strongly fortified Canaanite cities such as Megiddo, Beth-shean, Beth-shemesh, Gezer, and Jerusalem remained initially Canaanite. Later, in the New Testament period, there were purely Hellenistic cities in the land, including Tiberias, Sepphoris, Sebaste, Antipatris, and Scythopolis. It is clear that the constant contact with other cultures and religions must have sharpened their sense of them and their ability to discern. Israel derived much of its knowledge of God and the world from the Canaanites, the Egyptians, the Assyrians, the Babylonians, the Persians, and the Greeks. It eavesdropped very sensitively on the cultures and religions in its environment.

But those influences were always clarified, refined, placed in a new context, and thus altered in the direction of the biblical images of God and humanity. Israel did not adopt anything unquestioningly. It examined everything minutely, compared, made distinctions, critiqued, sharpened, altered, placed it all against a new background, and in that way created something new.

The State Is Not God

This new reflection on the idea of society would not have been possible without a new experience of God, of YHWH, the God who rescues and liberates. When Israel tried to describe its God, it could only repeat: our God is the one who liberated us from the slave state of Egypt. So when Israel calls YHWH its "LORD," it does not refer to a despot with a claim to submission but to its Creator and Liberator. YHWH had snatched this people from the hand of Pharaoh and traveled with it through the wilderness. YHWH bore it up and fed it and forgave its sins again and again. YHWH was a God of nearness, a God "who comes to our aid." While Israel often resisted God, it entrusted itself to its God over and over again and confessed with greater and greater clarity its belief that it must serve only this one God—in fact, that this God is the only one who exists.

This led to a de-divinization of the world, and for that very reason Israel could call into question the idea of the state as a mythic and therefore sacrosanct entity. It could demythologize the ancient Near Eastern state, which asserted that it was the absolute ruler, indeed, an untouchable god, and so lay a decisive foundation for the Western constitutional state.

According to faith, the Torah was given and revealed to Israel by God, but not as if it were something foreign and external to the world that had fallen from heaven. It was rather so that in it the wisdom of the world, the rationality of creation, and the laws of life are contained, put into words, and acknowledged as instruction that gives life. The Torah arose in history and comes to us by way of history—and yet it brings to light what the meaning of creation is, what is therefore written in the hearts of all people and all nations. But that inner truth of the world had to be drawn out of creation and history, and it had to find a place in the world where it could be held fast and never forgotten again. God willed that Israel should be that place.

Visible in a Particular Place

The link to a particular people is essential to the Torah; that is why it is itself so concrete. The instructions from Sinai are not an idealized image like Plato's ideal state. Israel always knew that, precisely because the

Torah is not a commandment imposed solely from without. Because it unveils the reality of creation, it grasps real life in detail. In Deuteronomy 22:8 we read: "When you build a new house, you shall make a parapet for your roof; otherwise you might have bloodguilt on your house, if anyone should fall from it." In the daytime it would be too hot on the flat roof of the house, but in the evening and at night it was pleasant to be there, and people often slept on the roof. Therefore a parapet was an important precaution. This is about protection of life in Israel. Even an accidental death must be avoided. Every person in Israel is the guardian of her or his brother and sister. The following regulation, from Deuteronomy 24:5, is equally concrete: "When a man is newly married, he shall not go out with the army or be charged with any related duty. He shall be free at home one year, to [make happy] the wife whom he has married." This commandment is not at all meant for the propagation of many children, perhaps as fodder for later wars. The verb "make happy" belongs, instead, to the sphere of the joy in living that broke forth in Israel at the great festivals.

Just look in the civil law code for a paragraph whose purpose is to "make one's wife happy," that is, one that speaks of happiness and joy in living. It is just as well that the civil law code does not speak of such things. It keeps to its own limits. But Israel's Torah is intended to bring to light the brilliance and beauty of creation. Its aim is for life to succeed. Exodus 23:4-5 points in the same direction:

> When you come upon your enemy's ox or donkey going astray, you shall bring it back. When you see the donkey of one who hates you lying under its burden and you would hold back from setting it free, you must help to set it free.

This too is about Israel's holiness, the glory of living the rationality of creation. The people of God is to be a healed creation; therefore rivalry and enmity within it must again and again be overcome. Exodus 23:4-5 not only shows Torah's tenderness for animals; it also attests that the Old Testament was already acquainted with the commandment to love one's enemy. But that love of enemy is not floating abstractly in some vacuum; it is practical and concrete.

Torah's instructions are thus concrete, and they are to be made visible in a concrete people, a real society. If we only profess in the creed that God is Lord but God's sovereignty is not tangible in real life, the creed remains an empty formula. If we only profess in the creed that God is the creator but God's creative sovereignty is not visible in a real piece of the world transformed by Torah, confession of the Creator will never persuade anyone.

For that very reason, Torah is tied to a particular, clearly defined people, in which it wills to embody itself. Through that people it is fixed firmly in the world forever. The meaning of creation, its wisdom, its reason, its logic can never again be lost to the world, because Israel exists.

That Israel is God's chosen people has always given offense to some. But election in the biblical sense means not preference but appointment to serve. Israel is in service to the other nations because it is the place within the world where the collected experience arising from worship of the true God is held fast and handed on. Perhaps a current problem can illustrate this service by the people of God.

At the end of the twentieth century we found that greater and greater quantities of atomic waste and other poisons were accumulating on the thin skin of our planet. These must be stored securely so that they will not do damage to future generations. But who will know, two hundred years from now, where such materials are stored throughout the world? Who will know how they are stored, what the various vessels contain, and what their condition is? In recent decades any number of conferences of scientists and specialists have been called to deal with this problem. Numerous suggestions have been made. One is that there must be people who are specially appointed and have no other task than to hand on knowledge of places where dangerous materials are stored, from generation to generation, so that there will not be a catastrophe in the world someday.

The task of the people of God is similar: it is to hand on, from generation to generation, the experiences of death and life that Israel has had throughout its long journey, so that this knowledge may never again be lost and thus the evils that might otherwise befall the world may be averted. So when Israel is called a chosen people, it means primarily that, through its knowledge of salvation, it holds the world in balance. Through its collected experiences, recorded in the Torah, it prevents the nations from sinking into the brutality and desolation of naked paganism.

The same is true for the church, the New Testament people of God. The Sermon on the Mount is not a new Torah, not a substitute for Israel's law; it is the fulfillment and perfection of the permanent gift of the Torah from Sinai. According to Matthew 5:17, Jesus says, "Do not think that I have

come to abolish the law or the prophets. I have come not to abolish but
to fulfill."

Values Require Communities

Everything I have just said about the binding of the Torah to a locality,
namely, that the universal moral law becomes visible in a particular
people, is true also of values. They too are locally rooted. They are tied
to the "places" of the history of Jewish and Christian enlightenment.
That is where they are anchored. If the anchor is pulled from its bed they
will drift into nowhere and be lost in the fog.

It would be naïve to suppose that particular basic ideas such as freedom or human dignity are self-evident and must appeal to everyone at
all times. They do appeal and enlighten, but only because they have been
fought for throughout history and because there are people who live
and defend them. Joseph Ratzinger spoke correctly when, in a 1992
speech in the rotunda of the Académie Française, he said, "Freedom can
abolish itself. Freedom can weary of itself when it has become empty.
The twentieth century has offered examples of a majority decision that
served to abrogate freedom."[6]

Values can only remain plausible and convincing from generation to
generation if they are experienced in real-life situations. How can we
make it believable for young people that protection of life is a crucial
and fundamental value if they do not see a place where children are
accepted and protected and where old people are not excluded but can
live in peace with the younger generation? The necessity of this real-life
context is the same for all values. Equality must be practiced. Solidarity
must be experienced. Human dignity must be made visible. Freedom
must be lived as freedom for good, down to the tiniest details of everyday
life. Values as mere "doctrine" would have no chance in the context of
social reality.

But all that is still inadequate. The history of Jewish and Christian
enlightenment incorporates an insight that is simply foundational: that
humanity can only be sustained in the long run if it preserves an awareness of human creaturehood or, more precisely, the acknowledgment
that God is master of life and the world. Only in this way was Israel able
to discover human dignity, and therefore the acknowledgment of God's
sovereignty is also at the center of the Torah.

To put it more clearly and more harshly: in the eyes of a society governed by functionality there can be no reason not to snuff out the lives
of mentally handicapped children who throughout their lives can do

nothing but drool—unless society is convinced that it has no right to do so because it is not the master of life and death, but God alone is master. The idea of human dignity cannot even arise, or it must quickly evaporate, without belief in God as master and creator of life.

The fact that by now, with our technical knowledge, we are in a position to kill children who would otherwise live with such mental handicaps before they are born, in more sterile and less obvious ways, changes nothing. On the contrary, it makes the whole matter all the more dangerous, because if I see a child being killed I can still be outraged, even if the victim itself is debilitated and unappealing. But if its removal is done almost invisibly, in a sterile medical situation, protest is suppressed before it starts.

The history of Jewish and Christian enlightenment includes still another insight: the poverty, weakness, entanglement, and guilt of human beings—and correspondingly, the possibility of forgiveness. Without the experience that in this world, despite all our sinning, there is forgiveness and restoration from God, people can all too easily become cynics. And cynics destroy society.

Church and State

It has probably become clear by now that, if there is to be a foundation of common experiences on the basis of which the people of God's knowledge can be preserved and protected, there must be living communities within the one people of God. But there is no need at all for the state to be transformed into the church and a pluralistic society into a theocracy. The clear separation of church and state has been recovered in the West in a long and painful history, and the process must never be reversed. Joseph Ratzinger wrote in 1965:

> Few things had hurt the Church so much in the last 150 years as its tenacious clinging to outmoded political-religious positions. The attempt to use the State as a protector of faith from the threat of modern science served more than anything else to undermine the faith. . . . The use of the State by the Church for its own purposes . . . has since Constantine been one of the most serious liabilities of the Church, and any historically minded person is inescapably aware of this.[7]

The church must not lay claim to the state for its own purposes, and in the same way, the state must not misuse the church to support its own interests. The church needs the state's protection in order to live its faith in freedom, and the state needs a multitude of believing communities as "the salt of society," because it lives altogether on the basis of presuppositions it cannot of itself guarantee or ground.

Thus the church best helps the state to fulfill its difficult and responsible tasks when it lives the values it has received as clearly and obviously as possible. If it accepts ambiguity, questionable compromises, and improper alliances, it damages itself and ultimately the state as well.

Chapter 23

The *Magnificat*:
Signal for a Revolution

The church's feasts have to be renewed over and over again; otherwise they become stiff and lose their living reality. That is true above all of Marian feasts. They are no longer a matter of course; rather, they provoke objections: There are so many of these Marian feasts. Do we really need them all? And despite all the church's denials, isn't it true that Mary is worshiped at those feasts? Above all, what does this Jewish girl have to do with our problems today—the injustices in society, the misery of the poor, the never-ending wars throughout the world?

The Liturgy's Response

The best answer to such questions comes from the liturgy itself. On Roman Catholic Marian feasts the gospel of the encounter between Mary and Elizabeth is very frequently used. Why this text in particular? Because of the words that Elizabeth says to Mary, of course: "Blessed are you among women" (Luke 1:42), and a little later, "and blessed is she who believed that there would be a fulfillment of what was spoken to her by the Lord" (Luke 1:45). Then Mary speaks her *Magnificat*, where she says of herself: "Surely, from now on all generations will call me blessed" (Luke 1:48). There is no text in the New Testament that is better suited to Marian feasts. It is therefore worthwhile to consider the *Magnificat* in more detail, for it is the basis for the church's praise of Mary and, still more, the basis for all the church's Marian feasts.

Mary as the Ultimate Object?

"Surely, from now on all generations will call me blessed!" Isn't that an embarrassing example of self-praise? No, because it is not primarily about Mary; it is about God's action. As one looks at Mary, praise is given for what God has done: *"for* the Mighty One has done great things for me, and holy is his name" (Luke 1:49).

In the year 1521, Martin Luther wrote a very moving and deeply beautiful interpretation of the *Magnificat*. I want to quote a small section from it, the one in which he speaks of the statement about Mary's being called blessed by all generations. Luther writes:

> Whoever, therefore, would show her the proper honor must not regard her alone and by herself, but set her in the presence of God and far beneath Him, must there strip her of all honor, and regard her low estate, as she says; he should then marvel at the exceeding abundant grace of God Who regards, embraces, and blesses so poor and despised a mortal. Thus regarding her, you will be moved to love and praise God for His grace, and drawn to look for all good things to Him, Who does not reject but graciously regards poor and despised and lowly mortals. Thus your heart will be strengthened in faith and love and hope.
>
> What, think you, would please her more than to have you thus come through her to God, and learn from her to put your hope and trust in Him, notwithstanding your despised and lowly estate, in life as well as in death? She does not want you to come to her, but through her to God.[1]

Note: Luther says here explicitly that we are to come to God "through her," that is, through Mary. He wants to emphasize that Mary is not the ultimate object of our worship but that looking at Mary must ultimately mean looking to God and giving God praise.

For Luther it is also clear that Mary is uttering not self-acclamation in the *Magnificat* but pure praise of God. The apparent praise of herself is built into Mary's confession that God has acted on her. It is not Mary who has done great things but the Lord who has done them in her. Certainly, Catholic Christians will add to what Luther says, affirming that

Mary spoke her yes, and without that yes the history of which the *Magnificat* speaks would not have reached its goal. In order to act, God needs a free human response.

Not So Sweet and Nice . . .

But what kind of history is this, in which Mary's yes at the end played such a crucial role? It is a history of the overturning of everything, and that is why the words Mary speaks in the *Magnificat* are not at all as "nice" as we might have expected, coming from her: the hungry will be filled while the rich stand by with empty hands. The poor will be exalted and honored, the powerful cast down from their thrones. These are not generalized truths about God that are being uttered here, not what God does again and again, everywhere in the world; this is about real events in the history of the people of God, about what God has already done in Israel.

Regrettably, most of the translations of the *Magnificat* are imprecise, particularly in this part of the text. The central statements should read:

> He has done mighty deeds with his arm.
> He has scattered those whose hearts are filled with pride.
> He has cast down the mighty from their thrones.
> He has brought honor to the lowly [i.e., the poor].
> He has filled the hungry with his gifts.
> He has sent the rich away with empty hands.
> He has embraced his servant Israel.

The corresponding verbs are not in the present tense, as some translations suggest.[2] They are in the aorist in Greek, which in this instance speaks of events in the past, of what God has already done in Israel. God has for a long time been doing mighty deeds in and for God's people, again and again. For that very reason it is plausible that God is doing so once more. God has embraced Israel, God's servant, and does so now, again.

A Revolutionary Song

That the mighty are cast down from their thrones and the poor and despised are raised up—words like those are found only on the lips of revolutionaries! Mary is, in fact, singing about a revolution that turns everything on its head. It began with Abraham. It happened as Israel revolted against the pharaoh and his theocratic state. It continually happened when Israel listened to God and opened itself to God's acting—the action of God that desires justice and peace in the world—through the example set by the people of God. This revolution would reach its culmination in Mary and her messianic child. What happened again and again in Israel, despite all its grumbling and all its resistance to God, happens now with Jesus, with a vehemence that transforms everything.

No, this is no nice, pretty song. Mary doesn't mince words; she speaks the unvarnished truth. She says: those who are concerned with only their own glory cannot accept the glorious works of God. Those who are occupied with only their own plans and self-optimization cannot recognize God's plan. Such people have no fear of God; they are simply staging their own selves and trying to build themselves up. Therefore in the end they stand there with empty hands. And this radical division between those who want only to put their own ideas into effect and those who desire what God wills runs throughout the history of the world and of Israel. In Jesus it will reach its summit.

Mary: Image of the People of God

So Mary praises not her own greatness and strength but the greatness of an Other: that of the God of her ancestors, the greatness of the God of Abraham, Isaac, and Jacob. She sings the song of the people of God. She sings of a great overturning that began with Abraham and now finds its culmination in Jesus.

Abraham believed not in himself and his own plans but in God's plan: that God would make him the progenitor of a great nation. So also Mary did not expect happiness in terms of her own wishes, dreams, and projections. The content of her life was God's ideas: what GOD planned for her. Therefore she can say, "the Mighty One has done great things for me." Those who exalt God in this way are not inhibited, impatient, and vicious, as Martin Walser suggested in his essay, "Ich vertraue. Querfeldein."[3] Such a one is, rather, truly human.

So the *Magnificat* speaks of God's deeds in Israel within history. This makes it clear that here Mary is not simply the young Jewish woman from Nazareth with her personal pathway in life. She is that, but at the same time she represents the people of God. She is the figure of faithful Israel. In her is concentrated all of Israel's history, just as it was in Abraham. In her and her child that history reaches its goal, its pinnacle. Therefore her song is at the same time the hymn of the whole people of God. It is our song, the hymn for us who live in the church and through faith have become sons and daughters of Abraham. It is true for us also that

> He has embraced his servant Israel,
>   in remembrance of his mercy,
> according to the promise he made to our ancestors,
>   to Abraham and to his descendants forever. (Luke 1:54-55)

Perhaps I should say something briefly about mercy: God's "mercy" here is not a particular generalized emotion such as exists in the ethical systems of all nations—the gracious gesture of someone in a better position who gives alms out of her or his abundance. At this point in particular we must consider the Hebrew background.

Mercy out of Fidelity to Israel

The *Magnificat* is immersed in biblical language. It plays over and over again on Old Testament texts. It is at home in a milieu dominated by a highly precise and differentiated culture of citation and allusion. That is: the hearers or readers knew which Old Testament textual contexts lay in the background. With "in remembrance of his mercy" they most surely recalled Psalm 98, which reads:

> The LORD has made known his victory;
>   he has revealed his vindication in the sight of the nations.
> He has remembered his steadfast love and faithfulness
>   to the house of Israel. (Ps 98:2-3)

Behind the words "steadfast love" in the English translation is the Hebrew word *ḥesed*. It refers to a communal attitude, or more precisely the helping action that arises from a relationship of fidelity. In Psalm 98:3 it means God's intervention on Israel's behalf, in accordance with God's promises (cf. Isa 52:10). In the *Magnificat* it means God's intervention corresponding to the oath God swore to Abraham. God's fidelity to community, to covenant, is at the same time pure love and pure mercy, but a love and mercy that proceed to action.

With what now happens in Jesus, God finally and definitively has mercy on God's people Israel and fulfills all the promises to the ancestors. "He has embraced his servant Israel," Jesus' mother sings. And God has done it not only then but "forever."

This fundamental experience Mary expresses at the end of her song of praise must become our own. Not only every individual among us but the church as a whole urgently needs God's merciful intervention. What the church needs first and above all is not structural reforms but God's intervention—and it needs people who perceive God's actions today and respond to them. Should not the misery of the people of God strike us in the gut and turn us around? We surely cannot praise Mary's yes to God and, while viewing the lack of faith around us, be concerned only for our personal well-being and that our private wishes be fulfilled.

Praise of Modesty?

But here at the end let us return to the beginning: in praying the *Magnificat* we can easily be deceived. Mary says in this hymn that God has looked on her "lowliness." That is quite often interpreted as a praise of littleness, a lauding of modesty, of unpretentiousness, of a hidden existence. Is Mary, in the *Magnificat*, praising modesty and taking a back seat?

Romano Guardini once said somewhere that we Christians should be humble but not modest. He put his finger precisely on the spirit of the *Magnificat*. This song does not speak about false modesty but says that God aids the oppressed to achieve their rights and tosses the oppressors down from their thrones. The *Magnificat* does not offer consolation in face of the miseries of this earth; rather, it speaks of the reversal of all conditions—now, today. It speaks of revolution and overthrow.

The place of this silent revolution about which Mary sings is Israel, is the church, is our congregations. Or we might say more cautiously: that is where it should be, at any rate, when they pray the *Magnificat* and are not reciting mere empty words. Our congregations are the place where people live together in nonviolence, solidarity, and unanimity, where they should constantly forgive one another. If that really happens, God's revolution will come about, and it will change our world.

Chapter 24

Faith: How Does It Work?

Do you know what the biggest problem is in writing a book or preparing a lecture? It is not that you can't think of anything to say. Usually you think of far too much, and the book is too thick and the lecture too long.

Nor is the biggest problem managing not to bore the readers or hearers. Not to bore them only calls for a little imagination, and anyone who as a child has played a lot and read a lot of books has plenty of imagination. No, the hardest thing is to give the book or the lecture a good beginning and, even more so, a good title. That often takes me hours.

For example, I wavered back and forth about what title I should give this chapter. The word "faith" had to be there, because we are experiencing the "Year of Faith." Pope Benedict celebrated its solemn opening in Rome on October 11, 2012. First I was going to call it "On the Nature of Faith." But then I drew back. Talking about the nature of faith—that would require twenty chapters. Besides, people talked in the 1920s about "the nature of faith." It sounds too pretentious.

No, I didn't want to give this chapter such a title. Then I thought of calling it "Faith: What Is It?" But that didn't please me, either. I would have had to speak in technical theological terms; for example, I would have had to show that faith is one of the three "cardinal virtues," that is, that faith, like Christian hope and Christian love, is pure gift. We cannot create faith in God, in God's words and deeds, of ourselves. Faith is, at depth, participation in the life of the triune God. It is pure trust, pure turning toward Jesus and, through him, to God the Father. Only the Holy Spirit can give us such faith.

So if I were to call the chapter "Faith: What Is It?" I would have to speak in the most sublime theological language. Of course, that is often necessary. We should never despise a good theology that subjects us to a "struggle with the concept." But I do not want to torture my readers with subtle theology just here. I want to speak quite practically about faith, for household use, you might say. And then the title occurred to me that stands at the head of the chapter: "Faith: How Does It Work?" I will write of it in seven points.

Faith Is Entry into a Long History

There is a definition of faith that used to be found in many catechisms. I myself learned it by heart when I was eleven years old. It was:

> What is faith?
> Faith means believing as true everything God has revealed and teaches us through the church to believe.

Please don't suppose I mean to question that definition. It is by no means false. It is even admirably brief and to the point. But it does not say everything. Above all, its deficiency is that it is very abstract. How does that happen, that God reveals God's self to us? God does not speak from heaven through a loudspeaker. As a rule, God does not whisper any private revelations into our ear either. Above all: God offers us no packaged instructions. So how is God revealed?

God has revealed God's self by leading people on a long road, on which they saw more and more clearly who God is and what God wills. A crucial station on the path was Abraham, who entrusted himself utterly to God and dared to leave his homeland and allow himself to be led by God into a new land. That is why we call him our "father in faith." And on this long road that began with Abraham there were many stations: Isaac, Jacob, Moses, Joshua, David, Josiah, Elijah, Elisha, Amos, Isaiah, Jeremiah, Ezekiel, John the Baptizer, and between and among them countless believers whose names we no longer know.

Finally, everything culminated in Jesus, who was truly human and yet one in whom God could entirely and finally express God's self, so that whoever listened to him heard God, and whoever saw him saw God's very self. Jesus not only followed Israel's path to its end; he himself is the way, he himself is the whole truth, and he is the fulfillment of all human searching for real life (John 14:6). And yet it is also true that without Israel's long path, Jesus himself would not have been possible, and Jesus' message would never have reached us if the church had not pursued his path still further. It is a long road, a long history with a lot of grumbling, many refusals, a great deal of resistance to God—but also one with profound trust, unflinching hope, holy men and women who made God the center of their lives and loved God by loving their brothers and sisters in the people of God.

Through all that God became more and more profoundly known. Faith is nothing other than entry into this long history of belief. Faith means learning from that history, entrusting oneself to it, living from it, entering on the way of the people of God.

In the *Magnificat*, the great revolutionary song Mary sang, we read at the end: "He has embraced his servant Israel, in remembrance of his mercy, according to the promise he made to our ancestors, to Abraham and to his descendants forever" (Luke 1:54-55). Sometimes when I pray these lines a shiver goes up my spine, and often I am seized with a profound joy. I am permitted to be a part of this history that began with Abraham. I may entrust myself to it. I am safe within it. I live from these promises. I find myself in the midst of this crowd of believers who are traveling through history toward God. It is a mighty multitude "that no one could count, from every nation, from all tribes and peoples and languages" (Rev 7:9). I may have aching feet. I may be lame. Perhaps I am limping along behind. But I am here.

That, then, was the first point: faith is an entry into a long history. Faith is participation in the path of the people of God. Now the second point.

Faith Needs an Environment

This second point is closely related to the first. Because faith is entry into a long history of belief, it cannot exist without the people of God, without the church, without community. I cannot believe alone, and I cannot come to believe alone.

There is a concept in modern biology that can deepen this insight. I am referring to the idea of the biotope or habitat. A biotope is a space for life. Plants and animals require a habitat that is appropriate for them if they are to live. Palms do not flourish in Greenland, whales do not multiply on glaciers, and blackberries do not grow in the desert. Some of our loveliest flowers need water meadows; when there are no more such meadows, the species dies out. Many butterflies require weeds that only grow on unproductive soils. If all we have are well-fertilized hayfields that are cut over five times a year and where only grass and dandelions grow, the consequence will be that throughout the region there will be almost no butterflies.

In the same way faith, if it is to grow, needs a biotope, an environment. For example, if a child is to grow in faith it needs believing parents for whom God is more important than anything else in the world. When it reaches puberty it needs people outside its own family who show it that faith is not lived only within its own family. It needs books that tell of faith in readable and even exciting language. The child must become acquainted with the great narratives in the Bible as well as with the life stories of the great saints. All that, and much more, belongs to the biotope of faith, the environment without which faith shrivels and suffocates.

This happened not long ago: a little girl from a First Communion group came to the pastor after Mass and said she wanted to be baptized. The pastor went to visit the parents to clarify things. The parents—she a physician, he a professor of education—took time for him and were very polite, but they explained firmly that at this time they did not want their daughter to be baptized or receive First Communion. "It's all her grand-mother's doing," they said. "Laura is with her every day because we are both overworked. Her grandmother talks to Laura about the Bible, Jesus, the church, the sacraments. Now Laura wants to be baptized and receive Communion. But we are against it. When it comes to religion, we don't want to impose on our daughter and steer her in one direction or another. Later, when she is eighteen, she can decide for herself whether she wants to be baptized and belong to a church. Until then we will raise her to examine things carefully and make critical comparisons. When she is grown up, she can decide for herself in complete freedom." Those were the words of the eight-year-old's parents.

"Decide for herself in complete freedom"? Wasn't the professor himself committing pedagogical malpractice? For a world filled with immoderate criticism of everyone and everything is something Laura will encounter sooner or later in any case. She will even be exposed to a society in which violence, egoism, denial, and refusal—the precise opposite of the Gospel—hold appalling sway. She will also learn her fill about unbelief. Anyone who, in the face of such a world, bars his or her child from the world of God and the happiness of childhood faith from the outset takes away that child's opportunity to be able to choose at all when the time comes.

It is a dangerous illusion to suppose that there is an ideologically neutral way to bring up a child, leaving the question of God open and instead restricting oneself to values such as critical distinction and beneficence. There is no such thing as an upbringing that leaves the great questions of life open, and this is so because in every upbringing, whatever it appears to be, the world is constantly being measured and judged. With every word and every sentence of our language, with every gesture and posture, we convey "the world" to our children, a world *already interpreted*. Whether we want to or not, we are constantly communicating our view of the world, either a world that broadens out toward God or one that has no room for God. There is no neutral language. Those who deliberately close the world of faith to their children are really the ones who are imposing their ideas on their children and manipulating them, because they are steering their children in the direction of unbelief. They are by no means raising them to be open to the world; they are denying them the breadth and freedom of faith.

Obviously we have to pay attention to our children's uniqueness, their own histories, their personhood. Obviously we must not force them to do something they do not want to do. No one can be compelled to believe, no adult and most certainly no child. Nor can one demonstrate faith; one can only live it openly. But if one is a believer, one dare not conceal from and deny one's child what one knows to be the truth about the world. Only those who perceive and experience the world of faith have the chance to come to believe. In that sense Laura's grandmother was by far the better educator. How should someone who has not gotten to know Jesus come to believe in him? How can someone who has never been fascinated by the life of a great saint sense what a longing for holiness might be? So faith needs an environment, a world in which it can breathe. It needs a biotope of Christian life. That brings me right to the center of my third point.

Faith Must Be Learned

My own time in elementary school fell within the years of National Socialism. At that time there was no more religious education in German schools; the Nazis had abolished it. But it did take place in the parishes, within the church itself. It was in a better place there than the schools can offer. I experienced it, in our city parish, as a very sound and thorough education in matters of faith. My catechism contained 286 questions and answers.[1] We were drilled on them, and I learned them all by heart. That was right and good. There is an elementary knowledge of the faith that one simply must learn. My old catechism is still on the shelf in my office.

But certainly a catechism on which one can be drilled is insufficient. One must become acquainted with people who believe, and must see in them how faith is lived. I grew up in Frankfurt am Main. When all the schools there were closed because of the Allied bombing raids, I was sent to relatives in the mountains. My sister Marianne was taken in by relatives in the Rhone valley and my brother Norbert by other relatives in Limburg; I lived with a somewhat older couple in Heppenheim (home town of the racecar driver Sebastian Vettel, for those who are interested!).

The move was a great thing for someone nine years old, because until that time I had intimate experience almost exclusively of my parents' faith. Now, suddenly, I lived with people who had been strangers to me before, and there I found the very same faith. I prayed with them; I listened to them talking together about church matters; I saw how they went every day, as a matter of course, to early Mass; I experienced what the sacraments meant to them. In particular, their attitude toward the sacrament of reconciliation impressed me deeply. This couple went to confession every month, and that Saturday was always like a feast day for them. They donned their best clothes and the husband shaved his whiskers. They did not say much before they went to church, but when they came back they emitted an exhilaration that was infectious.

I never heard them have a serious quarrel or say wounding words to each other, nor did they speak ill of other people. They had a sense of humor and exuded a serenity that made me feel good. The fact that they were both so gracious must have had something to do with their faith. They are long since dead, but I remain deeply grateful to them.

No one can learn all that from the catechism. You have to see it, experience it, take it into yourself, taste it. Faith must also be "learned" in this sense—through seeing and tasting. Then one's own decision for faith can gradually ripen. I come now to my fourth point.

Faith Lays Claim to the Whole of Life

One of the greatest dangers of our society is its segregation of various spheres or sectors of life. Sociologists tell us, rightly, that modern life plays itself out in very different worlds, that society is fragmented into subrationalities or equally weighted functional systems. But we can leave them to talk their professional jargon to one another. I am speaking simply about the spheres within which we live, which are drifting further and further apart. There is the sector of school, education, and training; the sector of profession or job and business life; the sector of free time on the weekends; and then, above all, there is the sphere of vacation, the supposedly "loveliest time of the year."

But there are a great many other sectors: those of politics, economics, science, law, medicine, art, sports. And then, alongside all the others, there is the religious sector. So all of life is divided into sectors and each has its own rules, its own particular vocabulary, its own behavioral norms, its own fashions—and its own time.

On Saturday an ordinary citizen finally has time to shop, turn on the washing machine, put the apartment or house in order, work in the garden, and take care of the necessary paperwork (paying bills, working on the tax return). On Sunday she or he—maybe, just perhaps—goes to church for an hour. Monday, it's back to work. If one is a believer, then, there is certainly one hour a week, and maybe a few minutes every day, for God.

But as our society is constructed, there is very little space for God *outside* this "religious" sector. Religion has thus become a subsphere, and faith is limited to a narrow sector of life—which means it is enduring a slow decline that may even lead to death, because faith demands the whole of life. You can't believe "a little bit" any more than you can be "a little bit" pregnant.

The people of Old Testament Israel knew that. Just as Jews do today, they recited the *Shema*, the "Hear, O Israel," daily. It begins:

> Hear, O Israel: the LORD is our God, the LORD alone. You shall love the LORD your God with all your heart, and with all your soul, and with all your might.
>
> [Write] these words that I am commanding you today in your heart. Recite them to your children and [murmur] them when you are at home and when you are away, when you lie down and when you rise. (Deut 6:4-7)

"Write these words in your heart" means that every Israelite should know God's instructions, the Torah, God's social order, by heart. "Recite them to your children" means repeat the Torah to your children again and again, until they know it by heart. The ultimate result will be that God's instruction will shape your whole life, every day, every hour; it will inform all your thinking. And the "you" addressed is not primarily the individual. That "you" is Israel. The people of God as a whole, its men and its women, and of course its growing youth as well, are to align themselves toward God.

Here, then, life is not cut up into sectors. All of life belongs to God, from morning to night, from the beginning of the year to its end, in the house and outside it. Quite obviously, the same is true of Christian faith: it must shape all of life. It *is* a way of life.

Surely you will be asking yourself: how can that be? When I work, I have to concentrate, or my work will go awry and I will even endanger others. And in my free time I can't be constantly thinking about God. Should I be praying when I am mowing the lawn or washing the car or the dishes? After all, I am not a comedian. There is some justification for such objections, and certainly the church has been aware of it. That is why there used to be a section in every catechism about so-called good intention. What is that?

"Creating a good intention" means that during the day, while I am working, I should think of God from time to time, entrust myself to God, ask God's help, pray that my work will be good, give thanks for the good and beautiful things I may have encountered—in short, that I live in the presence of God. This living in God's presence could be effected by tiny moments of looking toward God, just the time it takes to breathe deeply or turn on the computer. But such moments of making God present can run throughout the day like a string of pearls and give it meaning and clarity. Then faith is not just a sector of my life that is set apart; then it shapes my whole life.

But it is not only a matter of making God present during work and free time. Believers do not just want to live in God's presence; they want their faith to shape the world: their own environment, the world around them. Biblical faith, after all, is not something purely internal. It must give a shape to everything; it has within it the inextinguishable tendency to form a world, because faith is not otherworldly or unworldly; it contains a world.

Israel's Torah is the gigantic project of saturating not only one's own life but the whole environment with faith and bringing it under the rule of God. The Torah speaks of fields and how to sow them, of vineyards and fruit trees, of birds' nests and domestic animals, of houses and their walls, even of protective walls around roof terraces, of the human body and its illnesses, of shaving and cutting one's hair, and even says that it is forbidden to muzzle an ox that is drawing the thresher over the grain. Torah is about all creation: humans, beasts, plants, and even nonliving things. Nothing is left out; nothing may be excluded. The whole environment within which human beings live is to be subjected to God's rule so that the whole will have its dignity and identity.

This divine command to shape the world in terms of faith is, obviously, valid for Christians as well. They cannot believe in God as creator of the world and Christ as its redeemer and at the same time live in self-created chaos and freely chosen ugliness unworthy of human beings, for

> God desires not only to redeem souls
> but also bodies and clothing,
> eating, drinking, and sleeping,
> the house, its rooms,
> and the common life of its inhabitants,
> furniture and possessions,
> time and money.[2]

To repeat: real faith intends to shape the world, because it is about the whole human being, and that whole includes the surroundings in which the human being lives and into which each throws herself or himself.

The next point, the fifth, is intimately connected with what I have just been saying.

Faith Requires Ritual

I live in a house community with other people. Since our dwelling contains about ten rooms, we employ a house cleaner, a Turkish woman who is always happy and ready to help. Every year she observes the month's fast of Ramadan as a matter of course, and very correctly. During those thirty days she eats and drinks nothing until sundown, and above all, during that time she does not smoke, even though she is a heavy smoker. I have the greatest respect for the way this Muslim woman takes her way of life for granted, and I ask myself a little sadly: in these last decades, have we Christians in this country not lost something crucial in our lives? For a lived faith like hers necessarily requires established rituals, just as real life in general inevitably requires a whole host of rituals: bathing, brushing one's teeth, holding the door for others, shaking hands, greeting people, asking others for pardon, and much, much more.

Rituals function to unburden us and create order. For example, they make communication easier; they also give us something to hold on to within the chaos of life. But above all, they point to deeper contexts of meaning. Ultimately, their basis lies in the fact that the human being not only consists of spirit and soul but also has a body. No—we do not *have* bodies; we *are* bodies (just as we *are* souls). Therefore faith also necessarily includes the physical—what is visible, tangible, graspable, what leaps to the eye. And that, in turn, leads necessarily to Christian rituals.

In earlier days this visibility of faith was highly developed in the church. There was morning prayer, evening prayer, prayer before and after meals. We prayed the *Angelus* three times a day, wherever we were. There were signs of the cross, holy water, genuflecting in church, a crucifix in the living room and pictures of the saints, ejaculatory prayers, daily examination of conscience, the rosary. The church was always open, and one could go in and pray before the tabernacle. There were days of fasting and abstinence and regular confession. When I was little my mother always made the sign of the cross on my forehead before I left for school.

In the last few decades that has all vanished for many Catholic Christians; it has fallen out of use and is regarded as merely external or "just ritual" or even as old-fashioned. But that is a massive mistake. Faith needs ritual, embodiment, or it will disappear. The *Logos* of God became flesh, not pure internality. If Christians do not reclaim the physicality of their faith, Christianity in Europe, faced with the concreteness of Islam, will not have a chance.

Quite obviously, the external signs, gestures, and rituals of faith can change, but exist they must, just as a human being is a body and has a face. So don't be ashamed, the next time you go into the church, to genuflect, take holy water, remember your baptism in doing so, and don't start a conversation with the person next to you as if you were at the movies. You will see that faith is concrete and needs ritual. It needs signs to hold fast to, symbols that link us to believers throughout the world.

And now I arrive at my sixth point.

Faith Is Critical

By this I most certainly do not mean that it is a Christian's principal duty to criticize the church unceasingly. That has indeed become a new social game. Faith is regarded as emancipated if it subjects everything that happens in the church to suspicious examination. The bishops are favorite targets. After all, it is so nice to have scapegoats onto which one can shove every problem. Starting with oneself would be much more arduous. A standard strategy of current church criticism is to deny that one's own bishop is capable of dialogue and to accuse the pope of being incapable of shaping the faith "in accord with the times."

Here an important role is allotted especially to the "professional critics" who sense in every papal utterance a throttling of the "spirit of the Council," an unwillingness to reform, and even a contempt for human beings. Since these critics in particular are cultivated, flattered, and—as their own vanity prevents them from noticing—simply used, the church has become the "deformed church," especially in German-speaking countries; a lot of people want nothing more to do with it.

That is not at all the kind of criticism I mean by saying that faith must be critical. Faith should be critical of false gods, which of course exist just as surely today and with the same fake shimmer as long ago in Canaan. Our society has in the meantime developed in such a way that we are constantly being manipulated by thought patterns, value judgments, models, and worldviews that are profoundly unbelieving. For example, the author Dick Francis (1920–2010) remarks as an aside in one of his (best!) mysteries that "Historically, more people have died of religion than cancer."[3] So, as to the facts, how does Dick Francis know how many people have died of religion and how many of cancer? It could be that, if there were no faith in God or the divine, humanity would long since have perished of profound depression.

Then as to method: since the appearance of the successful works of the Swedish authors Maj Sjöwall and Peer Wahlöö mystery novels have been used more and more frequently to present ideologies to the world. If the action is exciting and the personalities are believable, an author can make highly effective propaganda for her or his worldview through this venue. It is most powerful if the corresponding ideologies are not openly stated, as in the quoted passage from Dick Francis; instead, they are spooned into the readers gently and almost unnoticeably. They drip imperceptibly into our veins.

Naturally, that happens not only in crime novels but just as much and still more often in online journalism, films, television series, newspapers, books, and even in news broadcasts. As helpful and necessary as our media are, in many ways they are also superficial, selective, and, especially in matters of "Christian faith," often positively featherbrained, if not deliberately intended to make us stupid. A Christian should know that not all factories are devoted to making consumer goods. There is a whole consciousness industry as well. Consequently, Christians must be critical.

It should also be said that critique in the sense of critical discernment has been essential to the people of God from the beginning. Since Abraham,

Israel has examined the religions surrounding it with the greatest care and radically refused everything in them that was untrue or unworthy of humans and of God. The early church did the same. It vehemently rejected the cult of the Greek gods and the Roman worship of the emperor. It was extremely critical in that regard. Christians even refused to participate in public meals on city festival days because they were connected to the imperial cult. With regard to the worship of the gods and the emperor, the church was quite ready to accept the accusation of atheism. Toward the gods of ancient society it did indeed want to be "godless."

But what the theologians of the early church took seriously and made their own was the critique of the gods found in ancient philosophy, the ethics of the Stoa, and much more. They made Paul's injunction a reality: "whatever is true, whatever is honorable, whatever is just, whatever is pure, whatever is pleasing, whatever is commendable, if there is any excellence and if there is anything worthy of praise, think about these things" (Phil 4:8). Quite obviously, Paul is here adopting words from the conceptual inventory of pagan ethics. So the Christians are to respect and even adopt the positive values they find in their environment. But they are to be critical toward everything that is contrary to the tradition of the people of God. Therefore, "test everything; hold fast to what is good; abstain from every form of evil!" (1 Thess 5:21-22).

We live today in the midst of a pagan society. We should have no illusions about that. In this situation it is an absolute necessity of life that we reflect on these basic principles laid down by Paul. We must know that much in our society, such as abortion, pre-implantation diagnosis, shifting partnerships, depreciation of marriage, euthanasia, and above all, the incessant public damage done to individual reputations, is incompatible with Christianity. Here Christians can only say, "We won't go along with it. We have our own ethic flowing from millennia of ancient experience, and with the Gospel behind it."

This means that there are areas in which Christian communities must be counter-societies. Otherwise they will make themselves superfluous, and Jesus' words will apply to them: "You are the salt of the earth; but if salt has lost its taste, how can its saltiness be restored? It is no longer good for anything, but is thrown out and trampled underfoot" (Matt 5:13).

Nevertheless, all that does not mean that Christians should withdraw into a ghetto. They must participate in everything that is positive in our society, and that is a great deal—and participate not as a rear guard, but as the *avant garde*. They can do it, because whenever they hold fast to their own tradition and the Gospel of Jesus Christ they are far in advance of society. So to my seventh and final point.

Each of Us Has a Personal History of Faith

We have seen that each of us must learn the faith. But faith must also grow. We do not simply "have" our faith; we grow into it, and that growth is not an automatic process in which one step follows another without effort. Not even trees grow automatically. There are times of drought during which a tree suffers; there are storms that shake it; there can be damage from insects, and storms may even break off large branches. Faith must become part of our existence, and that cannot happen without times of drought, crises, struggles. That is how faith grows.

Some time ago there was a crisis in a family that lives at some distance from here; it involved an eleven-year-old named Elizabeth. It occurred to her one day that faith had something to do with freedom.

It happened this way: A few days before Pentecost, while the whole family was gathered at the dinner table, Elizabeth's mother explained what the family would be doing on the day of Pentecost. Among other things, they would all go to the parish church for Mass on Pentecost Sunday and Pentecost Monday. When her mother had laid out the plans for the feast, Elizabeth raised her head and said, "I am not going to church on Pentecost." "Say what?" said her father. Her mother's face got red. "What do you mean?" she said. "You have to go to church on Pentecost." "I don't have to," said Elizabeth; she got up and disappeared. I won't rehearse the details of what happened during the next few days, but you can imagine the kind of dark clouds that gathered within the family. I will get right to the surprising turn the whole story took.

It seems that the grandmother lived on the floor above. The day after the confrontation, Elizabeth marched up to her grandmother and declared solemnly that she was not going to church on Pentecost. "I just don't want to," she said, "and when Mother says I have to, then I most certainly will not." The grandmother was an extraordinarily wise woman. She said to her granddaughter, "But you don't have to." "Oh yes," said Elizabeth. "You have to. And I don't want to have to." "Good," said the grandmother. "Let's call the pastor."

She went to the phone and had the good fortune to reach the pastor right away. She told him that little Elizabeth had a problem: she wanted to know whether anyone could be forced to go to Mass. "No," said the pastor, "we are fundamentally free in everything that has to do with faith." The grandmother handed the phone to Elizabeth, and the pastor repeated what he had told her grandmother: "Everything about faith is fundamentally a matter of freedom. If you don't want to, then you must not. You may only go if you are glad to." "Thank you!" said Elizabeth, and she disappeared. Her grandmother told her mother, "Now it is working in her. Leave her alone."

On the Saturday before Pentecost, Elizabeth suddenly appeared in the kitchen, where her mother was working. She shuffled around a bit and then said, "I think you need to iron my red dress a little." Her mother asked, "Oh, why? You aren't going to church." Elizabeth spread her feet firmly and said, "Yes, I am going to church. Not because you want me to. Everything about faith is fundamentally free. I have decided for myself that I am going to church tomorrow." End of a true story.

When I heard all this, I thought: that is absolutely normal in the development of a young person. It was at most surprising to hear how reasonably the grandmother and the pastor had acted and also, of course, that it all turned out so well. Elizabeth, while still so young, had learned something that many Christians take a whole lifetime to learn: we do not believe in God because we must, and we fulfill God's commandments and those of the church not as slaves but as free people, because we know that these commandments are our happiness and salvation, because we know that they are commandments *for the sake of life*. Faith is not meant to push us into a corner and put us in chains; it opens to us a broad horizon of freedom.

Most of us come to understand this only slowly through life: that faith in God and obedience and faithful doing of God's will are the supreme freedom. Probably eleven-year-old Elizabeth was taking the first step toward that important realization, namely, that God takes our freedom so seriously that God never forces us to do anything; instead, God knocks, respects our privacy, and almost never breaks open the door by force. But if God does that, for example, through an accident or an illness, it is only to help us to grasp the truth about our life.

After all I have said, I think there is no need to make a big point of the fact that crises in faith are necessary. They are needed in order to purify and deepen our faith. The most dangerous things in our lives are not crises of faith. Much more dangerous is a gradual crumbling of faith, a silent erosion, the slow decay of faith into dust, until one day we discover we have lost it. How does such a thing happen?

Usually it begins when we stop praying or our prayers become nothing but empty babbling that has nothing to do with the reality of our lives. Prayers from the heart, those that perhaps even battle with God, prayers that bring us happiness and peace, are a certain indication that our faith is alive. If there are no more such prayers within us, we are already on the path to unbelief.

There is one more criterion for beginning not to believe: quite simply, it is our Sunday participation in the Eucharist. Those who, without a serious reason (such as illness or advanced age), do not take part in the Sunday celebration of the Eucharist must know that their faith is in danger, or that at least they have a completely wrong image of church.

My father was a locomotive engineer who often worked the night shift. Again and again I saw how he came home on Sunday morning, tired out from his work, and went immediately to early Mass before he lay down to sleep. That impressed me more deeply than any sermon about the Sunday commandment. It was pure grace for me; I can't help it.

There are still many other criteria that show us how things stand with our faith, for example, the readiness, for Christ's sake, to forgive another who has wounded us, or a willingness to ask forgiveness when we ourselves have injured another. All that shows again that faith is not something purely internal. It expands from within. It tries to shape our lives. It is about our whole existence.

I have spoken about the slow crumbling of faith, and I have said that this subtle erosion is more dangerous than all the crises of faith that happen at one time or another. Let me add one final observation.

Living faith cannot exist without the Holy Spirit, and the Holy Spirit is not at all about putting us to sleep. The Spirit speaks to us; pushes us onward; tries to shake us awake, take us by the hand, and lead us to entirely new initiatives in faith. But we often resist with every means at hand.

For a while now psychologists and educators have been bandying about the notion of a "comfort zone." They say that nothing shapes a person as much as his or her comfort zone, where each of us has our order, our repose, our security. There we sit in a cage of habits. We invent a thousand reasons not to have to move. We use every means in our power to avoid leaving our comfort zone and daring anything at all. In theological terms, a Christian in her or his "comfort zone" also puts up barriers against the Holy Spirit, who tries to pull us out of our faith inertia, our snug belief, our deafness to the call of the Gospel.

When God calls us because God needs us, and we, out of fear and attachment to our comfort, say no, we are in a highly dangerous position. We are throwing away a chance to be generous before God and to gain breadth and freedom for our faith. Those who constantly resist the silent pressure of the Holy Spirit, however, slowly but surely undermine their own faith.

Still—I don't want to end this chapter with a listing of crises and erosions of faith. Rather, I want to encourage you to continue on the way of faith, bravely and in good spirits, or else to begin to believe anew. A few days ago a man I did not know at all, but with whom I by chance engaged in conversation, said to me, "I lost my faith at some point, because of the infinite misery in the world. I couldn't reconcile it with faith in a loving God. I haven't prayed for a long time. I've signed off on faith. But the strange thing is that I couldn't get rid of it. I was always uneasy. Somehow it kept coming up again and again. Then one day, when the whole thing had come over me again, I prayed: 'I don't know if you exist. I can't believe in you anymore. But if you exist, then do something; make it so that I can believe.' It was very strange: after praying I became quite calm. Somehow or other, there was a sudden peace, even happiness. Probably I have come back to faith, but at least I know now that faith requires radical prayer and one's whole existence."

That is not an edifying tale from a book. I have told it just as the man told it to me, sometimes hesitating, always reflective, and absolutely believable. His frank words moved me deeply. It is not so easy for men to talk about their faith. Besides, I was just then in a situation in which I had a strong personal need for such testimony. The man's witness strengthened my own faith. And in the Year of Faith, that may have been the most important thing—not only that we reflect on faith, not only that we deepen our faith, but that we witness to other people about God and what God has done for us. "God has done great things for us, and holy is God's name." Then, at last, our faith will have arrived at the place where its inmost center lies.

Chapter 25

The Bible in My Life as an Exegete

The topic assigned to me can only be understood biographically. But I absolutely do not want to offer you biographical effusions on the model of "the Bible and me." So I am going to fall back on an emergency tool: I will simply choose a biblical text and tell you about how it has been between me and that text over the years. Obviously it cannot be just any biblical text; it must have weight, and it must be one that was already important to me as a child, because the biographical element has to play some kind of role. At the same time, however, it must be a text by means of which I can show what moves me theologically now, in these years of my life.

Any number of texts present themselves, from the Old Testament, the gospels, the letters of Paul. But rather quickly, out of the 1,395 pages of my Bible, there arose a single text that has given me joy all my life long. Each of us has such texts in her or his life, ones that we perhaps encountered at an early age, looked at closely and intimately, and with which we have again and again engaged in conversation. For me it is the story of the wise men from the East told to us by Matthew (Matt 2:1-12) and read as the gospel on the feast of the Epiphany. How has this business of living with that text been for me? How did I encounter it? What has it done with me?

The Three Kings

When I was just a boy, maybe five or six years old, all that mattered to me was that, sometime after the birth of baby Jesus, three kings had come, after a long journey, to see Jesus and his parents. And so, sometime after Christmas, new figures were added to the crib: besides Jesus, Mary, Joseph, and the sheep, there were now three kings and—most important for a little boy—a camel. I even knew the names of those three kings: Caspar, Melchior, and Balthasar.

A few years later, when I had become an altar boy, I learned why they brought gold, frankincense, and myrrh as their gifts. They brought gold because Mary and Joseph were poor, frankincense to ward off the smell of the barn, and myrrh for the baby's health. That is how the curate explained it to us altar boys, and he even appealed to the great Thomas Aquinas for the information. He also told us that the three kings represented three parts of the earth: one came from Europe, one from Asia, and one from Africa. The last, the one from Africa, was the black king, the one I marveled at the most.

It is also part of my childhood memories that our family had a book of legends in which the three kings and their long journey could also be found. It told how at first each one traveled alone and how one day, led by God, they met in a *single* place and then journeyed on together. I also learned a Christmas carol that described their long journey and said:

> Behold the star we are bringing,
> A light from heaven so bright,
> And hear the song we are singing,
> A song of the holy night.
>
> We came from countries so distant,
> Through deserts and seas of world's night,
> Where everything still lies in darkness
> Because no one brings the earth light.
>
> We sought him in many great castles,
> Messiah, the king and the lord.
> Herod, he wanted to keep us,
> But we want to follow the star.
>
> And when we to Bethlehem came,
> In the land so holy, his home,
> The star above cried out one name
> That no one before us had known.
>
> The star led us to the manger,
> And between the beasts, in the straw
> There the saints sat all together
> And how happy the angels were.

And there was the child in the manger
Who smiled and greeted us dear,
And with him the host of the angels,
As friends they called us all near.

We fell to our knees to adore him
And praise the beautiful child
And each of us laid out before him
Our incense and myrrh and gold.

We wanted to offer him more,
And gave him our happiness all.
He drew a cross on our crowns
And smiled at us there in the stall.[1]

At school I also learned that, in times past, inns were quite often named for the three kings: the Crown, the Moor, the Golden Star, the Elephant— all of them allusions to the three kings, who from the Middle Ages onward had become an archetype for all those making long journeys. For me, as a child, that was all extremely graphic and fascinating. The three kings were part of my familiar world and had a solid place in the web of my childish faith.

The Magi from the East

Now for a big leap in time: already in religion class in high school I somehow learned that the biblical text does not speak about *kings*, but *magi*. When I began to study theology at the university, and read the gospels in their original language, in Greek, I saw that Matthew's gospel really does speak of *magoi*. That was the Greek name for Persian priests and also more generally for anyone from the East who was expert in Eastern medicine, philosophy, or religion. And those Eastern religions had a fascination for people in antiquity. A *magos* was a mixture of astronomer, astrologer, interpreter of dreams, magician, philosopher, and physician, but in any case a mysterious man.

Such *magoi*, I learned, sought the "child . . . born king of the Jews," and did so on the basis of their astronomical observations. "We observed his star at its rising," they said. "At its rising" was a technical astronomical term in antiquity. I also learned at that time that only Matthew tells the story of the star-seers, and neither Mark, Luke, nor John speak of it. Besides, Matthew does not say anything about *three* such seers; he simply says that Magi came from the East. It was only in the fourth century that Matthew's unstated number of Magi became *three* star-seers and then later three kings. In the Syrian church, I learned, even today there is veneration of *twelve* such seers from the East. The notion that they were kings appears first with the theologian Tertullian in the third century, with a reference to Psalm 72:

> May the kings of Tarshish and of the isles render him tribute,
>> may the kings of Sheba and Seba bring gifts.
> May all kings fall down before him,
>> all nations give him service. (Ps 72:10-11)

A Conjunction of Jupiter and Saturn?

During my theology studies I also noticed that there were various positions among biblical scholars about the interpretation of this gospel. Some said that the story Matthew tells is historically accurate to the last detail. Proof: in the years 7 and 6 BCE, that is, at about the time when Jesus was born, there were three so-called conjunctions, that is, an approach of planets to one another (from earth's point of view). More precisely, there was a conjunction of Jupiter and Saturn in Pisces, the sign of the fish. In antiquity the planet Jupiter was considered the royal star, and Saturn was the star of the Sabbath—which is to say, of the Jews. The sign of Pisces stood for the West. Would the star-seers of the East not have concluded that a new, powerful king had been born in the West, in the land of the Jews? Besides, the conjunction of Jupiter and Saturn had even been predicted by Babylonian astrologers, as can be established by texts from Babylon.

So star-seers from the East had taken to the road to honor the new king of the Jews, whom they apparently regarded as a rescuer and bringer of salvation. All this I heard in my theology studies in Frankfurt, from our professor of New Testament, Gerhard Hartmann, SJ, who tried in this way to explain the star of Bethlehem as a natural astronomical phenomenon. In his eyes the story of the star-seers in Matthew 2 was a documentary account.

An Invented Story?

Since I was very curious, I not only listened to the lectures but read a lot of literature about the Bible. I found that other biblical scholars were much more skeptical about the Matthean text. They asserted that it was an invented text, a story without any historical foundation, spun out of Jewish tales about Moses. As the pharaoh had sought the life of the newborn children of the Israelites, so now did King Herod. Others said that it was a legend of a common type: "rescue of the royal child." Still others said that the motif of a special star indicating the birth of a great ruler was very popular in antiquity. Similar stories had been told about Aeneas, Augustus, and Alexander the Great.

Besides this comparison with other narrative material, the critical exegetes argued as follows: why did Herod tell the *magoi*, "Go and search diligently for the child; and when you have found him, bring me word so that I may also go and pay him homage"? He could certainly have sent a spy, a secret messenger, after them. A crafty politician like Herod the Great would most surely have known how to manage that.

And why was the whole city of Jerusalem frightened at the news from the star-seers that a savior-king had been born to the people of God? Herod was not only unpopular in Israel; orthodox Jews hated him. In reality, Jerusalem would only have rejoiced at the news of a Messiah-king. Moreover, the star in Matthew 2:2, 9-10 is depicted not as a natural phenomenon but as a miraculous star, as is appropriate for a legend. Therefore, said the critical biblical scholars, the whole story is pure fiction. Matthew 2 is unhistorical, a pious invention, an artistic construct.

At that time this theology student found this divergence of opinions interesting but not particularly disturbing. I loved the story. It was beautiful, and because I saw it as beautiful, I felt it to be true, in a deep, indisputable sense that was connected to my faith in the Bible as a whole. At that time, in my first semesters of theology, I could not have said precisely what that truth consisted of, but I was convinced and sustained by it. In the long run, of course, it is not enough that one finds a biblical story beautiful or has an instinctive feeling that it is true. One must be able to say what constitutes the truth of a narrative.

The Liturgy as Key

Over the years it slowly became clear to me that neither the theory of the conjunction of two planets nor the all-too-simple psychology of the radical biblical critics is really capable of unlocking Matthew's narrative. The key to understanding is not given in astronomy or in a razor-sharp historical critique; it lies within the church's liturgy. The liturgy, from earliest times, has partnered the gospel about the Magi with the Old Testament reading from the beginning of Isaiah 60, which depicts the eschatological pilgrimage of the nations to Zion, that is, the journey of the Gentile nations to Jerusalem. It is only against the background of this biblical picture that one can understand the narrative about the coming of the star-seers. That text from Isaiah reads:

Arise, shine; for your light has come,
    and the glory of the LORD has risen upon you.
For darkness shall cover the earth,
    and thick darkness the peoples;
but the LORD will arise upon you,
    and his glory will appear over you.
Nations shall come to your light,
    and kings to the brightness of your dawn.
Lift up your eyes and look around;
    they all gather together, they come to you;
your sons shall come from far away,
    and your daughters shall be carried on their nurses' arms.
Then you shall see and be radiant;
    your heart shall thrill and rejoice,
because the abundance of the sea shall be brought to you,
    the wealth of the nations shall come to you.
A multitude of camels shall cover you,
    the young camels of Midian and Ephah;
    all those from Sheba shall come.
They shall bring gold and frankincense,
    and shall proclaim the praise of the LORD. (Isa 60:1-6)

This text from Isaiah 60 is only the finale of a grand theme that runs throughout the book of Isaiah. It begins as early as Isaiah 2:1-5, where we read that Mount Zion, with the house of the Lord, is established as the highest of mountains, and the nations are streaming toward it, that is, to the eschatological people of God. In Jerusalem they will learn to know the will of God and how to beat their swords into plowshares and their spears into pruning hooks. The world will finally have peace. This comes about because the nations arise and come to hear Torah from Jerusalem, the instruction of the Lord that goes forth from Zion.

This theme of the pilgrimage of the nations runs also through Deutero-Isaiah, chapters 40–55, and finally, Isaiah 60 again takes up Isaiah 2 and rounds off its grand vision. Both these visions, in Isaiah 2 and 60, are social in nature. They speak of the darkness that covers the peoples. It could scarcely be stated more succinctly or precisely: world society lives in chaos, confusion, and perplexity.

But the text immediately draws a counter-image: Israel, represented by the city of Jerusalem, will become the light of the world. Its lived social order will be a medicine for the nations' peacelessness. There is talk in the surrounding world about the fascination of this social order of the people of God. Because in eschatological Israel the right, longed-for society is visible, the Gentile nations come from everywhere to Zion, to see and experience for themselves how it can be possible for people to live together in peace and justice. That is what is meant by the radiance that goes forth from Zion. Ultimately, of course, it is the very radiance of God.

Isaiah 60:6 then says something astonishing and unexpected: the people who come from everywhere to Mount Zion "proclaim the praise [the splendid deeds] of the LORD." That is, they have understood that God is at work, and they see at last what God's plan for the world is. They are able to recognize its tangible presence in the life of the people of God, and that makes them capable of praising God and telling abroad what they have seen.

But the text says still more, and here it becomes quite concrete: in the new city is gathered "the abundance of the sea." That is not a vague, poetic image. The reference is to the valuable cargoes of merchant ships. Added to these are countless caravans with laden camels from Midian and Ephah, bearing precious goods, especially gold and frankincense. Thus the treasures of the nations will flood the land. In the distant background here is the image of an ancient Near Eastern empire in which vassal peoples were obligated to bring their gifts to the great king in huge processions every year or every three years. In reality those "gifts" were, of course, taxes or payments of tribute.

Even if the image of a procession of nations bringing tribute to Zion forms the background here, we must not interpret it as the capitalistic pipe dream of a tiny nation in decline. It is about the fulfillment of God's promises. What the Gentile nations bring to Zion, motivated by pure fascination, is the best they have. It is their knowledge, their experience of the world, their philosophy, their ethics, their art. They bring all their treasures into the eschatological city because they have understood that only there will they find a future and a hope.

The future city about which Isaiah speaks is thus not a special world and most certainly not a closed society. The gates of this city are open night and day. The city rejects nothing that is good, successful, or beautiful from among the nations. On the contrary: all that is constantly brought together, given its own identity, and handed on.

Because God respects the freedom of the nations, God needs a place in the world where the society God desires and has always dreamed of can take shape. Only in this way can the new thing God is creating be accepted in freedom. One can make a visual inspection of this new thing, can become acquainted with it in the place God has chosen, can associate oneself with it freely, and so can have a share in a new history that will become a blessing for the world.

I encountered this complex of ideas for the first time in the work of the Lutheran New Testament scholar Joachim Jeremias, whose lovely book, *Jesus' Promise for the Nations*,[2] I bought for myself when I was a theology student. There I also found for the first time the concept of the "eschatological pilgrimage of the nations," a phrase I had never heard before. That phrase, and what it means, were not present to the mind of the church at the time.

Jesus and the Gentiles

One day my student period came to an end. I had received my Habilitation in Würzburg, had been called to Tübingen, and of course now had to give lectures on the New Testament, for example, on Matthew's gospel. From that time it became more and more clear to me that the idea of the eschatological pilgrimage of the nations and the function of Israel as blessing for the world constituted the background for the story of the wise men from the East, not first in the church's liturgy, but already for Matthew himself.

The motif-complex of the pilgrimage of the nations lies behind many texts of the New Testament, far more than we suppose at first glance. Jesus himself accepted the theology of the pilgrimage of nations as a matter of course in all his work. He devoted himself entirely to working in Israel. Matthew 10:5-6 includes, as a saying of Jesus: "Go nowhere among the Gentiles, and enter no town of the Samaritans, but go rather to the lost sheep of the house of Israel." This saying ultimately refers to Jesus' own practice. In the time of his public activity he did not enter the major Gentile cities that lay within Israel. Tiberias, Sepphoris, Hippos, Scythopolis—we have no indication at all that he ever preached in those cities. When Jesus really did have something to do with a Gentile, such as the centurion at Capernaum or the Syro-phoenician woman, it is expressly noted as an exception to the rule. Why this meticulous concentration on Israel?

The answer is the Old Testament promise of the pilgrimage of the nations, which Jesus had profoundly internalized: first, the people of God itself must be gathered; first, Israel itself must accept the reign of God; first, the fallen dwelling of David must be rebuilt, as the Lord's brother James says in Acts 15:16-17. If Israel is not raised up again, the Gentiles cannot come. In that case, they have no chance.

The Pilgrimage of the Nations in the New Testament

Once one has understood this background to Jesus' activity, a good many post-Easter texts appear in a new light. I would like to demonstrate this very briefly in terms of *one* text, namely, Hebrews 12:18-24. There the people of God on Sinai and the New Testament people of God on Zion are contrasted:

> You have not come to [a mountain] that can be touched, a blazing fire, and darkness, and gloom, and a tempest, and the sound of a trumpet, and a voice whose words made the hearers beg that not another word be spoken to them. . . . But you have come to Mount Zion and to the city of the living God, the heavenly Jerusalem, and to innumerable angels in festal gathering, and to the assembly of the firstborn who are enrolled in heaven, and to God the judge of all, and to the spirits of the righteous made perfect, and to Jesus, the mediator of a new covenant, and to the sprinkled blood that speaks a better word than the blood of Abel.

This section is rhetorically stylized to the highest degree. It is the climax of the letter to the Hebrews. What kind of eschatology do we find here? The text represents an utterly present eschatology. As once the Old Testament Israel had approached Sinai, so now the New Testament community is to approach the heavenly Mount Zion, the true world beyond mere appearances. This real world, this dimension of ultimate salvation, is described this way: It is the true Zion, the city of the living God, the heavenly Jerusalem. Here there are myriad angels; here is the heavenly festal gathering, the heavenly *ekklēsia*, the archetype of the earthly *ekklēsia*. Here the already perfected righteous are assembled, and here, finally, is God, the judge, and Christ, the mediator of the new covenant.

To this heavenly Jerusalem, that is, this perfected, unsurpassable salvation, the believers, the Gentile Christians on their pilgrimage of nations, have already come. The Greek uses the perfect tense, which means this is a completed action. Certainly there is an eschatological reservation, since they have come to the "judge of all" people. They can still work out their salvation. And yet—they have already come. The author is thinking of baptism and, above all, of the worshiping assembly. When the earthly congregation gathers for Eucharist it is already in the midst of the heavenly assembly, among the angels, the righteous who have died, the heavenly Jerusalem. Then they are already standing before Christ and the throne of God.

That is pure present eschatology, and so we find expressed here the experience that with Jesus the ultimate, unsurpassable salvation has already arrived in the midst of history, and believers have arrived with him, the one who has died and been exalted to God, at the end of history. But above all, the text speaks about Mount Zion and the arrival of the Gentile Christians; it thus clearly presumes the notion of the pilgrimage of nations, even though this is not specifically expressed.

Many New Testament texts have the same background, and likewise Matthew 2 has the pilgrimage of the nations in mind. Matthew quite obviously saw in the coming of the Persian sages to worship Christ a prediction—even more, a distillation of what began after Easter: the coming of the Gentiles to Christ, to the church. His gospel is thus framed by the coming of the Gentiles as already announced in chapter 2 and the commission of the Risen One to the Gentile mission in Matthew 28:19-20.

In his Sermon on the Mount, one of the high points of Matthew's gospel, Jesus teaches eschatological peace. He cries out to the crowds, "Blessed are the peacemakers!" (Matt 5:9). And he teaches them absolute nonviolence, that is to say, what according to Isaiah 2 the Gentile nations will learn from Israel (Matt 5:38-41). Matthew thus means to say—and he thus summarizes it programmatically at the very beginning of his gospel—that since Jesus, the Messiah of Israel, has been born, the eschatological vision of the pilgrimage of the nations is being fulfilled. Now the Gentiles are coming to Zion. They are coming from far away. They are coming from among the nations. They are bringing their treasures with them. They are finding the resolution for their longings. They are finding in the messianic communities that have arisen since Jesus on the soil of Israel both rescue and salvation. They are coming from the world of the pagan religions and finding faith in Jesus Christ.

Thus for the New Testament communities the vision of Isaiah was no utopia, and the story of the wise men from the East was anything but just a well-shaped tale. The word "utopia" is, as we know, a construct. Thomas More created the Greek word as a title for his novel, *Utopia*, a critique of the state. Utopia means "no place, nowhere." But that is precisely what, for the New Testament communities, the vision of the pilgrimage of the nations was not. They were convinced that the fulfillment of the enormous vision of the pilgrimage of the nations had already begun. It had begun in the church that believes in Christ, the light of the world, and lives together, by his strength, in a new order of life, in peace. It had begun in the Gentiles who, all around the Mediterranean, were seeking entry into the church—seeking entry because they were attracted by the new life of the Christians, so clearly different from the life of the pagan Gentiles.

But not only the New Testament communities thought that way. So did the great early Christian theologians Justin, Irenaeus, Tertullian, Origen, and many others. So did the whole of the early church.

The Pilgrimage of the Nations in the Ancient Church

All that became more and more clear to me during my years in Tübingen. In 1985–86, in the midst of the time of the new peace movement, I took the trouble to investigate the reception of Isaiah 2 in the Greek and Latin fathers of the church. That is, I gathered together all the texts in which the theologians of the early church quoted Isaiah 2, and then I tried to see what they said about that text and its parallel in Micah 4:1-5.[3] The result was simply overwhelming for me. The early church fathers—the shift came only with Augustine—were all convinced that the great vision of the pilgrimage of the nations and the eschatological peace that would flow from it were already fulfilled or were in the process of fulfillment.

For the word of God, as the Gospel of Jesus Christ, had gone forth from Jerusalem. The Gentiles were coming and seeking entry into the Christian communities. And in those communities no one took up the sword any more, and no one practiced war; instead, they beat their swords into plowshares and their spears into pruning hooks. Justin had not the slightest hesitation in saying, in his *Apology* (here I am quoting directly): "And that it [the vision in Isaiah 2] did so come to pass, we can convince you" (Justin, *Apology 1*, 39). Justin knew, of course, that Isaiah's vision had not yet been fulfilled throughout the world. But it was so in the Christian communities, of which he says that they refuse to feel any kind of enmity toward their opponents. What an awareness those Christians must have had!—an awareness of something altogether new in the world, something that had come with Christ and in which they had a share. What pride speaks in such statements, and what assurance!

It would not be possible for me to read and discuss all the texts showing the reception of Isaiah 2 in the theologians of the ancient church that I occupied myself with in the mid-1980s. Instead, let me here only quote a text from the great theologian Origen. It is found in his *Contra Celsum* (5.33). The text presupposes that every local Christian community has become Zion, the "city on the hill" to which the Gentiles come. Origen writes:

> [We], all the nations come to [the house of the Lord], and [we], the
> many nations go forth, and say to one another, turning to the religion
> which in the last days has shone forth through Jesus Christ: Come,
> and let us go up to the mountain of the Lord, to the house of the
> God of Jacob; and He will teach us of His ways, and we will walk
> in them.

He thus quotes Isaiah 2 and asserts that in the church, the New Testament
people of God, the Zion theology of Isaiah 2 is being fulfilled. The Gentiles are already coming in. The eschatological peace is already reality.
Again: what an awareness! Would the theologians of the ancient church
not have been better advised to write more modestly?

Well, perhaps. But which is better? An immodesty that has understood
that Jesus could not have been the Messiah if messianic peace had not
begun in the world, or our current modesty, which has long since lost
hope that messianic peace can begin in this, our history, and therefore
transfers it to a transcendent heaven, thus disavowing Jesus as Messiah?
At any rate the theologians of the ancient church understood quite well
that the question whether the promises of Isaiah are already fulfilled is
ultimately about Jesus' character as Messiah. For the theologians of the
first centuries of our era what is essential and decisive is that in the New
Testament communities the Zion theology of Isaiah 2 was already becoming reality.

The Story of the Wise Men Is True

All that arose more and more within me during my time as professor
of New Testament in Tübingen. Thus the account in Matthew 2 that in
my childhood had been my beloved story of the three holy kings acquired an extraordinary depth for me. The narrative about the wise men
from the East now appeared to be itself a mighty vision that deserved
to be taken seriously in a social sense. Matthew 2 became for me a vision
of a church that does not reject its grounding in the Old Testament but
instead stands fast on the basis of Israel. Matthew 2 was now for me the
vision of a church in which all the treasures of the nations are gathered—
their experiences, their science, their wisdom.

As I slowly came to understand that, in many small steps, I knew that
this vision can and must not be only a "vision," for the narrative itself
says: *it has already begun*. The messianic reality, despite all its "not yet"
and all persecutions, has already begun. The church, as the eschatological

people of God, is called to be the place in which the radiance of the Lord shines forth, as depicted in the book of Isaiah.

And so I went on a search within the church. It would be better to say I was led. And one day I found the "child." I discovered people in the church who had come together out of many lands, led by the longing to experience church anew as something living, beautiful, full of promise. I found people who had brought their treasures with them, namely, their whole existence.

So now I feel much more secure than before in saying: Matthew's story is true, from beginning to end. It is true in every detail. And the longing for a living, youthful church has never been as great as it is today. That, then, was my history with this magnificent text, and it was at the same time part of my history with the Bible.

The Enchantment of Biblical Narratives

And now, in conclusion, I want to pose one more question that arises almost necessarily from what I have said and is fundamental to our dealing with biblical texts: what type of text is this section from Matthew 2 that I have deliberately spoken of at such length? Is it a documentary account? Most certainly not. Is it pure invention, a novelistic tale born of free imagination? Again, certainly not. But what is it? What should we call this kind of text, this peculiar kind of narrative?

There can be no doubt that Matthew 2 is partly a construct. There can be no doubt that it contains fictional elements. But it is not the product of unfettered imagination. The narrative is, as I have sought to demonstrate, nourished by the great vision of the pilgrimage of the nations, and the Matthean narrative says that this vision is already being fulfilled in the coming of the Gentiles into the church.

So the narrative deals with an intensely real event, namely, the miracle that surprised the young church exceedingly: that suddenly Gentiles from far distant places were streaming into the church, including highly gifted and learned women and men driven by longing for the true God and his messiah. That was a fact they experienced at close range, and the experience was now distilled in the narrative about the men from the East.

It is clear that here we have a unique kind of text, not the kind we would want to see on the front page of a serious newspaper: irreproachable documentation, pure facts, careful research. But neither is it the kind we encounter in the feature section, in a serial novel. No, it is a unique way of telling a story. It works with fictional, possibly also nonfictional, narrative elements, by the aid of which it distills real experiences of the people of God extending over a long period of time. There are a great many such narratives in the Bible.

When I began my studies we were all excited by the question of the historicity of such narrative texts in the Bible. In the foreground for us were the distinction of sources, genre criticism, historical criticism, the search for the historical Jesus. All of that was indeed worthwhile; we must not fall into the trap of fundamentalism. But somehow I have grown out of those questions. They are no longer so important to me. What interests me and many other exegetes now is the end text, the final version—not the prehistory of the text, but the text itself: its framework, its structure, its layout, its theology, its beauty, the enchantment of its sentences, where the text wants to lead me and what it wants to say to me, gently and yet urgently.

What stunning weight is in the mere statement that "when King Herod heard this, he was frightened, and all Jerusalem with him." Just try to write a sentence that is so brief and yet so full of reality. We are all frightened to our depths when we are confronted with God's truth.

I notice more and more, at my age, that I read texts of Sacred Scripture with a kind of "second naïveté." We hear them with a "first naïveté" in childhood. Then the texts are full of magic. Among theologians, in their studies, they are then taken apart, analyzed, dissected, scrutinized, brought within a system. Every theologian has to go through that phase. At any rate, I went through it, and I thoroughly enjoyed it.

But now I want to read my Bible quite simply again. I carry the burden of scholarship with me in my backpack. It is necessary, and we have to bring it along with us, because it helps us to understand the text in its final form. And yet in the end I want to be carried forward by the text itself and its fascination. I rejoice in it. I am frightened by its claim. I allow myself to be consoled by it. I live in it like a child whose mother tells it a story at bedtime.

Notes

Chapter 1

1. Karl Rahner, "Unterwegs zum neuen Menschen," first published in *Wort und Wahrheit* 16 (1961): 807–18, and under the title "Das Christentum und der 'Neue Mensch,'" in idem, *Schriften zur Theologie* 5 (Einsiedeln and Zürich, 1962), 159–79, at 175. English: "Christianity and the 'New Man,'" 135–53, in idem, *Theological Investigations* 5 (Baltimore: Helicon, 1966), at 149–50.

2. Leszek Kolakowski, "Der Anspruch auf die selbstverschuldete Unmündigkeit," 1–16, in *Vom Sinn der Tradition*, ed. Leonhard Reinisch (Munich: Beck, 1970).

3. Herbert Braun, *Jesus of Nazareth: The Man and His Time*, trans. Everett Kalin (Philadelphia: Fortress Press, 1979), 41–43.

4. Hans Conzelmann, *An Outline of the Theology of the New Testament* (New York: Harper & Row, 1969), 11.

5. I have not discussed Jesus' sayings against the rich in this chapter. I refer readers instead to Marius Reiser, *Der unbequeme Jesus*, Biblisch-Theologische Studien 122 (Neukirchen-Vluyn: Neukirchener Verlag, 2011), 115–36.

Chapter 2

1. Friedrich Nietzsche, *Untimely Meditations*, ed. Daniel Breazeale, trans. R. J. Hollingdale (Cambridge and New York: Cambridge University Press, 1997), 60.

2. The original is in Hermann Diels and Walther Kranz, *Die Fragmente der Vorsokratiker* (Berlin: Weidmann, 1951–52), DK22B12, "you cannot step into the same river twice, for fresh waters are ever flowing in upon you." The more common quotation, given above, is from Plato, *Cratylus* 402a.

3. *Corpus Inscriptionum Latinarum* 6, 26003. See also Hieronymus Geist, *Römische Grabinschriften* (Munich: Heimaran, 1969), no. 442. The Latin text reads: *Nihil sumus et fuimus mortales. Respice, lector: in nihil ab nihilo quam cito recidimus.*

4. Ibid., no. 436. The Latin text reads: *Bona vita vive, sodalis! Quare? Post obitum nec risus nec lusus nec ulla voluptas erit.*

5. Werner Peek, *Griechische Grabgedichte*, Schriften und Quellen der Alten Welt 7 (Berlin: Akademie-Verlag, 1960), 289.

6. Fernando Savater, *Tu, was du willst: Ethik für die Erwachsenen von Morgen* (Frankfurt and New York: Campus Verlag, 1993). The Spanish original is entitled *Ética para amador*. English: *Amador: In Which a Father Addresses His Son on Questions of Ethics*, trans. Alastair Reid (New York: Henry Holt, 1994).

7. Aldous Huxley, *Brave New World* and *Brave New World Revisited*, Harper Perennial Modern Classics (New York: HarperCollins, 2005), 101.

8. Ibid., 40.

9. Address by Israeli President Ezer Weizman to the Bundestag and Bundesrat of the Federal Republic of Germany (January 16, 1996). Accessible at: www.jewishagency.org.

Chapter 3

1. See Arye Ben-David, *Talmudische Ökonomie. Die Wirtschaft des jüdischen Palästina zur Zeit der Mischna und des Talmud*, 1 (Hildesheim and New York: Olms, 1974), 300, 306.

2. Moses Hadas, *Imperial Rome* (New York: Time, Inc., 1965), 84–85.

Chapter 4

1. Bracketed text from author's translation.—Trans.

2. Thus NRSV and most English translations.

3. Herbert Will et al., *Glauben*, Kursbuch 93 (Berlin: Rotbuch, 1988), 204.

4. Translation © Brigitte Dubiel, at http://german.about.com/library/blgzauberl.htm, accessed March 16, 2013.

5. Article in the *Frankfurter Allgemeine Zeitung* 153, no. 5 (July 4, 2012), on an exhibit in the Pergamon Museum in Berlin.

6. Translator's note: the German wordplay on "Heil" (salvation) and "Heilung" (healing) is not reproducible in English.

Chapter 5

1. Erich Fried, *Gedichte*, 13th ed. (Munich: Deutscher Taschenbuch Verlag, 2007), 78.

2. Mary W. Blundell, *Helping Friends and Harming Enemies: A Study in Sophocles and Greek Ethics* (Cambridge and New York: Cambridge University Press, 1989), 26. For the reference to Blundell and her research I am indebted to Marius Reiser, "Love of Enemies in the Context of Antiquity," *New Testament Studies* 47 (2001): 411–27. See also idem, *Der unbequeme Jesus*, Biblisch-theologische Studien 122 (Neukirchen-Vluyn: Neukirchener Verlag, 2011), 95–100.

3. Bertolt Brecht, "The Mask of Evil," trans. H. R. Hays, in Brecht, *Poetry and Prose*, ed. Reinhold Grimm and Caroline Molina y Vedia (New York: Continuum, 2006), 114–15.

4. Hesiod, *Works and Days*, ll. 353–54.

5. Augustine, Sermon 340, 3, in idem, *The Works of Saint Augustine* 9 (306–340A), "On the Saints" (Brooklyn, NY: New City Press, 1994), 293–94.

6. Luise Rinser, *Zölibat und Frau*, 3rd ed. (Würzburg: Echter Verlag, 1967).

7. Augustine, "Homily 10 on the First Epistle of John" (1 John 5:1-3), 7.

8. Tertullian, *Apologeticum* 39.

Chapter 6

1. *Der Spiegel* 41 (2001): 160.

2. For what follows, see, for example, Martin Walser, *Ich vertraue. Querfeldein. Reden und Aufsätze* (Frankfurt: Suhrkamp, 2000), 11–19.

3. Arthur Schopenhauer, "Religion: A Dialogue," 1–24, in *The Essays of Arthur Schopenhauer*, trans. T. Bailey Saunders (Teddington, Middlesex: Echo Library, 2006), 22.

4. Aleksandr Solzhenitsyn, *August 1914. The Red Wheel: A Narrative in Discrete Periods of Time* (New York: Farrar, Strauss, and Giroux, 1989), 466.

5. José Saramago, "Im Namen Gottes ist das Schrecklichste erlaubt," *Frankfurter Allgemeine Zeitung* 220, 52 (September 21, 2001).

Chapter 7

1. *Die Bibel in gerechter Sprache*, ed. Ulrike Bail et al. (Frankfurt: Gemeinschaftswerk der Evangelischen Publizistik, 2006).

2. Joachim Jeremias, *The Eucharistic Words of Jesus*, trans. from the second German ed. by Arnold Ehrhardt (Oxford: Basil Blackwell, 1955).

Chapter 8

1. See Peter Handke, *Prosa, Gedichte, Theaterstücke, Hörspiele, Aufsätze* (Frankfurt: Suhrkamp, 1969).

2. Friedrich Nietzsche, *Thus Spoke Zarathustra: A Book for All and None*, trans. Adrian Del Caro and Robert B. Pippin (Cambridge and New York: Cambridge University Press, 2006), 71.

3. Friedrich Nietzsche, *Human, All Too Human: A Book for Free Spirits*, part 2, trans. Paul V. Cohn (New York: Macmillan, 1913), No. 98: "Theatricality and Honesty of Unbelievers," 54.

4. Joseph Ratzinger, *Introduction to Christianity*, trans. J. R. Foster (New York: Herder & Herder, 1971), 213–14.

5. Cf. Immanuel Kant, *Critique of Practical Reason*, A 54: "He [i.e., someone who must make a conscientious decision in a difficult situation] judges, therefore, that he can do a certain thing because he is conscious that he ought, and he recognizes that he is free, a fact which but for the moral law he would never have known." Quoted from Thomas Kingsmill Abbott, trans., *Kant's Critique of Practical Reason and Other Works on the Theory of Ethics* (London: Longmans, Green & Co., 1879), 165. It seems that the dictum "you can because you should [or: you must]" was later abstracted from this text. At any rate, in 1942 Walter Schmidkunz issued a collection of quotations from Kant in the *Münchner Lesebogen*, no. 11, under the title *I. Kant, Du kannst, denn du sollst. Vom Ethos der Pflicht* ["I. Kant. You can because you should. The Ethics of Obligation"]. The title phrase does not appear among the quotations. I am grateful to Fr. Giovanni Sala, SJ, of Munich, for this information.

6. I owe this phrasing to Prof. Dr. Ludwig Weimer.

7. Benedict XVI, encyclical *Spe salvi* (November 30, 2007), §38.

Chapter 9

1. Ernst Käsemann, "Begründet der neutestamentliche Kanon die Einheit der Kirche?," *Evangelische Theologie* 11 (1951–52): 13–21; repr. in idem, *Exegetische Versuche und Besinnungen* 1, 4th ed. (Göttingen: Vandenhoeck & Ruprecht, 1965), 214–23. Translated as "The Canon of the New Testament and the Unity of the Church," 95–107 in idem, *Essays on New Testament Themes*, trans. W. J. Montague (London: SCM; Philadelphia: Fortress Press, 1964).

2. Flavius Josephus, *Bell.* 2, 12.3, §232; *Ant.* 20, 6.1, §118.

3. *Ant.* 18, 2.2, §§29–30.

4. Gerhard von Rad, *Old Testament Theology*, vol. 1: *The Theology of Israel's Historical Traditions* (Louisville: Westminster John Knox, 2001), 207.

Chapter 10

1. See chap. 9, n. 1 above.

2. This has now been demonstrated by David Trobisch in his book, *Die Endredaktion des Neuen Testaments. Eine Untersuchung zur Entstehung der christlichen Bibel*, Novum Testamentum et orbis antiquus 31 (Fribourg: Universitätsverlag; Göttingen: Vandenhoeck & Ruprecht, 1996). English: *The First Edition of the New Testament* (Oxford and New York: Oxford University Press, 2000). In many parts of this lecture I have relied on his pathbreaking work, which seeks to clarify the most important part of the history of the canon not with reliance on early church authors but through an investigation of the manuscript evidence.

3. Origen, *Commentary on John* 10.107 (Sources chrétiennes 157, 446). Origen is here referring to the eating of the paschal meal according to Exodus 12:7-10 and interpreting the text allegorically. My translation relies on Marius Reiser, *Bibelkritik und Auslegung der Heiligen Schrift. Beiträge zur Geschichte der biblischen Exegese und Hermeneutik*, WUNT 217 (Tübingen: Mohr Siebeck, 2007), 127.

4. Ernst Käsemann, "Paulus und der Frühkatholizismus," in idem, *Exegetische Versuche und Besinnungen* 2, 2nd ed. (Göttingen: Vandenhoeck & Ruprecht, 1965), 239–52, at 248. English: "Paul and Early Catholicism," 236–51, in *New Testament Questions of Today*, trans. W. J. Montague (Philadelphia: Fortress Press, 1969), at 245–46.

Chapter 11

1. Irenaeus, *Adv. Haer.* 3, 3.3.

2. Following Georg Schwaiger, "Papsttum I," *Theologische Realenzyklopädie* 25 (Berlin and New York: de Gruyter, 1995), 647–76, at 649.

3. Jürgen Roloff, *Die Kirche im Neuen Testament* (Göttingen: Vandenhoeck & Ruprecht, 1993), 163–65.

4. Cf. Rudolf Pesch, *Die biblischen Grundlagen des Primats*, QD 187 (Freiburg: Herder, 2001), esp. 66–69.

5. Ibid., 26.

Chapter 13

1. Karl Prümm, *Christentum als Neuheitserlebnis. Durchblick durch die christlich-antike Begegnung* [*Christianity as Experience of the New: Perspective on the Encounter between Christianity and Antiquity*] (Freiburg: Herder, 1939).

2. Adolf von Harnack, *Die Mission und Ausbreitung des Christentums in den ersten drei Jahrhunderten* (Leipzig: J. C. Hinrichs, 1902); English: *The Mission and Expansion of Christianity in the First Three Centuries*, trans. James Moffatt (New York: Putnam, 1908).

3. Julian, *Epistula ad Arsacium*, in Sozomenos 5, 15–16. Translation in Julian the Apostate, *Works*, 3 vols., trans. Wilmer Cave Wright, LCL (New York: Macmillan; London: Heinemann, 1913, 1923), vol. 3, *Letters*, 22: To Arsacius, High-priest of Galatia. By "atheism," Julian means Christianity!

4. This is a favorite text that is quoted to death on the Internet, unfortunately without reference to the original.

5. Walker Percy, *The Message in the Bottle: How Queer Man Is, How Queer Language Is, and What One Has to Do with the Other* (New York: Farrar, Strauss, and Giroux, 1975), 6.

6. The following reflections on the theology of the Easter Vigil rest largely on a text by Dr. Arnold Stötzel of Munich, which I am grateful to be able to draw upon.

7. Consequently, in his great apology, *The City of God*, Augustine devoted a long section to listing the real and attested miracles that had happened in his neighborhood: *De civitate Dei* 22, 7–8.

Chapter 14

1. Quotations are from Adolf von Harnack, *Das Wesen des Christentums*, GTB 227 (Gütersloh: Gütersloher Verlagshaus Mohn, 1977). The lecture texts were translated into English and published as *What Is Christianity*, trans. Thomas Bailey Saunders (London: Williams and Norgate; New York: Putnam, 1901). English quotations are from that publication.

2. Harnack, *What Is Christianity*, 60–61.

3. Ibid., 154.

4. Ibid., 66.

5. Ibid., 125–26.

6. Anonymous, in the anthology, *Dem Führer: Gedichte für Adolf Hitler* (Stuttgart and Berlin: Georg Truckmüller, 1939).

7. Quoted by Johann Neuhäusler, *Kreuz und Hakenkreuz. Der Kampf des Nationalsozialismus gegen die Katholische Kirche und der kirchliche Widerstand* (Munich: Verlag der Katholischen Kirche Bayerns, 1946), 251.

8. *Corpus inscriptionum Judaicarum* 1404; this translation by K. C. Hanson and Douglas E. Oakman at http://www.kchanson.com/ancdocs/greek/theodotus.html. The *archisynagogos* was the head (*archōn*) of the synagogue.

9. Joseph Ratzinger, *Theologische Prinzipienlehre. Bausteine zur Fundamentaltheologie* (Munich: Wewel, 1982), 266. English: *Principles of Catholic Theology: Building Stones for a Fundamental Theology* (San Francisco: Ignatius Press, 1987), 253.

Chapter 15

1. Peter Stuhlmacher, *Der Brief an Philemon*, EKK 18, 2nd ed. (Zürich: Benziger; Neukirchen-Vluyn: Neukirchener Verlag, 1981), 74.

Chapter 16

1. Karl Otto Conrady, *Das große deutsche Gedichtbuch. Von 1500 bis zur Gegenwart*, 2nd ed. (Munich and Zürich, 1991), 495.

2. See Georg Braulik, "Gibt es 'sacramenta veteris legis'? Am Beispiel der Beschneidung," 369–401, in idem and Norbert Lohfink, *Liturgie und Bibel. Gesammelte Aufsätze*, Österreichische Biblische Studien 28 (Frankfurt: Peter Lang, 2005).

3. Romano Guardini, "Das Gleichnis vom Säemann," in idem, *Wahrheit und Ordnung*, Universitätspredigten, vol. 7 (Würzburg: Fränksche Gesellschaftsdruckerei, 1956), [3–13]; 159–69.

4. Reinhold Schneider, *Winter in Wien. Aus meinen Notizbüchern 1957/58*, 6th ed. (Freiburg, Basel, and Vienna: Herder, 1961), 129–31.

Chapter 17

1. Jean-Paul Sartre, *Le Diable et le bon Dieu X*, 4 (Paris: Gallimard, 1951), 267. English in idem, *The Devil & the Good Lord, and Two Other Plays* (New York: Vintage Books, 1962), 141.

2. Martin Walser, *Ich vertraue. Querfeldein. Reden und Aufsätze* (Frankfurt: Suhrkamp, 2000), 9–21.

Chapter 19

1. Isak Dinesen, *Babette's Feast and Other Anecdotes of Destiny* (New York: Vintage Books, 1993), 3.

2. Ibid., 41.

Chapter 20

1. Bertolt Brecht, *Mother Courage and Her Children*, trans. Eric Bentley (New York: Grove/Atlantic, 1955), 105–6.

2. Lothar Zenetti, *Auf Seiner Spur: Texte gläubiger Zuversicht*, 3rd ed. (Mainz: Matthias-Grünewald, 2002).

3. "Wer möchte leben ohne den Trost der Bäume!" So Günter Eich begins his poem, "Ende eines Sommers" (End of a Summer) in idem, *Botschaften des Regens. Gedichte* (Frankfurt: Suhrkamp, 1955; repr. 1983), 7. English: *Rain's News*, trans. Teo Savory (Santa Barbara, CA: Unicorn Press, 1968); excerpted in *Pigeons and Moles: Selected Writings of Günter Eich*, trans. Michael Hamburger (Columbia, SC: Camden House, 1990), 11.

Chapter 21

1. *Sura* 19.30–33 is somewhat different. There Jesus, while still in the cradle, says, "I am a servant of GOD. He has given me the scripture, and has appointed me a prophet. . . . And peace be upon me the day I was born, the day I die, and the day I get resurrected." Apparently this presupposes that Jesus dies like any other human and will be raised on the Last Day.

2. *Summa theologiae* I-II, q. 109, a. 1, ad 1.

Chapter 22

1. They are individual compound words in German, which, more often than in English, can attach an adjective to a noun to form a single word.—Trans.

2. Robert Spaemann, *Über Gott und die Welt. Eine Autobiographie in Gesprächen* (Stuttgart: Klett-Cotta, 2012), 245.

3. Ernst-Wolfgang Böckenförde, *Die Entstehung des Staates als Vorgang der Säkularisation* (Stuttgart: Kohlhammer, 1967), repr. in idem, *Recht, Staat, Freiheit. Studien zur Rechtsphilosophie, Staatstheorie und Verfassungsgeschichte*, stw 914 (Frankfurt: Suhrkamp, 1991), 92ff., at 112. English in idem, *State, Society, and Liberty: Studies in Political Theory and Constitutional Law* (New York: Berg/St. Martin's Press, 1991), 45. Italics in original.

4. Michael Walzer, *Exodus and Revolution* (New York: Basic Books, 1985); see esp. pp. 3–4, 6–7, 17, 78–79, 112–13, and *passim*.

5. Hartmut von Hentig, *Ach, die Werte: über eine Erziehung für das 21. Jahrhundert* [*Oh, Values: Educating for the Twenty-First Century*] (Munich: Carl Hanser Verlag, 1999), 34.

6. For the English translation of the Académie Française address, see Joseph Cardinal Ratzinger, "Freedom, Law, and the Good: Moral Principles in Democratic Societies," in idem, *Values in a Time of Upheaval* (New York: Crossroad, 2006), 45–52, at 50.

7. Joseph Ratzinger, *Ergebnisse und Probleme der dritten Konzilsperiode* (Cologne: Bachem, 1965), 31–32. English: idem, *Theological Highlights of Vatican II*, trans. Henry Traub, Gerard C. Thormann, and Werner Barzel (New York and Mahwah, NJ: Paulist Press, 1966), 144.

Chapter 23

1. Martin Luther, *Works*, vol. 21 (St. Louis: Concordia Publishing House, 1955–2012), 295–358.

2. [This is true of most German translations but does not apply to English versions.—Trans.] For a correct German translation of the aorist verbs in the *Magnificat*, see Norbert Lohfink, "Was heißt das—Armenfrömmigkeit? Erörtert am Beispiel des Magnifikat," 13–22, in idem, *Lobgesänge der Armen. Studien zum Magnifikat, den Hodajot von Qumran und einigen späten Psalmen*, SBS 143 (Stuttgart: Katholisches Bibelwerk, 1990).

3. See chap. 17, n. 2 above.

Chapter 24

1. *Katholischer Katechismus für das Bistum Limburg* (Bischöflicher Ordinariat Limburg an der Lahn, 1936).

2. Derived from a prayer by Günther Krasnitzky, in *"Damit wir Deiner Spur folgen." Eine Auswahl aus den Gebeten von Günther Krasnitzky* (Urfeld am Walchensee: Akademie für Glaube und Form der Integrierten Gemeinde, 1988), 140.

3. Dick Francis, *Straight* (New York: Jove/Putnam, 2003), 125.

Chapter 25

1. The text of the German original is by Georg Thurmair, the melody by Adolf Lohmann.

2. Joachim Jeremias, *Jesu Verheißung für die Völker*, 2nd ed. (Stuttgart: Kohlhammer, 1956). English: *Jesus' Promise to the Nations* (Philadelphia: Fortress Press, 1967).

3. Cf. Gerhard Lohfink, "'Schwerter zu Pflugscharen.' Die Rezeption von Jes 2,1-5 *par* Mi 4,1-5 in der Alten Kirche und im Neuen Testament," *Theologische Quartalschrift* 166 (1986): 184–209.

Index of Biblical Citations and Other Ancient Literature

Old Testament

New Testament

Index of Proper Names